CONSUMER LENDING

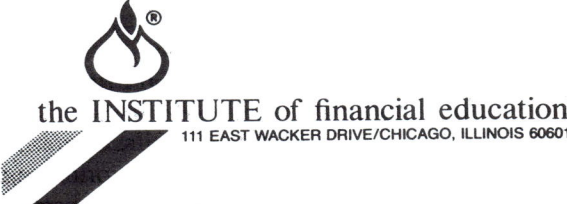

© 1987 by The Institute of Financial Education
Second Edition
All rights reserved.
Printed in the United States of America

7890/54321

United States Copyright is not claimed for any material taken from United States Government sources.

No part of this publication may be reproduced, stored in a retrieval system or transmitted, in any form or by any means, electronic, mechanical, photocopying, recording or otherwise without the written permission of the publisher.

The George E. Cole® forms, reprinted with permission of Boise Cascade Corporation, are applicable only for use in Illinois and while Boise Cascade Corporation believes the forms were an accurate representation of applicable law at the time of the most recent printing of the forms, it is possible that they have become outdated as a result of changes in the law. Accordingly, the Boise Cascade Corporation makes no representation as to their legal sufficiency or accuracy.

ISBN 0-912857-36-6
Library of Congress Catalog Card number: 86-82604

Contents

Foreword		vii
Acknowledgments		ix
Chapter 1	**Consumer Credit: Past, Present and Future**	2
	History of Consumer Installment Credit	
	Consumer Credit Categories	
	Types of Consumer Credit	
	Users of Consumer Credit	
	Providers of Consumer Credit	
	The Future: Marketing's Importance	
	Determining Customer Needs	
	Delivering Products and Services	
Chapter 2	**Types of Loans and Credit Insurance**	30
	Consumer Loan Policies	
	Types of Loans	
	Credit Insurance	
Chapter 3	**Laws and Regulations Affecting Consumer Loans**	60
	Regulations Protecting Lenders	
	Regulations Protecting Consumers	
Chapter 4	**Interest**	104
	The Nature of Interest	
	Simple Interest	
	Finance Charge and Annual Percentage Rate	
	Appendix	

Chapter 5	**Loan Evaluation**	**138**
	Purpose and Policy	
	The Six Cs of Credit	
	Taking the Application	
	Verifying Personal Credit Information	
	Analyzing Credit Information	
	Notifying the Applicant of the Credit Decision	
	Underwriting Indirect Loans	
Chapter 6	**Establishing and Perfecting Security Interest in Collateral**	**186**
	Loans Secured by Collateral	
	Establishing a Valid Security Interest	
	Perfecting Security Interest	
	Attachment vs. Perfection	
	Perfecting Security Interest when Making Indirect Loans	
	Terminating the Financing Arrangement	
Chapter 7	**Document Preparation and Loan Closing**	**216**
	Promise to Repay	
	Truth-in-Lending Disclosures	
	Documents for Loans Secured by Personal Property	
	Documents for Loans Secured by Real Property	
Chapter 8	**Servicing Consumer Loans**	**248**
	Maintaining Security Interest and Insurance on Collateral	
	Processing Consumer Loan Payments	
	Consumer Loan Reports	
	Servicing Indirect Loans	
	Credit Cards	
	Handling Inquiries	
Chapter 9	**Collection Procedures and Remedies**	**280**
	Consumer Loan Delinquency	
	Classifying Delinquent Borrowers	
	The Collections Policy	
	Collections Devices and Tools	

                Special Problems
                Remedial Payment Plans
                Collateral Acquisition
                Charge-off Procedures

Chapter 10 Consumer Lending and Bankruptcy   320
                Historical View of Bankruptcy Laws
                Overview of Consumer Bankruptcy
                Chapter 7 Bankruptcies: Liquidation
                Chapter 13 Bankruptcies: Repayment

Glossary   **350**

Index   **374**

Foreword

Explosive is a good way to describe both the past and current demand for consumer credit. Between 1980 and 1987, total outstanding consumer credit doubled from under $300 billion to nearly $600 billion. Savings institutions are one of the major lenders contributing to this dramatic growth, increasing their outstanding consumer installment credit nearly twice as fast as total average percentage changes nationwide. This rapidly growing consumer credit market provides many opportunities for financial institutions to enter or to expand their services in this area. The new edition of this Institute textbook is designed to contribute to the success of consumer lending programs by providing the necessary educational support and assistance.

Consumer Lending provides a comprehensive orientation to consumer credit needed by all lending personnel. Representing a major revision, this second edition covers the explosive growth in consumer credit demand since the first edition was published in 1981. Also, the expanded range of lending services since 1981 is covered. While specifically written for use in The Institute's educational programs, the text also is a valuable resource book for all consumer lending professionals.

In addition to an introduction to the basics of consumer credit, the text is rich with practical everyday work examples. The first four chapters present fundamental consumer credit facts, terms and concepts—the language of consumer credit.

This includes a study of the history of consumer credit and marketing's role in providing consumer lending services. Also included is a comparison of credit providers, the types of consumer loans and credit insurance, consumer credit laws and regulations, and how to calculate interest. The last six chapters present a thorough analysis of the activities, duties and tasks performed in credit evaluation, document preparation, perfection of security interest, loan closing, servicing and collections. The last chapter reviews the Federal bankruptcy law as it impacts on consumer credit operations. From cover to cover, *Consumer Lending* is designed to meet the needs of today's lending department by providing practical help for the professionals who fulfill this challenging job and who want to do it well.

Dale C. Bottom
President
The Institute of Financial Education
January, 1987

Acknowledgments

John L. Schmidt, AIA	Vice President of Operations
Naomi W. Peralta	Director of Instructional Design
P. Gerald McEnany	Instructional Project Manager
Ed Rozalewicz	Writer
Robert W. Brown	Director of Design
Gail Rafter Meneley	Vice President of Marketing
Jean Lou Hess	Project Coordinator, Editor
Matthew Doherty	Designer
Gayle Paprocki	Production Coordinator
Sandra Clay	Production Assistant
Ruby Dau-Schmidt	Word Processing Operator
Yvette Harris	Word Processing Operator
Beverly Johnson	Word Processing Operator

The Institute thanks the following individuals who reviewed portions of the manuscript:

Ralph Burton, Vice President, Phoenix Federal Savings, Muskogee, Oklahoma

Blair C. Holman, Glendora, California

Neil Lukatch, Chicago, Illinois

Michael D. Joehnk, Department of Finance, College of Business, Arizona State University, Tempe, Arizona

C. P. (Pete) Jorgensen, Vice President Consumer Loans, Home Federal Savings, Tucson, Arizona

Dennis P. Schenk, Vice President Consumer Loan Director, St. Paul Federal Bank for Savings, Chicago, Illinois

William W. Tennent III, Senior Vice President Commercial Banking, Security Federal Savings, Richmond, Virginia

Also, The Institute appreciates the cooperation of:

Tom Toft, SAF Systems and Forms

Wayne F. Bengtson, Program Director, Consumer Lending, United States League of Savings Institutions

L. Joseph Salm, Vice President and Director, United States League of Savings Institutions

In addition, The Institute of Financial Education recognizes the earlier contributions of all those involved with the first edition of this text entitled *Consumer Lending for Savings Associations*.

CONSUMER LENDING

1

Consumer Credit: Past, Present and Future

Objectives

After studying this chapter, you should be able to:
- ☐ Explain the demand for consumer credit in terms of historical background and economic influences;
- ☐ Identify and describe the three categories of consumer credit;
- ☐ Compare and contrast the three means of obtaining consumer credit;
- ☐ Describe four consumer characteristics that influence credit use;
- ☐ State four reasons why consumers use credit;
- ☐ List and describe five major providers of consumer credit;
- ☐ Define the term marketing;
- ☐ Describe four ways to determine customer needs and cite the advantages and disadvantages of each;
- ☐ Describe the employee skills needed to meet customer needs;
- ☐ Explain four ways of delivering financial services and how each way can benefit both the lender and the consumer.

INTRODUCTION

This chapter provides a brief historical overview of consumer credit, discusses present trends and finally, through a discussion of marketing activities, briefly considers the future of consumer credit.

The history of consumer credit in this country had its beginning in the early 1900s. Since then, consumer credit has been used increasingly to encourage consumer purchases. The demand for consumer credit has never been greater than it is today. This is true partly because the persons born in the 1950s and 1960s are currently at the stage of their lives during which they are most likely to use consumer credit. The changing economic conditions since 1970 have also had an important influence on the pace of consumer credit use.

Consumer characteristics are directly related to the use of consumer credit and are important marketing considerations for financial institutions. By affecting the types of consumer loans sought by customers, consumer characteristics influence the structure of an institution's entire consumer credit program.

Many institutions provide consumer credit and competing institutions usually have a direct affect on each other's credit services. Although federally chartered savings institutions have offered certain types of consumer credit since the 1930s, they are fairly new providers of most types of consumer loans. The Depository Institutions Deregulation and Monetary Control Act of 1980 (DIDMCA) authorized savings institutions to diversify their lending programs by expanding consumer lending opportunities—and challenges. Further deregulation occurred in 1982 with the passage of the Garn-St Germain Depository Institutions Act.

The marketing of consumer lending products and services entails a broad scope of activities and requires a great deal of planning. Although most employees in the lending department are not directly involved with market planning, the policies and procedures that govern their everyday work activities evolve from such planning. An awareness that their daily routines have been designed with various marketing goals in mind can help lending employees gain a better understanding of their institution's entire consumer lending program, develop a more positive attitude, feel better informed about their own positions, and generally become more efficient and productive.

HISTORY OF CONSUMER INSTALLMENT CREDIT

In the early 20th century, mass production techniques were developed to bring down the cost of manufacturing high-priced items such as automobiles. These techniques, along with the introduction of installment purchasing, brought high-priced items within the reach of average consumers. As in the early 1900s, today most consumers do not have enough available cash to purchase high-priced items such as cars or large appliances. They need a schedule of monthly payments that spreads the cost of these expensive items over a period of time.

During the 1920s, the use of credit gained wide consumer acceptance. The amount of credit outstanding rose from $1 billion at the end of World War I to more than $3 billion at the end of 1929. The demand for installment credit dropped during the Depression but recovered to its pre-1929 level by 1936. Installment credit outstanding reached $6 billion dollars in 1941, but declined to $2 billion in 1944. This was due to the fact that during World War II consumer goods were limited, the use of installment credit was restricted, and consumers generally had enough income to pay cash for the items they needed or could acquire. After the war, installment credit quickly recovered its prewar level, and by 1955 installment credit outstanding was estimated to be $29 billion.

Since World War II, U.S. consumers have exhibited a trend of rising expectations and desires to improve their standard of living. They have been more willing to borrow from future income to satisfy current needs and desires. Consumer debt levels have risen steadily. Total consumer installment credit outstanding surpassed $180 billion by 1970, $300 billion by year-end 1980, $460 billion by year-end 1984 and had crossed the $500 billion mark by mid-year 1985 (see Figure 1-1).

Installment credit, however, is only one part of consumers' total debt. As shown in Figure 1-2, consumers' total borrowings amounted to nearly $2 trillion at year-end 1984. Of this total, about 70% of each household's indebtedness was comprised of home mortgage loans; about 24% was in the form of installment consumer credit; and about 6% of consumer debt was noninstallment consumer credit.

The relatively short history of consumer credit reveals several positive benefits that have accrued to the consuming public.

- Credit can be used to purchase more goods and services than ever before.
- The standard of living in the United States has improved.
- Consumers can select from a greater number and variety of goods than in the past.
- Manufacturers can market their products more profitably to a larger U.S. population.

Thus, the growth in consumer credit can be seen as an integral part of an expanded economy.

CONSUMER CREDIT CATEGORIES

Lenders often group consumer loans into three categories: single payment or installment; open-end or closed-end; and secured or unsecured. These categories are important to lenders because they affect how the loan program is marketed, administered and priced to reflect the costs and risks involved.

Installment or Single Payment

The two basic payment methods for consumer credit are installment and single payment. *Installment credit* plans are repayment plans that involve two or more future payments. Payments are scheduled at periodic intervals (for example, monthly, quarterly or semiannually) and continue until the full amount of the loan is repaid. Therefore, these plans allow consumers to obtain or enjoy the benefits of goods or services while paying for them in small amounts over a specified period of time.

Single-payment credit refers to repayment plans in which full payment for a good or service is made in one lump sum. This sum is paid at a future date agreed upon by both consumer and creditor.

FIGURE 1-1
Consumer Installment Credit Outstanding, 1930–1984 (in billions/years)

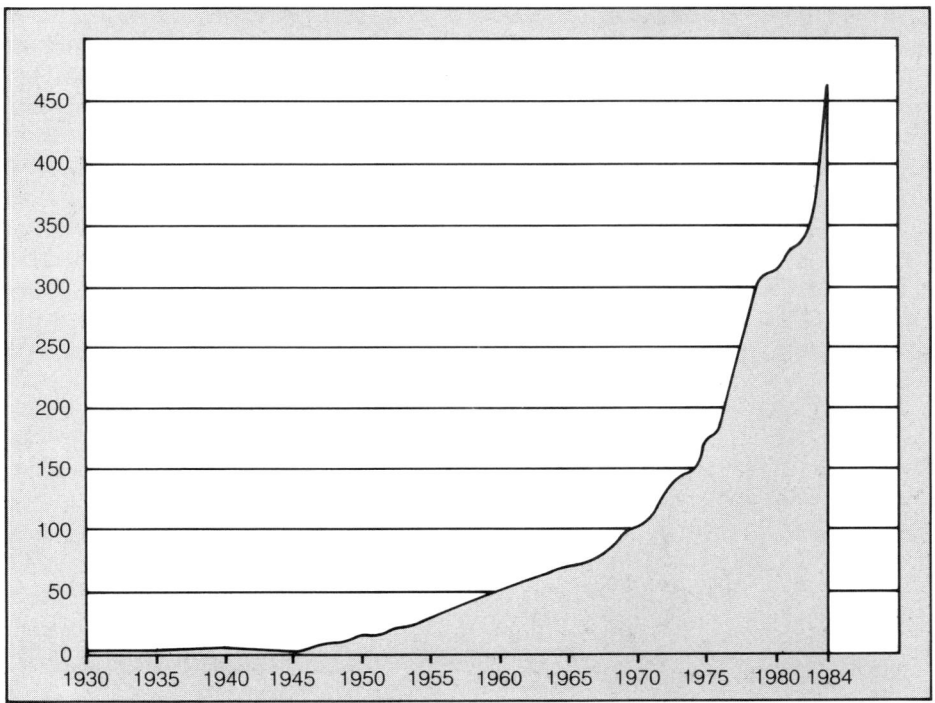

Source: *Consumer Installment Credit,* Board of Governors of the Federal Reserve System.

With both credit arrangements, the consumer can immediately enjoy the good or service; however, a lump-sum payment may be difficult for some consumers to make, especially for high-priced items. Originally, single payment plans were used by consumers who were short of cash at the moment but expected more income in the near future. For example, farmers who were low on cash just before harvesting their crops would try to work out a verbal agreement with merchants for the purchase of necessary goods with repayment in the fall after harvest. Today, single payment consumer credit is used mostly for convenience, to enable the consumer to obtain a good or service without requiring immediate payment. It includes single payment loans from commercial banks (such as 90-day notes), retailers' charge accounts with balances paid in 30 days or less and service credit such as bills owed to hospitals or physicians, etc.

FIGURE 1-2
Consumer Debt Outstanding, Relative Amounts, 1984

Home Mortgages
$1,332 billion

Installment
$461 billion

Noninstallment
$117 billion

Source: Federal Reserve Board.

Of these two credit plans, the installment arrangement is the more common. It represents approximately four-fifths of total outstanding consumer credit.

Open-end or Closed-end

The frequency of payments and the flexibility of a loan are determined by whether it is an open-end or closed-end loan. With *open-end credit*, a consumer is permitted to purchase goods or services on credit up to a certain dollar amount. This dollar limit is set by the lender and is based on the financial capacity and credit reputation of the consumer.

Consumers can draw against their line of credit without having to make specific arrangements for each purchase and can make payments that most closely reflect their financial capabilities at a particular point in time. As the loan balance is reduced, the amount of available credit increases back to the predetermined limit. Also, the line of credit remains available (open) indefinitely until either the borrower or lender cancels it.

Closed-end credit is a fixed-term credit arrangement. In

contrast to open-end credit, the specific amount of credit to be extended, the length of time for repayment and the payment amounts are established before the actual purchase.

Relatively expensive items such as automobiles are usually purchased under closed-end type of credit. For example, if a consumer decided to purchase an automobile on credit, the loan agreement would be prepared prior to the delivery of the car. The agreement specifies the amount of the loan, the monthly payment, the length of time for repayment and the specified interest rate.

Additional purchases cannot be automatically attached to the original credit amount of the closed-end arrangement. Once the terms are agreed on, a consumer makes regular payments for the length of time specified. If a consumer wishes to purchase other goods or services on credit before the original agreement is satisfied, another agreement must be negotiated with the creditor.

Secured or Unsecured

A third way to categorize consumer credit is by the security for repayment that the lender may require. In this category, a loan may be either secured or unsecured credit. To obtain *secured credit*, a consumer must offer some form of collateral to secure the promise of future payments. *Collateral* can be an item of tangible or intangible value that is owned or is being purchased with loan funds by the individual, such as an automobile, real estate, household furniture, a boat, a mobile home or a deposit account.

There are important reasons for the existence of secured credit. A creditor may want some form of collateral as a precaution against unforeseen circumstances that could prevent a consumer from following through on a promise to repay a loan. When repayment terms are not fulfilled, the creditor can take action to repossess the pledged collateral and sell it to obtain the money promised by the debtor. Even if a creditor determines that the borrower's financial status and credit worthiness are adequate, the creditor may insist on a pledge of collateral in addition to the debtor's promise to repay. Lenders typically require collateral for purchase money loans, where the loan proceeds are used to finance the purchase of such items as autos, boats and RVs.

> Jack Jones, a consumer, has a credit card with a $500 open line of credit. In effect, he can purchase five items today, five tomorrow and six the next day if, collectively, the total of these purchases does not exceed $500. A separate credit agreement is not necessary for either each item or each day's accumulated purchases. Jack receives a monthly billing statement that lists the purchases for that billing period. The minimum payment amount and the total dollar amount for all purchases or other transactions are indicated on the statement, along with the amount of available credit still remaining. Mr. Jones has the option of paying the minimum, the total or any amount in between at the time he is billed. Therefore, the repayment method under an open-end arrangement is flexible.

Unsecured credit does not involve a pledge of collateral. The only security for full repayment is the debtor's promise to repay the executed note. This type of credit may be extended to consumers possessing a good reputation for repaying creditors. The consumer's credit history may even include several previous loans with the lender. Generally, with unsecured credit, consumers borrow less money for a shorter period of time and at a higher interest rate than they can on a secured basis.

TYPES OF CONSUMER CREDIT

The three means of obtaining consumer credit are retail, service and direct loans. While all credit use involves the immediate possession of a good or service to be paid for at a future time, the means by which credit is extended is based on two major factors in the credit transaction: the nature of the item acquired and the number of parties involved in the purchase transaction. Retail credit may be used for a wide array of consumer goods and may involve either two or three parties. Service credit and direct loans involve the user of the service or borrower and the provider of the service or loan.

Retail Credit

Retail credit is used in the sale of retail goods, or goods purchased solely for consumption. Also known as merchandise credit, retail credit plans are devised and provided by retail merchants in order to sell merchandise and collect for sales within a relatively short time. Retail credit is commonly offered by major, nationwide retailers but may also be offered by local department or discount stores that maintain their own credit systems.

Two parties are involved in the actual retail credit transaction: the retailer and the consumer. Normally, cash is not exchanged at the time of purchase, but payment is expected within a short time period.

Financing of retail credit, however, can be accomplished via the involvement of either two or three parties. When only two parties are involved, the business owner finances the credit by carrying the customer's account for a short time until payments are received. When three parties are involved, financing arrangements can be made with private credit card companies such as American Express, Visa or MasterCard. Retailers receive almost immediate payment for customers' purchases from the credit card company in exchange for an agreed-upon percentage discount or fee.

Open-end retail credit can be categorized as either installment or single payment credit. *Retail revolving credit* is an open-end arrangement in which a customer is permitted to purchase goods or services in return for an agreement either to make full payment within 25 to 30 days or monthly payments including interest. Interest charges are added for the privilege of using this type of credit. The customer may still make additional purchases on the revolving credit ac-

> Shirley Smith may purchase a small appliance on credit. She presents her credit card to the sales clerk, signs an agreement promising to pay for the appliance at a future date and takes the appliance home. This entire transaction took place between Shirley Smith and the sales clerk, and cash was not involved at the time of purchase.

count as long as the balance does not exceed a predetermined dollar amount. All retail revolving credit is most commonly used in department store purchases involving high-priced items. Retail credit can be secured by the items being purchased.

In *retail installment credit*, a buyer and seller may agree to extend payment for the goods over a longer period of time than for retail revolving credit. For the privilege of delayed payment, a carrying charge is generally levied on the customer. One or many items may be involved, and the installment account may be secured by an additional agreement on the merchandise purchased.

The single payment credit arrangement is sometimes referred to as *retail open charge credit*. A consumer acquires goods with the promise to pay in one lump sum, usually within a 30- to 60-day period. The consumer usually pays no additional fee for the privilege of the delayed payment.

Service Credit

A second means of obtaining consumer credit is through a service credit arrangement. A *service credit* arrangement is used by consumers to acquire the benefits derived from nontangible items or services. Service credit outstanding is the amount owed by individuals to professional practitioners and service establishments. Legal advice and medical or dental care are examples of services that can be obtained with this type of credit transaction.

Service credit involves repayment methods similar to those used in retail credit. Usually only two parties are involved in a service credit transaction.

Direct Loan

The third means of obtaining consumer credit is with a direct loan. A *direct loan* is used when a consumer obtains cash (money) in exchange for a promise to repay the debt by a predetermined future date. The most common form of a direct loan typically pertains to a purchase money transaction and involves three parties: the buyer, the seller and the provider of credit.

> Joe Streeter wants to purchase an automobile from Frank Wheels. Mr. Wheels (the seller) will not accept credit; instead he asks for $3,000 in cash for the car. Since Mr. Streeter (the buyer) only has $1,000 in cash, he needs an additional $2,000 to buy the car. Mr. Streeter goes to ABC Savings and Loan to obtain a $2,000 auto loan. ABC Savings will let Mr. Streeter have the $2,000 auto loan if he agrees to repay it in monthly installments over a two-year period and pledges the car as collateral. He agrees and gets the money he needs to purchase the car. Note that the actual purchase of the car involved three parties: Joe Streeter, Frank Wheels and ABC Savings. However, the cash credit transaction took place between Joe Streeter (buyer) and ABC Savings. As far as Frank Wheels was concerned, he was paid in full when the automobile was purchased.

USERS OF CONSUMER CREDIT

Who are consumer credit users, and what are they like? Consumer credit exists because people want it and use it. Research has shown that some people are greater users of credit than others. Certain consumer characteristics have been shown to be directly related to the use of credit. These characteristics influence not only the amount but the type of credit a consumer demands. Consequently, providers of consumer credit should be aware of these consumer characteristics and understand how they influence the existing or potential use of credit.

Consumer Characteristics

The following four consumer characteristics have been found to influence the actual and potential use of consumer credit.
- level of family income;
- age;
- stage of family life cycle; and
- level of education.

Family Income

The level of family income (total income per household) has a direct effect on the amount of credit used. People with higher incomes generally can afford to take on more credit than those with lower incomes: theoretically at least, the higher the level of family income, the greater the capacity for repayment. A family with a higher income is more likely to request credit and is more likely to request larger amounts of credit. Determining the amount of debt a person can handle will be covered in Chapter 5.

Figure 1-3 shows the correlation among three of the four factors that determine mean and median consumer debt outstanding. In particular, notice the relationships between income and percentage of families and dollar amount outstanding. Figure 1-3 refers to mean and median dollar amounts. The mean refers to the arithmetic average of all reported amounts. The median amount refers to the middle value, above and below which lie an equal number of reported amounts.

Age

Age affects the amount of credit a person uses (see Figure 1-3). People between the ages of 25 and 64 tend to use credit most often. Within that age bracket, outstanding consumer debt generally increases with the age of the head of the family until age 44, and then begins to decline. According to the 1983 survey cited earlier, families most likely to have consumer debt outstanding are headed by someone between the ages of 35 and 44.

Stage of Family Life Cycle

The stage of family development (family life cycle) is a category based on consumer characteristics such as marital status, number and age of children, age of the primary wage earner and working status of the wage earner (that is, working, retired or unemployed). These factors influence the needs and buying habits of consumers and affect the level of credit used. For example, families with younger children may have a greater need for appliances, automobiles, homes and other high-priced items that are typically financed. A family with older children may already have a home and other high-priced items, but may need to provide college educations for the children and may desire vacation travel and other forms of entertainment requiring a high level of credit

FIGURE 1-3
Correlation Between Consumer Debt and Selected Family Characteristics

Characteristic	Percent of families	Consumer debt outstanding (dollars)	
		Mean (dollars)	Median (dollars)
Family income (dollars)			
Less than 5,000	33	2,834	677
5,000–7,499	40	1,919	573
7,500–9,999	48	4,152	1,006
10,000–14,999	54	3,452	1,451
15,000–19,999	66	4,295	1,639
20,000–24,999	72	4,149	2,336
25,000–29,999	72	4,632	2,929
30,000–39,999	77	5,138	3,594
40,000–49,999	80	7,079	4,365
50,000 and more	75	12,772	5,529
Age of family head (years)			
Under 25	64	3,584	2,263
25–34	77	4,781	2,265
35–44	79	6,673	3,030
45–54	71	5,780	3,152
55–64	57	6,325	1,700
65–74	31	3,537	943
75 and over	15	1,117	308
Life-cycle stage of family head			
Under 45 years			
Unmarried, no children	64	4,864	1,900
Unmarried, no children	86	4,877	2,949
Married, with children	83	5,922	3,076
45 years and over			
Head in labor force	66	6,403	2,949
Head retired	27	2,967	677
All ages			
Unmarried, with children	65	4,433	1,135
All families	62	5,400	2,382

Source: *Federal Reserve Bulletin*, December 1984.

use. When children move out on their own and the parents are at their peak earning levels, the level of credit use may subside.

Level of Education

Traditionally, an individual's level of education has a significant influence on the amount of income earned (see Figure

1-4). Higher-paying jobs typically demand higher levels of education. Individuals with higher incomes can handle more debts. Therefore, individuals with more education would possess a greater capacity to incur and repay debt than those with lower levels of education, assuming they secure employment consistent with their education.

Why Consumers Use Credit

Consumer credit must serve some purpose or satisfy some need. Basically people use credit for four reasons:
- as a forced savings;
- as a convenience;
- to facilitate the consumption of future income; and
- to facilitate the purchase of high-priced items.

Using credit and incurring outstanding debts provide a strong incentive for some people to save to avoid defaulting on their payments. Often, people who otherwise find it almost impossible to make regular deposits into a savings account are able to make monthly payments to a creditor because they are committed to pay their debts in ways that add to their personal assets.

Credit also serves as a convenience for many consumers. For example, Judy Brown may walk into a store and see something she would like to purchase. If she does not have enough cash for the item, she can purchase the item on credit. In this situation, the use of credit is more readily available than cash, making it possible to immediately obtain the good. However, because it makes instant purchasing convenient, credit may also encourage impulse buying.

Consumers sometimes use credit because they anticipate that their income will increase. In an economic sense, they are currently consuming future income. In other words, consumers are spending money they do not have now, hoping or knowing they will have it in the future. For example, Larry White is told that he will be receiving a higher salary in six months due to a job promotion. Larry has been thinking of getting a new car, but he could not afford the monthly payments. Larry reasons that if he cuts back on some of his other expenses, he can purchase the car now with the anticipation of more income in six months. His purchase decision is affected by the potential availability of credit.

Credit also facilitates the purchase of high-priced items. Many consumers do not have the large amounts of savings needed to purchase high-priced items with cash; however, they often can afford to make smaller monthly payments. Consequently, they will make a credit rather than a cash purchase.

PROVIDERS OF CONSUMER CREDIT

Commercial banks, consumer finance companies, credit unions, savings institutions and retail firms are the major providers of consumer credit. All of these institutions, except retail firms, are known as *financial intermediaries*. Intermediaries serve as a link between individuals and others with surplus funds (savers and investors) and the credit market (mortgage loans and other investments).

Financial intermediaries use the funds deposited with them to make investments. Retail firms are not considered financial intermediaries since their main function is to sell retail items and only provide credit to facilitate the purchase of these items. Money invested by retail firms, in most cases, would be reinvested in the firm itself. Retail firms do not act as a link between depositors' funds and the credit market and, therefore, do not act as intermediaries.

Commercial Banks

Commercial banks are privately owned and operated financial intermediaries chartered by a state or federal agency. Their main purposes are to facilitate commerce (buying and selling) and promote industry, to provide a safe place for deposited funds and to aid in the transfer of those funds by check and credit extension. They are the oldest form of financial intermediary in the United States and serve the widest variety of businesses, government entities and individuals.

Commercial banks did not always extend consumer credit. Before 1930, over 50% of their lending activity was directed toward businesses. The remainder was dedicated to real estate transactions. However, during the 1930s, bank interest in consumer lending was stimulated by the increase in demand for consumer credit and the success of government

FIGURE 1-4
Average Income and Level of Education Compared, 1983

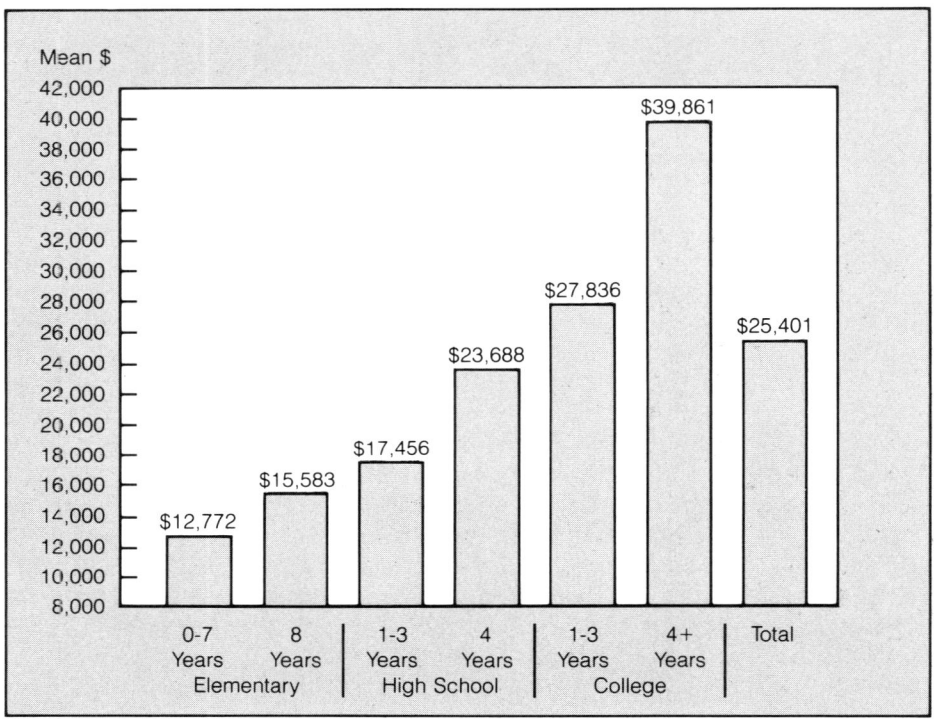

Source: Bureau of Statistics.

loan programs such as the FHA Title I Home Improvement Loans. By 1940, approximately 5,000 banks were actively making consumer loans. By the end of World War II (1945), as a result of an increased consumer demand for goods, this number had increased to 11,000.

Commercial banks presently hold approximately 43% of outstanding consumer installment credit (see Figure 1-5). Although the role of commercial banks as providers of consumer credit is not expected to change, different size banks may focus on different markets and priorities in the future. Large commercial banks are expected to become primarily concerned with serving commerce and industry as they were in earlier years, with smaller banks serving the local community and concentrating on the financial needs of individuals and households.

Consumer Finance Companies

A *consumer finance company* is a state-regulated company whose main purpose is to make installment credit available to consumers. Such financing is offered directly to consumers through direct cash loans or through the purchase of installment retail sales paper from dealers or retailers whose customers buy automobiles or other goods for which they pay over a period of time. Consumer finance companies are the second largest providers of consumer installment credit (see Figure 1-5).

Finance companies vary in size from small companies with a single office to large chains with many branch offices across the country. Some are independently owned while others are subsidiaries of manufacturers, bank holding companies, insurance companies or conglomerate firms. Finance companies obtain their funds by competing with the other businesses in the funds markets—they may sell their own

---

FIGURE 1-5
Total Assets of Financial Intermediaries at Year-end (billions of dollars)

Financial Intermediary	1960	1965	1970	1975	1980	1985*
Commercial Banks	$257.6	$377.3	$576.2	$964.9	$1,703.7	$2,460.3
Savings Institutions:						
Savings Associations	71.5	129.6	176.2	338.2	630.7	952.2
Savings Banks	40.6	58.2	79.0	121.1	171.6	325.7
Total	112.1	187.8	255.2	459.3	802.3	1,277.9
Life Insurance Companies	119.6	158.9	207.3	289.3	479.2	812.0
Private Pension Funds	38.1	73.6	110.4	186.6	412.5	655.2
State and Local Pension Funds	19.7	34.1	60.3	104.8	198.1	397.2
Finance Companies	27.6	44.7	64.0	98.8	191.3	331.7
Money Market Funds	. . .	. . .	. . .	3.7	74.4	207.5
Investment Companies	17.0	35.2	47.6	42.2	58.4	251.5
Credit Unions	6.3	11.0	18.0	36.9	71.6	135.3
Total	$598.0	$922.6	$1,339.0	$2,186.5	$3,991.5	$6,528.6

*Preliminary.
Sources: CUNA International, Inc.; Federal Home Loan Bank Board; Federal Reserve Board; Institute of Life Insurance; Investment Company Institute; National Council of Savings Institutions; United States League of Savings Institutions.

Reprinted with permission from *Savings Institutions Sourcebook*. Copyright © 1986 by the United States League of Savings Institutions.

stock, issue commercial paper or bonds, or they may borrow from banks.

State laws often limit the maximum rate of interest permitted on finance company loans, as well as the size of loans these companies can make. Annual interest rates for cash loans can vary from over 36% on the smallest loans, because of the high operating costs involved, to under 18% on larger, secured loans. The relationship between maximum authorized rates and the demand for various size loans also influences the size of loans made by finance companies. When rates are regulated, the lender may find loans that are less than a certain size unprofitable to provide.

Credit Unions

Credit unions are cooperative financial organizations chartered by the state or federal government for the purpose of collecting savings from members and making loans to other members. Members of credit unions have a common bond such as one or more of the following: place of employment; membership in the same labor union, religious congregation or club; or place of residence. Credit unions derive most of their income from consumer loan repayments by members and are dependent on this source of income for dividends to distribute to their savers.

The types of loans and investments that credit unions can make vary, although most unions specialize in consumer loans for home improvements, educational expenses or automobiles. Some credit unions also offer first and second mortgage loans and issue credit cards.

As of 1986, credit unions were the third largest providers of consumer installment credit (see Figure 1-5). Their growth is generally attributed to low operating expenses and low default rates that have enabled them to offer low interest rates to members. Credit unions frequently receive free office space provided by a sponsor; are exempt from state taxes because of their cooperative nature; and often receive free management services, all of which contribute to low operating expenses. However, larger credit unions, where more members use the services on a regular basis, are usually staffed with paid personnel because a more consistent schedule and longer working hours are necessary.

Savings Institutions

Savings and loan institutions are state or federally chartered financial intermediaries that accept deposits from the public and invest those deposits primarily in residential mortgage loans. They collect interest from borrowers and pay out the major portion of this interest to savers as a return on their deposits. Until recently, federally chartered savings institutions had limited opportunity to offer various forms of consumer credit. However, as a result of recent legislation (see Figure 1-6), savings institutions are rapidly increasing their share of consumer installment loans and currently rank fourth as providers of consumer installment credit (see Figure 1-5).

Savings institutions have the potential to play a substantially greater role than they already do as providers of consumer installment credit. Since the early 1980s, federally chartered savings institutions have capitalized further on their existing services and investigated new offerings to establish a competitive balance with other financial institutions. Further growth is expected because, in general, savings institution depositors have characteristics that enhance the possibility of their becoming consumer loan customers, too. A 1984 U.S. League of Savings Institutions Savers Survey revealed that savings institution depositors tend to be more highly educated and earn higher incomes than members of the average household.

State-chartered savings banks are nearly all *mutual* in form, though a few have converted to stock form. (Federal savings banks may select either a mutual or stock charter when organized or when converted to federal status.) They invest savings primarily in mortgage loans, stocks, bonds and other securities. Originally started in Philadelphia and Boston in 1812, most mutual savings banks are still located in the New England and Mid-Atlantic states, with a few in the West and Midwest.

In the past, unlike other financial institutions, mutual savings banks did not use deposits to extend credit. Rather, they invested in long-term securities, primarily bonds. Eventually they found it profitable to extend credit in the form of mortgage loans. Now, although their lending activity is still primarily real-estate oriented, they are also permitted to provide other forms of credit. Mutual savings banks have, in fact, become intense competitors for consumer credit in several northeastern states. They held over $10 billion in

FIGURE 1-6
New Powers for Federally Chartered Thrifts

New powers	DIDMCA	Garn-St Germain
	(Effective March 31, 1980)	(Effective October 15, 1982)
Consumer loans	Consumer loans up to 20% of total assets	Consumer loans up to 30% of total assets
	Educational loans up to 5% of total assets	
	Issue credit cards	
Commercial loans	Commercial real estate up to 20% of total assets	Commercial real estate loans up to 40% of total assets
	Unsecured construction loans up to 5% of total assets	Other commercial loans up to 5% of total assets prior to January 1, 1984 (7.5% of total assets for savings banks) and up to 10% of total assets thereafter
		Equipment leasing up to 10% of total assets
Transaction accounts	NOW accounts from individuals and nonprofit organizations	NOW accounts from governmental units
		Demand deposits from persons or organizations that have established "a business, corporate, commercial or agricultural loan relationship" with the institution

outstanding consumer installment credit at the end of January, 1986.

Retail Firms

Retail firms are businesses that facilitate the transfer of consumer goods from the manufacturer to the consumer. The most familiar type of retail firm is the large-scale, nationwide department store. These stores specialize in selling retail goods to consumers and generally extend retail rather than cash credit. According to Federal Reserve statistics, these retail companies follow closely behind savings and loans as providers of consumer installment credit.

Retail credit can be traced back to the colonial period when companies first extended credit to facilitate the purchase of large items. One of the first to provide consumer installment credit for its products was the Singer Sewing Machine Company. On a smaller scale, general stores in small towns often extended credit to their customers by merely keeping a record of the customer's name and the amount of purchase.

Retail firms extend credit to increase sales volume and to develop customer loyalty. When customers use credit they tend to purchase more goods and usually purchase higher-quality, higher-priced items. Also, consumers usually prefer to buy at the stores with which they have established credit relationships. For some department stores, at least half of all sales are credit sales.

Although the cost of extending credit is expensive, most retail firms, especially the larger concerns, must offer some form of credit to compete effectively. Thus, credit is often seen as a key factor in maintaining a high sales volume.

Automobile financing is an important segment of retail lending. The large automobile manufacturers have wholly owned credit subsidiaries that purchase installment contracts from their auto dealers. Automobile credit subsidiaries assist sales by offering a low interest rate for certain models or for limited periods of time. Also, some automobile companies form additional subsidiaries to provide other types of consumer credit and mortgages.

Nationwide credit card companies such as American Express, Diners Club and Carte Blanche are also considered retail lenders. These are essentially travel and entertainment companies that require all charges to be paid in full on a 30-day basis.

Gasoline companies are another provider of consumer credit. They extend credit for the same reasons as retail firms: for customer convenience, to increase sales volume and to build customer loyalty. Gasoline companies provide only revolving credit. Between 1980 and 1986, their holdings of revolving credit remained stagnant at around $4 billion. With over $500 billion of overall consumer installment credit outstanding in 1986, gasoline companies today hold less than 1% of the total consumer installment credit outstanding.

THE FUTURE: MARKETING'S IMPORTANCE

Regardless of the type of credit or the type of provider, consumer credit must be a service that consumers value and will use. The function of determining consumers' credit needs and designing and promoting desirable credit services is marketing. *Marketing* is a management function; its purpose is to identify and provide at a profit the financially related services that customers want and need. Marketing activities include: researching customer needs; selecting from alternative ideas; and planning, implementing, distributing, servicing, evaluating, and revising products and services.

Since a documented need and desire for consumer credit exists, lending institutions want to become invovled in this profitable area. However, offering various forms of consumer credit regardless of the consumer's credit history, income, family size and other characteristics is extremely risky. And ignoring the demands of the economic and competitive environment within which a financial institution must operate is equally risky. Therefore, for any financial institution to be successful in the consumer credit area, it must be ready to undertake a complete marketing effort.

DETERMINING CUSTOMER NEEDS

There are many ways of determining customer needs. Some are more cost effective than others.
- Personal contact allows needs to be directly observed and communicated.
- Telemarketing (or telephone marketing) allows consumer needs, questions and answers to be voiced.
- Printed materials that request a reply can be sent by mail.
- Statistics of recorded buying patterns or responses from a particular group can be studied.
- Consumer complaint information can be analyzed.

Personal Contact

Personal contact is the most direct way of discovering a potential or existing customer's needs. It can also be the most expensive method, although costs can be controlled with proper market planning. Personal contact affords many advantages. It provides lending personnel with the greatest amount of information about the customer. Not only can the lender listen to the customer, but also observe the customer's mannerisms, facial expressions and gestures. These observations can then be interpreted for further information about the customer's needs and wants.

Customer contact personnel must be able to use personal contact to discuss fees and services knowledgeably. Personnel well versed in their institution's products are likely to give customers a favorable impression of professionalism.

Telemarketing

Determining and servicing customer needs over the telephone can be very profitable for lenders. The telemarketing of products and services can be handled in two ways. With *inbound telemarketing* the lender's telephone number is advertised (for example, a toll-free number) and incoming customer calls are handled. With *outbound telemarketing* the lender's employees call potential or existing customers to stimulate business. Both telemarketing methods have advantages and disadvantages and require that employees master telephone communication skills.

Financial institutions that use telemarketing have found that inbound telemarketing attracts new customers and provides a chance to cross-sell additional services to existing customers. Many members of the young, affluent market are attracted to the convenience of using the phone to get information about a service.

Some lenders who use inbound telemarketing ask customers who call in to answer a few profile questions such as, "What motivated you to call?" Profile questions may disclose to the lender some useful statistics. For example, the lender could determine the percentage of callers who were not current customers and would not have even considered the lender before they learned of the toll-free number.

Outbound telemarketing is most effective when used to cross-sell additional services to existing customers. Lenders have successfully used this method as a follow-up to direct mail advertising.

Customers have cited the following advantages of conducting business over the phone.
- It allows them to do their banking business from their homes.
- It saves them time.
- It provides them with personal service and immediate answers to their questions.

Customers who do not like to be contacted by phone say that they are reluctant to give out personal financial information over the phone. Some financial institutions are now trying to develop a method to prove to the customer that the call is indeed from the financial institution.

By Mail

Marketing by mail to prospective and existing customers is a fairly inexpensive way to make targeted audiences aware of a financial product or service. Unfortunately, generating more than a small percentage of responses can be difficult. Typically, prospective customers who receive unsolicited mail spend only a few seconds glancing at it before they dispose of it. To increase the number of responses that can result in approved loans, lenders need to spend time developing a market plan.

A mail marketing plan needs to address several issues:
- when should the campaign be launched;
- what products and services will be emphasized;
- who will be contacted; and
- how will questions be answered and services rendered.

Using Statistics

Statistical summaries are often used to target or segment a market that management hopes will be responsive to the services offered. Statistics can be used empirically to derive a credit screening or preapproval process. (Credit screening is explained in further detail in Chapter 5.) Marketing managers often study statistics before implementing a telephone, mail or advertising campaign; in fact, all methods of determining customer needs can be enhanced by the use of statistics.

Certain types of statistics are more useful for marketing specific products and services than others. When distribution is local and market conditions differ from national norms, the local institution understands and caters to the basic habits of the area's people.

In this situation, local market statistics are helpful. Examples include specific types of loans. For products with a widespread demand that are distributed nationally, statistics from national research may be useful. Examples of such products include credit cards and automated teller machine cards.

DELIVERING PRODUCTS AND SERVICES

Four ways of delivering financial services to consumers are maintaining branch offices, word-of-mouth referrals, credit cards and participating in an ATM network. Today, financial services are being successfully marketed in ways beyond the "brick and mortar" method of maintaining numerous branch offices. Instead of waiting for customers to walk in some aggressive lenders are actively involved in finding loans to make. For example, a lender may market its products by word-of-mouth referrals from dealers, realtors, lawyers, financial consultants and other institutions not offering the product. Word-of-mouth referrals from professionals in the community encourage customers to accept and ask for new, innovative products and services.

Another way to deliver services is through credit cards. With credit cards, the lender must perform only a single act of judgment: the initial approval of a line of credit. From that single decision, an endless series of transactions is possible. Once the lender has become efficient, there is potential for delivering much more than merely small, unsecured loans. The credit card can be used in conjunction with other services—i.e., deposits and other forms of investments.

Lenders also can deliver consumer loan services by participating in a shared, national ATM network. By participating in such a shared system, lenders can penetrate new markets while generating user fee income from owned ATMs. Because there are so many institutions that have ATM cardholders, the potential for user fees is great.

SUMMARY

Consumer installment credit was first widely used to purchase high-priced items such as sewing machines and automobiles in the early twentieth century. Its use has accelerated tremendously since World War II, with outstanding obligations reaching over $500 billion by mid-1985. Throughout history, the demand for credit was, and still is, directly related to economic conditions that affect consumers' income level and the availability of goods to consumers.

The three categories of consumer credit are installment or single payment; open-end or closed-end; and secured or unsecured. The terms installment and single payment refer to the method of payment at some future date. Open- and closed-end consumer credit refer to the continuity of credit extended under one credit arrangement. Secured and unsecured consumer credit refer to the existence or nonexistence of collateral used to insure full payment at some future date.

The three means of obtaining consumer credit are through retail, service and direct loans. All three involve the immediate possession of a good or service to be paid for at some future date. Two major features that distinguish these means from one another are the characteristics of the item acquired and the number of parties involved in the purchase of the item.

Level of family income, age, stage in the family life cycle and years of education are four consumer characteristics that influence the volume of credit use. There are four general reasons for using credit: credit is a forced savings, a convenience, a facilitator of the consumption of future income and a facilitator in the purchase of high-priced items.

The five major providers of consumer credit are commercial banks, consumer finance companies, credit unions, savings institutions and retail stores.

Marketing affects all financial decisions. Lenders use market planning throughout all stages of the loan cycle. Marketing includes determining customer needs and delivering products and services in an efficient, cost effective way that will generate profits. Several ways of determining customer needs are personal contact, telemarketing, mail and the analysis of statistics. Employee cross-selling is a very effective way to determine and market services. All methods involve an attempt to create an awareness of the financial services available to people who are potentially interested and who will have the desire and ability to take some action.

Creating value for the customer is important when delivering lending services. Lenders need fast, cost-efficient delivery systems to enhance customers' perceptions of the value of their services. Such systems include branch offices, word-of-mouth referrals from community professionals, credit cards and ATMs linked to several services.

CHAPTER QUESTIONS

1. List four reasons why consumers use credit.

2. State how the level of family income, age, stage of family life cycle and level of education relate to the potential use of consumer credit.

3. Differentiate between open-end and closed-end credit.

4. Describe the three basic means of obtaining consumer credit, and note how they are used.

5. List and describe the roles of the five primary providers of consumer credit.

6. Define the term marketing.

7. Cite the advantages and disadvantages of determining customer needs in person, over the telephone, by mail and from statistics. Discuss the employee skills necessary for each method.

8. Explain three ways of delivering financial services and how each can benefit both the lender and consumer.

2

Types of Loans and Credit Insurance

Objectives

After studying this chapter, you should be able to:
- ☐ Differentiate between direct and indirect loan origination;
- ☐ Describe three factors that are usually included in consumer loan terms;
- ☐ Evaluate six forms of collateral commonly used to secure consumer loans;
- ☐ Identify common loan features of at least ten specific consumer loans;
- ☐ Cite four benefits a savings institution might gain from offering a credit card program;
- ☐ Differentiate between the single-account and two-account approaches to handling overdraft loans; and
- ☐ Identify nine types of insurance designed to reduce both lender and borrower risk.

INTRODUCTION

By the time a customer enters a savings institution to apply for a consumer loan, the institution has already completed extensive planning that enables it to offer credit arrangements acceptable to both customers and the institution. What types of loans best fit customers' needs? What collateral, if any, is required to secure the loans? What is the proper interest rate to charge so that the loans are profitable for the lender and still attractive to borrowers? What insurance is needed to protect both the customers and the institution? These and many other questions were answered during the actual development of a successful consumer lending program.

Consumer loans offered by savings institutions can be classified in many different ways, including purpose, terms and origination method. Every institution does not offer all types of consumer loans. Understanding the key characteristics of loans will help to distinguish among the many types of consumer loans and to explain the benefits of a specific loan program to customers.

The first part of this chapter provides an overview of the loan characteristics that should be considered when developing a consumer lending program. Features such as origination methods, loan terms and security considerations are explained as they apply to consumer loans.

The second part of the chapter describes a variety of specific consumer loans that federally chartered savings institutions have the authority to make. First, an explanation is given of the traditional nonmortgage loans that many federally chartered savings institutions have offered for some time that can now be offered as consumer loans or under other loan authorizations. Then, consumer loans are explained, and credit cards and overdraft loans are discussed. The chapter concludes by presenting the particular types of credit insurance that are related to consumer lending.

CONSUMER LOAN POLICIES

The three means of consumer credit are retail, service and direct loan.

The goal of a consumer loan program is to be profitable. At the same time, it must meet state and federal legal requirements. In pursuing its goal, management has several options to consider when choosing the specific characteristics, or policies, of the loans it will offer. Loan policies that must be decided upon include origination method, terms and acceptable collateral to the lender. Of course, loan policies should be structured to be profitable to the lender also.

Loan Origination

Even though many different lenders offer numerous types of consumer loans, there are only two basic methods of loan origination: direct origination and indirect origination.

In direct loan origination, a loan is negotiated between a consumer and a lender and is considered a direct loan. Usually a customer directly contacts a lender, completes an application and is interviewed by a loan officer. The loan officer conducts a credit investigation, makes the decision to approve or reject the application and, if approved, closes the loan. A direct loan does not have to be closed by an employee of the lender or at the lender's place of business. As long as the consumer has directly applied to the lender for the loan, it can be closed by a servicing agent or at a location other than the lender's office and still be considered a direct loan.

In contrast, an *indirect loan* is any loan originated by a dealer, retailer, or seller of goods and services to finance the purchase of those goods and services. Indirect loans are also called third-party loans or dealer paper because the loans are assigned or sold to a lender by a third party. For example, a consumer could apply for a loan to finance an automobile purchase at the car dealer. In this case, the dealer will contact the lender. In the indirect loan origination method, a loan is indirectly provided by a lender to the customer in a process that usually involves three parties: a lender, a dealer and a consumer. Automobile, mobile home, recreational vehicle, home improvement and appliance loans are frequently originated through indirect lending.

With the indirect method of origination, the lender may lose some accuracy or quality in receiving all of the pertinant information about the borrower or transaction. Although indirect lending may offer a potential for greater loan volume, the risks are also greater than with direct lending because the lender does not have personal contact with the borrower.

Although credit cards have some characteristics of both direct and indirect origination, they usually are considered direct loans.

Loan Terms

Before granting a consumer loan, the most important criteria to assess are the borrower's credit standing and ability to repay the loan. This information will determine whether a loan should be granted and how the loan terms should be arranged.

Loan terms are usually comprised of three factors. These are the loan amount, loan maturity (the time within which the loan must be repaid) and interest rate charged. Loan terms are determined by both legal restrictions and lender policy. Specific loan limits, loan-to-value ratios and maturities may be prescribed by the particular loan authority under which the loan is structured. For example, a lender's policy may allow lending up to 80% of the suggested value for a used automobile as stated in the National Automobile Dealers Association Used Car Guide. If the dealer is asking a purchase price for the auto that is higher than the suggested value, the buyer may be seeking a loan that is over the lender's acceptable loan-to-value ratio. In addition, the maturity, loan amount and interest rate can be flexible or fixed (open-end or closed-end) depending upon the lender's policy.

If not limited by regulation, the maximum loan amount is usually based on a combination of the borrower's ability to repay the loan and the lender's established policy. For example, an institution's policy may determine that the maximum auto loan for used cars not more than three years old is $10,000 with a maturity not to exceed 48 months.

The maturity of a consumer loan is based on factors such as regulations, lender policy, borrower's financial ability and the nature of the collateral securing the loan. For secured loans, the type of collateral used and the length of time it retains its value will affect the length of time granted to repay the loan.

Interest rates charged for consumer credit vary depending upon the type of loan. Generally, a higher risk loan means a higher interest rate. For example, an unsecured loan (one not secured by collateral) may require a higher interest rate than a secured loan. The length of time allowed to repay a loan also affects the interest rate. Longer maturities tend to carry higher rates because of increased risk to both the borrower and the lender. The longer the loan maturity, the greater the chance that the borrower may become unable to repay the loan. For lenders, both interest rate risks and the market value risks of holding a loan increase with longer maturities. Because of inflation's impact on increasing prices, however, maturities on most types of consumer loans have increased in recent years.

Consumer Loan Collateral

While consumer loans can be unsecured, many are secured, or collaterized, by real or personal property, guarantors or co-makers, insurance policies, stocks, bonds and other negotiable instruments. The nature of the collateral used to secure consumer loans requires unique considerations and involves unique risks that distinguish consumer lending from mortgage lending. For example, the collateral used for most consumer loans quickly depreciates in value. Also, such collateral is usually transported easily and, (other than real property or when otherwise attached) in the event of default, repossession may prove difficult.

The two most common types of collateral used to secure loans are real property and personal property. *Real property* is land along with any buildings or other objects permanently affixed to it. *Personal property* includes objects that are not permanently affixed to land. Some examples of personal property include appliances, cars, boats and television sets. Most often personal property is used as collateral to secure consumer loans. Special attention must be given to the value of the collateral, in other words, the dollar amount for which the collateral can realistically be sold.

The value of collateral can either appreciate or depreciate. Real property tends to increase, or appreciate, in value over a period of time. Land is not normally subject to the same kind of physical deterioration as personal property, but its value is affected by location, supply and demand, and overall economic conditions. The structures and items permanently affixed to a parcel of land are subject to wear and tear, but, because much emphasis is placed on the land, the value of real property tends to remain relatively stable or even increase.

Personal property usually depreciates, or loses value over a period of time, because it is subject to wear and tear (physical depreciation). The analysis of a consumer loan secured by personal property requires more attention on the part of the lender than one secured by real property. A loan secured by depreciating collateral will require a shorter maturity than a loan secured by collateral with an anticipated long life or collateral that appreciates in value. Unless the maturity of the loan matches the expected life of the personal property being financed, the value of collateral securing the consumer loan may actually decrease to a point where its value is less than the loan's principal balance (the portion of the loan amount not repaid). If this situation occurs, the borrower may feel there is little incentive to repay the loan and may decide to stop making payments altogether. Also, there might not be enough value remaining in the collateral if it has to be sold to repay the loan. Because of the possibility of this situation occuring, most lenders consider the financial strength of the borrower to be more important than the collateral itself.

Other forms of collateral used to secure loans are insurance policies, stocks, bonds and other negotiable instruments. When an individual pledges an insurance policy as collateral, the policy's value can be based on either the face amount or the cash value (surrender value). Typically, lenders will take physical possession of the collateral when it is in the form of stocks, bonds or other negotiable instruments. Because the value of such collateral fluctuates daily, an agreement for additional collateral should be required in case the value falls below a set minimum. If the loan will be used for investment purposes, the lender must also be aware of loan amount limits, called margin requirements, that are set by the Federal Reserve Board. These limitations depend on the type of security (common stock, corporate or Treasury bonds) that will be purchased with the loan proceeds. For example, if Mr. Leverage wants to finance the purchase of $1,000 of common stock, he would be required to pledge collateral having a value of at least $500.

A loan can also be secured by a *guarantor*, an individual or entity, who promises to make payments to the lender in the event the borrower defaults on the loan. Borrowers are considered to be in default when they do not make the payments necessary to repay the loan. Lenders request guarantors when they want additional assurance from one or more financially competent individuals that the debt will be repaid. In the case of a young borrower, the guarantor is often a parent or other close relative. In other situations, the guarantor may be a business partner, neighbor or friend. The guarantor's signature is an indication of his or her belief that the borrower will be able to repay the debt. In the event the borrower cannot repay the debt, the lender will look to the guarantor for repayment.

Loan Profitability

The dollar amount per loan is extremely important in determining loan profitability. The primary reason loan departments are volume oriented is that most costs involved in acquiring and maintaining loans are fixed, regardless of the dollar amount per loan. No matter how small or large the dollar amount of the loan, the lender's total cost will remain the same because similar procedures and labor efforts are required for all loans.

When lenders calculate the profitability of a loan program they are concerned with four costs.
- The cost of funds including bad debts. This represents the interest rate lenders pay to obtain money that they can lend.
- The acquisition cost. This represents the marketing and administrative costs involved with making loans.
- Servicing costs. These represent the costs of collecting, receiving and handling payments.
- Liquidation costs. These pertain to computing pay-offs, releasing liens on secured loans and other administrative costs that are necessary when loans are paid off.

After lenders have determined the total costs for their loan program, they concentrate on lowering the cost per dollar loaned by increasing the volume and loan size if possible. While the total cost of a loan remains the same, the cost per dollar loaned does not. Assume, for example, the total lender's cost of making a loan is $50. Forest Savings and Loan has 50 loans totaling $50,000, while Pearson Savings and Loan has 25 loans totaling $20,000. The total cost of the loans to Forest Savings is $2,500 (50 loans times $50 per loan). This amount is 5% of the total dollars ($50,000) extended as loans. Thus, Forest spent five cents out of every dollar to make its loans. The total cost to Pearson is $1,250, (25 loans time $50 per loan). This amount represents 6.25% of the total dollar amount ($20,000) of loans made. Pearson spent over six cents per dollar on loan costs, which is over one cent more than Forest spent.

The important variable here is volume. The average dollar amount of each loan extended by Forest was $1,000, while the average dollar amount per loan extended by Pearson was $800. The cost per dollar was lower for Forest than for Pearson. Cost per dollar loaned partly explains why loans for smaller amounts frequently carry higher interest rates than loans for larger amounts. However, if a lender extends a large volume of loans, this will also affect the interest rate of its large and small loans.

TYPES OF LOANS

Federally chartered savings institutions have long been able to offer a variety of loans in addition to first mortgage loans. Some types of loans being offered include the following: equity (junior mortgages), home improvement, mobile home, deposit account and education. The following section describes these traditional nonmortgage loans along with the consumer and credit card loans that savings institutions have been granted authority to offer by the Depository Institutions Deregulation and Monetary Control Act of 1980 (DIDMCA).

Traditional Nonmortgage Loans

The specific types of traditional nonmortgage loans are home improvement, mobile home, deposit account and education loans. These loans are grouped under the heading of "traditional" because they were the only loans, other than first mortgage loans, that federally chartered savings institutions could offer prior to the DIDMCA of 1980.

Home Improvement Loans

Home improvement loans provide funds for repairing, altering or restoring residential structures. Examples of home improvements include room remodeling or additions, swimming pools, siding installations, energy conservation alterations, and new furnaces or air conditioning systems.

Home improvement loans can be classified as either government-insured or conventional. Government-insured loans are authorized for savings institutions under Title I of the National Housing Act of 1934 and are insured by the Federal Housing Administration (FHA). Conventional home improvement loans are authorized for federally chartered institutions by the Home Owner's Loan Act of 1933. A conventional home improvement loan program (without government or private insurance) is conducted according to an institution's own plan; that is, an institution develops its own policies and procedures in compliance with federal and state laws and regulations. Home improvement loans are originated as either direct or indirect loans and are typically offered as installment loans.

Homeowners especially seek home improvement loans in times of high inflation, such as those experienced in the 1970s and early 1980s. As home prices continue a general trend upward, many homeowners prefer to remodel or add to a present home rather than to purchase another home at a higher price. As of year end 1984, FSLIC-insured savings institutions held nearly $5.6 billion in home improvement loans.

The earliest home improvement loan program was the Federal Housing Administration Title I program authorized in 1934. The Federal Housing Administration is a government agency within the Department of Housing and Urban Development whose purpose is to stabilize the home mortgage market. The FHA does not extend loans but functions as an insuring agency on loans made by lenders under prescribed conditions. The FHA insures a lender for up to 90% of the loss sustained on an individual loan. The total payments to any one lender are limited to a maximum of 10% of the institution's total FHA-insured loan portfolio. The FHA requires the institution to pay a premium for this insurance protection. However, savings institutions are attracted to the FHA program because their losses are reduced when a borrower does not repay the loan.

All federally chartered and most state-chartered institutions are permitted to make FHA Title I loans. Institutions wishing to make these loans must qualify with the FHA as approved lenders by meeting all FHA procedural requirements and using the prescribed FHA forms. The FHA furnishes procedures manuals, updates the manuals with regular bulletins and provides required forms. In addition, the U.S. League of Savings Institution's *Federal Guide* contains up-to-date FHA regulations.

Most home improvement loan programs are conventional rather than FHA. Conventional loans are more flexible than FHA Title I loans. The FHA imposes restrictions on lenders to prevent them from extending loans for various purposes, such as the construction of a swimming pool or the installation of a burglar alarm. Lenders offering their own home improvement loan plans are not subject to FHA restrictions.

Terms for home improvement loans can differ depending upon the loan amount, lender policy and existing state laws. An institution now has the option under FSLIC regulations to choose the lending authority under which it will categorize home improvement loans. Home improvement loans may be made under the FSLIC authority for Nonconforming Secured Loans and Loans Without the Requirement of Security, the real estate lending authority or the new consumer loan authority. Each authority has its own restrictions and requirements for loan terms.

Savings institutions can invest in either secured or unsecured home improvement loans. A secured loan generally uses the real property on which the improvements will be made as collateral. **Loans secured by liens on real estate may still be considered as consumer credit under FSLIC regulations. In this case, however, "the association relies substantially upon other factors, such as the general credit standing of the borrower, guaranties, or security other than the real estate or mobile home as the primary security for the loan."**[1] Today, many lenders display more flexible attitudes toward extended maturities in structuring home improvement loans to allow for interest rate and payment adjustments during the term of the loan. Also, there are no geographical lending area restrictions except those imposed by the lender or state regulations.

Each lender can determine a policy for securing conventional home improvement loans. The Federal Home Loan

Bank Board (FHLBB) requires no security on home improvement loans made by federally chartered institutions. However, as a precautionary measure, institutions usually establish a specific loan amount over which the loan must be secured. The FHA requires that loans over $2,500 be secured by a lien on the real property.

Deposit Account Loans
A *deposit account loan* is extended to a consumer who pledges a portion of his or her funds deposited with the institution as security for the loan. Authority for deposit account loans originally was granted by the Home Owners' Loan Act of 1933 which has been amended several times.

A saver who borrows against deposits pays interest. This interest rate is usually between 2% and 4% above the interest rate the lender pays on the deposit account. During the term of the loan, the deposit account is still accumulating earnings, and in effect, the borrower (saver) is only paying between 2% and 4% interest on the loan. For this reason, deposit account loans are very appealing to consumers (see Figure 2-1).

A consumer might want a deposit account loan for two basic reasons: to avoid loss of earnings on the deposit account and to leave a savings program undisturbed. Some deposit accounts do not pay earnings to the date of withdrawal, and others have penalties for early withdrawal. Since the saver loses earnings if money is withdrawn from the account, it is often wiser to take out a loan for the desired amount using the deposit account as security.

Deposit account loans are the safest type of loan that lenders can make because they are secured 100% by a customer's money. According to FHLBB regulations concerning deposit account loans, a savings institution cannot lend a sum of money that exceeds the balance in the deposit account. Also, the institution must charge the borrower a rate of interest that is at least 1% per year more than the effective yield paid on the collateralized deposit account, including the effects of compounding.

Deposit account loans became very popular in the 1970s. Total loans outstanding for savings institutions increased from $1.5 billion in 1974 to $6 billion in 1979, with the greatest increase taking place between 1977 and 1979. This may have been due to the introduction of new savings plans requiring

FIGURE 2-1
Deposit Account Loan Form

SAVINGS ACCOUNT LOAN

NAME AND ADDRESS	☐ DO ☐ DO NOT CHARGE OFF AT NEXT EARNINGS DATE.					LOAN NO.
	INSTALLMENTS OF	FIRST PAYMENT DUE	INT ONLY ☐	LUMP SUM ☐	PRE-AUTH. ☐	DATE OF MATURITY

DATE OF NOTE	ANNUAL INTEREST RATE	SAVINGS NUMBER	SAVINGS BALANCE	APPROVED BY	CHECK NUMBER
	%		$		

DISCLOSURE SAVINGS ACCOUNT LOAN

ANNUAL PERCENTAGE RATE The cost of your credit as a yearly rate	FINANCE CHARGE The dollar amount the credit will cost you	Amount Financed The amount of credit provided to you or on your behalf	Total of Payments The amount you will have paid after you have made all payments as scheduled
%	$	$	$

You have the right to receive at this time an itemization of the Amount Financed
☐ I want an itemization. ☐ I do not want an itemization.
Your payment schedule will be:

Number of Payments	Amount of Payments	When payments are due
	$	
	$	
	$	

☐ This loan payable on demand, disclosure assumes 1 year maturity.
VARIABLE RATE: The Annual Percentage Rate may increase during your loan only if the interest rate paid on your pledged savings account increases. Your loan rate will be increased to ______% above whatever the rate that is being paid on your pledged savings account. Any increase will be in the form of higher payments. If, hypothetically, your loan was for $1500 at 10% for 12 months with payments of $131.88 and the rate immediately increased to 12% your payment would increase to $133.28.
Security: You are giving a security interest in your savings account number:
☐ ______________

Prepayment: If you pay off early, you will not have to pay a penalty.

See the Note on the right for any additional information about nonpayment, default, any required payment in full before the scheduled date, and prepayment refunds and penalties.

e means an estimate

11801-8 (8/85) CSLDWA-1
©SAF Systems and Forms, Inc.

NOTE

In this Note the words You, and Your mean anyone who signed it. Our, We and Us mean

To repay your loan you promise to pay us $______________
plus simple interest on your unpaid balance at the annual rate of ________ per cent.
You will pay this amount in ______ ☐ monthly ☐ quarterly ☐ semi-annual payment(s) of $__________ each and a final payment of $__________. We can require you to pay immediately the unpaid balance of your loan plus unpaid interest at any time we choose. The FINANCE CHARGE shown is estimated assuming that you will make all payments on the due date.
Your payment(s) are due on the same day of the month starting ______________, 19____.
Your interest rate will be increased only if the rate paid on your pledged savings account increases. Your loan rate will increase to ______% above whatever the rate that is being paid on your pledged savings account.

You pledge your account #______________ in our institution as security for your loan. You promise to us that you are the rightful owner of this account; that there are no current lawsuits, bankruptcy proceedings, other security instruments or transfers to a third party that would affect the security interest we are establishing here. We may withdraw from this account any amount due without sending you a notice or making a formal complaint or protest of your nonpayment at any time.

By signing below, you acknowledge receipt of a completed copy of this Note and Disclosure Statement.

______________________ SEAL

______________________ SEAL

high minimum balances and severe penalties on withdrawals. In 1979, deposit account loans represented 40% of all nonmortgage loans made by savings institutions.

At year-end 1983 and 1984, deposit account loans outstanding were $3.2 and $3.9 billion, respectively. Today, some institutions are questioning the profitability of continuing to offer deposit account loans because of the administrative costs involved. Consumers still find such loans practical when the early withdrawal penalties exceed the costs to borrow.

Mobile Home Loans

A *mobile home loan* is a nonmortgage loan made to an individual for the purchase of a mobile home. It is secured by the lender's lien on the mobile home. A *lien* is a claim that a lender has upon the property of another as security for the payment of a debt or charge. Technically defined, a mobile home is a movable, portable dwelling without permanent foundation, designed for year-round living. A mobile home today is officially referred to as a "manufactured home," although mobile home is still the common marketplace term.

Mobile home loans, like home improvement loans, can be classified as either government-insured or conventional. FHA-insured mobile home loans are authorized by Title I of the National Housing Act of 1934 to facilitate the financing of mobile home purchases. Savings institutions also may offer mobile home loans insured by the Farmers Home Administration (FmHA) or guaranteed by the Veterans Administration (VA). VA assistance takes the form of a guarantee to the lender on loans with low downpayments. Institutions are also authorized by the Housing and Development Act of 1968 to invest in conventional (own plan) mobile home loans. By mid-1986, mobile home loans outstanding exceeded $25 billion.

During 1985, the nationwide average price of a new single family home surpassed $100,000, while the average price of existing single family homes climbed over $90,000. It is no wonder that mobile homes have once again become a widely accepted substitute for the traditional, single family home. Figure 2-2 shows that mobile homes reached their peak of popularity in the early 1970s. However, they continue to add to the housing stock. Since 1980, mobile home shipments have accounted for over 20% of the total annual number of new, single-family units.

Improvements in quality have increased mobile home acceptance. Since 1969, the building codes, safety standards and construction requirements to which all manufacturers must adhere have helped to maintain a specified level of quality.

The expandable mobile home is a recent manufacturing innovation that adds more space to the standard mobile home by means of a fold-out section. Once a unit is placed in its permanent position, the fold-out section can be expanded by the use of sliding, unfolding or tip-out hydraulic devices. Double-wide and triple-wide mobile homes offer another spacious alternative. This type of home consists of two or more separate sections that are joined into a single unit at the mobile home site.

FIGURE 2-2
Mobile Home Shipments

		% of Private Starts	
Year	Number of Units	Total	Single-family†
1960	103,700	8.3%	9.4%
1965	216,470	14.7	18.3
1970	401,190	28.0	33.0
1971	496,570	24.2	30.1
1972	575,940	24.4	30.6
1973	566,920	27.7	33.4
1974	329,300	24.6	27.0
1975	212,690	18.3	19.2
1976	246,120	16.0	17.5
1977	277,000	13.9	16.0
1978	275,900	13.7	16.1
1979	277,400	15.9	18.9
1980	221,600	17.1	20.6
1981	240,900	22.2	25.5
1982	239,600	22.6	26.6
1983	295,800	17.4	21.7
1984	295,600	16.9	21.4
1985*	283,500	16.3	20.9

*Preliminary.
†Single-family conventional homes and mobile homes.
Sources: Department of Commerce; Manufactured Housing Institute; National Conference of States on Building Codes and Standards.

Reprinted with permission from *Savings Institutions Sourcebook*. Copyright © 1986 by United States League of Savings Institutions.

The larger loan amounts and longer maturities required for mobile home loans make this very specialized form of lending quite unlike other traditional nonmortgage loans. Federally chartered institutions can lend up to 90% of the borrower's total cost and offer a maturity of up to 20 years. Higher mobile home prices require longer terms, which, in turn, permit more manageable monthly payments; thus, maturities often range from 15 to 20 years (see Figure 2-3).

FHLBB regulations issued in 1980 allow institutions more flexibility in offering mobile home loans and structuring loan terms. For example, there are now no geographical lending area restrictions for loans originated by savings institutions. In addition, federally chartered institutions have the authority to make mobile home loans with an interest rate and payment adjustment flexibility similar to the flexibility of home improvement loans.

In the past, most mobile home loans were originated on an indirect basis. Today, an increasing number of these loans are made on a direct basis. Direct origination makes adjustable interest rate and payment arrangements more feasible and easier to structure.

Mobile home loans are usually secured by a chattel, or personal property, lien on the mobile home itself. In the process of extending credit, however, institutions have the option of utilizing the flexible provisions of the consumer loan authority or other mobile home lending authorities. If an institution relies substantially on the general credit standing of the borrower, guaranties or security other than the mobile home as the primary security for the loan, the loan is considered consumer credit. If primary security is placed on the mobile home itself, the loan is not considered consumer credit, but rather a real estate loan.

Education Loans
The Housing Act of 1964 and subsequent amendments provided authority for federally chartered savings institutions to make loans for the purpose of financing a college or vocational education. A few state legislatures had previously provided authority for their respective state-chartered institutions to make education loans. Today, a number of government-sponsored and private education loan programs exist, funded through federal or state agencies or private organizations.

Lenders can, if they choose, sell student loans in the secondary market as a source of liquidity. The Student Loan Marketing Association (Sallie Mae) is a government-sponsored, private corporation created to increase the flow of funds into student loans by aiding the purchase of student loans in the secondary market. This also alleviates subsequent servicing requirements for student loans.

Federal legislation created several programs which insure, guarantee and/or provide assistance for education loans. The Higher Education Act of 1965 was designed to provide student loan insurance and federal guarantees to lenders meeting the requirements set forth in the act. This

FIGURE 2-3, Side 1
Mobile Home Loan Application

FIGURE 2-3, Side 2
Mobile Home Loan Application

IMPORTANT
VOLUNTARY INFORMATION FOR GOVERNMENT MONITORING PURPOSES
COMPLETE FOR DWELLING RELATED LOANS ONLY

Notice to Applicant(s) For A Loan Related To A Dwelling

The following information is requested by the Federal government to monitor compliance by the lender with Federal statutes which prohibit lenders from discrimination on these bases against applicants for a loan or other service. The lender is required to note race and sex, on the basis of sight and/or surname, if the applicant(s) choose not to do so.

APPLICANT		CO-APPLICANT	
*Race/National Origin	*Sex	*Race/National Origin	*Sex
☐ 1. American Indian or Alaskan Native	☐ Male	☐ 1. American Indian or Alaskan Native	☐ Male
☐ 2. Asian or Pacific Islander	☐ Female	☐ 2. Asian or Pacific Islander	☐ Female
☐ 3. Black ☐ 4. White		☐ 3. Black ☐ 4. White	
☐ 5. Hispanic ☐ 6. Other - (specify) _____		☐ 5. Hispanic ☐ 6. Other - (specify) _____	

I decline to furnish all or part of this information _____ Initial

I decline to furnish all or part of this information _____ Initial

*Lender: If either applicant or co-applicant chooses not to designate either race or sex information, you must do so, to the extent possible, based on sight and/or surname. To designate any information that you have provided, please enclose it with parenthesis ([X]).

AGREEMENT

The undersigned hereby declare and represent that they have read the foregoing Application, that all statements made therein are complete and true to their knowledge, that all financial and credit information of value to the consideration of this Loan Request has been given and that the statements are made and information given as an inducement to the Lender to grant the Loan for which this Application is made. The Applicant(s) authorize the Lender, or his Agent, to verify the information contained herein and to make such additional normal inquiries as reasonably may be related to or associated with this Application, from credit bureaus and from employers, creditors, and references listed on this Application.
The Applicant(s) understand that the Lender may at its option, cancel any Commitment or Loan granted if: Application contains any false or misleading information or in its opinion, the credit investigation discloses an unsatisfactory credit record.

Accepted:

Applicant _____ Date _____ Co-Applicant _____ Date _____

BELOW IS FOR DEALER/OFFICE USE
MOBILE HOME DESCRIPTION

UNIT PURCHASED	TRADE-IN
NEW ☐ SINGLE WIDE ☐	SINGLE WIDE ☐
USED ☐ DOUBLE WIDE ☐	DOUBLE WIDE ☐
YEAR ___ MAKE ___	YEAR ___ MAKE ___
MODEL ___ SIZE ___ X ___	MODEL ___ SIZE ___ X ___
MODEL NO. ___ SERIAL NO. ___	MODEL NO. ___ SERIAL NO. ___
NO. OF BEDROOMS ___ BATHS ___	NO. OF BEDROOMS ___ BATHS ___
EXTRA EQUIPMENT ___	EXTRA EQUIPMENT ___

INSURANCE DETAIL

☐ MOBILE HOME PHYSICAL DAMAGE PACKAGE $ _____
☐ FLOOD INSURANCE
☐ FIRE, THEFT & CASUALTY
☐ COMPREHENSIVE
☐ VSI
☐ CREDIT LIFE
☐ ACCIDENT & HEALTH
☐ OTHER
TOTAL INSURANCE COST $ _____

INSURANCE TO BE PLACED BY ☐ INSTITUTION ☐ PURCHASER ☐ DEALER
IF INSURANCE PLACED BY OTHER THAN INSTITUTION, PLEASE PROVIDE AGENT'S:
NAME _____ PHONE ( ) _____
ADDRESS _____

PURCHASE DETAILS

CASH SELLING PRICE INCLUDING TAX, ON-SITE DELIVERY
AND EXTRA EQUIPMENT $ _____
DOWN PAYMENT – CASH $ _____
  TRADE-IN $ _____
  LESS AMOUNT OWED $ _____
  NET TRADE-IN $ _____
TOTAL CREDITS FOR DOWN PAYMENT   (–) $ _____
UNPAID BALANCE $ _____
INSURANCE EXPENSE (From insurance detail)   (+) $ _____
OTHER (Describe) _____   (+) $ _____
AMOUNT TO BE FINANCED $ _____
PLUS FINANCE CHARGE   (+) $ _____
AMOUNT OF NOTE $ _____

PAYABLE IN ___ MONTHLY INSTALLMENTS OF $ ___
AND ___ MONTHLY INSTALLMENTS OF $ ___   APR ___ %
(NOTE: REQUIRED TIL AND OTHER DISCLOSURES MUST BE GIVEN CUSTOMER)

DEALER COSTS DISCLOSURE		DISPOSITION	
NEW	USED	Loan ☐ Approved	☐ Simple
Dealer Cost $ ___	*Wholesale Value	☐ Rejected	☐ Add On
Freight Cost $ ___	$ ___	☐ Customer Notified ___ %	☐ Discount
$ ___	$ ___	☐ Dealer Notified	Interest Rate

*IF USED, WHOLESALE VALUE (COST) WAS DETERMINED FROM
☐ VALUATION GUIDE   OR   ☐ APPRAISAL (ATTACH COPY)
AUTHORIZED SIGNATURE _____

001370

MOBILE HOME LOAN APPLICATION

legislation also resulted in the development of state insuring programs.

Among the current education loan programs are the National Direct Student Loan Program, the Guaranteed Student Loan Program and the Federally Insured Student Loan Program. The agencies sponsoring such programs promise to reimburse the lender for specified sums of money in the event students do not repay the loans. Lenders should be aware, of course, that loans are only as safe as the agency or organization guaranteeing their repayment.

Both federally sponsored and state-sponsored programs have requirements that specify who is eligible for a loan, the maximum guaranteed amounts, repayment methods and the amount of subsidies involved, if any. The loan limits set forth in the requirements change periodically (usually annually). While the student is in school, the federal government pays the interest on the loan if adjusted family gross income is under a specified amount or the family demonstrates need. Graduate students also are able to borrow. Students begin payments six months after graduation or when they cease to be at least half-time students.

In a slightly different arrangement, parents may borrow on behalf of dependent students. Loan repayments on parent education loans begin 60 days after the money is disbursed by the institution. Parents are responsible for interest accrued during the 60-day period.

In addition to interest, institutions may charge an origination fee on student loans. The institution may or may not elect to collect this fee from students. However, the U.S. Department of Education requires lenders to report all fees, collected or not collected.

Savings institutions receive a special allowance from the federal government to cover the administrative costs of maintaining federally guaranteed loans before repayment. The allowance amount is figured as a percentage of the unpaid balance of the loans. The percentage rate is based on the 13-week Treasury bill rate and the allowance is paid quarterly. Education loans outstanding at FSLIC-insured institutions at year-end 1983 and 1984 were nearly $2.5 billion and almost $3.8 billion, respectively. Although education loans are not very profitable for lenders to make and maintain, particularly in times of low interest rates, the secondary market does provide a source of liquidity. The number of education loans outstanding will probably continue to increase as tuition fees do.

Consumer Loans

Consumer loans were authorized for federally chartered institutions by the Depository Institutions Deregulation and Monetary Control Act of 1980. As stated earlier, the FHLBB regulations specifically define a consumer loan as "a secured or unsecured loan to a natural person for personal, family or household purposes." Such a loan is a type of consumer credit and may be either an open- or closed-end loan. The consumer loans described in this section are automobile, equity, recreational vehicle, marine, aircraft, furniture/appliance, personal and check credit.

Automobile Loans

The largest single category of consumer loans is automobile loans. They comprise nearly 40% of all outstanding consumer credit. Commercial banks presently provide the greatest amount of automobile credit in terms of total dollar volume.

Consumers purchasing automobiles often use credit because of the small cash outlay required. For new car purchases, consumers generally can put down about 10% in cash and take out a loan for the remaining amount. Loans can also be obtained to finance used car purchases. The maximum loan amount for used car loans is commonly determined in one of the following two ways, although some lenders may use other guidelines. One way is to limit the loan amount to 80% of the purchase price. Another way is to set the limit based on the National Automobile Dealers Association Used Car Guide, or other current price guide, that lists the value of automobiles according to the model and year. The maximum loan amount can then be set at a particular percentage of the listed value.

The maturity on an automobile loan can range from 12 to 60 months, with the most frequently used terms being 42-48 months. Rising automobile prices and interest rates on loans have contributed to a trend toward longer maturities. Today, shorter-term loans result in monthly payment amounts that are too high for many consumers. A longer term increases the time a borrower has to pay off the loan and reduces the amount of each monthly payment; however, it also increases the risk to the lender due to the depreciating value of the collateral.

Savings institutions need to consider the intended purpose and anticipated use of the car when making an automobile loan. As a consumer loan, an automobile loan cannot be made for commercial purposes. In addition, if the car is to be driven extensively, the value of the car may quickly decline. Lenders are concerned about the extent of use because the loan is secured by the car. The very nature of an automobile causes it to physically deteriorate over a period of time, and, as the car deteriorates, it also loses value. If a borrower should stop making payments on a loan, there may not be enough value left in the car to pay it off. As a result, lenders must consider this fact when setting the loan limits and credit requirements.

Dependency on any collateral for repayment is not a good practice because the collateral is only a precaution or added security against default. Lenders should be primarily concerned with a borrower's willingness and ability to repay the debt. Carelessness on the part of the lender can be very costly, since not only is the automobile quickly depreciating in value, but also it may be difficult to locate if the borrower should default on the loan.

Equity Loans
Equity is the portion of real property owned by an individual. When purchasing a home, an individual's total equity is equal to the actual downpayment. Thereafter, a homeowner's equity increases in two ways: first, as the loan is repaid (thereby reducing the balance owed) and second, as the market value of the home appreciates. An *equity loan*, also known as a second or junior mortgage loan, uses a homeowner's equity as security for this multipurpose loan.

This type of loan became popular in the 1970s when the upward trend of home prices sparked homeowner interest in utilizing the new found, additional equity in their homes as a way of borrowing money. For example, if Mary Jones purchased a home for $90,000 and borrows $60,000, she will have a $30,000 equity in the house. Then, if Mary needs $10,000, she could borrow the sum in the form of an equity loan, secured by a second mortgage on the home (the $60,000 loan being the first mortgage). However, in the event the borrower defaults, the lender in first position (the one holding the first lien) must be paid in full before the lender in second lien position receives payment.

Liens other than first liens are commonly referred to as junior liens. Junior liens can be second, third, fourth, or as many mortgages as a property's value can secure. Each subsequent level of mortgage (second, third, and so on) has less priority than the one before. For this reason lenders generally believe it to be a prudent practice not to accept lower than a second lien position. Prior to the 1980 regulations, a federally chartered savings institution could only take a junior lien position if it also held the first lien.

The total dollar amount of loans secured by the same real property is limited to a percentage of the property's value. Federal regulations require that an institution keep records of all liens on a subject property as evidence that the loan-to-value ratio on the property has not been exceeded. If the total loan amount exceeds 90% of the real property value, private mortgage insurance is required. *Private mortgage insurance* (PMI) protects the lender from a loss on a specified percentage of the unpaid loan balance. A premium, which is usually expressed as a monthly figure and added to the borrower's monthly loan payment, is required on this type of insurance. Regulations state that loans over 90% of the property value must be insured down to 80%. The actual percentage covered by private mortgage insurance is the difference between the loan-to-value ratio and 80%. Thus, if the loan-to-value ratio were 95%, the lender would have 15% (95 minus 80) coverage in case of default. If the unpaid balance of the loan were $50,000 and the borrower defaulted, the lender would receive $7,500 (15% of $50,000) from the private mortgage insurance company. The remainder of the loan balance ($50,000 minus $7,500) would be collected through legal means. Private mortgage insurance can be canceled when the unpaid loan balance is down to 80% of the property value.

Equity loans are a readily accessible means of financing current consumer needs. Equity loans are made for a variety of purposes including debt consolidations, tuitions, vacations and investments. The demand for these loans is increasing as home prices continue to rise and homeowners' equity increases. Equity lines of credit that can be accessed through credit cards are increasing in popularity because of the convenience they provide for consumers.

Lenders welcome the increasing demand for equity loans for several reasons. Those lenders providing residential mortgage loans can adapt equity loan programs easily, often using the same fundamentals, personnel and equipment. The profitability of equity loans is enhanced by a low delinquency rate and the fact that the security backing the loan, the property, is generally appreciating in value.

Recreational Vehicle Loans
Recreational vehicles (RVs) are units built or mounted on a chassis and intended for travel, vacationing, camping and other temporary living. The fact that recreational vehicles are intended for travel differentiates them from mobile homes, which are intended for permanent residence.

According to the Recreation Vehicle Industry Association, there are over seven and one-half million recreational vehicles on the roads today. Most of their owners live in the Western United States, are married homeowners, and have a strong willingness and ability to repay their loans. For every new unit sold, there are about six used units sold, which explains why over half of all recreational vehicle loans are paid off before maturity. Actually 70% of the RV owners who sell their units purchase another, more expensive unit, so the average life of an RV loan is only about four years. Lenders financing these vehicles usually require downpayments of between 20% and 25% and offer maturities ranging from five to eight years for direct loans and seven to 12 years for indirect loans. Almost three-quarters of the RV consumer loans are indirect loans arranged through dealers.

The recreational vehicle market is tied closely to inflation, energy expenses and the consumer confidence index. Notice the drop in RV shipments (from manufacturers to dealers) during the years 1973-1974 and 1977-1980 as shown in Figure 2-4. These years were periods of economic recession. Usually consumers purchase fewer recreational vehicles during bad economic periods and more during good times, and loan activity fluctuates accordingly. Lenders entering the RV market should be aware of this behavior, because RV lending is volume oriented. If the market for recreational vehicles is slow for a period of time, the demand for loans decreases; loan volume also decreases; and cost per dollar loaned increases, causing profitability to decrease.

Marine Loans

Marine loans are used to finance the purchase of boats. Typical marine loans range from $3,000 to $100,000. New boats require about a 20% downpayment, and older or used boats, require a larger downpayment. The loan term generally extends up to 10 years or longer for both new and used boats although the average life of a boat loan is less than four years. Boat owners often trade their boats every three or four years whether they were purchased new or used. This explains the relatively short average loan life.

There are over 13 million boat owners in the United States. Marine loans have become increasingly popular in regions of the country with a convenient access to water. Boat values in these areas usually remain high because of consumer demand.

One advantage of extending loans to purchase large, new boats, particularly those valued over $35,000, is that they do not depreciate quickly. In some instances, they may even

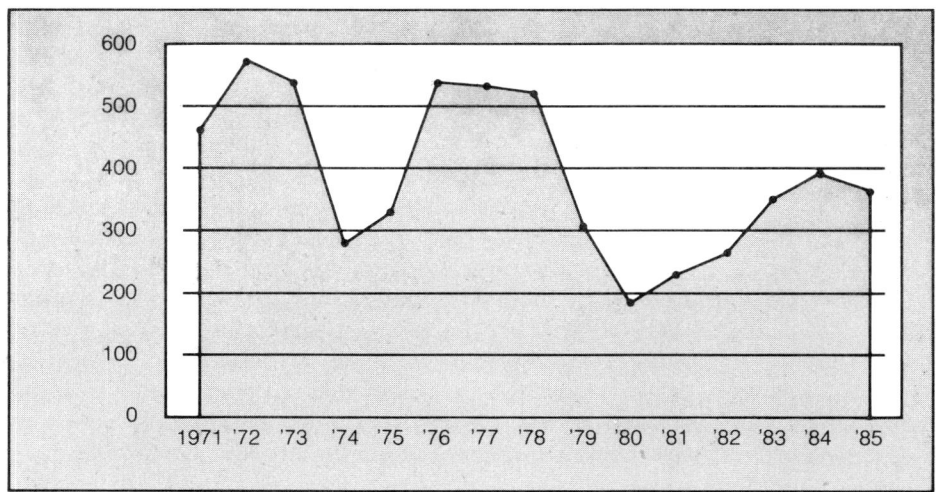

FIGURE 2-4
Total RV Shipments (in thousands)

Source: *Recreational Vehicle Financing: A Survey of Lenders 1985 Experiences*, Recreation Vehicle Industry Association, Reston, VA.

increase in value. However, new boats usually depreciate significantly in the first year. The amount of depreciation depends on a boat's characteristics. Older boats have an advantage over newer ones in that their value remains relatively stable. A mistaken belief about used boats is that they will not last through the life of the loan used to finance them. Most older boats have a lifespan of at least 40 years.

A marine loan is usually secured by the boat that is financed. An aid to help lenders determine the current market value of this collateral is the *Used Boat Price Guide* and the *New Boat Price Guide*.[3] Regardless of the value of the collateral, lenders must protect themselves by carefully analyzing the borrower.

Aircraft Loans
Financing can be obtained for both new and used aircraft. Most aircraft have a relatively low rate of depreciation because the life expectancy of an aircraft is long. This enables lenders to offer loans with maturities of seven years or more. The value of a used aircraft is commonly determined by contacting established aircraft dealers.

There are five major considerations lenders must be concerned with before using a price guidebook or talking with aircraft insurance agents.

- The lender should determine whether or not the aircraft will be stored in a hangar when not in use. Planes exposed to the weather may suffer more physical deterioration than planes stored in a hangar. The rate of depreciation generally relates to the rate of deterioration.
- Regular certified maintenance checks are important. The Federal Aviation Administration (FAA) requires all aircraft to have periodic inspections based upon the number of hours the aircraft is in the air. Logs must be kept on the maintenance and flying hours. Lenders should inspect these logs. The lender must assure the borrower meets FAA regulations both to protect the borrower and to maintain the value of the aircraft.
- The lender should determine if the borrower has proper insurance coverage on the aircraft (covered later in this chapter).
- The lender should be aware of the aircraft's wing construction. Aircraft with cloth wing construction

require more maintenance than those with a metal covering.
- Lenders should consider the high costs of ongoing required maintenance when analyzing whether a borrower is qualified.

Lenders with extensive aircraft lending experience offer aircraft loans nationwide. Since competition with specialists in aircraft lending makes it difficult to be successful in some geographical areas, aircraft lending is one of the least popular types of consumer loans among savings institutions. Also, to effectively offer aircraft loans, lenders should employ a specialist in this lending area. Aircraft loans comprise only a small percentage of total consumer loans, but their average dollar size is comparable to boat loans, suggesting a low cost-per-dollar when making these loans.

Furniture and Appliance Loans
To acquire appliances, television sets or furniture for the interior of the home, consumers often use credit cards. However, they may obtain purchase money financing with furniture and appliance loans. Loan amounts for furniture and appliances are generally very small; consequently, small loan companies and some manufacturers provide most of the financing for these items. The average loan amount is about $500, with loans usually ranging from $100 to $2,500 or more. The term of the loan will depend on the amount of the loan and the borrower's capacity to repay. Due to the small loan amounts, many lenders have found this loan activity unprofitable and finance furniture and appliance purchases under credit card programs.

Personal Loans
These loans are made for the purposes of debt consolidation, vacations, and sometimes for the purchase of furniture, appliances and other durable goods. Personal loans are generally not secured by the items being financed. This fact distinguishes them from the other types of closed-end consumer loans.

Personal loans are often for small amounts, which make them less profitable than most other consumer loans. Since personal loans are often unsecured, the terms of these loans are based solely on the borrowers' character and capacity to repay them. If a borrower defaults, there is no collateral to recover as repayment for the debt. Due to the high administrative costs of providing small personal loans, some lenders may not permit installments and require a single lump-sum payment, which reduces the cost of maintaining the loan and processing payments.

Today the vast majority of small personal loans are in the form of credit card or revolving credit loans.

Check Credit

Check credit plans involve setting up a loan account for the specific purpose of writing checks. Checks are issued solely to serve the loan account. When consumers write checks, they are automatically writing themselves loans. These loan plans are also known as lines of credit.

Loans generated under check credit programs are unsecured, but sometimes they are secured by deposit accounts or real and personal property. The line of credit extended can vary depending on the creditworthiness of the applicant and whether or not collateral is provided. Consumers tend to make larger purchases under check credit plans than with overdraft plans (discussed in the next section) because of the different purposes of the two plans. The check credit plan is specifically set up for loan purposes, whereas the overdraft plan is usually intended to help the consumer avoid having an insufficient checking account balance.

Consumer Leasing

A *lease* is a contract that specifies the conditions by which an owner conveys the possession and use of an asset to another. The lease is a financing contract between a *lessee* (user of the asset) and a *lessor* (owner of the asset). Unlike a loan agreement, the leased asset is never owned by the lessee during the term of the lease.

Leasing provides advantages for both the lessor and the lessee. The lessor, by owning the asset, is able to take advantage of tax laws that permit investment tax credits and depreciation to reduce taxable income. The tax benefits enjoyed by the lessor can be passed to the lessee in the form of rental charges that are lower than interest costs would have been had the asset been purchased with a loan. The lease payments are further reduced below what a loan would be because the estimated value of the asset at the end of the lease, called the *residual value*, also is taken into consideration. After the term of the lease ends, the lessor can sell the asset.

For savings and loans, vehicles represent an attractive market for leasing. By 1990 between 50% and 75% of all new vehicles purchased will be leased, as customers become aware of the financial attractiveness of leases.

Credit Cards and Overdraft Protection

Credit cards and overdraft protection are two types of consumer loans that have become very popular. The following section describes how these loans work and discusses some of the lenders' considerations for providing them.

Credit Cards

Credit cards are a type of open-end revolving loan. Credit cards facilitate the transfer of funds from financial institutions to sellers of goods or services. After obtaining lines of credit for various amounts, consumers receive small instant loans at the moment they use their credit cards. Federally chartered savings institutions were authorized to offer credit cards by the DIDMC Act of 1980.

Financial institutions' involvement with credit card programs began with commercial banks in the 1950s. Commercial banks felt credit card operations provided four primary benefits.

- A credit card operation was a means of generating consumer installment credit since it provided consumers with an additional source of credit. Banks were experts in extending credit to consumers, and credit cards were just an innovative offshoot of this activity.
- Credit cards offered an opportunity to remove smaller, unprofitable loans from the installment loan department. The costs of small, closed-end installment loans made them difficult to offer at a profit. Banking officials felt that the costs of making loans would be greatly reduced by issuing credit cards because the service costs of extending credit would be shared with the merchant at the point of purchase.
- Credit cards provided a complete service to bank customers. Customers who did not use closed-end installment credit normally used cash or personal checks at the point of purchase. The existence of credit cards, however, provided customers with a reasonable alternative to paying by cash or check.

- Credit cards appealed to merchants. Small merchants in particular saw credit cards as a means of eliminating bad personal checks. Also, merchants could stop using their own credit system and could let the banks handle all the responsibility for repayments. For those merchants who did not have credit systems of their own, the acceptance of bank credit cards was an opportunity to increase sales.

When merchants decide to accept a credit card, they sign an agreement with a financial institution. The merchant deposits the receipts from the credit card transactions for face value less the merchant discount imposed by the bank. This discount, or fee, varies among merchants but averages around 2.5%. In return for the percentage received from the merchant, the financial institution provides the merchant with support, accounting and collection services. The merchant's bank interchanges transactions with the cardholder's institution. An interchange fee is paid by the merchant's bank to the card-issuing institution.

The most common credit card systems in use today can be used for purchases of goods and services in the United States and other countries and may also be used to obtain cash advances from participating financial institutions.

Since credit cards are a type of open-end revolving loan, customers receive lines of credit that enable them to purchase items valued up to a predetermined dollar limit. Cardholders receive periodic statements (usually monthly) listing all of their purchases and other transactions. They can pay the balance in full to avoid paying interest. Or, cardholders may pay a portion of the balance that exceeds a specified minimum. Then they will incur interest on the unpaid balance. Customers that use the card to obtain cash advances pay interest from the date each cash advance was made. To summarize, credit cardholders benefit from three conveniences:
- paying for purchases once a month by converting individual purchase transactions into a monthly bill;
- obtaining small loans conveniently (cash advance); and
- extending payments for purchases.

There are two types of card users: convenience users and those who extend their balances beyond the initial installment. Convenience users (those who pay their accounts in full when billed) in essence have a "free" loan because interest is not charged until after the statement is issued and the due date is passed. These customers pose a problem for credit card companies. The convenience users are, in effect, not paying for the convenience of a credit card even though the issuing company is incurring costs by offering credit. About 50% of the gross volume generated by credit cardholders goes interest free to convenience users. To cover the costs generated by convenience users, the other cardholders may be charged a higher rate of interest on an unpaid balance and/or the lender may accept lower profits than if there were no convenience users. To reduce losses, many credit card companies have started charging annual fees to all cardholders. These fees are charged whether or not the card is used.

Savings institutions can offer credit card services in one of three ways: as card issuers, agents or participating agents. Card issuers assume all responsibility for evaluating the applicant and transferring funds and assume profits or losses incurred by the service. Agents solicit customer applications on behalf of the card issuer. Agents may receive a solicitation fee and have their name appear on the card. Participating agents transfer a portion of the outstanding funds and share in the profit or loss on their accounts. The responsibility of evaluating the applicant varies in different situations.

Institutions thinking of offering credit cards have, of course, much planning to do. Developing strategies for marketing, distributing, pricing, approving, servicing and collecting are major initial and ongoing necessities. It is especially important to develop effective procedures for handling billing disputes and evaluating credit worthiness in order to keep delinquencies and bankruptcies to a minimum.

The credit card market is extremely competitive. The majority of credit worthy customers who desire a card already have one or more cards. These cardholders do not readily switch from their present institution without costly giveaways, such as low or no annual fees, lower interest rates, value adding services like telephone and discount shopping, insurance protection or risky higher lines of approved credit.

A number of other factors tend to limit the profitability of credit card operation. Consumer movements in many areas are trying to lower or limit the interest rate charged on credit cards. Convenience users, too, put a significant dent in the institution's yield. Institutions initially issuing credit cards are likely to experience higher than average amounts of defaults, and collection workouts are more difficult than for other loans because the cardholder can continue to charge purchases until the card is revoked. Defaults usually occur when the cardholder has reached his or her credit limit. Maintaining security and preventing credit card fraud are ever growing concerns also.

Institutions that plan and implement their own credit card programs must also be able to monitor their own operations and be able to spot and correct any customer or profit related problems quickly. Institutions that plan ahead are usually flexible enough to change with market demands and to foster in their customers' minds an ongoing sense of value regarding their services. When they offer credit cards that customers perceive as valuable, institutions have an excellent chance to cross-sell other profitable services that will develop loyal customer relationships.

Overdraft Protection
Overdraft revolving credit is actually protection against overdrawn checking accounts. A customer with such an arrangement is given a line of credit and allowed to write checks up to a specified amount over the balance in his or her checking account. Since overdraft protection offers the availability of an unsecured loan, considerations and precautions adopted in normal lending operations should be used in providing this service.

Many savings institutions have adopted overdraft protection plans to compliment their NOW account services. Basically, when overdraft protection is combined with a NOW account, the customer need not worry about accidently writing a check for more than his or her available balance. Customers can be spared much embarrassment by institutions that offer overdraft revolving credit. This credit arrangement facilitates the purchase of smaller items, but is not intended to replace longer-term, closed-end credit arrangements.

Overdraft revolving credit tied to a NOW account can be handled by either the single-account or two-account approach. The single-account approach treats the loan as a negative balance in the account. If the balance becomes negative, the customer is charged interest at a specified rate (one that is usually lower than that on a closed-end unsecured loan). If a deposit is made to the account while the balance is negative, it frequently eliminates the loan. When the balance is positive, the customer earns interest at the NOW account rate. The single-account approach generally does not provide

> Customer Joan Rogers currently has $500 in her NOW account. She also has overdraft protection consisting of an open line of credit for $1,000 with First Savings on her NOW account. Joan wants to purchase a television set for $900, so she writes a check for $900 and gives it to the merchant. The following steps take place:
>
> | Transaction | Balance |
> | --- | --- |
> | Checking account balance | $500 |
> | Check is written and deducted from the account | −$900 |
> | Account becomes overdrawn | −$400 |
> | First Savings transfers funds from open line of credit to cover the overdraft | $400 |
> | Checking account balance after the transaction | 0 |
> | Ms. Rogers now has a loan of | $400 |
> | Ms. Rogers has available credit in the overdraft plan of | $600 |
>
> Overdraft protection is convenient since Joan has easy access to the line of credit. She does not have to apply for a loan every time she makes a purchase and overdraws her NOW account.

for billing and minimum loan payments. An institution should develop a system by which it can monitor accounts near the credit limit. Then inspections can be made to locate customers who make little or no attempt to reduce loan balances.

With the two-account approach, the loan account is separate from the NOW account. Funds are transferred from the loan account to the NOW account to accommodate an overdraft. Usually, for both single-account and two-account methods, funds are transferred in multiples of a specified amount (for example, $50 or $100). A separate loan statement requiring a minimum payment amount is provided monthly. Accounts using the two-account approach are easier for the institution to monitor. Customers may prefer this arrangement because the balances in the loan and NOW accounts are computed separately. The two-account feature also enables

MasterCard or VISA to cover the overdraft with a cash advance. In this case the credit card would be used in place of the loan account.

CREDIT INSURANCE

Since lenders accept a certain amount of risk when lending money, they take precautions to insure repayment of the debt. Analyzing a borrower's financial position, requesting collateral and recommending insurance are three ways lenders can prevent losses. This section describes the types of credit insurance commonly used with consumer loans.

Consumer loan insurance can be classified according to who or what is insured: borrower, collateral or loan transaction. Insurance plans that focus on the borrower provide loan payments if the borrower dies or becomes physically disabled. Often lenders receive a substantial portion of the premium from credit life and accident and health insurance as commissions from the insurer. In many cases, a lender's projected percentage of borrowers who will purchase insurance greatly affects the interest rate charged and the profitability of the loan. Lending institutions have been criticized for being less concerned with qualifying the borrower than with generating commissions. Insurance plans that focus on losses resulting from collateral destruction can be obtained by the borrower for vehicles, mobile homes and home improvements. Other types of insurance that pertain to the collateral securing the loan transaction are nonfiling, warranty and skip insurance. Insurance that protects only the lender from losses on repossession is also available.

Credit Life Insurance

Credit life insurance insures a borrower in the event of death. If death occurs, the insurance benefits will pay the lender the loan balance due. Credit life usually takes one of three forms: decreasing, level or joint.

Decreasing life is the most common form of credit life insurance. The policy begins on the first day of the loan term and ends when the loan is repaid fully. Throughout the life of the policy, the amount of coverage equals the outstanding loan balance. The most common type of decreasing life insures the gross amount of the loan (principal balance plus up to 60 days of interest). In the event the insured borrower should die, the insurance company would pay the lender the outstanding principal balance on the loan. The unearned interest portion would go to the borrower's estate. If the account should be over 60 days past due, the insurance normally would not cover the entire amount. When offered in conjunction with open-end credit (for example, a credit card), the insurance premium is based on the outstanding balance and added to the monthly bill.

Level life is the least common form of credit life insurance. The primary difference in this coverage is that it stays the same over the life of the loan. For example, if a borrower took out $10,000 worth of coverage, upon death of the borrower the insurance company would pay a total of $10,000 regardless of the outstanding balance. The amount in excess of the loan balance would go the borrower's estate. Thus, the coverage does not decline as with decreasing life.

As more couples depend on two incomes to support a household, *joint life coverage* is becoming popular. The policy is written insuring both the husband and wife and can provide either a decreasing or level amount of coverage. Insurance benefits are paid upon the death of either one of the insured.

Accident and Health Insurance

Accident and health insurance provides monthly loan payments to the lender on behalf of the borrower (the insured). The benefits are paid for a prescribed period of time if the borrower loses income as a result of an accident or illness.

The insurance coverage usually takes effect on either a retroactive or an elimination basis. Under a retroactive policy, the insured is required to have been off work for a certain number of days before the coverage is triggered. Benefits, however, are paid from the first day of disability (retroactively). Under an elimination policy, the coverage also does not take effect until the insured has been off work for a certain number of days; however, it is not retroactive. Since the illness or injury of a nonincome-producing member of the borrower's family can also put undue strain on the budget, coverage is advisable, where available and affordable, on dependents as well as on the borrower. This minimizes the lender's risk of loss.

Physical Damage Insurance

While lenders should look to the borrower's earning power for the repayment of a loan, the continuing value of the collateral behind the loan must also be considered. A borrower's motivation to continue making payments can be significantly reduced if the financial obligation outweighs the value of the secured assets. If a loan is not repaid, the lender hopes to salvage some value from the collateral, especially if there is a good secondhand market for well-maintained merchandise. If there is a chance that some damage to the collateral might occur over the life of the loan, then insurance should be recommended. Insurance policies to cover physical damage are written for automobiles, boats, recreational vehicles and aircraft.

Dual interest coverage offers protection for up to 100% of the value of the collateral. Both the lender and the borrower, who is presumed to have some equity in the item, are covered. The common coverage includes both comprehensive and collision protection on automobiles. Comprehensive insurance covers most sudden losses in the value of vehicles other than losses due to collision. Such coverage generally includes fire, theft, damage from falling objects and vandalism. Collision provisions cover accidents in which the vehicle collides with another vehicle or object. One hundred percent of all losses are covered under the comprehensive provisions, although some plans include a $50 deductible. Typical collision coverage will pay 100% of all losses in excess of an initial deductible amount, usually $200 or $250.

Comprehensive and collision coverage may be combined to offer protection against almost any kind of physical damage. However, protection against the premature loss of value to the collateral as a result of abusive treatment is generally not offered. In the event of a claim for damages, only the actual cash value of the claim, reduced by any deductibles, will be paid by the insurance company. Thus, the character of the borrower and the physical life expected from the item are considered by the lender in making a credit decision.

Nonfiling Insurance

Available for most types of secured loans, nonfiling insurance is primarily for the benefit of the lender. For this reason, unlike the insurance plans previously described, the cost of the premium is not passed on to the borrower. The protection that *nonfiling insurance* provides is to insure the lender against a loss that results from unintentional errors or omissions in the filing or recording of a security interest.

To protect its interest in a property, a lender needs to file or record a security interest in the piece of property (personal or real). This filing protects innocent third parties who might buy the property from the owner or who might lend funds against it as collateral without knowing that another creditor already has an interest in it.

Skip Insurance

The purpose of *skip or Vendors Single Interest (VSI) insurance* is to protect the lender from losses caused by the borrower changing the property securing the loan, embezzlement or someone hiding the collateral. Other acts also included are those that make it impossible to locate or recover the collateral. This coverage is primarily used for collateral that is movable. The institution will also often be reimbursed from the insurance company for some repossessing costs (costs incurred in acquiring the collateral).

Warranty Insurance

This type of insurance protects the lender and the borrower from losses sustained from the misrepresentation of goods by the seller. Misrepresentation is generally a violation of two implied warranties, merchantability and fitness for a particular purpose. According to the Uniform Commercial Code (Sec. 2-314 and 315) merchantible goods should "pass without objection in the trade under contract," should be "fit for the ordinary purposes for which such goods are used," should be "adequately contained, packaged and labeled as the agreement may require," and should "conform to the promises or affirmations of fact made on the container or label if any." An example of misrepresentation would be a car dealer who has tampered with an automobile's odometer.

Some warranty insurance policies protect the lender and the borrower against faulty merchandise, unfulfilled warranties and other claims and defenses against the seller of the merchandise. Most policies, however, are only extensions of the written warranties provided by the manufacturer.

Flood Insurance

This type of insurance protects both the borrower and the lender from loss of property due to flood damage. In 1968, Congress established the voluntary National Flood Insurance Program to provide coverage at subsidized rates. To change this voluntary program into a required one, the Flood Disaster Protection Act was passed in 1973. One provision of this act prohibits federal financial assistance for damage due to floods for communities not participating in the program.

Property owners in identified flood areas are required to buy flood insurance if they have a real estate secured loan with a federally supervised, regulated or insured financial institution. All mobile home and certain home improvement loans fall under the flood insurance requirements. FHA requires flood insurance on all Title I property improvement loans located in flood areas, whether secured or unsecured. On conventional, noninsured home improvement loans, the FHLBB requires that only those loans secured by the property meet the flood insurance requirements.

Aircraft Insurance

Aircraft insurance is similar to collision and comprehensive coverage on automobiles since it protects against all physical damage from any external cause. In contrast to automobile protection, however, the deductible feature on aircraft policies usually varies, depending on whether or not the aircraft is in use. The deductible amount should not exceed 10% of the face amount of the policy. The lender should insist upon both on-the-ground and in-the-air coverage to insure adequate protection. Hull insurance for the full value of the aircraft is generally required for the entire term of the loan.

All hull policies contain a clause that the maximum settlement will be based on the value of the aircraft at the time of loss. Because of this, the lender should make certain that the loan balance decreases at least as rapidly as the depreciation of the aircraft, so that the owner always has a true equity position. A lender's loss payable endorsement form may also be required.

Aircraft insurance policies generally contain many exclusions that can be significant for the lender's protection. Large losses can be prevented by dealing only with quality insurers and carefully reviewing the insurance policy. Following are examples of three exclusions:
- flight outside of the continental United States;
- unlicensed pilots (or pilots uncertified to fly that particular type of plane); and
- excessive weight of cargo or persons on board.

Marine Insurance

Marine insurance policies are designed for two classes of boats: outboard motor insurance for boats that generally are hauled on land, and yacht insurance for boats that are not hauled on land (for example, yachts, cruisers, inboard speedboats and sailboats). Risk hull insurance should be required because it protects against loss due to fire, lightning, stranding, sinking, collision and hurricanes. Marine insurance can also cover outboard motors that are lost overboard.

To protect the lender, insurance policies on marine craft that are transported on land usually contain a long form loss payable endorsement that includes a breach of warranty. This protects lenders from losses sustained as a result of defective marine craft.

For all marine craft, the minimum amount of coverage should be the actual cash or replacement value. If a salvage value (the dollar amount the asset is estimated to be worth at the end of its useful life) is included in the replacement value, the insurance amount should be that much greater. Salvage liens taking priority over the lender's lien may exist, and, in the event of a claim, the lender risks losing the amount designated as salvage value. Lenders also may require protection and indemnity insurance that insures the boat owner against personal injury and property damage losses.

SUMMARY

A loan is an extension of cash credit to be repaid with a finance charge. The installment loans described in this chapter are commonly secured by real or personal property and are originated on a direct or indirect basis. The term and loan amount can be flexible or fixed, open- or closed-end. Loan terms (loan amount, maturity and interest rate) are affected by characteristics of the borrower and the collateral, purpose of the loan, laws and regulations, and lender policy.

Specific types of loans now offered by federally chartered savings institutions can be divided into three groups: traditional nonmortgage loans, consumer loans, and credit card and overdraft protection. Traditional loans are the only loans other than first mortgage loans that federally chartered institutions were authorized to offer prior to the Depository Institutions Deregulation and Monetary Control Act of 1980.

Traditional nonmortgage loans include home improvement, deposit account, mobile home and education loans. These loans differ in purpose and involve different forms of collateral for security. Home improvement and mobile home loans can be insured by the FHA, and home improvement loans can also be sold in the secondary market.

Consumer loans include automobile, equity, recreational vehicle, marine, aircraft, furniture and appliance, and personal loans. These loans can be secured or unsecured and may involve depreciating collateral. Lenders should be knowledgeable about the behavior of the collateral's value when structuring loan terms. However, for all types of consumer loans presented in this text, major emphasis should be placed on borrowers' credit worthiness to repay the debt and not on collateral value.

Check credit plans involve the setting up of a loan account for the specific purpose of writing checks. Customers writing checks under this arrangement are in effect writing themselves loans. Credit cards are a type of revolving loan (open-end) in which the customer receives a line of credit and can purchase items up to a predetermined dollar limit. Overdraft credit works in a similar fashion, but the medium used is checks rather than plastic cards.

To help reduce risk and increase protection for both the borrower and lender, credit insurance can be obtained. Insurance provides protection in the event unforeseen circumstances either prevent a borrower from repaying a debt or cause damage to the collateral held as security. The nine types of credit insurance described in this chapter are credit life, accident and health, physical damage, nonfiling, skip, warranty, flood, aircraft and marine.

CHAPTER QUESTIONS

1. Explain why a lender might be reluctant to use insurance policies, stocks and bonds, or negotiable instruments as collateral.

2. Why are consumer loans volume oriented?

3. Describe three factors that affect consumer loan terms.

4. How does a mobile home loan differ from a conventional single-family mortgage loan?

5. Cite four potential benefits an institution might gain from offering a credit card program.

6. Explain the lender's benefits in providing RV and boat loans.

7. Distinguish among decreasing, level and joint credit life insurance.

8. Differentiate between nonfiling and skip insurance.

FOOTNOTES

[1]See CFR Section 561.38.
[2]See CFR Section 545.45 and Special Management Bulletin S-226, dated September 2, 1983, by the United States League of Savings Institutions.
[3]Published by BUC International Corporation, 1881 N.E. 26th Street, Fort Lauderdale, Florida 33305.

3

Laws and Regulations Affecting Consumer Loans

Objectives

After studying this chapter, you should be able to:
- [ ] Explain the major purposes behind consumer credit regulations;
- [ ] Describe the restrictions that federally chartered institutions must observe when offering consumer loans;
- [ ] Describe three limitations that federal institutions must observe when offering consumer leasing;
- [ ] Describe three aspects of consumer lending commonly addressed by state laws;
- [ ] Assess the legal obligations a lender incurs when making indirect consumer loans;
- [ ] Identify the scope of the Equal Credit Opportunity Act; and
- [ ] State the major points and provisions of the laws protecting consumers who take on a consumer loan.

INTRODUCTION

Both federal and state governments write consumer credit laws and oversee subsequent regulations with the intent of providing protection. This legislation helps protect lenders against taking excessive risks and insures that they provide credit in an equitable manner. Some laws and regulations are also designed to protect the availability of credit to consumers, to provide disclosure of loan terms so that borrowers can form comparisons and to require lenders to follow practices that respect consumer privacy. In these ways, laws and regulations protect both lending institutions and the public.

Federal legislation regarding consumer credit operations at savings institutions is directly regulated by the Federal Home Loan Bank Board (FHLBB) and the Federal Savings and Loan Insurance Corporation (FSLIC). But many other federal agencies also have an effect on the consumer credit operations of savings institutions. Depending on the type of loan involved, a lender should be aware of policies generated by the Federal Reserve Board (FRB), the Federal Trade Commission (FTC), the Office of Education, the Department of Housing and Urban Development, the Federal Aviation Administration and the Department of Defense.

Although present federal involvement in the field of consumer credit is extensive, the individual states developed the original body of consumer legislation. Today, the individual states are still primarily responsible for such matters as interest rate regulation, creditor rights and remedies, and credit insurance.

Chapter 3 provides a basic overview of consumer credit regulations by summarizing their purposes and the effects they have on everyday decision making. The chapter is divided into two parts. The first part describes the laws that protect lenders, such as authorizing savings institutions to offer consumer loans and placing limits on loan amounts. It also describes the statutory lender liabilities that may be incurred when granting credit. The second part of the chapter describes the laws that protect consumers. Laws pertaining to documentation, disclosure, credit reporting, collection and privacy are covered. Although many of the laws that protect lenders and consumers are interrelated, grouping them by purpose makes them easier to understand. Since the laws are lengthy and complex, this text will describe only their most important features. Readers desiring greater detail should refer to the actual regulations cited in this chapter's appendix.

REGULATIONS PROTECTING LENDERS

In the early 1980s, two significant laws greatly expanded savings institutions' consumer lending authority. These two laws were the Depository Institutions Deregulation and Monetary Control Act of 1980 (DIDMCA) and the Depository Institutions Act of 1982 (Garn-St Germain). Based on these laws, the FHLBB and the FSLIC developed guiding regulations regarding consumer loans made by federally chartered savings institutions. (See the lenders' regulations section of this chapter's appendix.)

DIDMCA and Garn-St Germain

A primary purpose of the DIDMCA was to make competition among financial institutions more equitable. The Act was not intended, however, to alter the primary role of savings institutions which is to provide home mortgage financing. Therefore, restrictions were placed on the amount of consumer loans a savings institution could make in order to insure that adequate funds would continue to be available for housing. For this reason, regulations based on the 1980 law limited institutions' ability to be fully competitive in the marketplace.

The Garn-St Germain Act of 1982 and subsequent amendments have eliminated many of these earlier restrictions. Remaining restrictions generally pertain to percentage-of-assets limitations, documentation and disclosure. The following paragraphs briefly discuss the basic guidelines of the Garn-St Germain Act.

Percentage-of-assets

As a result of the Act and amendments, federally chartered institutions are now able to make consumer loans up to a maximum dollar amount outstanding of 30% of an institution's assets. However, there is a further limiting factor. Investments in corporate debt securities and commercial paper, which often are made for hedging purposes, must also be included in this 30%-of-assets category. To protect themselves against possible losses in one type of investment, institutions will often *hedge* by making counterbalancing transactions in other types of investments. In determining whether the 30%-of-assets limitation has been reached, all consumer loans and investments in commercial paper and corporate debt securities must be added together.

Institutions do have some flexibility, however, in observing this 30% limitation. Loans that are not classified as consumer loans need not be added into this total. Institutions are permitted to classify individual loans under different sections of the regulations so long as such loans conform to all the regulations of those sections. In other words, an institution approaching its 30%-of-assets limitation for consumer loans could reclassify its consumer loans as real estate secured loans, for example, if those loans also met all the regulated qualifications for that class.

An important element in these decisions is the definition of consumer loans given in section 561.38 of Title 12 of the U.S. Code. This source restricts consumer loans to those made to a natural person (as opposed to an entity such as a corporation) for personal, family or household purposes. There are no restrictions as to whether the loan is secured or unsecured, or to the type of collateral that may be used to secure it. Regulations do specify, however, that in order to be classified as a consumer loan, the loan must be granted on the

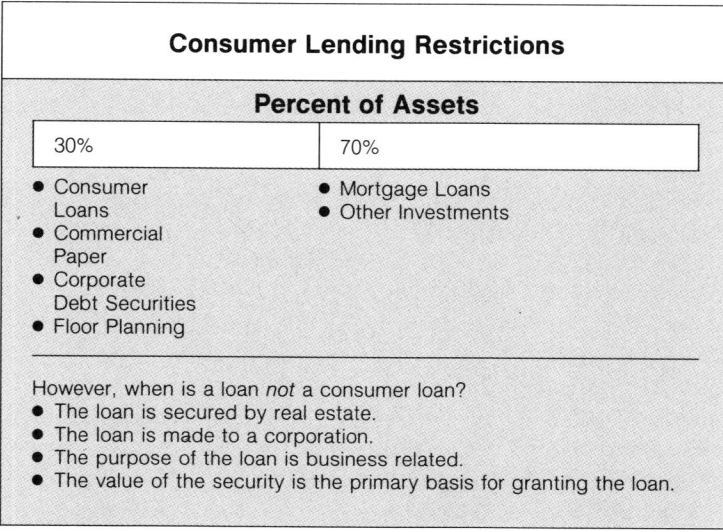

basis of factors *other* than the value of real estate or a mobile home used as the primary security. Alternate factors that may be used in underwriting include the credit standing, capacity and character of the borrower, or guarantees or securities on property other than real estate or mobile homes. To document that these loans are appropriately designated as consumer loans, institutions should keep evidence that demonstrates their compliance with such other factors in their files.

Thus, even though a loan is secured by real estate or a mobile home, it may be classified as a consumer loan if other factors provided the basis for the actual extension of credit and the institution has documented that these were the deciding factors. In fact, depending upon the institution's policies and underwriting rules, the loan may be classified either as a consumer loan or a real estate loan. Generally, complying with consumer loan regulations is simpler than meeting all real estate loan regulations.

One other type of loan is part of the 30%-of-assets calculation. Under the consumer lending authority, federal institutions are permitted to make loans to dealers to finance inventory. These loans are called *floor planning*. Lenders who provide credit for floor planning are more likely to receive, in turn, the dealer's highest quality indirect loans, or paper, than are lenders who do not provide inventory financing. The dealers included under this authority must be sellers of consumer goods, and only goods incident to personal, family or household purposes may be floor planned. Also, FHLBB regulations no longer require a savings institution's board of directors to approve dealers before establishing a business relationship with them. When inventory loans are considered commercial loans (as when they are used strictly to acquire goods intended for retail sale to consumers), they fall within the 30%-of-assets limitations for consumer lending rather than the stricter limitations for commercial loans.

Similar expansions in powers can be seen in the two areas: the maximum dollar amount of an unsecured loan to a single borrower and geographical restrictions. This maximum dollar amount was limited until 1983, at which time the limitation was removed. As of June 8, 1983, specific limitations on unsecured loans to one borrower no longer exist. All institutions may make up to $500,000 in outstanding loans to one individual. (Of course, an institution may establish its own written policies to limit the amount of unsecured credit it will extend to one individual.) Also, previous geographic restrictions as to lending territories have been dropped from the regulations. Now, only state law can restrict lending territories.

Scheduled Items
The FSLIC has established specific rules for classifying loans on which the consumer has become delinquent in making payments. Regulations define when loans become *scheduled items*, that is, items classified as slow or a loss.

Slow consumer credit is subdivided into two types: closed-end and open-end. Closed-end consumer credit is slow when it has been delinquent for 90 to 119 days (four monthly payments). Open-end consumer credit is defined as slow if it has been delinquent 90 to 179 days (four to six billing cycles). In both instances, a payment is considered an amount equal to 90% or more of the contractually required payment.

There are exceptions to these classifications. If a loan is well secured, supported by a valid guarantee or insured, or if claims have been filed against a solvent estate, the loan does not have to be classified as slow.

Consumer credit classified as a loss is defined as closed-end

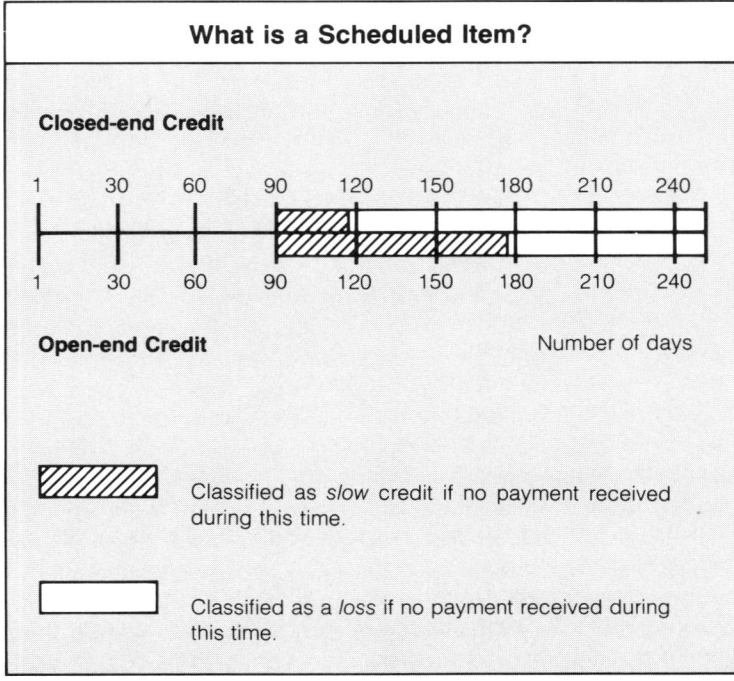

consumer credit that has been delinquent 120 days or more (five payments or more) and open-end consumer credit delinquent 180 days or more (seven billing cycles or more).

Consumer credit classified as "slow" must be included in an institution's scheduled items. Scheduled items are an important concern to the institution's management as well as to regulators. The amount of scheduled items reflects the soundness of an institution's loan portfolio. Scheduled items negatively affect the institution's profits and, if ignored, might cause regulators to reassess the institution's investment authority. Auditors look at scheduled items when evaluating whether an institution has poor underwriting practices or is taking excessive risks. Additionally, if a loan reaches a delinquent status that classifies it as a loss, the loan amount outstanding must be charged off against the institution's current earnings.

Credit Cards, Deposit Account Loans and Education Loans
Two additional consumer loans authorized for federal institutions are credit cards and loans on deposit accounts. Unlike the other consumer loans previously described, credit cards and deposit account loans at savings institutions are not subject to the percentage-of-assets limitations. In addition, education loans are considered consumer loans but are not calculated as part of the consumer lending total. Instead, they are considered a specific loan type, and federal institutions are limited to offering educational loans that do not exceed 5% of their assets.

The FHLBB excludes credit cards from its definition of consumer loans under section 545.50 of Title 12, Code of Federal Regulations. As a result, credit cards are not subject to many of the other restrictions imposed for consumer loans. However, the FSLIC does include credit cards in its definition of consumer credit under section 561.38 and, therefore, subjects them to the regulations pertaining to scheduled items and losses.

Consumer Leasing
Federal institutions are permitted to provide consumer leasing that fits the defined purpose of consumer loans as stated under section 545.50. Institutions providing consumer leasing must abide by three important limitations specified in section 545.53. First, the lease must be a "net lease." Second, the lease must be a "full-payout" lease. And third, no more than

20% of the institution's return may come from the residual value of the property at the end of the initial term of the lease.

First, then, under a *net lease*, the lessee assumes responsibility for the payment of all charges and expenses such as taxes, insurance and maintenance. In other words, institutions are required to play a passive role in the lease transaction (making a loan secured by a lease). This is in contrast to an *operating lease* in which the lessor or manufacturer is responsible for maintenance and services.

This is a handicap to the institution in that excluded items such as those listed above generally represent an important part of any sound leasing agreement. Therefore, institutions that provide leasing services will need assurances that the lessee will assume responsibility for all of the items or that lessees will arrange for them to be provided by a separate leasing company operating in the lessee's behalf.

A *full-payout lease*, the second requirement, means that the total payment stream of the lease rental payments alone should cover the cost of the leased asset, the cost of financing, the lessor's overhead and a rate of return acceptable to the lessor. This contrasts to a *nonpayout lease*, in which the lessor's profits are in part dependent on the lease being renewed or on finding a second lessee to take over payment of the remaining expenses.

The third restriction relates to the value of property securing the loan. It states that no more than 20% of the return on the loan is to be realized from the residual value of the property at the end of the initial term of the lease. Recall from the previous chapter that the residual value is the value of the leased asset at the end of a lease. The higher the residual value, the lower the lease rental payments will be. For example, assume a new car cost $14,500, and, if leased, the lessor would receive a total of $16,000 in lease rental payments over the full term of the lease. Consequently, to further lower the monthly lease rental payment, a residual value of over 20% of the $16,000 ($3,200) could not be established. This restriction is intended to emphasize the importance of basing leasing decisions on the credit worthiness of the lessee and not on the residual market value of the leased property. Also, it is intended to discourage institutions from offering leases that generally have higher risks or are of shorter duration thereby requiring extensive remarketing efforts (such as operating leases). The overall purpose of these three requirements is to limit the lending institution's exposure to risk.

State Regulations

A recent trend in federal consumer credit legislation has been to have federal laws supplement state laws rather than displace them completely. State laws are displaced by federal laws only if the state law is less stringent than the federal law. If the state law is more stringent, it takes priority.

There are several key areas of state consumer credit regulation that are of importance to savings institutions. These include:
- usury;
- consumer warranties and contractual capacity; and
- the Uniform Consumer Credit Code.

Usury

The most common area of state regulation affecting consumer credit transactions involves interest rates. Some states have adopted usury statutes that set maximum interest rates that may be charged on a loan. Typically, these interest rate ceilings vary depending on the nature of the loan. For example, the rate ceiling for consumer loans secured by real property may be lower than that for unsecured loans.

Institutions found guilty of usury violations are subject to losing all interest from the transaction. If interest has already been paid, twice the amount of interest paid may be recovered by the borrower.

State and federal usury regulations were complicated by Title V of the DIDMCA. This title contained a federal overrule of state usury ceilings on mortgages (Section 501), business and agricultural loans (Section 511) and other loans made by federally insured institutions (Sections 521-524). The overrules were permanent in some cases and temporary in others. On the other hand, for a time, individual states could override the federal rules by passing specific legislation for that purpose. For example, the time line for overrides on residential mortgage loans for states was April 1, 1983. For business and agricultural loans, the federal overrule expired automatically on that same date but could have been overridden sooner by specific state action. For other loans, the federal overrule is permanent but can be overridden by specific state action at any time in the future.

The intent of the Title V federal overrules was to lessen two problems with state usury ceilings that had emerged in the high interest rate environment of 1978-80. First, ceilings on certain types of credit were preventing lenders from raising rates in line with increases in their cost of funds. Second, competitive problems arose when state ceilings prevented some institutions from charging the same high rates that banks were permitted to charge under the current bank regulations.

The combination of high interest rates (high costs) and restrictive state usury ceilings (low returns) created an economic quandary for savings institutions. Under these conditions, some lenders became unwilling to extend credit, even at their state's maximum, because their own cost of funds had risen sharply. Restricted lending programs hurt business, the real estate market and consumers. Some business firms were unable to finance their operations, and builders were unable to sell new homes because buyers were unable to obtain mortgage loans. Consumers, too, experienced difficulty in financing automobiles and other needed items.

At that time certain popular opinions prompted the desire for federal intervention. One widely held opinion was that most state ceilings were not flexible enough to avoid the credit allocation problems that surfaced in the high interest environment of 1979-83. The states were not expected to change their ceilings as quickly as conditions warranted. Reportedly, several states feared that relaxing usury ceilings would expose consumers to lenders who might charge them exorbitant interest rates. And finally, with the deregulation of interest rates on deposits held by federally insured institutions, some thought the U.S. Congress should loosen restrictions for loans as well. Despite the call for federal intervention and a loosening of usury restrictions, Congress acknowledged the states' historical role in setting usury ceilings by allowing states to override any or all sections of Title V as described above.

Consumer Warranties and Contractual Capacity

Another area of consumer credit commonly regulated by state law is that of consumer warranties and contractual capacity. State consumer warranty statutes relate to "implied" warranties. An *implied warranty* insures that a product is fit for consumption even though there is no written statement to that effect. Contractual capacity statutes describe individuals who cannot be legally bound by a contract. Factors such as insanity, age and mental capacity can directly affect an individual's legal responsibility for a contract. Lenders need to be aware of warranty and contractual capacity statutes since they may have an impact on the credit worthiness of a borrower and defenses available to a consumer in a given transaction.

The Uniform Consumer Credit Code
At one time most credit laws were established by states, but this proved not totally satisfactory. Therefore, in 1963, the National Conference of Commissioners on Uniform State Laws initiated a study to develop a set of consumer credit laws that could be adopted by all states. As a result of this study, the American Bar Association approved the Uniform Consumer Credit Code (UCCC) in 1969. Only a few states have adopted the Uniform Consumer Credit Code in its entirety, although several have passed statutes containing various elements of the UCCC.

Specific purposes of the UCCC include the following:
- to set finance-service charges and vary interest rate ceilings to assure an adequate supply of consumer credit;
- to foster competition among providers of consumer credit;
- to protect consumers from unfair lending practices; and
- to encourage the development of sound consumer credit practices.

The primary objective of the UCCC is not to make all state consumer credit statutes uniform but to pull together and clarify the various laws and regulations within a state.

Lender Liability

In addition to complying with FHLBB regulations and federal statutes, savings institutions need to be aware of the legal liabilities they may incur when extending consumer credit through direct or indirect loans. In particular, the following three statutes relate to lender liability:
- The Uniform Commercial Code—Holder-in-Due-Course Rule;

- The Magnuson-Moss Warranty Act; and
- The Bankruptcy Reform Act of 1978.

The Uniform Commercial Code—Holder-in-due-course Rule

The Uniform Commercial Code is an extensive body of business-related laws that has been adopted by 49 states (the exception being Louisiana). One key area of the UCC that affects consumer lending is the holder-in-due-course rule. Originally, the holder-in-due-course rule stated that subsequent purchasers of a promissory note were not subject to any claims regarding the initial transaction. For example, assume Martin Zellerman purchased and financed a new automobile through a local dealer. The dealer, needing cash, sells Martin's note to a local lending institution. Two months later Martin discovers a defect in the auto and refuses to make payments until the defect is repaired. Although the dealer is still legally liable for defective mechanisms, under the original holder-in-due-course rule, Martin must continue to make payments to the institution since the institution is not subject to claims against the dealer. Should legal action be required to repair the defect, Martin's only recourse would be against the dealer.

In order to give consumers another source of recovery, the Federal Trade Commission has amended the holder-in-due-course rule outlined in the Uniform Commercial Code. In effect since 1976, this regulation states that sellers of goods and services cannot take or receive a consumer credit contract unless the contract specifically states that all holders of the contract (note) are subject to claims against the seller.

The regulation also requires sellers of goods and services to insure that the consumer credit contract contains specific language. This language must be printed in at least 10 point, boldface type. The language reads as follows:

**NOTICE
ANY HOLDER OF THIS CONSUMER CREDIT CONTRACT IS SUBJECT TO ALL CLAIMS AND DEFENSES WHICH THE DEBTOR COULD ASSERT AGAINST THE SELLER OF GOODS OR SERVICES OBTAINED WITH THE PROCEEDS HEREOF. RECOVERY HEREUNDER BY THE DEBTOR SHALL NOT EXCEED AMOUNTS PAID BY THE DEBTOR HEREUNDER.**

Only the seller has a specific legal obligation to insure that the proper language is made part of the contract. Technically, savings institutions are not legally responsible for insuring that the language above is made part of the contract. However, the FTC's holder-in-due-course rule applies not only to contracts that are purchased from dealers but also to contracts that are originated on an indirect basis and in which there is an affiliation or referral situation between the creditor and the seller. Therefore, if the lender provides the seller with contract forms to be used for financing, the lender must either require the dealer to have its own contracts or revise the provided contracts to include the required notice.

The net result of including the above notice in a contract is that the lender, in effect, assumes the role of the seller in being responsible for the implied warranty. Therefore, an institution should carefully scrutinize the product being sold. In addition, an institution should carefully analyze the dealer (seller) on the basis of ethical standards, service capacity and financial stability. Also, as a safeguard, lenders generally should take extra care before financing extended warranties. Extended warranties should have a contingent servicing plan in case the dealer goes out of business before the extended warranty expires.

The Magnuson-Moss Warranty Act
Enacted in December 1976, the Magnuson-Moss Warranty Act protects consumers against fraudulent or misrepresented warranties issued by manufacturers and sellers of consumer products. For the purposes of this Act, consumer products are defined as tangible personal property used for personal, family or household purposes.

The Magnuson-Moss Warranty Act regulates the way that warranties are structured, written, displayed and captioned. Warranties must be identified as full or limited and must be written in a language easily understood by consumers. If the warranty is limited, written specifications of the limitations must be included.

Purchasers of goods may sue sellers or manufacturers if they feel a warranty does not comply with this Act, and, if successful, the purchaser may recover legal fees as well as damages. Lenders holding dealer paper subject to this Act are liable for any claims against the dealer under the FTC holder-in-due-course rule. Institutions should be aware of any warranties expressed by dealers with whom they do business and should inspect the warranties to insure compliance with the Magnuson-Moss Warranty Act.

Federal Bankruptcy Laws
A number of state and federal laws affect debtors who are unable to repay their debts and seek relief through bankruptcy. Two of the most significant today are the Bankruptcy Reform Act of 1978 and the Bankruptcy Amendments and Federal Judgeship Act of 1984.

The two main purposes of the Bankruptcy Reform Act of 1978 were to help severely troubled debtors receive a discharge of existing debts through the courts and to provide these debtors with the opportunity for a fresh start. This Act set forth procedures for obtaining a discharge of debt or for allowing debtors to arrange an easier repayment plan. Provisions of this and later acts are covered in the federal bankruptcy code.

One effect of the Bankruptcy Reform Act of 1978 was to make it easier for consumers to declare bankruptcy and more difficult for creditors to collect money owed them. Some abuses resulted from the Act, however, because it did not include either a financial responsibility requirement or a requirement that affordable debts be paid after a petition for bankruptcy was filed. Thus, persons with high net incomes were able to use bankruptcy to eliminate debts that they might actually have been capable of paying in whole or in part.

The Bankruptcy Amendments and Federal Judgeship Act of 1984 was an attempt to prevent debtor abuses of these types. The law also was intended to speed the bankruptcy process through the courts by shortening the time periods for debtor actions. A third purpose was to encourage debtors to choose the option of repayment (Chapter 13) rather than discharge (Chapter 7) since there are advantages to creditors and debtors in Chapter 13 over Chapter 7 filings. Therefore, the 1984 law mandates that bankruptcy courts inform debtors of the two options and their consequences. In general, the 1984 law imposed more restrictions on debtors. (These laws also are covered further in Chapter 10.)

In collecting payments from insolvent borrowers, lenders must follow procedures set forth under federal law. Therefore, lenders should know the bankruptcy process in order to insure that their consumer loan policies and collection procedures can minimize consumer credit losses.

REGULATIONS PROTECTING CONSUMERS

The increasing use of consumer credit after World War II triggered concern regarding the effectiveness of laws governing consumer credit transactions. Incidents of excessive finance charges and abusive and fraudulent credit practices, coupled with difficulty in legal prosecution, led many states to develop and adopt laws to alleviate these problems.

The resulting regulations have been designed and amended to provide consumers with two major types of protection: protection for prospective borrowers and protection for consumers who already have obtained credit. Of course, many of the laws directed to these two concerns are interrelated since their intention is to provide for the fair application of all credit practices. (See the consumer protection regulations section of this chapter's appendix.)

Enacted in 1968, one of the first major pieces of federal legislation in this category was the Consumer Credit Protection Act. It contained several titles which have themselves become known as acts and which are described in the following sections.

Protection for Prospective Borrowers

The laws protecting prospective borrowers have two primary purposes. One is to prevent discrimination on the basis of race, color, religion, sex or national origin when consumer credit is being extended. The second purpose is to insure that adequate and timely disclosures on credit provisions are given to consumers so that they can make intelligent comparisons among various available credit terms. In order to prevent discrimination the following acts were developed:
- Fair Housing Act of 1968;
- Equal Credit Opportunity Act;
- Community Reinvestment Act; and
- Truth-in-Lending Act.

Fair Housing Act of 1968

The purpose of the Fair Housing Act of 1968 is to insure fairness and consistency in real estate lending practices. Specifically, the Act prohibits discrimination against people seeking housing credit on the basis of race, color, religion, sex or national origin. Although this Act primarily concerns first mortgage loans for the purchase of a dwelling, it also applies to home improvement and second mortgage loans, both of which can be considered forms of consumer credit.

Three consumer lending practices are specifically prohibited by the Fair Housing Act of 1968. The Act states that it is illegal to discriminate:

- by denying credit intended for purchasing, constructing, repairing or maintaining a dwelling;
- by arbitrarily fixing loan terms such as the amount, interest rate, duration (time) or other conditions of loan (in other words, the same loan terms must apply to all applicants); or
- by extending or denying credit, and/or adjusting the terms of a loan for reasons pertaining to the race, color, religion, sex, or national origin of the present or prospective residents of a dwelling for which a loan is being negotiated.

Equal Credit Opportunity Act

The Equal Credit Opportunity Act (ECOA) was added to the 1968 Consumer Credit Protection Act late in 1975. The primary purpose of ECOA is to prohibit consumer credit lenders from discriminating on the basis of sex, marital status, race, color, religion, national origin or age. In addition, credit applicants cannot be discriminated against because all or part of their income is derived from a public assistance program or because they have exercised any right in good faith under the Consumer Credit Protection Act.

ECOA delegated to the Federal Reserve Board the power to issue regulations to implement the statute. The Board's regulation, known as Regulation B, specifies that "a creditor shall not discriminate against an applicant on a prohibited basis regarding any aspect of a credit transaction."

Two important points of this provision require emphasis. First, all applicants and all types of consumer credit are subject to ECOA. Second, all aspects of a credit transaction

are subject to ECOA provisions. A credit transaction consists of all activities and procedures from initial inquiries to the application and credit evaluation process through the collection process. Specific procedures and policies subject to ECOA include:
- credit information gathering and use;
- credit investigation procedures;
- standards of credit worthiness;
- conditions of credit;
- furnishing of credit information;
- revocation, alteration or termination of credit; and
- collection procedures.

To safeguard against any unintentional errors in the processing of loan requests, the FHLBB requires institutions to prepare and make public clearly written, nondiscriminatory loan underwriting standards concerning all types of loans. All lending personnel must be aware of ECOA's requirements and their institution's commitment to equitable credit practices. Because of the very broad scope of this law, lenders must make constant efforts to insure compliance.

Community Reinvestment Act
The Community Reinvestment Act (CRA) of 1977 was enacted as Title VIII of the Housing and Community Development Act of that same year. This Act requires regulatory agencies to examine financial institutions to insure that they are meeting the credit needs of their respective communities. The FHLBB is responsible for issuing regulations and guidelines and for inspecting member institutions to insure that they are in compliance with CRA.

Under CRA, an institution is required to prepare a CRA statement that discloses all types of credit available to designated lending territories and includes a description of the institution's community involvement efforts. Statements must be reviewed annually by the institution's board of directors. The public has the right to comment on an institution's community activities, and these comments, along with CRA statements for the past two years, must be kept on file at the institution. A "CRA Notice" also must be on display at each office.

A savings institution may be penalized if the FHLBB determines that it is not fulfilling its obligations to the community. This penalty may be FHLBB denial of institution applications for branches, mergers, deposit facilities and charters, or FHLBB restrictions on the amount of funds the institution may borrow from federal agencies.

Truth-in-Lending Act, Regulation Z
The Truth-in-Lending Act (TIL), the Truth-in-Lending Simplification and Reform Act, the Consumer Protections Rule and the Electronic Funds Transfer Act were intended to provide consumers with understandable disclosures on credit transactions.

As part of the Consumer Credit Protection Act, TIL became effective in 1969. Its purpose is to encourage comparison shopping by credit consumers and to increase consumer understanding about the actual cost of credit. The Act requires that consumers receive extensive disclosures about the details of consumer credit transactions before they take place.

The Federal Reserve Board has the authority to issue rules and regulations to implement TIL. All lenders must comply with these rules and regulations as outlined in Regulation Z. Because the regulations are lengthy and quite detailed, only a basic overview of the main points is covered in this chapter. The following four major points are contained in TIL.

- The annual percentage rate (APR) and finance charges must be disclosed.
- All disclosures must be given to the borrower before the contract is signed.
- The consumer must receive a copy of the contract.
- Whenever credit is secured with the consumer's principal residence as collateral, or a sale is made of the consumer's home, a three-business day-right of rescission (cancellation) takes effect (see Figure 3-1).

Although different detailed disclosure lists are required, depending on whether the credit transaction is open-end or closed-end, five important numerical disclosures apply for all loans.

- The amount financed. This is ordinarily the borrower's loan amount less any prepaid finance charge.
- The payment schedule, or the size, number and due dates of all scheduled payments. The payment stream includes principal, interest, any other finance charges and any insurance premiums paid in the installments.

FIGURE 3-1
Notice of Right to Cancel

NOTICE OF RIGHT TO CANCEL

_____LOAN NO._____
(Identification of Transaction)

Your Right to Cancel
You are entering into a new transaction to increase the amount of credit provided to you. We acquired a mortgage, lien, or security interest on your home under the original transaction and will retain that mortgage, lien or security interest in the new transaction. You have a legal right under federal law to cancel the new transaction, without cost, within three business days from whichever of the following events occurs last:

(1) the date of the new transaction, which is_____; or
(2) the date you received your new Truth in Lending disclosures; or
(3) the date you received this notice of your right to cancel.

If you cancel the new transaction, your cancellation will apply only to the increase in the amount of credit. It will not affect the amount that you presently owe or the mortgage, lien, or security interest we already have on your home. If you cancel, the mortgage, lien or security interest as it applies to the increased amount is also cancelled. Within 20 calendar days after we receive your notice of cancellation of the new transaction, we must take the steps necessary to reflect the fact that our mortgage, lien, or security interest on your home no longer applies to the increase of credit. We must also return any money you have given to us or to anyone else in connection with the new transaction.

You may keep any money we have given you in the new transaction until we have done the things mentioned above, but you must then offer to return the money at the address below. If we do not take possession of the money within 20 calendar days of your offer, you may keep it without further obligation.

How to Cancel
If you decide to cancel the new transaction, you may do so by notifying us in writing, at

You may use any written statement that is signed and dated by you and states your intention to cancel, and/or you may use this notice by dating and signing below. Keep one copy of this notice because it contains important information about your rights.

If you cancel by mail or telegram, you must send the notice no later than midnight of_____
(date)

(or midnight of the third business day following the latest of the three events listed above). If you send or deliver your written notice to cancel some other way, it must be delivered to the above address no later than that time.

I WISH TO CANCEL

_____   _____
Consumer's Signature   Date

I/We Received **Notice of Right to Cancel** in Duplicate this Date_____, 19_____.

_____   _____
(Signature)   (Signature)

43022-3 (12/81*)
Right of Rescission (Refinance)   SAF Systems and Forms, Inc.

- The total of payments. Defined arithmetically, this is the sum of all the payments called for in the payment schedule.
- The finance charge. Defined arithmetically, this is the total of payments less the amount financed.
- The annual percentage rate.

Basically, for open-end credit, lenders must provide disclosures to the consumer about:

- when and how a finance charge is levied and calculated;
- periodic rates and balances affecting the finance charge and corresponding APR;
- when and how other charges are imposed;
- conditions and methods for the acquisition of property used to secure payment;
- the minimum periodic payment required;
- the consumer's rights regarding disputed billing errors;
- what to do in case of errors or inquiries about a bill; and
- outstanding balances at the start and end of the billing cycle along with the amounts and dates of all transactions, payments and finance charges that occurred during the period.

Semiannually, creditors are also required to send a statement to their credit customers outlining the procedure to follow in the event of an error or inquiry about their bill (see Figure 3-2).

In 1970, Congress added provisions to the TIL Act relating to the issuance and use of credit cards. These provisions state that credit cards may be issued only in response to a request or upon renewal of an existing card. Further, card holders are only liable for unauthorized use of credit cards in amounts not to exceed $50. However, card holders cannot be held liable at all if the credit card issuer has not adequately notified card holders of their potential liability. Should a card issuer dispute a card holder's claim that use of a credit card was unauthorized, the card issuer has the responsibility to disprove the customer's claim.

The disclosure requirements for closed-end consumer credit vary according to the nature of the loan and often include matters such as demand features, prepayment provisions, late charges and statements regarding assumption of the loan.

FIGURE 3-2
Periodic Disclosure Statement/Billing Errors and Inquiries

> **IN CASE OF ERRORS OR INQUIRIES ABOUT YOUR BILL**
>
> Send your inquiry in writing [**at creditor's option:** on a separate sheet] so that the creditor receives it within 60 days after the bill was mailed to you. Your written inquiry must include:
>
> 1. Your name and account number (if any):
>
> 2. A description of the error and why (to the extent you can explain) you believe it is an error; and
>
> 3. The dollar amount of the suspected error.
>
> If you have authorized your creditor to automatically pay your bill from your checking or savings account, you can stop or reverse payment on any amount you think is wrong by mailing your notice so that the creditor receives it within 16 days after the bill was sent to you.
>
> You remain obligated to pay the parts of your bill not in dispute, but you do not have to pay any amount in dispute during the time the creditor is resolving the dispute. During that same time, the creditor may not take any action to collect disputed amounts or report disputed amounts as delinquent.
>
> If you have a problem with property or services purchased with a credit card, you may have the right not to pay the remaining amount due on them if you first try in good faith to return them or give the merchant a chance to correct the problem. There are two limitations on this right:
>
> 1. You must have bought them in your home state or, if not within your home state, within 100 miles of your current mailing address; and
>
> 2. The purchase price must have been more than $50.
>
> However, these limitations do not apply if the merchant is owned or operated by the creditor, or if the creditor mailed you the advertisement for the property or services.
>
> This is a summary of your rights; a full statement of your rights and the creditor's responsibilities under the Federal Fair Credit Billing Act will be sent to you both upon request and in response to a billing error notice.

Source: *Federal Guide*, Consumer Protection Unit, Regulations Section, Sec. 226.7.

Truth-in-Lending Simplification and Reform Act

After its passage, the Truth-in-Lending Act was amended a number of times and was, as a result, sometimes difficult to interpret. Required disclosures were not only difficult to complete, but consumers had difficulty in understanding them. This defeated the original purpose of the Truth-in Lending Act, which was to "assure meaningful disclosure of credit terms." As a result of these complications, Congress enacted the Truth-in-Lending Simplification and Reform Act, effective in 1980.

One of the primary objectives of this Act was to reduce the number of required disclosures so that it was easier for consumers to understand disclosure statements.

There are two major points in the TIL Simplification and Reform Act. One covers information that must be included in "federal boxes." The other specifies that disclosures be written in simple English.

Loan documents must include four federal boxes that segregate and highlight the amount financed, APR, finance charge and total of payments. Writing disclosures in simple English is a special challenge, because writing a disclosure that is easy to understand and, at the same time, legal and enforceable in a court of law is often quite difficult.

Consumer Protections; Unfair or Deceptive Credit Practices
Issued by the FHLBB, the Consumer Protections rule became effective on January 1, 1986. It covers both consumer loans and certain equity loans made by savings institutions that are members of the Federal Home Loan Bank System. The FHLBB requirements are similar to those issued by the Federal Trade Commission for its respective lending groups.

The rule contains six provisions that prohibit the use of four specific contract provisions and the pyramiding of late charges. In addition, these provisions require that disclosure be given to potential cosigners of consumer credit obligations. Each of these provisions will be discussed separately.

1. *Cognovit or Confession of Judgment* is the first prohibited clause. It declares the borrower's consent to future judgments against the borrower for the amount owed in case the borrower defaults on a loan. It waives both the borrower's right to prior notice and the right to be heard in a formal legal proceeding. A contract cannot require a borrower to waive these rights.
2. *Wage Assignment* is a contract clause between a borrower and a lender stating that, upon default, the lender has the right to obtain a specific portion of the borrower's wages from a specific employer without notice or hearing. Wage assignments differ from wage garnishments in that garnishments require a court judgment while an assignment does not. Most states, including all states that have adopted the Uniform Consumer

Credit Code, already have restrictions on the use of wage assignments. They are now prohibited at the federal level.
3. *Security Interest in Household Goods* is a contract clause giving a lender a nonpossessory lien on personal property. Nonpossessory refers to those situations where the lender does not have actual physical possession of the collateral. The provision prohibits the taking of a security interest in household goods unless they are part of a purchase money transaction in which the household goods securing the loan are being purchased with the loan proceeds.
4. *Waiver of Exemption* is a contract clause allowing a lender to waive a borrower's protection under state law from the attachment of real or personal property. The provision that prohibits lenders from disregarding exemptions does not apply to real or personal property that secures the loan.
5. The rule also prohibits a lender from engaging in any practice or accounting method that would result in *pyramiding late charges,* that is, charging multiple late charges for one late payment.
6. The rule also requires lenders to disclose in writing to potential cosigners that they will have to repay the loan if the borrower does not. This protection for cosigners prohibits the misrepresentation of the nature or extent of cosigner liability. It also forbids the failure to disclose that liability. The rule further requires that cosigners be informed fully **before** becoming obligated.

Although the FHLBB and the FTC use different broad definitions regarding who is considered a cosigner, a *cosigner* is usually defined as an individual who signs a legal document on an equal basis with the signer. On a promissory note, all cosigners are individually and jointly liable for repayment of the full debt. Typically, cosigners include any person whose signature is requested as a condition for granting credit to a consumer but who does not receive goods, services or money. A lender usually requests a cosigner after reviewing a loan application and deciding that additional security is necessary. Whenever a lender requires a guarantor or cosigner on a loan application, the lender must provide the cosigner with a proper notice (see Figure 3-3).

FIGURE 3-3
Notice To Cosigner

DATE _____

LOAN# _____

NOTICE TO COSIGNER

You are being asked to guarantee this debt. Think carefully before you do. If the borrower doesn't pay the debt, you will have to. Be sure you can afford to pay if you have to, and that you want to accept this responsibility.

You may have to pay up to the full amount of the debt if the borrower does not pay. You may also have to pay late fees or collection costs, which can increase this amount.

The creditor can collect this debt from you without first trying to collect from the borrower. The creditor can use the same collection methods against you that can be used against the borrower, such as suing you, garnishing your wages, etc. If this debt is ever in default, that fact may become a part of your credit record.

THIS NOTICE IS NOT THE CONTRACT THAT MAKES YOU LIABLE FOR THE DEBT.

45959 (11/85)
COSIGNER NOTICE

SAF Systems and Forms, Inc.
1-800-323-3000

Electronic Funds Transfer Act

This Act, implemented through Federal Reserve Board Regulation E, established the rights and responsibilities of financial institutions and their customers with regard to electronic funds transfers. As defined in Regulation E, "an *electronic funds transfer* (EFT) consists of any transfer of funds, other than transactions originated by paper instruments, that is triggered through the use of an electronic terminal, telephone equipment, computer, or magnetic tape and orders or authorizes an institution to debit or credit an account."

As providers of consumer credit, savings institutions are subject to the provisions of this Act only in so far as preauthorized EFTs are concerned. *Preauthorized EFTs* are activities authorized by consumers in advance, such as when a transfer of funds occurs and recurs at regular periodic intervals. For example, preauthorized loan payments made through the automatic transfer of funds from a customer's savings or checking account are subject to this Act.

There are four conditions that cover disclosures required for EFT transactions.
1. Disclosures must be conducted when the customer contracts for EFT services.
2. Disclosures providing information similar to that of a receipt are required every time a customer initiates an EFT.
3. Disclosures containing preauthorization from the customer, including stop payment provisions on transfers, are required.
4. Institutions must provide periodic statements to customers on all customer accounts affected by EFT.

In some cases, institutions may have to comply with both Regulations E and Z when providing required disclosures to customers. For example, if an institution provides a line of credit that can be accessed from an automatic teller machine (ATM), it must provide customers with disclosures that are in accord with both Regulations E and Z.

Protection for Current Borrowers

Many of the legal protections provided for prospective borrowers also cover lender actions after credit has been granted. The previous section outlined certain disclosures that are required both when a customer applies for credit and after credit has been granted. This section explains the following four acts (see Figure 3-4) that generally come into play only after credit has been extended:
- Fair Credit Reporting Act;
- Fair Credit Billing Act;
- Fair Debt Collection Practices Act; and
- Right to Financial Privacy Act.

Fair Credit Reporting Act

Enacted in 1971, the primary purpose of the Fair Credit Reporting Act is to regulate the consumer credit reporting industry. In particular, it regulates how credit information is obtained and the conditions under which information later is disclosed to others. Prior to this law's enactment, consumers

FIGURE 3-4
Federal Statutes Relating to Consumer Credit

Act	Year Enacted	Importance for Consumer Credit Transactions	Reference Sources
Truth-in-Lending Act (TIL)	1968	Requires disclosures pertaining to credit terms to facilitate credit term comparisons by consumers.	*Federal Guide*, Volume 2, Consumer Protection Unit
Fair Housing Act	1968	Prohibits discrimination in real estate secured credit transactions on the basis of race, color, religion, sex or national origin.	*Federal Guide*, Volume 2, FHLB System Law and Regulation Unit
Fair Credit Reporting Act	1971	Provides a means to regulate consumer reporting industries in terms of how credit information is obtained and what is disclosed.	*Federal Guide*, Volume 2, Consumer Protection Unit
Fair Credit Billing Act (part of Truth-in-Lending Act)	1974	Provides consumers with the opportunity to question billing statements in error.	*Federal Guide*, Volume 2, Consumer Protection Unit
Equal Credit Opportunity Act (ECOA) as amended	amended 1976	Prohibits discrimination in credit transactions on the basis of sex, marital status, race, color, religion, national origin and age.	*Federal Guide*, Volume 2, Consumer Protection Unit
Magnuson-Moss Warranty Act	1976	Requires full explanation of manufacturers' warranties in language easily understood by consumers.	15 U.S.C. §2301, 16 C.F.R., Part 700 ef. seq.
Uniform Commercial Code "Holder-in-Due-Course Rule"	1976	Requires all consumer credit contracts to specifically state the liability of all holders of the contract for all claims against the seller.	*Federal Guide*, Volume 2, Consumer Protection Unit
Community Reinvestment Act (CRA)	1977	Requires the preparation of statements indicating institution involvement in the community and the posting of notices stating consumer rights to obtain a copy of the statement.	*Federal Guide*, Volume 2

Act	Year Enacted	Importance for Consumer Credit Transactions	Reference Sources
Bankruptcy Reform Act	1978	Sets forth procedures for discharging debts of insolvent debtors.	Title II of the U.S. Code
Electronic Funds Transfer Act	1978	Requires disclosures on transactions triggered through the use of an electronic terminal, telephone equipment, computer or magnetic tape.	*Federal Guide*, Volume 2, Consumer Protection Unit
Right to Financial Privacy Act	1979	Prohibits federal government investigation of consumer financial information without proper documentation.	*Federal Guide*, Volume 2, Consumer Protection Unit
Truth-in-Lending Simplification and Reform Act	1980	Simplifies disclosures required under the Truth-in-Lending Act of 1969.	*Federal Guide*, Volume 2, Consumer Protection Unit
Depository Institutions Deregulation and Monetary Control Act	1980	Expands consumer lending authority for federally chartered institutions.	*Federal Guide*, Volume 2
Garn-St Germain Depository Institutions Act	1982	Enhances the authorities for federally chartered institutions.	*Federal Guide*, Volume 1
Consumer Protections; Unfair or Deceptive Credit Practices	1985	Prohibits the use of four contract provisions, pyramiding late charges and requires disclosure to potential cosigners.	12 C.F.R., Part 535

had little recourse if inaccurate disclosures about their credit history were made by reporting agencies.

The consumer credit reporting industry consists of credit bureaus, investigative reporting companies and similar organizations that gather and report consumer information. The Fair Credit Reporting Act limits distribution of such information. A credit reporting facility may release information only upon the written consent of the consumer and/or when it is assured that the party requesting the information will use it for constructive purposes, such as to determine a consumer's eligibility for credit and/or employment. The Act also limits what may be reported. Information deemed "ancient history" is not to be included in such a report. For instance, bankruptcies occurring 14 years prior and judgments seven years prior to the credit report request may not be reported.

The Act also requires that certain types of disclosures be made to consumers and that consumers be given an opportunity to rectify inaccurate reports. In the event a lender denies a loan request due to adverse conditions exposed by credit sources, the applicant must be informed in writing of the nature of the adverse conditions and the sources. Upon receipt of the adverse disclosure, the applicant has the right to pursue the source and to challenge any information reported by the source that the consumer claims is inaccurate. If an adverse condition is in error, it must be erased from the records of the source providing the information. Also, unresolved disputes about credit use must be recorded as such.

Lenders are subject to both civil and criminal liabilities under this Act. Those found in violation of the Fair Credit Reporting Act are subject to monetary penalties and/or imprisonment.

Fair Credit Billing Act
Supplementing the 1971 Consumer Protection Act, the Fair Credit Billing Act passed in 1974 provides consumers with the opportunity to question the accuracy of amounts billed to them by creditors. The borrower has the right to question the accuracy of the billing statement by writing to the lender within 60 days of receiving the statement. Between the time the lender receives the borrower's letter and the time the lender responds, the borrower is not required to submit payment for the disputed amount. Penalties for nonpayment of disputed amounts during this time are prohibited.

Fair Debt Collection Practices Act
This Act, effective as of 1978, was designed to eliminate abusive debt collection practices by collectors and to promote state action to protect consumers from such practices.

Savings institutions are subject to this Act only if they are considered debt collectors. An institution is a debt collector for those debts in which:
- it is acting as a third party in a reciprocal service agreement whereby it is required to collect debts other than its own; or
- it uses a name other than its own (in writing or orally) that would give the appearance a third party is collecting the debt.

The Fair Debt Collection Practices Act outlines practices that are considered abusive collection activities. These include threatening to use violence, using obscene language, and making excessive phone calls to debtors and/or third parties. The hours of the day that telephone contact may be made with the debtor are also limited, and restrictions are placed on communications with persons other than the borrower.

The following debt collection procedures are prohibited:
- mentioning to persons, other than the debtor, that the debtor owes money;
- using postcards for collection procedures;
- collecting a debt on attorney or other collection agency stationery when it is used with the intent of making the debtor think a legal firm is involved when it is not; and
- making statements that imply that repossession, foreclosure or a lawsuit is imminent when there are no intentions or plans to take these actions.

Debt collectors in violation of the Act are subject to penalties arising out of civil action suits and class action suits.

Right to Financial Privacy Act
In effect since 1979, this Act attempts to insure a degree of consumer privacy by establishing certain procedures for government investigators who attempt, for law enforcement purposes, to gain access to an institution's records. Federal agencies or departments seeking the financial records of customers must follow these rules. Foremost among them is customer notification of the investigation. The customer then has the opportunity and right to protest such action through judicial proceedings. A customer is defined by this Act as an

individual who or a partnership comprised of five or fewer individuals who use or used any service offered by the lender.

Government agencies may gain permissive access to customer records by presenting institutions with one of the following documents:
- written customer authorization;
- administrative subpoena;
- search warrant;
- judicial subpoena; or
- formal written request.

Despite receiving any one of the above documents, institutions are prohibited from releasing records until the government produces a Certificate of Compliance certifying that the agency complied with the requirements of this Act.

SUMMARY

One purpose of the Depository Institutions Deregulation and Monetary Control Act of 1980 and the Garn-St Germain Depository Institutions Act of 1982 is to enhance the competitive position of all financial institutions. To this end, DIDMCA and Garn-St Germain authorize broader consumer lending powers for federally chartered savings institutions. These broadened consumer lending powers have been implemented primarily through FHLBB regulations that present guidelines and requirements for offering consumer credit at federally chartered institutions.

In addition to complying with FHLBB and FSLIC regulations, institutions also must comply with the various federal statutes affecting consumer credit. The primary sources of federal consumer credit law are the Consumer Credit Protection Act of 1968 and the Equal Credit Opportunity Act of 1975. These acts cover all phases of consumer credit and are designed to curb unfair credit practices, primarily through disclosure requirements and lender restrictions. Other acts affecting consumer credit operations include the Fair Credit Reporting Act, the Right to Financial Privacy Act, the Fair Housing Act of 1968 and the Community Reinvestment Act. See Figure 3-4 for a summary of the laws relating to consumer credit. The appendix accompanying this chapter list these laws.

Lenders are legally liable for claims and defenses against sellers and manufacturers of goods and services. Therefore, savings institutions must be especially cautious when making indirect loans through dealers and sellers. Lenders should be aware of any warranties covering dealer products and services. In addition, the dealer's reputation and financial stability should be thoroughly researched.

Finally, lending personnel need to be thoroughly familiar with their own state laws affecting consumer credit. Aspects of consumer credit that are commonly regulated by state statutes include interest rates, implied warranties and contractual capacity.

CHAPTER QUESTIONS

1. What are the major purposes of consumer credit regulations regarding both lenders and borrowers?

2. What are the primary factors on which an institution should rely when it is making consumer loans?

3. Explain how the 30%-of-assets limitation for consumer loans affects federally chartered institutions.

4. Define the terms slow consumer credit and consumer credit classified as a loss, and explain why they should be kept to a minimum.

5. Describe three limitations that federal institutions must observe when offering consumer leasing.

6. Describe three areas of consumer credit commonly regulated by state laws.

7. When making indirect consumer loans, why is it important that a lender carefully screen the dealer as well as the products that the dealer sells?

8. Why is it necessary for lending personnel to be aware of the Equal Credit Opportunity Act and what it covers?

9. List four major points included in the Truth-in-Lending Act and five required numerical disclosures that apply to all closed-end loans.

10. Explain, in terms of borrower benefits, any three of the six provisions contained in the Consumer Protections; Unfair or Deceptive Credit Practices rule.

11. List four acts that protect borrowers after a consumer loan has been made, and briefly describe any one of them.

APPENDIX

Regulations for Federal Associations

Title 12 U.S. Code 1464 (c)(2)(b)—Total investment authority
545.31—Election regarding classification of loans
545.32, 545.33 and 545.34—Loans secured by borrower-occupied property
545.42—Home improvement loans
545.45—Manufactured home financing
545.47—Overdraft loans
545.50—Consumer loans (previously 545.7-10)
545.51—Credit card operations
545.52—Loans on savings accounts
545.53—Consumer leasing
545.7-4—Education loans

FSLIC Regulations
561.38—Consumer credit definition
561.39—Open-end consumer credit
561.40—Closed-end consumer credit
561.15—Scheduled items
561.16a—Slow consumer credit
561.16b—Consumer credit classified as a loss
563.46—Charge off of consumer credit classified as a loss
563.9-3—Loans to one borrower

For a list of TIL amendents, see Special Management Bulletins:
S-226 dated September 2, 1983; S-233 dated May 21, 1984; S-244 dated September 23, 1985; S-251 dated June 2, 1986 and S-252 dated June 3, 1986 by the United States League of Savings Institutions

Consumer Protection Regulations

Title 15, U.S. Code—Consumer Credit Protection Act
Part A—General Provisions
Section 1601—Truth-in-Lending Act
Part B—Credit Transactions
Part C—Credit Advertising
Part D—Credit Billing
Section 1666—Fair Credit Billing Act
Part E—Consumer Leases
Section 1667—Consumer Leasing Act of 1976
Section 1681—Fair Credit Reporting Act
Section 1691—Equal Credit Opportunity Act
Section 1692—Fair Debt Collection Practices Act
Section 1693—Electronic Funds Transfer Act

Federal Reserve System Rules Title 12, Code of Federal Regulations
Part 226—Truth in Lending (Regulation Z)
Part 227—Unfair or Deceptive Acts or Practices; Credit Practices
Part 213—Consumer Leasing (Regulation M)
Part 202—Equal Credit Opportunity (Regulation B)
Part 205—Electronic Funds Transfers (Regulation E)
Part 535—Consumer Protections; Unfair or Deceptive Credit Practices

Special Management Bulletin S-246
dated December 2, 1985 by the United States League of Savings Institutions

Federal Trade Commission Title 16, Code of Federal Regulations
Part 600—Statements of General Policy
Part 433—Preservation of Consumer's Claims and Defenses
Part 444—Credit Practices

4
Interest

Objectives

After studying this chapter, you should be able to:
- ☐ Define the term *amortization* and explain how to use an amortization table to find a loan's required monthly payment;
- ☐ Describe the basic concept underlying simple interest;
- ☐ Compare and contrast three methods of interest calculation that are based on either a 360 or 365 day year;
- ☐ Compute the finance charges lenders can assess on open-end credit accounts using the adjusted balance, previous balance and average daily balance methods;
- ☐ Differentiate between the United States Rule and the actuarial method of determining earned interest; and
- ☐ Define annual percentage rate (APR) and explain why it is important.

INTRODUCTION

All lending employees should be able to explain and perform the calculations necessary to determine interest charges on consumer loans. Computers cannot always be relied on to calculate borrowing costs because there are times when computers are inoperative. Customers are frustrated when, in response to an inquiry, they hear, "The computer is down," or "The computer made an error on your account." Also, when lending personnel understand the calculations basic to consumer lending, they can offer explanations to customers and answer customer questions more easily.

This chapter describes the most common type of interest charged on consumer loans today: simple interest. Also, add-on interest and discount interest are introduced. The different methods used to determine when interest begins to accrue and ways to determine the principal balance on which interest will be charged are discussed. The purposes of finance charges and the annual percentage rate (APR) and how to calculate them also are explained. The United States Rule and the actuarial method of determining earned interest as well as the calculation of monthly payments are reviewed. Finally, the chapter discusses how to calculate loan pay-offs and interest rebates on prepaid loans. This chapter includes an Appendix that has additional information about add-on interest, discount interest and the Rule of 78s.

THE NATURE OF INTEREST

In a consumer credit transaction, the consumer borrows a sum of money and agrees to repay it at a later time. The consumer also agrees to pay the lender interest for the use of the borrowed funds. *Interest* is the dollar amount charged for the use of the money; it is expressed as a percentage of the total dollar amount of the loan. The amount of money borrowed is the *principal*.

The lender establishes a *repayment schedule* that details how the debt will be repaid. The repayment schedule reflects the terms of the loan that both the borrower and lender find mutually acceptable. Over a mutually acceptable period of time, the borrower typically makes equal payments in monthly installments. Part of each installment payment reduces the outstanding principal and part of each payment pays off the accrued, or earned interest. This process of reducing principal and paying interest through equal installments at specific intervals over a set period is called *amortization*. As the principal gets smaller, the interest that accrues each month is also reduced. Generally, installment payments are made monthly or quarterly.

Factors That Affect Interest Totals

The amount of interest paid depends on the following factors:
- the loan amount, also called principal;
- the loan term or loan maturity;
- the stated annual interest rate;
- the repayment schedule; and
- the method used to calculate interest.

The *loan term* is the total length of time allowed for repayment of a debt. It generally is expressed as a portion or multiple of one year. The interest rate is stated as a percentage of the loan amount, or principal. At any given interest rate, the greater the principal, the longer the term of the loan, and the less frequent the repayment schedule, the larger the

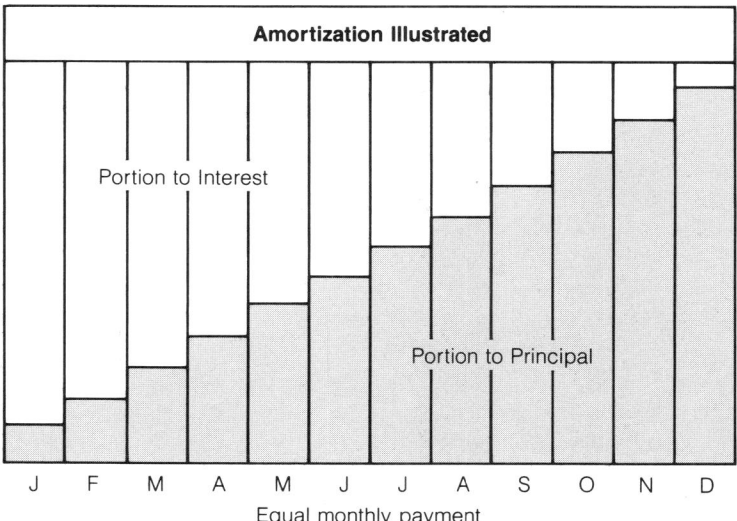

Amortization Illustrated

Portion to Interest

Portion to Principal

J F M A M J J A S O N D
Equal monthly payment

total amount of interest will be. The method used to calculate interest also affects the total amount of interest over the life of the loan.

Methods of Interest Computation

The relationship among the principal, interest rate and term can be expressed in the following interest formula:

$$\text{Interest} = \text{Principal} \times \text{Rate} \times \text{Term}$$

This formula is used for all three methods of interest calculation commonly used in consumer lending. The three methods are simple, add-on and discount. Each type has a different approach for determining when to calculate and add interest during the term of the loan. See Figure 4-1 for a comparison of add-on, discount and simple interest.

FIGURE 4-1
Comparison of Three Methods of Calculating Interest

	ADD-ON	DISCOUNT	SIMPLE
Calculation of Interest	Interest is precomputed and added to loan amount.	Interest is precomputed and subtracted from loan amount.	Interest is computed on the outstanding principal balance.
Recognition of Interest	Earned interest is recognized according to the Rule of 78s.	Same as Add-on	Earned interest is recognized according to the United States Rule or actuarial method.
Rebates	Rebates are necessary because the outstanding loan balance reflects both principle and interest.	Same as Add-on	No rebates are necessary because the outstanding loan balance reflects principle only.
Total Interest Amount	$I = P \times R \times T$	$I = P \times R \times T$	I = Monthly Payment × # of Mos. in Term −P
Monthly Payment Amount	$\dfrac{P + 1}{\text{Number of Payments}}$	$\dfrac{P + 1}{\text{Number of Payments}}$	Use amortization tables

Since interest represents income for lenders, lenders are concerned with receiving and accounting for interest as it is earned. This process is called *recognition of income*. Consumers, too, are concerned with knowing the amount of interest they pay because it can represent a tax deduction. As of July 1986, however, tax proposals would eliminate deductions for consumer loan interest.

This section includes explanations of add-on interest and discount interest. Further explanations and examples follow in the Appendix to the chapter. Simple interest is thoroughly discussed in the next section.

Add-on Interest
Using the *add-on interest* method, interest is computed by using the interest formula to calculate the interest charge for the term of a loan and adding that charge to the principal of the loan. The borrower agrees to repay the principal plus interest. The dollar amount of each monthly installment is determined by dividing the principal plus interest by the number of payments to be made. The number of payments equals the number of months in the loan term.

Add-on interest is also called precomputed interest; the borrower knows the total amount of interest to be paid at the beginning of the loan term. This feature, as well as the relative ease of calculating the monthly payment amount made add-on interest popular with lenders.

Consumers, however, have begun to view add-on interest with a critical eye. Some consumer complaints have led to legal actions prohibiting the use of add-on interest in some areas. Consumers mainly object to the precomputation of interest. Using the add-on method, interest is calculated on the full principal amount for the entire loan term. However, borrowers only have use of the full principal amount until the first payment is made. With every subsequent payment, they have less and less of the principal amount to use but must continue to pay interest on the full amount.

Discount Interest
Like add-on interest, the *discount interest* method uses the original principal amount to calculate the total interest for the loan. Unlike add-on interest, however, the interest determined by the interest formula is **subtracted** from the principal to obtain the net loan amount.

Using the discount interest method, the total interest and

the monthly payment amount can be calculated easily by hand. However computerized lending operations are growing, and hand calculations are no longer performed regularly. The popularity of discount interest has been declining. Today, the discount interest method is most often used with short-term business loans which have a loan term of one year or less and no intermediate payments.

SIMPLE INTEREST

Simple interest is a method of calculating interest in which the amount of interest is calculated on the outstanding principal balance of a loan for each given period. It has become increasingly popular among consumers. The basic concept underlying simple interest is that interest is paid only on the amount borrowed for the length of time during which the borrower has full use of the credit. As the principal is reduced, less interest accrues. Thus, as each payment is made on a closed-end loan (discussed later in this chapter), a larger portion of the amount goes toward reducing the principal balance and a smaller portion pays off the interest. This happens because the loan is repaid in equal payments while the interest is charged on a decreasing principal balance so the dollar amount of interest decreases with each payment.

Simple interest can be applied to any kind of loan; open-end or closed-end. Recall that open-end loans, or open-end credit, offer credit used until a certain, prearranged borrowing limit is reached. Closed-end loans are repaid in equal monthly installments. The basic concept behind simple interest is easily seen in closed-end noninstallment loans to which the basic interest formula is applied. Consider the effect of simple interest in the following examples: A loan of $5,000 is made for two years at 16%. Assume that no monthly payments are made and that the total amount of the loan plus interest is due at the end of two years. Using the basic formula (Interest = Principal × Rate × Term), interest is calculated by multiplying $5,000 by 16% by two years or $5,000 × .16 × 2. The amount of interest in this case is $1,600, so that at the end of the second year the total amount due will be $6,600.

If the term of the loan is shorter, the amount of interest charged will be less given an equal principal and an equal interest rate. Suppose the $5,000 loan discussed above is repaid at the end of three months. To determine the amount of interest, the principal is multiplied by the rate and then multiplied by one-fourth (or 3/12) since three months is one-fourth of a year ($5,000 × .16 × .25). The total amount due will be $5,200. In these uncomplicated examples, the simple interest calculation for an entire closed-end loan is relatively straightforward.

In most cases, however, loans are repaid gradually on a monthly basis, and interest is charged per month on the unpaid principal. Credit card interest provides a clear example of the required calculation for open-end loans. Most credit cards charge simple interest that is computed as follows: The annual interest rate is divided by 12, such as 18%/12, to arrive at a 1.5% per month rate on an annual rate of 18%. This monthly rate is then applied to charges outstanding each month. The exact amount is determined by considering the number of days as a fraction of a month with each "month" assumed to have 30 days. For example, $1,000 incurring an 18% finance charge for 15 days (one-half of a month or .5) can be computed as follows:

$$\begin{aligned}\$1{,}000 \times (.18/12 \times .5) &= \$1{,}000 \times .015 \times .5 \\ &= \$15 \times .5 \\ &= \$7.50\end{aligned}$$

Determining Days in a Year

An actual calendar year contains 365 or 366 days; however, some financial institutions use a 360-day year to calculate interest and some use a combination of both 360 and 365 days. There are three common methods of determining the number of days on which to calculate interest in a year:
- exact interest-exact time;
- ordinary interest-exact time; and
- ordinary interest-ordinary time.

In all three methods, the basic interest formula remains unchanged. Only the method of determining the time period for the loan's interest charges differs. As will be demonstrated, the method of counting days affects the total amount of interest on the loan even when the rate and term are the same.

Exact Interest-Exact Time

The *exact interest-exact time* method of calculating interest is based on a 365-day year and uses the exact number of days that interest is earned or owed. In leap years this method uses 366 days. It is also known as the 365/365 method. Consider the following example:

Bob Friendly borrows $900 on September 11. He agrees to repay the loan, with 13% interest, on December 14. How much interest will Bob owe?

To solve this problem, first determine the exact number of days the loan will be outstanding. September 12 is day 254 of the year and December 14 is day 348. Subtracting 254 from 348 leaves 94 loan days. The interest on Bob's loan can be calculated by using the basic interest formula: $900 × .13 × 94/365 equals $30.13. If Bob invests $900 in a long-term certificate of deposit paying 13% simple interest, he could also use the exact interest-exact time method to determine the value of his account for any time period of less than one year.

Ordinary Interest-Exact Time

The *ordinary interest-exact time* method of calculating interest is based on a 360-day year and uses the exact number of days interest is earned or owed. Using 360 instead of 365 days simplifies calculations and results in a slightly higher yield. This method is called the 365/360 method of calculating interest.

If we substitute this method in the previous loan example, Bob will owe more interest: $900 × .13 x 94/360 equals $30.55. The exact number of days has remained the same, but it now represents a slightly larger proportion of a shorter year.

Ordinary Interest-Ordinary Time

The *ordinary interest-ordinary time* method of calculating interest is based on a 360-day year with each month having exactly 30 days. Using this method results in a slightly higher yield than considering 365 days in a year. It is called the 360/360 method of calculating interest. Assuming each month has 30 days simplifies interest calculations. Borrowers will be charged interest for 30 days in any month, regardless of whether or not that month has 30 days (e.g., February has 28 days and July has 31 days). Some financial institutions use this method to calculate interest on loans but generally do not use it for deposits.

Applying this method to the previous loan example, the interest on Bob's loan is calculated in the following way: First, determine the number of days the loan will be outstanding based on ordinary time. Bob borrows on September 11 and promises to repay his loan on December 14. Remember that the ordinary time method assumes each month has 30 days. To determine the number of loan days in this case, consider the number of days left in September as 19 (30-11); the number of days in October and November as 60 (even though October actually has 31 days); and the 14 days in December, for a total of 93 days. Then use the basic interest formula to calculate Bob's interest: $900 × .13 × 93/360 equals $30.22.

Calculating Monthly Payments

Today, most consumer loans are repaid in equal monthly payments with part of the payment used to reduce the principal and part used to pay off the accrued interest. There are various ways to calculate monthly payments. For closed-end loans, amortization tables enable lenders to compute the required monthly payment that will repay the loan in full over its term. For open-end loans or credit, various methods are used to arrive at the principal balance that will be assessed finance charges. With simple interest the United States Rule or the actuarial method can also be used to determine earned interest and then to calculate monthly payments. The United States Rule is based on the time when payment is received, and the actuarial method is based on a preset time period.

Closed-end Loans

Closed-end loans usually require borrowers to repay the debt in equal monthly installments. Since the computations involved in obtaining these figures are complicated and lengthy, lenders rely on precalculated amortization tables (see Figure 4-2) or programmable calculators. An *amortization table* shows the monthly payment amount needed to amortize, or pay off, a borrowed sum at a given interest rate over a period of time. For example, if Pamela Green qualifies to borrow $1,000 for one year at 15% simple interest, and agrees to repay the loan in 12 equal payments, the amortization table in Figure 4-2 can be used to determine her monthly payment. The figure at the point on the table where 15% and 12 months intersect is $90.26.

FIGURE 4-2
Simple Interest Monthly Amortization Table

Basic Monthly Payment Table for a Loan of $1,000

MOS.	12%	12¼%	12½%	12¾%	13%	13½%	14%	14½%	15%
2	507.52	507.67	507.83	507.99	508.14	508.46	508.77	509.09	509.40
3	340.03	340.17	340.31	340.45	340.59	340.87	341.15	341.43	341.71
4	256.29	256.42	256.55	256.68	256.81	257.08	257.34	257.60	257.87
5	206.04	206.17	206.30	206.42	206.55	206.81	207.06	207.31	207.57
6	172.55	172.68	172.80	172.92	173.05	173.30	173.54	173.79	174.04
7	148.63	148.75	148.88	149.00	149.12	149.36	149.61	149.85	150.09
8	130.70	130.82	130.94	131.06	131.18	131.42	131.66	131.90	132.14
9	116.75	116.86	116.98	117.10	117.22	117.46	117.70	117.94	118.18
10	105.59	105.71	105.82	105.94	106.06	106.30	106.53	106.77	107.01
11	96.46	96.58	96.69	96.81	96.93	97.16	97.40	97.64	97.87
12	88.85	88.97	89.09	89.21	89.32	89.56	89.79	90.03	90.26
13	82.42	82.54	82.65	82.77	82.89	83.12	83.36	83.59	83.83
14	76.91	77.02	77.14	77.26	77.37	77.61	77.84	78.08	78.31
15	72.13	72.25	72.36	72.48	72.59	72.83	73.06	73.30	73.53
16	67.95	68.07	68.18	68.30	68.42	68.65	68.88	69.12	69.35
17	64.26	64.38	64.50	64.61	64.73	64.96	65.20	65.43	65.67
18	60.99	61.10	61.22	61.34	61.45	61.69	61.92	62.15	62.39
19	58.06	58.17	58.29	58.41	58.52	58.76	58.99	59.23	59.46
20	55.42	55.54	55.65	55.77	55.89	56.12	56.35	56.59	56.83
21	53.04	53.15	53.27	53.39	53.50	53.74	53.97	54.21	54.44
22	50.87	50.99	51.10	51.22	51.34	51.57	51.81	52.04	52.28
23	48.89	49.01	49.12	49.24	49.36	49.59	49.83	50.06	50.30
24	47.08	47.20	47.31	47.43	47.55	47.78	48.02	48.25	48.49
25	45.41	45.53	45.65	45.76	45.88	46.12	46.35	46.59	46.83
26	43.87	43.99	44.11	44.23	44.34	44.58	44.82	45.05	45.29
27	42.45	42.57	42.69	42.80	42.92	43.16	43.39	43.63	43.87
28	41.13	41.25	41.36	41.48	41.60	41.84	42.08	42.31	42.55
29	39.90	40.02	40.14	40.25	40.37	40.61	40.85	41.09	41.33
30	38.75	38.87	38.99	39.11	39.23	39.46	39.70	39.94	40.18
31	37.68	37.80	37.92	38.04	38.16	38.39	38.63	38.87	39.11
32	36.68	36.79	36.91	37.03	37.15	37.39	37.63	37.87	38.11
33	35.73	35.85	35.97	36.09	36.21	36.45	36.69	36.93	37.17
34	34.84	34.96	35.08	35.20	35.32	35.56	35.80	36.05	36.29
35	34.01	34.13	34.25	34.37	34.49	34.73	34.97	35.21	35.46
36	33.22	33.34	33.46	33.58	33.70	33.94	34.18	34.43	34.67
37	32.47	32.59	32.71	32.83	32.95	33.20	33.44	33.68	33.93
38	31.77	31.89	32.01	32.13	32.25	32.49	32.73	32.98	33.22
39	31.10	31.22	31.34	31.46	31.58	31.82	32.07	32.31	32.56
40	30.46	30.58	30.70	30.82	30.94	31.19	31.43	31.68	31.93
41	29.86	29.98	30.10	30.22	30.34	30.59	30.83	31.08	31.33
42	29.28	29.40	29.52	29.65	29.77	30.01	30.26	30.51	30.75
43	28.73	28.85	28.98	29.10	29.22	29.47	29.71	29.96	30.21
44	28.21	28.33	28.45	28.58	28.70	28.94	29.19	29.44	29.69
45	27.71	27.83	27.95	28.08	28.20	28.45	28.70	28.94	29.20
46	27.23	27.36	27.48	27.60	27.72	27.97	28.22	28.47	28.72
47	26.78	26.90	27.02	27.14	27.27	27.52	27.77	28.02	28.27
48	26.34	26.46	26.58	26.71	26.83	27.08	27.33	27.58	27.84
49	25.92	26.04	26.17	26.29	26.41	26.66	26.91	27.17	27.42
50	25.52	25.64	25.77	25.89	26.01	26.26	26.52	26.77	27.02
51	25.13	25.26	25.38	25.50	25.63	25.88	26.13	26.39	26.64
52	24.76	24.89	25.01	25.13	25.26	25.51	25.76	26.02	26.27
53	24.40	24.53	24.65	24.78	24.90	25.16	25.41	25.67	25.92
54	24.06	24.19	24.31	24.44	24.56	24.82	25.07	25.33	25.58
55	23.73	23.86	23.98	24.11	24.23	24.49	24.74	25.00	25.26
56	23.41	23.54	23.66	23.79	23.92	24.17	24.43	24.68	24.94
57	23.11	23.23	23.36	23.48	23.61	23.87	24.12	24.38	24.64
58	22.81	22.94	23.06	23.19	23.32	23.57	23.83	24.09	24.35
59	22.53	22.65	22.78	22.91	23.03	23.29	23.55	23.81	24.07
60	22.25	22.38	22.50	22.63	22.76	23.01	23.27	23.53	23.79

Reprinted with permission of The Financial Publishing Company, Boston, Massachusetts.

Basic Monthly Payment Table for a Loan of $1,000

MOS.	12%	12¼%	12½%	12¾%	13%	13½%	14%	14½%	15%
61	21.98	22.11	22.24	22.36	22.49	22.75	23.01	23.27	23.53
62	21.73	21.85	21.98	22.11	22.24	22.49	22.75	23.02	23.28
63	21.48	21.60	21.73	21.86	21.99	22.25	22.51	22.77	23.03
64	21.24	21.36	21.49	21.62	21.75	22.01	22.27	22.53	22.80
65	21.00	21.13	21.26	21.39	21.52	21.78	22.04	22.30	22.57
66	20.78	20.90	21.03	21.16	21.29	21.55	21.82	22.08	22.35
67	20.56	20.69	20.81	20.94	21.07	21.34	21.60	21.86	22.13
68	20.34	20.47	20.60	20.73	20.86	21.12	21.39	21.65	21.92
69	20.14	20.27	20.40	20.53	20.66	20.92	21.19	21.45	21.72
70	19.94	20.07	20.20	20.33	20.46	20.72	20.99	21.26	21.52
71	19.74	19.87	20.00	20.13	20.27	20.53	20.80	21.06	21.33
72	19.56	19.69	19.82	19.95	20.08	20.34	20.61	20.88	21.15
73	19.37	19.50	19.63	19.77	19.90	20.16	20.43	20.70	20.97
74	19.19	19.32	19.46	19.59	19.72	19.99	20.25	20.53	20.80
75	19.02	19.15	19.28	19.42	19.55	19.82	20.08	20.36	20.63
76	18.85	18.98	19.12	19.25	19.38	19.65	19.92	20.19	20.46
77	18.69	18.82	18.95	19.09	19.22	19.49	19.76	20.03	20.30
78	18.53	18.66	18.79	18.93	19.06	19.33	19.60	19.87	20.15
79	18.37	18.51	18.64	18.77	18.91	19.18	19.45	19.72	20.00
80	18.22	18.36	18.49	18.62	18.76	19.03	19.30	19.58	19.85
81	18.08	18.21	18.34	18.48	18.61	18.88	19.16	19.43	19.71
82	17.93	18.07	18.20	18.34	18.47	18.74	19.02	19.29	19.57
83	17.79	17.93	18.06	18.20	18.33	18.60	18.88	19.16	19.43
84	17.66	17.79	17.93	18.06	18.20	18.47	18.75	19.02	19.30
85	17.52	17.66	17.79	17.93	18.07	18.34	18.61	18.89	19.17
86	17.40	17.53	17.67	17.80	17.94	18.21	18.49	18.77	19.05
87	17.27	17.40	17.54	17.68	17.81	18.09	18.36	18.64	18.93
88	17.15	17.28	17.42	17.55	17.69	17.97	18.24	18.52	18.81
89	17.03	17.16	17.30	17.43	17.57	17.85	18.13	18.41	18.69
90	16.91	17.04	17.18	17.32	17.45	17.73	18.01	18.29	18.58
91	16.79	16.93	17.07	17.20	17.34	17.62	17.90	18.18	18.47
92	16.68	16.82	16.95	17.09	17.23	17.51	17.79	18.07	18.36
93	16.57	16.71	16.85	16.98	17.12	17.40	17.68	17.97	18.25
94	16.46	16.60	16.74	16.88	17.02	17.30	17.58	17.86	18.15
95	16.36	16.50	16.64	16.77	16.91	17.19	17.48	17.76	18.05
96	16.26	16.40	16.53	16.67	16.81	17.09	17.38	17.66	17.95
97	16.16	16.30	16.43	16.57	16.71	17.00	17.28	17.57	17.85
98	16.06	16.20	16.34	16.48	16.62	16.90	17.18	17.47	17.76
99	15.96	16.10	16.24	16.38	16.52	16.81	17.09	17.38	17.67
100	15.87	16.01	16.15	16.29	16.43	16.71	17.00	17.29	17.58
101	15.78	15.92	16.06	16.20	16.34	16.62	16.91	17.20	17.49
102	15.69	15.83	15.97	16.11	16.25	16.54	16.82	17.11	17.41
103	15.60	15.74	15.88	16.02	16.16	16.45	16.74	17.03	17.32
104	15.52	15.66	15.80	15.94	16.08	16.37	16.66	16.95	17.24
105	15.43	15.57	15.71	15.85	16.00	16.28	16.57	16.87	17.16
106	15.35	15.49	15.63	15.77	15.92	16.20	16.49	16.79	17.08
107	15.27	15.41	15.55	15.69	15.84	16.12	16.42	16.71	17.00
108	15.19	15.33	15.47	15.62	15.76	16.05	16.34	16.63	16.93
109	15.11	15.25	15.40	15.54	15.68	15.97	16.26	16.56	16.86
110	15.04	15.18	15.32	15.46	15.61	15.90	16.19	16.49	16.78
111	14.96	15.10	15.25	15.39	15.53	15.82	16.12	16.41	16.71
112	14.89	15.03	15.17	15.32	15.46	15.75	16.05	16.34	16.64
113	14.82	14.96	15.10	15.25	15.39	15.68	15.98	16.28	16.58
114	14.75	14.89	15.03	15.18	15.32	15.62	15.91	16.21	16.51
115	14.68	14.82	14.96	15.11	15.26	15.55	15.84	16.14	16.44
116	14.61	14.75	14.90	15.04	15.19	15.48	15.78	16.08	16.38
117	14.54	14.69	14.83	14.98	15.12	15.42	15.72	16.02	16.32
118	14.48	14.62	14.77	14.91	15.06	15.36	15.65	15.95	16.26
119	14.41	14.56	14.70	14.85	15.00	15.29	15.59	15.89	16.20
120	14.35	14.50	14.64	14.79	14.94	15.23	15.53	15.83	16.14

The basic interest formula can be used to calculate the principal and interest portions of Pamela's first month's payment of $90.26.

$$\text{Interest} = \text{Principal} \times \text{Rate} \times \text{Term}$$
$$= \$1{,}000 \times .15 \times \tfrac{1}{12} \text{ (1 month)}$$
$$= \$12.50$$

Thus, $12.50 of Pamela's first month's payment of $90.26 is used to pay off the accrued interest and the remaining $77.76 ($90.26 minus $12.50) is used to reduce the principal.

Since Pamela repaid $77.76 of the principal with her first payment, her outstanding balance is now $922.24 ($1,000.00 minus $77.76). To find the interest portion for the second month, the interest is calculated using the new outstanding principal balance as follows:

$$\text{Interest} = \$922.24 \times .15 \times \tfrac{1}{12}$$
$$= \$11.53$$

Each succeeding month's interest is computed from the outstanding principal balance until the principal is repaid in full (see Figure 4-3). These calculations may also be used to determine how much interest has actually been paid at any point in the loan's history.

FIGURE 4-3
Simple Interest Amortization Schedule ($1,000 at 15% for 12 months)

MONTH	OUTSTANDING PRINCIPAL BALANCE	PRINCIPAL	INTEREST	AMOUNT OF PAYMENT
1	$1,000.00	$77.76	$12.50	$90.26
2	922.24	78.73	11.53	90.26
3	843.51	79.72	10.54	90.26
4	763.79	80.71	9.55	90.26
5	683.08	81.72	8.54	90.26
6	601.36	82.74	7.52	90.26
7	518.62	83.78	6.48	90.26
8	434.84	84.82	5.44	90.26
9	350.02	85.88	4.38	90.26
10	264.14	86.96	3.30	90.26
11	177.18	88.05	2.22	90.26
12	89.14	89.13	1.12	90.25
		$1,000.00	$83.11	$1,083.11

Open-end Loans or Credit

Unlike a closed-end loan, open-end loans or credit can be used until a certain prearranged borrowing limit is reached. Borrowers will be charged a finance charge for the extended credit. Truth-in-lending legislation requires that open-end creditors tell borrowers the method of calculating the finance charge and when finance charges begin to accrue. This information is necessary to calculate the borrower's payments.

Creditors use different methods to determine the loan balance on which finance charges will be assessed. Some creditors assess finance charges after subtracting payments made during the billing period. This is called the *adjusted balance method*. Other creditors give no credit for payments made during the billing period. This is called the *previous balance method*. Under a third method—the *average daily balance method*—creditors add borrowers' balances for each day in the billing period and then divide by the number of days in the billing period. Figure 4-4 compares these three methods of calculating payments. Figure 4-5 shows a sample disclosure that describes six different billing methods that are variations of the three methods discussed.

The Truth-in-Lending Act requires creditors to disclose to borrowers when finance charges begin to accrue. This disclosure clarifies how much time borrowers have to pay their bills before a finance charge is added. Some creditors, for example, give borrowers a 30-day "free ride" to pay their balances in full before imposing a finance charge. A local retailer might offer delayed finance charges on purchases made with its

---

FIGURE 4-4
Comparison of Three Billing Methods

	Adjusted Balance	Previous Balance	Average Daily Balance
Monthly Interest Rate	1½%	1½%	1½%
Previous Balance	$400	$400	$400
Payments	$300	$300	$300 (payment on 15th day)
Interest Charge	**$1.50** ($100 × 1.5%)	**$6.00** ($400 × 1.5%)	**$3.75** ($250 × 1.5%)

own credit card. By contrast, on all cash advances and credit lines other than credit cards, the finance charge typically starts the day the cash is disbursed.

It should be noted that the truth-in-lending law does not set the rates or tell the creditor how to make interest calculations; it only requires that the creditor disclose the method that will be used and when the finance charges will begin to accrue. To comply with these requirements, lending personnel should be able to explain terms to their customers.

United States Rule

The *United States Rule* determines interest based on the daily outstanding principal balance for the period between the receipt of payments. For example, if a borrower makes two payments 15 days apart, interest on the second payment is computed for 15 days using the outstanding principal balance during that time.

The Rule lends itself well to a coupon payment system in which borrowers are supplied with a book of coupons. One coupon is submitted with each payment. If a payment is missed, earned interest is collected from the next payment made. Consequently, first a portion of the next payment is applied to interest; then the remaining portion is used to reduce the outstanding principal. The final payment amount is adjusted to reflect the accumulated interest still owed.

Actuarial Method

The *actuarial method* determines earned interest for a set period of time based on the outstanding principal balance for that period, regardless of when payments are received. As under the United States Rule, payments are first applied to the interest, then to the principal. Lenders often use the actuarial method with a monthly billing system, which makes it possible to calculate interest on the outstanding principal for the entire month.

If a borrower misses a payment under the actuarial method, the interest is still calculated for the full month. The next payment made is applied first to the accrued interest, and the remainder (if there is any) is used to reduce the principal. This reduces the outstanding principal balance for the following month.

If a payment made after a skipped payment is not large enough to cover all the accrued interest, the remaining

FIGURE 4-5
Disclosure of Six Billing Methods

1. Average Daily Balance Method (including current transactions)
We take the beginning balance of your account each day, including unpaid finance charge from a previous billing period, and subtract any insurance premiums, any returned check fees, any late payment charges, any payments as of the day we receive them and any credits as of the date we issue them. We add any new purchases as of the date they were made. This gives us the daily balance. Then, we add up all the daily balances for the billing cycle and divide the total by the number of days in the billing cycle. This gives us the "Average Daily Balance."

2. Average Daily Balance Method (including current transactions)
We take the beginning balance of your account each day and subtract any insurance premiums, any returned check fees, any late payment charges, any unpaid finance charges, any payments as of the day we receive them and any credits as of the date we issue them. We add any new purchases as of the date they were made. This gives us the daily balance. Then, we add up all the daily balances for the billing cycle and divide the total by the number of days in the billing cycle. This gives us the "Average Daily Balance."

3. Average Daily Balance Method (excluding current transactions)
We take the beginning balance of your account each day, including unpaid finance charge from a previous billing period, and subtract any insurance premiums, any returned check fees, any late payment charges, any payments as of the day we receive them and any credits as of the date we issue them. We do not add in any new purchases. This gives us the daily balance. Then, we add all the daily balances for the billing cycle together and divide the total by the number of days in the billing cycle. This gives us the "Average Daily Balance."

4. Average Daily Balance Method (excluding current transactions)
We take the beginning balance of your account each day and subtract any insurance premiums, any returned check fees, any late payment charges, any unpaid finance charges, any payments as of the day we receive them and any credits as of the date we issue them. We do not add in any new purchases. This gives us the daily balance. Then, we add all the daily balances for the billing cycle together and divide the total by the number of days in the billing cycle. This gives us the "Average Daily Balance."

5. Adjusted Balance Method
We take the balance you owed at the end of the previous billing cycle (the "Previous Balance"), including unpaid finance charge from a previous billing period, and subtract any insurance premiums, any returned check fees, any late payment charges, any payments received and credits issued during the present billing cycle. This gives us the "Adjusted Balance".

6. Adjusted Balance Method
We take the balance you owed at the end of the previous billing cycle (the "Previous Balance"), and subtract any insurance premiums, any returned check fees, any late payment charges, any unpaid finance charges, and any payments received and credits issued during the present billing cycle. This gives us the "Adjusted Balance."

accrued interest is added to the outstanding principal balance. This process is called *capitalization* or negative amortization. It results in a compounding of interest, since the overdue interest from one month's underpayment has been added to the principal balance on which interest calculation is made the following month. A comparison of the United States Rule and the actuarial method is shown in Figure 4-6.

Capitalization can also occur if the first payment date is scheduled for more than 30 days after the loan closing with all remaining payments scheduled at one-month intervals. To avoid capitalization, the interest for the time over the first 30 days often is collected at the loan closing. This interest also may be added to the first payment amount or added to the principal and spread equally over the rest of the payments.

In recent years, many states have passed laws prohibiting capitalization of interest, or negative amortization. To comply with these laws, lenders separate interest earned but not collected from principal. Payments are first applied to uncollected interest; then to the current month's interest; then to principal. If interest is not capitalized, an adjustment must be made to the final payment to recover any uncollected interest.

FIGURE 4-6
Comparison of United States Rule and Actuarial Method

UNITED STATES RULE	ACTUARIAL METHOD
■ Unpaid earned interest is collected from future payments.	■ Unpaid earned interest is capitalized (added to the outstanding principal balance).
■ Interest is calculated between receipt of payments.	■ Interest is calculated for each time interval scheduled between payments.
■ Payments are applied first to earned interest then to principal.	■ Same
■ Adjustments are made for accumulated interest with the last payment.	■ Continuous adjustments are made for early and late payments throughout loan term.
■ Used most frequently with payment coupons and regularly scheduled payments.	■ Used most frequently with monthly billing.

Since interest is calculated for a given period under the actuarial method, lenders do not charge additional interest if payments are late.

FINANCE CHARGE AND ANNUAL PERCENTAGE RATE

Certain disclosures are required for both open-end credit and closed-end credit. Under truth in lending, lenders must disclose, in writing and before any agreement is signed, the finance charge and the annual percentage rate.

The Finance Charge

Finance charges are "all charges payable directly or indirectly by the borrower and imposed directly or indirectly by the creditor as an incident to or as condition of the extension of credit."[1] Finance charges include charges payable by the borrower, seller or any other person on behalf of the borrower to the creditor or a third party. They include charges such as interest, activity fees, points, finders' fees and credit investigation fees. If the lender requires the borrower to obtain insurance, the insurance premiums also must be included as finance charges. These include credit life insurance premiums; accident, health, loss of income, or property damage insurance premiums; and premiums for insurance protecting the creditor. Federal regulations require disclosure of all finance charges. Certain state statutes also have disclosure requirements for finance charges.

For example, borrowing $1,000 for a year might cost a consumer $100 in interest. If there were also a service charge of $15, however, the total finance charge would be $115. Disclosure laws and regulations can help the borrower learn the full cost of credit before signing the loan papers.

Annual Percentage Rate

The *annual percentage rate* (APR) is defined by Truth-in-Lending Regulation Z as "a measure of the cost of credit, expressed as a yearly rate, which relates the amount and timing of payments made."[2] The APR takes into account the amount of interest and all other types of finance charges. In other words, the APR is the percentage cost of credit on a yearly basis. The APR is the consumers' key to comparing costs, regardless of the amount of credit, type of interest charged or the length of time they have to repay their loans.

Annual percentage rates can be approximated using the constant ratio formula (see Figure 4-7). This formula shows the relationship of finance charges to the loan principal for a given loan term. It is used only for approximating. The formula for calculating the actual APRs on closed-end loans is complicated and requires a knowledge of higher mathematics to execute. Because of the calculation's complexity as well as the importance of accurately representing the APR, lenders formulate APR by using precalculated tables that were specially designed by computer programs.

Tolerance Range for Closed-end Loans
Regulation Z (explained in Chapter 2) requires that the APR stated by lenders on all loans be accurate within a given range. For federal savings institutions, this range, called the *tolerance range*, is ⅛ of 1% of the figures as computed by FHLB examiners. For example, when the exact APR is determined to be 10⅛%, a disclosed APR from 10% to 10¼% (or the decimal equivalent), would comply with the regulation.

The APR for an irregular transaction is considered accurate if it varies in either direction by not more than ¼ of 1% from the actual APR. This tolerance range is intended for complex transactions involving more than one advance or disbursement; irregular payment periods; or irregular payments amounts (other than an irregular first period or an irregular first or final payment). It may also be used in transactions involving increasing payment schedules where by contract the borrower is committed to several series of payments in different amounts. It does not apply, however, to variable rate loans where the initial disclosures are based on a regular amortization schedule over the life of the loan, even though payments may later change because the interest rate may change.[3]

APR for Simple Interest Loans
For simple interest loans without other finance charges, the APR is the same as the simple interest rate. This is because interest is calculated on the declining principal balance. However, when there are additional finance charges over the

> Jack Kruger borrows $1,000 for one year and pays a finance charge of $100. If he keeps the entire $1,000 for the whole year and then pays it back all at once, with simple interest, he will pay an APR of 10%. But, if he repays the $1,000 plus the finance charge (a total of $1,100) in 12 equal monthly installments, as he would with add-on interest, he does not really get to use the $1,000 for the whole year. In fact, he gets to use less and less of that $1,000 each month. In this case the $100 charge for credit results in an APR of 18%.
>
> If the lender initially deducts the $100 finance charge, leaving Jack with $900, and Jack agrees to repay $1,000 in 12 equal monthly installments, the APR will be over 20%. In this case, using the discount interest method, Jack gets to use less and less of only $900 each month, yet is paying a finance charge based on $1,000.

simple interest rate the APR increases due to an increased ratio of the total finance charge to the original principal.

Finding APR for simple interest loans with finance charges is facilitated by using the Federal Reserve's APR tables (see Figure 4-8). Rounding of numbers is permitted. Actually lenders may use any accurate source in determining APRs, but there is an advantage to using the Federal Reserve's tables. Good faith conformance to these tables (and the

---

FIGURE 4-7
Approximating APR Constant Ratio Formula

$$APR = \frac{2 \left(\begin{array}{c} \text{\# of payment} \\ \text{periods} \\ \text{in one year} \end{array} \times \text{Finance Charges} \right)}{\text{Loan Principal} \left(\begin{array}{c} \text{Total \# of} \\ \text{payments} \\ \text{made} \end{array} + 1 \right)}$$

FIGURE 4-8
Simple Interest Annual

RATE TO BE DISCLOSED	15.000	15.250	15.500	15.750
Maturity Years	Prepaid Finance Charge Divided by Amount of Loan			
5	0.00275	0.00822	0.01365	0.01904
6	0.00320	0.00956	0.01586	0.02210
7	0.00362	0.01081	0.01793	0.02496
8	0.00401	0.01198	0.01985	0.02763
9	0.00438	0.01307	0.02164	0.03010
10	0.00472	0.01408	0.02329	0.03238
11	0.00504	0.01501	0.02483	0.03449
12	0.00533	0.01587	0.02624	0.03644
13	0.00560	0.01667	0.02754	0.03823
14	0.00585	0.01740	0.02874	0.03987
15	0.00608	0.01808	0.02984	0.04137
16	0.00629	0.01869	0.03084	0.04274
17	0.00648	0.01926	0.03176	0.04399
18	0.00666	0.01977	0.03259	0.04513
19	0.00682	0.02024	0.03335	0.04616
20	0.00697	0.02066	0.03404	0.04710
21	0.00710	0.02105	0.03466	0.04795
22	0.00722	0.02140	0.03523	0.04871
23	0.00733	0.02171	0.03574	0.04941
24	0.00743	0.02200	0.03620	0.05003
25	0.00752	0.02226	0.03661	0.05059
26	0.00760	0.02249	0.03698	0.05109
27	0.00767	0.02270	0.03731	0.05154
28	0.00773	0.02288	0.03761	0.05194
29	0.00779	0.02305	0.03788	0.05230
30	0.00784	0.02320	0.03812	0.05262
31	0.00789	0.02333	0.03833	0.05291
32	0.00793	0.02345	0.03852	0.05316
33	0.00797	0.02356	0.03869	0.05339
34	0.00800	0.02365	0.03884	0.05359
35	0.00803	0.02374	0.03898	0.05377

Source: Truth in Lending, Regulation Z, Annual Percentage Rate Tables

16.000	16.250	16.500	16.750	17.000
0.02438	0.02968	0.03494	0.04016	0.04534
0.02829	0.03442	0.04049	0.04650	0.05247
0.03193	0.03882	0.04564	0.05239	0.05906
0.03531	0.04290	0.05041	0.05782	0.06515
0.03844	0.04668	0.05481	0.06284	0.07076
0.04134	0.05017	0.05887	0.06746	0.07592
0.04401	0.05338	0.06261	0.07170	0.08065
0.04647	0.05633	0.06604	0.07558	0.08497
0.04872	0.05904	0.06917	0.07913	0.08892
0.05079	0.06151	0.07204	0.08237	0.09252
0.05268	0.06377	0.07465	0.08532	0.09579
0.05440	0.06583	0.07703	0.08800	0.09876
0.05597	0.06770	0.07919	0.09043	0.10145
0.05740	0.06940	0.08114	0.09263	0.10388
0.05869	0.07094	0.08291	0.09462	0.10608
0.05986	0.07233	0.08451	0.09641	0.10805
0.06092	0.07358	0.08595	0.09803	0.10983
0.06187	0.07471	0.08725	0.09948	0.11142
0.06273	0.07573	0.08841	0.10078	0.11285
0.06351	0.07664	0.08945	0.10194	0.11413
0.06420	0.07746	0.09039	0.10299	0.11527
0.06482	0.07820	0.09122	0.10392	0.11629
0.06538	0.07885	0.09197	0.10475	0.11719
0.06588	0.07944	0.09264	0.10549	0.11800
0.06632	0.07996	0.09323	0.10615	0.11872
0.06672	0.08042	0.09376	0.10673	0.11936
0.06707	0.08084	0.09423	0.10725	0.11992
0.06738	0.08120	0.09464	0.10771	0.12042
0.06766	0.08153	0.09501	0.10812	0.12086
0.06791	0.08182	0.09534	0.10848	0.12125
0.06813	0.08208	0.09563	0.10880	0.12160

Federal Reserve's instructions for using them) establishes compliance with Regulation Z, even if the figures in the table are later judged to be incorrect and outside of the tolerance range.

To use the Federal Reserve's tables, lenders must compute the prepaid finance charge as a ratio of the original principal. Insurance must be reflected in the APR only if it is mandatory. If insurance is optional, it is not disclosed as interest and does not effect the APR. For example, suppose Bill Tate borrows $6,000 at 15% for five years, and the lender requires Bill to pay a total of $175 for prepaid credit life insurance and other charges. In this case, the finance charge is divided by the original balance, resulting in a factor that can be found in an APR table.

Factor = Prepaid Finance Charge/Original Principal
= $175/$6,000
= .02917

Looking at the table, the first number equal to or greater than the factor .02917 is located in the sixth column. This gives an APR of 16.250%.

APR on Open-end Loans
APR can be calculated for open-end loans according to the guidelines given in Regulation Z.[4] The same 1/8 of 1% tolerance range applies to open-end loans. There are several types of finance charges on open-end loans including the following: one constant periodic rate, two or more periodic rates, fixed fee per balance and fixed fee. Each type of finance charge requires a slightly different formula for computing the APR.

If the finance charge for a given period is figured according to a single rate that remains constant throughout the year, the APR is computed by multiplying that rate by the number of periods in the year. Thus, if the finance charge is 1.5% per month, the APR is 18%. The following illustrates one constant periodic rate:

APR = Periodic Rate × Number of Periods in One Year
= 1.5 × 12
= 18%

A different formula is needed to calculate APR if the finance charge is figured for a given period according to two or more periodic rates. In this instance, the APR is computed by dividing the total amount of the finance charge by the sum of the balances to which different rates were applied and then multiplying by the number of periods. For example, if the total finance charge is $29.00 and the sum of the balances is $2,200, the APR equals 15.82%. This is found by using the following formula for two or more periodic rates:

$$\text{APR} = (\text{Total Periodic Finance Charge}/\text{Sum of Balances}) \times \text{Number of Periods in One Year}$$
$$= ((\$4 + \$7 + \$8 + \$10))/((\$400 + \$500 + \$600 + \$700)) \times 12$$
$$= (\$29/\$2{,}200) \times 12$$
$$= 15.82\%$$

Lenders sometimes apply a fixed finance charge according to the size of the outstanding principal balance for the period. For example, a lender might offer the following arrangement: If the outstanding balance is less than $150, the finance charge is $2; if the outstanding balance is between $150 and $300, $3; between $300 and $600, $5; and between $600 and $900, $7. In this case, the APR is figured by dividing the total finance charge by the median balance (the halfway point) in the appropriate balance range and multiplying by the number of periods in one year. Thus, if the finance charge for the period is $5 and there are 12 such periods, the median balance is $450 ([halfway between $600 and $300]/2 + $300), and the APR is 13.33%. The formula for the fixed fee per balance method is as follows:

$$\text{APR} = (\text{Total Periodic Finance Charge}/\text{Median Balance for Range}) \times \text{Number of Periods in One Year}$$
$$= (\$5/\$450) \times 12$$
$$= 13.33\%$$

There are restrictions in the use of the fixed fee per

period, or fixed fee, method of calculating finance charges. Lenders may also charge these fees only if the loan balance drops below an established minimum. Fixed fees are used when the amount of the finance charge based on periodic rates or balances is not sufficient to cover the costs involved in handling the loan transactions.

When a fixed fee is used alone, the APR is simply the relationship of finance charges to the outstanding balance multiplied by the number of periods in one year.

$$APR = (Periodic\ Finance\ Charges/Outstanding\ Balance) \times Number\ of\ Periods\ in\ One\ Year$$

When the fixed fee is charged in addition to periodic rates or a flat fee per balance, then the fixed fee is added to the total finance charge, and the corresponding annual percentage rate formula is used.

Lending personnel should inform prospective borrowers that the APR is only one of several important factors to consider when selecting a loan. Consumers need to be informed of all the terms before they can make an intelligent choice. For example, suppose Cathy Lynch needs to borrow $6,000 to purchase a car. After deciding which car to purchase, she calls three local lenders and obtains the following information:

	APR	Length of Loan	Monthly Payment	Total Finance Charge	Total Cost
Lender A	14%	3 years	$205.07	$1,382.52	$7,382.52
Lender B	14%	4 years	$163.96	$1,870.08	$7,870.08
Lender C	15%	4 years	$166.98	$2,015.04	$8,015.04

Which lender should Cathy choose? That depends partly on what she needs.

The lowest cost loan is available from Lender A (see the last column on the chart). If she were looking for lower monthly payments, however, Cathy could choose to pay off the loan over a longer length of time as Lenders B and C have offered. She would then have to pay more in total costs. A loan from Lender B—at 14% APR for four years—charges about $488 more finance charges than Lender A's loan. The same four-year loan term is even more expensive from

Lender C; the 15% APR would add another $145 to the finance charges as compared with Lender B.

By considering all the terms, Cathy will be better able to choose the loan that best suits her needs and know in advance the full cost of the loan.

Early Repayment

Consumer loans are often repaid in full before their due date. When a loan is paid off early, the borrower asks the lender for a payoff figure. This payoff figure is affected by the way in which the lender recognizes when interest is earned and added. With simple interest, earned interest may be determined using either the United States Rule or the actuarial method. In either case, the borrower is not penalized for prepayment since interest is paid only on the balance outstanding for the length of time the amount is owed.

By contrast, when the borrower has an add-on loan, or when rebates must be granted on prepaid credit life and/or disability insurance premiums, the Rule of 78s (explained in this chapter's Appendix) is used to calculate the rebate.

SUMMARY

Due to disclosure requirements under consumer protection laws, consumers are becoming increasingly more knowledgeable about the costs of borrowing and how these costs are calculated. Thus, lending personnel must be able to explain to consumers how their institutions compute all borrowing costs and charges. Consumers should understand the basic interest formula:

$$\text{Interest} = \text{Principal} \times \text{Rate} \times \text{Term}.$$

The term of the loan is affected by the method—either 365/365, 365/360 or 360/360—which the lender uses to determine the length of the loan. Also, lenders use different methods to determine the principal balance on which interest will be charged. For simple interest, amortization tables are used to find the monthly installment payment needed to pay off a loan at a given interest rate over a specified period of time.

CHAPTER QUESTIONS

1. Define the term amortization and explain how to use an amortization table.

2. Differentiate among three methods of calculating interest that use different number of days in a year.

3. Compute the finance charge a lender would assess on the this open-end credit account using the adjusted balance, previous balance and average daily balance methods.

	Adjusted Balance	Previous Balance	Average Daily Balance
APR	21%	21%	21%
Previous Month's Balance	$1,000	$1,000	$1,000
Payments	$ 700	$ 700	$ 700 made on the 15th day
Finance Charge	_____	_____	_____

(Show the principal amount on which the finance charge is assessed under each method.)

4. Compare and contrast the United States Rule and the actuarial method of determining earned interest on a loan based on simple interest.

5. Figure the APR for a $5,000 loan at 12% simple interest for four years with an annual service charge of $15.

FOOTNOTES

[1] Truth-in-Lending Act, Title 15, U.S. Code, Section 1605
[2] Truth-in-Lending Regulation Z, Title 12, Code of Federal Regulations, Part 226.22

[3]Truth-in-Lending Regulation Z, Title 12, Code of Federal Regulations, Part 226.22

[4]Truth-in-Lending Regulation Z, Title 12, Code of Federal Regulations, Part 226.14

APPENDIX

In the past, the add-on interest and discount interest methods for computing interest on consumer loans were used regularly in addition to the simple interest method. Today, a combination of consumer preference, computerized operations and changing state laws have made the add-on and discount methods far less popular than the simple interest method for computing interest. However, where still allowed by state laws, the add-on interest method sometimes is used for indirect auto loans, and the discount interest method still has commercial loan applications. This appendix briefly explains each method and provides examples for further clarification.

Also covered in the appendix is the Rule of 78s. Lenders might use the Rule of 78s to recognize when interest is earned with the add-on and discount interest methods. Also, the Rule of 78s can be used to rebate prepaid credit life and disability insurance premiums whenever a loan is paid off early.

Add-on Interest

Using the add-on interest method, interest is computed by determining the interest charge for the loan term and adding that charge to the principal of the loan. The borrower agrees to repay the principal plus interest. When only one payment is involved, this method produces the same effective interest rate, or APR, as the simple interest method. When two or more payments are to be made, however, use of the add-on method results in a higher APR because the borrower does not have use of the total amount of principal for the entire loan term.

For example, Pamela Green borrows $1,000 for one year at 15% add-on interest from Sunnyside Federal Savings and Loan. The total amount of interest on her loan is determined by using the basic interest formula:

$$\begin{aligned} \text{Interest} &= \text{Principal} \times \text{Rate} \times \text{Term} \\ &= \$1{,}000 \times .15 \times 1 \\ &= \$150. \end{aligned}$$

The net loan amount equals the principal amount plus the total interest.

$$\begin{aligned} \text{Net Loan Amount} &= \text{Principal} + \text{Interest} \\ &= \$1{,}000 + \$150 \\ &= \$1{,}150 \end{aligned}$$

The monthly payment amount is figured by dividing the net loan amount by the number of months in the loan term. In this example the loan term is 12 months.

$$\begin{aligned} \text{Monthly Payment} &= (\text{Principal} + \text{Interest})/\text{Number of Months} \\ &= \$1{,}150/12 \\ &= \$95.83 \end{aligned}$$

Thus, Pamela must make 12 payments of $95.83 to pay off her loan.

Discount Interest

Using the discount interest method, the interest formula is applied to the original principal balance to calculate the total interest for the loan. Then the interest is *subtracted* from the principal. The borrower receives the difference between the principal loan amount and the interest amount.

Applying the discount method to the example of Pamela Green and her $1,000 loan at 15% for one year, the total interest equals $150. With discount interest, Pamela only receives $850, but she agrees to repay $1,000 to the lender in monthly installments of $83.33.

$$\begin{aligned}\text{Net Loan Amount} &= \text{Principal} - \text{Interest} \\ &= \$1{,}000 - \$150 \\ &= \$850\end{aligned}$$

$$\begin{aligned}\text{Monthly Payment} &= (\text{Principal} + \text{Interest})/\text{Number of Months} \\ &= \$1{,}000/12 \\ &= \$83.33\end{aligned}$$

Figure 4-9 compares the relative cost of credit to Pamela Green using the three methods of calculating interest. Discount interest has the highest APR because the interest is deducted from the original principal amount ($1,000 − $150) at the beginning of the loan term. Add-on interest has the next highest APR because the interest is charged on the original loan amount for the full loan term, even though Pamela only had full use of the funds for a limited time. Simple interest has the lowest APR because the interest is charged only on the outstanding principal balance.

The Rule of 78s

The *Rule of 78s* is a method of recognizing the earned portion of add-on interest for any given period by applying predetermined factors to the total interest for the loan term. A declining ratio is applied to a fixed-loan amount to determine interest earned for the period. The Rule of 78s is also called the *sum-of-the-digits method*.

The Rule of 78s is authorized by law in several states as a means of calculating rebates of finance charges when a loan is paid off early. The rule provides the percentage of the total interest amount that is to be returned to the borrower.

The rule is particularly useful for determining unearned interest on prepaid loans made under add-on or discount interest methods. In these cases, the outstanding loan balance reflects both principal and interest. When the loans are prepaid, a rebate of unearned interest often is necessary. The unearned interest is subtracted from the outstanding loan balance to arrive at the payoff figure, which will eliminate the debt.

FIGURE 4-9
Comparison of APRs on a $1,000 Loan at 15% for One Year

	ADD-ON	DISCOUNT	SIMPLE
Loan Principal	$1,000	$850	$1,000
Total Interest	$150	$150	$83.11
Constant Ratio Formula	$\dfrac{2(12 \times \$150)}{\$1{,}000(12+1)}$	$\dfrac{2(12 \times \$150)}{\$850(12+1)}$	$\dfrac{2(12 \times \$83.11)}{\$1{,}000(12+1)}$
APR	27.69%	32.58%	15.34%

In the Pamela Green example illustrating the add-on interest method, the borrower has use of the full principal amount ($12/12$ths) only for one month of the 12-month loan term. Then the first payment is made. During the second month she has use of $11/12$ths of the principal amount; the third month, $10/12$ths, and so forth. During the twelfth month she has use of only $1/12$th of the principal. During the early months of the loan term, Pamela Green has use of a greater portion of the principal, and she must pay more interest than later in the loan term. Since she has 12 times more money available to use during the first month than during the last, she must pay 12 times more interest for the first month than for the last.

The first step under the Rule of 78s, is to add up all the digits for the number of payments scheduled to be made. For Pamela's loan, a loan to be repaid in 12 monthly installments, the numbers one through 12 are added together (1 + 2 + 3 + 4 + 5 . . . + 12) to equal 78. The answer is "the sum of the digits" and explains how the rule was named. For Pamela's loan, her total interest is divided into 78 parts for payment over the term of her loan. The lender earns $12/78$ths of the total interest in the first month, $11/78$ths of the total interest in the second month, $10/78$ths in the third, and so on.

This leaves $1/78$th of the interest earned in the last month (which is $1/12$ of the first month's interest). The top number in the fraction represents the number of payments left to satisfy the debt.

The total interest on Pamela's loan is $150. Twelve seventy-eighths of the total interest amount is earned interest for the first month. In this case, the earned interest is $23.08 ($^{12}/_{78}$ × $150 = $23.08).

Using the add-on method, Pamela's monthly payment is $95.83. By applying the Rule of 78s, the earned interest and principal portions of each month's payment can be determined (see Figure 4-10). In Pamela's case $72.75 of the first month's payment ($95.83 minus $23.08) is allocated to repayment of principal. Note that throughout the loan term the payment amount remains constant. However, the amount allocated to repayment of principal increases, and the portion of the payment applied to interest decreases.

Of course, the Rule of 78s can also be applied to loans with terms longer than one year. Instead of computing the sum of the numbers of the payments in the term, (because this is a tedious task), the following formula may be used:

Sum = ½ the Number of Payments × (Number of Payments + 1)

FIGURE 4-10
Add-On Interest Amortization Schedule, Using the Rule of 78s ($1,000 at 15% for one year)

BEGINNING BALANCE	PAYMENT NUMBER	PAYMENT AMOUNT	INTEREST	PRINCIPAL
$1,150.00	1	$95.83	$23.08	$72.75
1,054.17	2	95.83	21.15	74.68
958.34	3	95.83	19.23	76.60
862.51	4	95.83	17.31	78.52
766.68	5	95.83	15.38	80.45
670.85	6	95.83	13.46	82.37
575.02	7	95.83	11.54	84.29
479.19	8	95.83	9.62	86.21
383.36	9	95.83	7.69	88.14
287.53	10	95.83	5.77	90.06
191.70	11	95.83	3.85	91.98
95.87	12	95.87	1.92	93.95
Total 0		$1,150.00	$150.00	$1,000

For example, suppose Pamela's brother Jim takes out a $5,000 loan at 15% add-on interest for three years. His interest for the loan is $2,250, and he agrees to repay the principal and interest totaling $7,250 in 36 monthly installments of $201.39. Apply the Rule of 78s using the sum formula based on 36 payments.

$$\begin{aligned} \text{Sum} &= \tfrac{1}{2}(36) \times (36 + 1) \\ &= 18 \times 37 \\ &= 666 \end{aligned}$$

The amount of interest earned from the first month's payment is 36/666ths of $2,250 or $121.61. The remainder goes toward repayment of the principal.

Now suppose that after paying as scheduled for 30 months Jim earns extra income and decides to pay off his loan early. A rebate of the unearned interest must be calculated. First, Jim's outstanding loan balance is figured by multiplying the monthly payment amount ($201.39) by the number of payments remaining (36 minus 30 equals 6).

$$\begin{aligned} \text{Outstanding Loan Balance} &= \text{Monthly Payment Amount} \times \text{Number of Payments Remaining} \\ &= \$201.39 \times 6 \\ &= \$1{,}208.34 \end{aligned}$$

Second, the rebate is calculated using the sum formula from the Rule of 78s.

$$\begin{aligned} \text{Sum} &= \tfrac{1}{2} \text{ the Number of Payments Remaining} \times (\text{Number of Payments Remaining} + 1) \\ &= \tfrac{1}{2}(6) \times (6 + 1) \\ &= 3 \times 7 \\ &= 21 \end{aligned}$$

The six payments remaining on Jim's loan represent 21/666 of the interest charged on the loan. Thus, multiplying the total interest amount, $2,250, by 21/666 equals the rebate amount, $70.95. This amount represents unearned interest as a result of prepayment.

Third, the final payoff figure is computed by subtracting the rebate amount from the outstanding loan balance:

$$\text{Payoff} = \text{Outstanding Loan Balance} - \text{Rebate}$$
$$= \$1{,}208.34 - \$70.95$$
$$= \$1{,}137.39$$

To satisfy the debt, Jim Green must pay $1,137.39. Similarly, the Rule of 78s may be used to compute a borrower's rebate of prepaid insurance premiums. For example, if Jim pays an additional amount monthly for credit insurance, he is entitled to a rebate of the unearned premium.

The interest paid under the Rule of 78s is usually different than interest paid under the simple interest declining balance method. How much the interest will vary when it is computed under the Rule of 78s depends on the length of the loan, the rate of interest charged and the timing of the prepayment. Under the Rule of 78s, the lender earns approximately three-fourths of the finance charge during the first half of the loan term. This gives the lender a higher loan yield for early payoffs (before mid-term) and a lower loan yield for later payoffs (after mid-term) than it would obtain from a simple interest loan. Because simple interest loans have a constant yield throughout the loan term, lenders find them easier to manage in a portfolio than loans under the Rule of 78s.

ADDITIONAL CHAPTER QUESTIONS

1. Using both the add-on and discount interest methods, give the formulas and calculate the total interest amount and the net loan amount for a $4,000 loan at 11% for three years.

2. Carol Anderson obtains a $1,500 loan from a local lender. She is charged 14% add-on interest and agrees to repay the loan in 12 monthly installments. Using the Rule of 78s, calculate the interest and principal portion of Carol's second monthly payment.

3. Explain the principle underlying the Rule of 78s.

4. To purchase a new boat, Jim Beatty obtains a loan for $4,500 at 13% add-on interest for 48 months. Using the Rule of 78s, what will be the outstanding loan balance, rebate figure and payoff amount if Jim decides to prepay the loan after 33 months?

5

Loan Evaluation

Objectives

After studying this chapter, you should be able to:
- Describe the benefits of fulfilling a borrower's needs within the limits of an institution's lending policies;
- Define the six Cs of credit;
- State the relationship between the information on an application and the four critical borrower characteristics;
- Explain the proper way to take a loan application;
- State how and why personal credit information should be verified;
- Identify at least seven warning signals of possible fraud;
- Describe five different methods to analyze credit information on an application;
- State how an applicant should be notified of a credit decision;
- Explain the importance of evaluating a dealer; and
- Differentiate between buying dealer paper with full recourse or with repurchase conditions.

INTRODUCTION

The consumer loan evaluation process begins when a lender receives a loan application. With a direct loan, a loan applicant is in direct contact with a lender. This contact may be by mail, telephone or face-to-face interview with lending personnel. With indirect loans, however, potential borrowers may not even be aware of the lender's role in evaluating their applications since their primary contact is with a dealer. Dealers generally complete loan applications for potential borrowers and forward them to lenders.

The loan evaluation process is the same for both direct and indirect loan origination. This chapter describes this evaluation process in detail, including establishing the loan purpose, matching the borrower's needs to established loan policies, understanding and applying the six Cs of credit, taking applications, verifying personal credit information, analyzing credit information and notifying the borrower of the credit decision.

This chapter also examines some additional factors, such as buying dealer paper and evaluating new dealers, that must be considered by lenders making indirect loans. The peculiarities involved in taking applications for indirect loans are discussed.

PURPOSE AND POLICY

There are several reasons for lending personnel to become aware of an applicant's particular needs. Lending personnel must verify that the applicant's request can be satisfied with a loan that the lender is legally authorized to make. For example, if the request is for a consumer loan, it must, by definition, be a loan to a natural person for personal, family or household purposes. Also, the applicant must be old enough to enter into a binding contract as determined by state laws.

Lending personnel must also ascertain whether the loan terms requested (purpose, principal amount, length of loan term, type of collateral, etc.) fall within policy guidelines and authority of the institution. For example, if an applicant requests a loan for a business purpose, it could not be classified as a consumer loan. If the lender makes commercial loans, the applicant should be directed to that department.

After an applicant's loan request has been successfully evaluated based on legal criteria and lender policy guidelines, it should be evaluated from a needs point of view. The loan should have the following qualifications:
- good for the lender since it should be profitable;
- good for the consumer because it provides a needed source of funds; and
- good for the community because it stimulates cash flow among local businesses.

Sometimes a loan type other than what was requested may better suit the needs of the customer. For example, the applicant might be asking for an installment loan to cover a personal need that occurs regularly, such as paying for tuition or funding an IRA. The loan counselor would then have an opportunity to suggest a line of credit, which might better suit the customer's needs than an installment loan. The counselor also might be able to cross-sell other financial products that would suit the customer's needs, such as certificates of deposit for an IRA. In another situation, a particular loan request might put too heavy a financial strain on the applicant's resources. In this case, the loan would not be meeting the applicant's needs, and the loan counselor might find it necessary to deny the loan request.

Consumer lending personnel should be aware of the major underwriting differences between mortgage loans and consumer loans. When evaluating a mortgage loan, there is sufficient time to verify, with written confirmation, everything on the application. With consumer loans, there is not enough time to verify everything in writing, so other methods of verification must be used. There is more emphasis on checking the collateral associated with mortgage loans than with consumer loans. When evaluating a consumer loan, the ability and willingness to repay the loan are emphasized.

THE SIX Cs OF CREDIT

Most creditors, regardless of whether they are regulated, deregulated or nonregulated, consider the following six Cs of credit before deciding to provide a loan:
- character;
- capacity;

- capital;
- collateral;
- conditions; and
- competition.

The first four refer to critical characteristics for determining the borrower's willingness and ability to repay a loan. They reflect personally on the borrowers. The last two refer to factors that affect both the borrower and the lender, factors beyond their immediate control.

Character

Character refers to the borrower's reputation for repaying debt and is determined from the borrower's credit history. Character is the key factor in any lending function. It refers to the borrower's apparent or historically demonstrated willingness, determination and commitment to pay, even during hard times. It reflects the applicant's integrity and honesty. An applicant may have more than enough capacity, capital and collateral to repay a loan and, yet, still be a potential problem for a lender, if, in spite of everything else, the borrower lacks the basic willingness to repay.

Evidence of character can be found in the applicant's past credit history. The applicant's reputation for repaying debts can be verified by a credit check. If the applicant is found to have been delinquent frequently on past loans, this signifies that the repayment of debt has not been a high priority. In this case, the loan is probably too risky for the lender to justify granting.

Another way to determine character is by talking to others with whom the customer has previously done business. Because a determination of character may be based on subjective criteria, it is often more difficult to ascertain character than to verify the other Cs of credit. It is difficult to measure the intangible personal qualities and attributes that will result in a sense of obligation and a willingness to fulfill a loan agreement. Despite this difficulty, lenders must evaluate character because consumer loans should be made to individuals based primarily on an individual's credit worthiness rather than on collateral.

Capacity

Capacity refers to an applicant's ability to repay a loan according to a schedule. Capacity is determined by verifying the applicant's total income and total expenses and subtracting the latter from the former. The applicant's unallocated, regular income should be sufficient to make the scheduled payments and leave a margin for unexpected fluctuations in total income or expenses. In a well-structured loan, a lender's perception of the ability of a borrower to make payments is a major consideration in granting the loan.

To properly evaluate capacity, loan personnel must obtain accurate, verifiable income information from an applicant. A lender must also determine whether or not a stated level of income will be maintained for at least the term of the loan. When the continuance of sufficient income is in doubt, as in the case of an elderly person who plans to retire before the end of the loan term, a lender may look for other evidence of capacity, such as capital owned by the applicant.

When gauging capacity, a lender should verify all obligations an applicant may have because an obligation or debt that is not listed on an application might impair an applicant's ability to repay. Lending personnel must attempt to verify that an applicant has not omitted any major expenses that would exceed policy guidelines.

Capital

Capital refers to the assets or items of value owned by an applicant that could be a possible source of debt repayment. Each applicant should be able to show evidence of some reserve capital, either in the form of a checking account or some other type of liquid deposit or investment. This provides a financial buffer in case the applicant experiences a temporary shortfall in regular earnings—for example, a period of illness or unemployment. Capital can also be used for unexpected expenses that would otherwise strain the capacity of the borrower's regular income to meet all monthly obligations. Capital can thus act as an extra safety reserve or cushion that enables repayment. Should the borrower default, capital may be used to satisfy a judgment. In other words, when character and capacity prove insufficient and there is inadequate collateral value, or a loan is unsecured, capital may be the only resource from which payments can be extracted.

The desired amount of reserve capital should be determined on the basis of factors such as loan amount, earning level, past history of earnings, applicant's character and type of collateral, if any. When evaluating a loan request, capital is often more important than collateral. This is especially true in cases where character has changed, capacity falls or the collateral could depreciate rapidly. In such cases, the individual's net worth must be evident.

Collateral

Collateral refers to something of value—either tangible or intangible—such as an automobile or certificate of deposit, that can be used to secure a promise of future payments. A lender can repossess collateral if a loan is not repaid. Collateral is often in the form of an item being purchased by the borrower with the proceeds of the loan (purchase money); it can be viewed as a back-up source of repayment. If an applicant fails to live up to a loan agreement, collateral can be repossessed and sold. The proceeds, however, will rarely be sufficient to fully repay loan and repossession costs.

In most states, if the collateral's value is less than the loan payoff amount and repossession occurs, the borrower is still obligated to make up the deficiency; but such deficiencies are usually difficult to collect. Therefore, a lender should not use collateral to counterbalance an applicant's weaknesses in character, capacity or capital. In the extremely rare event that a lender is able to sell collateral for more than the loan payoff balance plus repossession costs, most state laws require that any remaining funds be returned to the borrower.

Lenders may require collateral when they perceive an applicant as a marginal risk. However, if the collateral's market value, depreciation and expected useful life are balanced against an excessive loan amount and/or an unrealistically long term, the lender really has little more than an unsecured loan. Because the ability to recover the collateral's value is uncertain, an individual's credit worthiness is more important in loan evaluation. This is the reason why 10-year auto loans do not exist. At some point, the loan balance would exceed the market value of the financed car, and the borrower would have little incentive to continue making payments.

Loan terms and conditions should be structured to match collateral values and expected value fluctuations. Ideally, lenders prefer collateral that maintains or appreciates in value during the loan term. Loans secured with real property that will appreciate, such as a home, are preferred over loans secured with personal property that will depreciate in value, such as an automobile.

Conditions

Conditions refer to the economic climate affecting both the borrower and the lender. Conditions include inflation; interest rates; seasonal demand for an item (i.e., a boat or pool); availability and price of gasoline (this caused the sharp drop in demand for recreational vehicles in the late 1970s); or prospects for continued employment opportunities where the borrower lives. Additional borrower conditions include stability of residence and employment. Conditions such as these can affect a borrower's capacity to repay and, therefore, should be taken into consideration when evaluating a loan application. Conditions also affect lenders' decisions as to types of loans and loan terms offered. Under some conditions, certain loans will cease to be mutually beneficial or appealing to both borrowers and lenders.

Competition

Competition refers to the rivalry between two or more businesses striving for the same customers or market. Competition is the final characteristic that lenders consider when evaluating a loan application. Competition among lending institutions affects a particular lender's decision on whether or not to offer a particular type of loan. A lender may decide, after careful consideration of all costs and risks involved, that it cannot match competitors' terms and still be profitable. By contrast, a lender might advertise a loan type that it believes will be profitable after assessing the competition. Competition between lenders provides customers with choices. With commercial loans, competition must be viewed from two

Consumer Lending

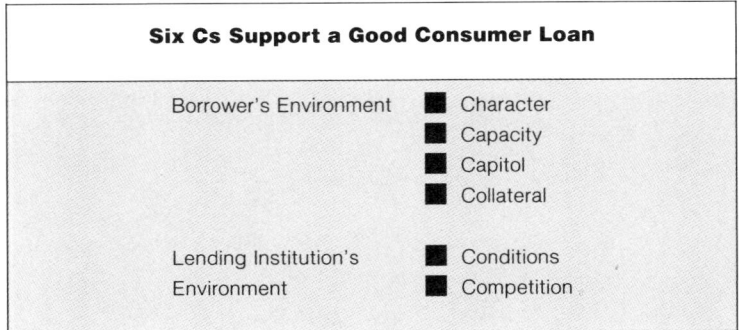

sides: both the lender's competition and the business borrower's competition affect loan decisions and evaluations.

TAKING THE APPLICATION

Consumer credit personnel receive many inquiries from people shopping for consumer loans. Common inquiries concern the types of loans that are available and the terms of the loans such as: interest rates, annual percentage rates and monthly payment amounts. Regulation B defines a *loan application* as "an oral or written request for an extension of credit that is made in accordance with procedures established by a creditor for the type of credit requested." Discouraging applicants from making inquiries or completing an application is expressly forbidden by Regulation B. In addition, if a person calls a lender to inquire about a type of loan that the lender does not offer, the consumer credit department is required to inform the caller of his or her right to file a loan application and to obtain a written copy of the lender's underwriting standards. The lender then must accept and process the application if one is filed. These requirements are discussed in greater detail later in this chapter.

Application Interview

A consumer credit department may accept applications by mail, over the telephone or in an interview with a consumer loan officer. At the prospective borrower's request, an application may be sent by mail to be completed, signed and returned to the consumer credit department. Applications taken by telephone require a clerk or consumer loan officer to ask the prospective borrower for the information needed to complete the application form. In this instance, the applicant usually signs the form at the time funds are disbursed.

If the prospective borrower visits the lender, an interview is conducted by a consumer loan officer. The officer either asks the applicant to complete the application form, or orally requests the information and completes the form for the applicant. As was explained in Chapter 3, Regulation B requires that all applicants be provided with an Equal Credit Opportunity Act (ECOA) Notice (see Figure 5-1). This notice may be printed on the application form or included with the letter stating the credit decision. In addition, all applicants must receive a copy of the lender's underwriting standards if they request one.

The setting and time of an interview are important. Many people will be a little nervous (and worried about rejection) when applying for a loan. Therefore, the consumer loan officer should begin the interview by smiling, introducing himself or herself and greeting the applicant by name. The officer should explain the importance of obtaining accurate information and briefly describe how the information is used to make a credit decision. The loan officer should ask questions in a conversational manner to make the applicant comfortable. A well-handled, face-to-face interview is more

---

FIGURE 5-1
ECOA Notice

You are hereby provided the following "Equal Credit Opportunity Act" notice as required under Section 202.9(a)(2) of Regulation B of the Consumer Credit Protection Act.

The Federal Equal Credit Opportunity Act prohibits creditors from discriminating against credit applicants on the basis of race, religion, national origin, sex, marital status, age (provided that the applicant has the capacity to enter into a binding contract); because all or part of the applicant's income derives from any public assistance program; or because the applicant has in good faith exercised any right under the Consumer Credit Protection Act. The Federal Agency that administers compliance with this law concerning this creditor is:

If there are any major factors which you feel could substantially affect this evaluation of your application, we would be pleased to discuss them with you.

Authorized Signature   Date
45023 (1/80)   SAF Systems and Forms
Statement of Reasons for Denial of Credit and ECOA Notice

148   Consumer Lending

FIGURE 5-2, Side 1
Consumer Loan Application

Chapter Five 149

FIGURE 5-2, Side 2
Consumer Loan Application

than a courtesy; it can lead to better loan decisions. A skillful interviewer can alleviate any of the applicant's hesitancy about providing information on personal financial matters and make the applicant feel at ease about requesting credit.

An interview provides an excellent opportunity for a consumer loan officer to identify an applicant's need for other services. The officer may suggest services such as credit life insurance, NOW accounts or other deposit services. Cross-selling helps establish an applicant as a loyal customer. Customer loyalty has been found to be closely related to the number of account relationships between the customer and the institution.

The Application Form

Application forms vary; however, they all request similar information. Figure 5-2 is an example of a basic consumer loan application form. A lender has important reasons for requesting all the information that is included on an application form. Each bit of information tells the lender something about either the borrower's character, capacity, collateral or capital (see Figure 5-3). Careful loan evaluation requires that all necessary information be obtained and inserted on the application form.

Since the information on the application is used to evaluate the loan, a large percentage of the underwriting process can take place during the application interview. Verification of the information at that stage serves as a check on the applicant's honesty and gives the loan officer a chance to further analyze the data. Therefore, lending personnel must refrain from rendering any opinions during the application process as to whether the loan will be approved or rejected. Similarly, employees who take loan applications but who do not have approval authority must refrain from turning down or discouraging a loan applicant or giving assurances that the loan will probably be approved.

If an applicant asks the loan officer for an opinion about how the information being supplied will be evaluated, the loan officer should remain neutral and encourage completion of the application. The officer should emphasize that decisions are not based on the response to any single question, but that all the information on the form is taken into consideration before a decision is made. If the loan officer believes that the application may be rejected, it is appropriate to ask the applicant for any other sources of income or capital that have not been listed or for the name of a co-applicant who might be available if the applicant does not qualify for the loan alone.

Applicants should not be discouraged unless the institution does not offer the type, terms or purpose of the requested loan, or the applicant does not qualify because he or she does not meet the lender's written policy requirements, such as minimum income or required number of credit references. In these circumstances, the lender may have a loan product, other than the one requested, that suits the applicant's needs. For example, the consumer loan officer (or application form) asks applicants to give the intended purpose of the loan, loan amount and length of time needed to repay the loan. FHLBB regulations broadly state that consumer loans can be made for personal, family or household purposes, but cannot be made for commercial purposes or to businesses. Institutions should make reasonable efforts to insure that credit is extended for personal, family or household purposes, although applicants will usually reveal a more specific purpose for obtaining a loan, such as the purchase of a car or a major household appliance.

The applicant completes the personal information section of the application, giving full name, age, address and phone number. According to Regulation B, creditors cannot request the sex of the applicant nor require courtesy titles (such as Miss, Ms., Mrs. or Mr.). A previous address should be given if the individual has resided at the present address for less than two years. Addresses can help to pinpoint the identity of applicants when conducting credit searches (for example, John Smith of 121 N. East Avenue is not the same person as John Smith of 412 N. West Ave., and each may have different credit reputations). The applicant's social security number and the number and ages of dependents are listed as further evidence of applicant identity.

At least two years of employment information is also needed. This information includes the name, address and phone number of employer; length of employment; type of business; and applicant's position or title. This information helps to identify employers who then can be contacted to verify salary and length of employment. The type of business, the applicant's position in it and length of employment

FIGURE 5-3
Application Information and Borrower Characteristics

Borrower Characteristic	Loan Request	Personal Information	Assets/Income	Liabilities Obligations Credit Reference
Character	Sets forth a guideline for placing emphasis on credit reputation on similar loans.	Helps identify applicant and place of employment for credit investigation.		Provides information that may reveal tendencies to over extend debt and past and present credit reputation.
Capacity	Sets forth a guideline in determining a borrower's ability to repay.		Provides information on borrower's financial ability to repay debt.	Provides information as to how much income is used to pay debts.
Collateral	Sets forth a guideline for determining sufficient collateral value.		Provides a list of items that might be pledged as security.	Provides information concerning ownership of assets. (Are there other loans secured by this collateral?)
Capital	Sets forth a guideline as to applicant's capital position in relation to loan size.		Provides a list of possible sources of repayment in the event of loan default.	Provides information as to the net worth of applicants.

Real Estate Owned	Insurance	Personal References	Agreement	Description of Collateral
		Provides a source of direct inquiry about applicant's reputation.	Serves as permission to investigate character.	
Provides possible collateral source.	Provides information regarding the protection of collateral against damage or loss.			Provides identification of pledged property.
Provides detailed information on the status of real estate capital.	Provides information that reveals possible additional capital.			

can help lenders to determine the applicant's income stability and potential.

Applicants are asked to state whether or not there are any judgment liens against them or if they have filed for bankruptcy within the past seven years. A *judgment lien* is a charge against the real or personal property of a debtor as a result of a final ruling by a judicial court. Judgment liens give creditors a security interest in a debtor's property and can include the right to acquire and retain possession of the property until the debt is satisfied. A judgment lien may be released when the debtor pays the creditor in full and the court issues a full satisfaction and release of the judgment statement. A *bankruptcy* is a legal proceeding in which a debtor's assets are administered by a court to pay creditors. Acquiring information on judgment liens and bankruptcy helps a consumer loan officer determine an applicant's credit character.

Personal and employment information concerning a co-applicant may be required. A *co-applicant* is a person who requests credit along with an applicant. Both applicant and co-applicant are contractually liable for repayment of the debt. A spouse, for example, may be a co-applicant. However, for open-end credit, the lender can request information on a spouse only if the spouse is a joint signer and is contractually liable. The spouse's income can also be considered if the applicant resides in a community property state or relies either on the spouse's income or on alimony or child support from the spouse, or former spouse, as a basis for repayment.

Assets are tangible and/or intangible items of value that help determine a borrower's capital. Information that might be required about assets on the application includes:
- available balances of checking and deposit accounts;
- net worth of a business (for self-employed individuals);
- current market value of any vehicles and whether or not they were financed;
- the total value of other personal property;
- the current value of any stocks and bonds owned; and
- a description and estimated value of any real estate owned.

An applicant should list all income that is received on a regular and consistent basis. Income is generally expressed as a monthly figure. The most common sources of income are base earnings, bonuses, commissions, dividends and interest. Base earnings refer to income for work performed during regularly scheduled working hours. Information on all sources of income helps the consumer loan officer determine an applicant's capacity to repay the loan.

Consistency is the key factor in determining the types of income other than regular wages that should be included on the application. Lenders cannot exclude irregular income derived from sources such as part-time employment or public assistance programs. Income from alimony, child support or maintenance payments, however, is included only if the applicant requests that it be considered as income.

Regulators cite various factors that may form the basis for determining consistency. According to the consumer protection unit of the *Federal Guide*: "Factors that a creditor may consider in determining the likelihood of consistent payments (income) include but are not limited to, whether the payments are received according to a written agreement or court decree; the length of time that the payments have been received; the regularity of receipt; the availability of procedures to compel payment; and the credit worthiness of the payor, including the credit history of the payor when available to the creditor under the Fair Credit Reporting Act or other applicable laws."[1]

Real estate owned usually pertains to the applicant's primary residence, although additional real estate owned should also be listed. In each case, the property should be described, and the amounts of the mortgage loan and total monthly payment amount should be detailed. If the mortgage has been paid in full, that should be indicated in this section.

Information on all past and current creditors is requested in the section on liabilities, obligations and credit references. This information helps the consumer loan officer determine the applicant's character or reputation for repaying credit, as well as current obligations against the applicant's capital.

Consumer loan officers ask applicants if they are married, separated or unmarried and indicate this on the front of the loan application (see Figure 5-2, Side 1). According to ECOA, loan officers may not ask for further information concerning marital status. The applicant's marital status indicates which of several follow-up steps must be taken by the loan officer. On secured loans where the borrower is married, for instance, the spouse jointly owns the collateral and must sign a security agreement. If the spouse does not sign this agreement, the lender may have difficulty acquiring the collateral upon default, except in community property states. In community property states, both spouses do not have to sign the legal document unless real estate or a vehicle titled in both names is offered as security. Otherwise, in community property states, either signature will bind both spouses to the debt.

The reverse side of the application form (see Figure 5-2, Side 2) contains three sections. First, personal references are required. These references may be used to help locate a borrower in the event of default. Second, an applicant's signature in the agreement section certifies that all the information given is true and accurate. The signature also gives the lender the authority to verify credit references. The third section contains space for the lender's use: to list finance charges and the APR, to describe the collateral and to compile the credit analysis information.

On applications for secured credit, a description of the collateral and whether or not the collateral is insured for loss or damage should be noted on the application form (see Figure 5-2, Side 2). A description is necessary both to determine the value of the collateral and to help identify it. Since lenders generally require physical damage insurance, the applicant must indicate whether or not the collateral is insured. If it is not already insured, the lender notifies the applicant of the insurance requirement.

Experienced loan officers often are able to focus on certain clues about the applicant that can indicate a poor credit risk. Sometimes further investigation by the officer or explanations from the applicant may be necessary. For example, if an applicant is unable to present acceptable identification when completing the application form, the loan officer should try to determine why. Applicants who have declared bankruptcy or who have had judgment liens against them should explain the circumstances of these actions. Lenders should avoid applications made by minors under the legal age of consent in their state since minors cannot make valid contractual arrangements. If inadvertently made, contracts with minors may not be enforceable and the lender would suffer a loss.

The most suspicious applicants are those who are in a great hurry to have their credit approved, possibly without much investigation into their credit histories. These applicants might appear at the day's closing time, usually at the end of the week. Their application forms seem to depict the perfect borrower, and, upon first investigation, everything seems in order. However, a thorough check often will reveal false credit sources or inaccurate references or other information that should arouse the loan officer's suspicions.

Experience and the prudent use of standard policies are the best protections against bad risks. Lenders should caution their less-experienced loan officers to watch for deceptive applicants. Consumer loan employees also should remember to follow written policies and procedures and to refuse to rush through credit approvals or to take shortcuts.

Consumer Loan Register

A consumer loan register is a chronological listing of every loan application received by a lender. Information recorded in the register may include the date of each loan application, name and address of the borrower, loan amount, interest rate and APR. The monthly loan payment amount, the finance charge, and the purpose and type of the loan may also be listed. Other information is added as the loan application is processed and closed: the date of approval or denial, the loan account number and the date of loan closing. The information can be written into a log book by hand or entered into a computer that prints out a register report.

The consumer loan register serves as a complete and convenient reference for both FHLB examiners and the institution. FHLB examiners select certain consumer loan accounts from the register to be examined for compliance with ECOA and other regulations. The institution uses the register for in-house audits and to answer customer inquiries on the status of loans.

VERIFYING PERSONAL CREDIT INFORMATION

The information obtained on a loan application is critically important for evaluating the credit characteristics of a borrower. Thus, every application must be completed in full with all data verified. If necessary, the information on the application may have to be used to help locate delinquent borrowers or to catch and stop con artists. Collectors also might trace delinquent borrowers through other credit sources, by checking driver's license numbers or by contacting personal references. Discrepancies between reported and verified information or the presence of nonverifiable information may be indications of fraud and should be scrutinized carefully.

On receipt of a completed and signed application, the consumer loan officer identifies specific information for the credit clerical staff to verify. The type of information that is actually verified depends upon the lender's policies and procedures and the particular application. The following information usually requires verification: past and current employment, repayment history, savings and checking account balances, the value of the collateral, and whether or not there are any judgment liens or other liens on the collateral.

Since timely credit processing and decision making are important, consumer loan officers must be selective in the type of information that is marked for verification on any single application. To save time, the officer may choose not to verify application data that seem reasonable. Loan officers experienced in evaluating credit often develop an ability to focus on information that seems doubtful or suspicious and which should be investigated further and verified. While careful verification reduces risk for lenders, it must be balanced against another need—prompt response. The more information that must be verified, the longer it takes to process the application. However, the desire for a prompt response should not be used as an excuse to bypass a skillful and necessary investigation.

Sources of Credit Information

Generally, most sources used by lenders for credit information provide accurate reports. True credit information is not created; it is factual data that is accumulated, stored and reported in a timely manner and should be obtainable at a low cost to the lender. Opinions about the applicant's ability to repay are not acceptable.

The most common sources of information are the lender's own files and records, the records of other financial institutions and lenders, employers, credit reporting agencies and applicants' financial statements. Lenders usually request information by mail, by telephone, or by asking the applicant to submit proof, such as a current paycheck stub or income tax return. Mail inquiries are generally quite complete and can be obtained at a relatively low cost. Telephone inquiries can be made more quickly but may be less complete and more costly. They are generally used to verify specific information. Asking the applicant to prove given information is often faster than verifying by mail. At times, certain types of information are not easily obtained over the telephone, and the loan officer will need to turn to other methods for timely verification. For example, some companies will not disclose an employee's income or other private information over the telephone; but income can be quickly verified from a current paycheck stub. Employment status can be checked by looking up the telephone number of the company in a phone directory, calling the company and asking to speak to the applicant.

In-file information is data stored within the institution in the form of existing and past deposit and/or loan accounts. These historical account records can help to determine applicant character and may also provide a verification of capital (for example, deposit account balances). In-file information is an excellent source of data because it is easily accessible and quickly obtained at a low cost.

Direct inquiry refers to information obtained through contact with specific, qualified parties. Examples of direct inquiry include writing to financial institutions for verification of customer account balances, phoning employers to verify employment status and calling past creditors to verify a customer's past repayment performance. Direct inquiry is a good method for quick, brief, specific information verification. On the other hand, information thus obtained is often incomplete, subject to duplication and costly because considerable time may be spent collecting small bits of information.

Credit reporting agencies are a good credit information source for lenders because they specialize in their function: to collect and store information on the credit histories of individual borrowers. Agencies gather information from financial institutions, employers, creditors, public records, landlords, collection agencies and other credit reporting agencies. The credit history they compile is then made available to lenders at a fee. Three basic types of credit reports are issued by these agencies. One is the *in-file report*. This report lists all information that the agency has on the applicant in question. Another is a *trade report* that provides a record of past and current credit accounts. A trade report shows the name of the creditor; the date the account was opened or the loan was closed; the highest credit balance; and the loan amount, present balance, past due amounts and whether there were any late payments. A *special report* gives only specific information requested by a lender.

Credit reports can be relayed by mail, orally over the telephone or via computer terminal. Computer terminals can provide direct access to the credit reporting agency's records over telephone lines. The credit clerk keys in the lender's identifying number and the names of applicants about whom information is requested. The information is relayed to the lender's computer terminal, which then has the credit reports printed out in a matter of seconds.

Another source for credit information is financial statements supplied by the applicant. For a self-employed individual applying for personal credit, the lender will want to evaluate the applicant's credit capacity by obtaining copies of federal income tax returns or profit and loss statements. These forms provide information about an applicant's income. An important point regarding income from self-employment is that only reported income can be considered. Since consumer loan officers are concerned about the consistency and stability of income, loan officers may ask to see these forms for a period of several years (usually at least two years). The longer period takes into account fluctuations in income level and helps to discover their cause, such as economic conditions or personal reasons. Usually the applicant is asked to explain the particular reasons for significant fluctuations in income.

Investigating the Ownership and Value of Collateral

Although the emphasis during evaluation is on the borrower's character and capacity, some efforts need to be devoted to investigating the value of the collateral for a secured loan. The ownership of the collateral can be verified from title reports, certificates of title and certificates of title registration. *Title reports*, obtained for real property, identify the owner of the property, give a description of the property and indicate if there are any liens against the title. *Certificates of title* are evidence of ownership for automobiles, recreational vehicles and, in some states, boats. *Certificates of registration* are evidence of ownership for aircraft. Besides listing the owner, certificates of title and of registration give a description of the property and list any liens against it.

Additional sources for verifying collateral ownership are state and federal agencies that record ownership information, since these documents are considered public ownership information; the secretary of state records ownership of automobiles and other types of motor vehicles; and the Federal Aviation Administration records aircraft ownership.

To obtain title reports and other information on real property, lenders typically employ companies that specialize in title search and/or title insurance. Title reports from title insurance companies are commonly called *commitments for title insurance*. Title insurance companies report on the condition of the title and, when appropriate, offer a title insurance policy termed a Policy of Insured Real Title (PIRT) for a small fee. A similar title search should also be done for aircraft.

In addition to establishing the ownership of collateral, lenders will often try to verify value. Physical inspection can determine that the collateral exists and is in good condition. Guidebooks that list the value by make, model and year of automobiles, mobile homes, boats and so on should also be consulted to obtain a current value.

Detection of Fraud

Financial crime is a growing problem that concerns all lenders. One type of crime that is of special concern to credit departments is fraud. Institutions and lenders of all sizes may experience fraud losses that reduce profits. These losses eventually must be passed on to consumers in the form of higher borrowing costs. Lending personnel should be aware of the characteristics of a possibly fraudulent applicant and the types of discrepancies on an application that may indicate a potential fraud.

Inconsistent Identification

Since the credit decision rests heavily on the character and performance of the applicant, the person's identification must be verified. When the data about an individual is inconsistent, the information may be false.

Inconsistent identification used to obtain a loan might consist of stolen or fake IDs. Seeing the applicant in a face-to-face interview and requesting picture IDs can reduce the opportunities for applicants to use lost or stolen IDs. Also, lending personnel should be aware of certain indicators on standard IDs that suggest that the document might be counterfeit or fake.

FIGURE 5-4
Correct Social Security Numbers

SS#	STATE ISSUED	SS#	STATE ISSUED
001 to 003	New Hampshire	440 to 448	Oklahoma
004 to 007	Maine	449 to 467	Texas
008 to 009	Vermont	468 to 477	Minnesota
010 to 034	Massachusetts	478 to 485	Iowa
035 to 039	Rhode Island	486 to 500	Missouri
040 to 049	Connecticut	501 to 502	North Dakota
050 to 134	New York	503 to 504	South Dakota
135 to 158	New Jersey	505 to 508	Nebraska
159 to 211	Pennsylvania	509 to 515	Kansas
212 to 220	Maryland	516 to 517	Montana
221 to 222	Delaware	518 to 519	Idaho
223 to 231	Virginia	520	Wyoming
232 to 236	West Virginia	521 to 524	Colorado
232, 237 to 246	North Carolina	525, 585	New Mexico
247 to 251	South Carolina	526 to 527	Arizona
252 to 260	Georgia	528 to 529	Utah
261 to 267	Florida	530	Nevada
268 to 302	Ohio	531 to 539	Washington
303 to 317	Indiana	540 to 544	Oregon
318 to 361	Illinois	545 to 573	California
362 to 386	Michigan	574	Alaska
387 to 399	Wisconsin	575 to 576	Hawaii
400 to 407	Kentucky	577 to 579	Dist of Columbia
408 to 415	Tennessee	580	Virgin Islands
416 to 424	Alabama	580 to 585	Puerto Rico
425 to 428, 587	Mississippi	586	Guam
			American Samoa
429 to 432	Arkansas		Philippine Islands
433 to 439	Louisiana	700 to 729	Railroad

Following are a few common discrepancies that can be easily checked. Social Security numbers and employer W-2 ID numbers can be cross-checked against charts that list each state's assigned prefix or code (see Figures 5-4 and 5-5). Most state driver's license numbers begin with the first letter of the driver's last name. Fake work IDs may list a company phone number that is connected to a "boiler room" answering service, or belong to a friend or relative of the applicant. The company name and/or address may be fictitious. The authenticity of a work ID can be checked by looking up the company in a telephone or business directory, comparing the two numbers and calling the published telephone number instead of the one supplied by the applicant.

Characteristics of a Fraudulent Applicant
Lending personnel should be alert to spot certain characteristics of an applicant or application that signal the possibility of fraud. Three general areas have to do with the applicant's behavior during the interview, with data on the applicant's residence and with financial data.

Regarding the applicant's behavior during the interview, the loan officer should watch for the following behavior.
- The applicant does not seem to be nervous or anxious about getting the loan. Remember that most applicants are at least a little apprehensive about a possible rejection.
- The applicant does not engage in small talk. Lending personnel often direct the loan interview. Since the application should be taken in a conversational manner, some small talk naturally occurs.
- The applicant appears hesitant to provide specific information.
- The applicant uses titles, such as doctor or CPA to intimidate or rush lending personnel.

The loan officer should be alert for possibly fraudulent information about where the applicant lives or can be reached. Some of this information is listed below.
- The phone number prefix does not match the prefix used for the given address.
- Post office boxes as mailing addresses make locating an applicant difficult. If a rural route is given, the applicant should be asked for directions.
- Phone number verification calls are answered by some-

FIGURE 5-5
W-2 Employer ID Numbers

Numbers will always be shown as 2 digits-space-7 digits, the two digit prefix number corresponds to the district where the number was issued per the list below:

Dist/City	State	Code	Dist/City	State	Code
Aberdeen	South Dakota	46	Jackson	Mississippi	64
Albany	New York	14	Jacksonville	Florida	59
Albuquerque	New Mexico	85	Little Rock	Arkansas	71
Anchorage	Alaska	92	Los Angeles	California	95
Atlanta	Georgia	58	Louisville	Kentucky	61
Augusta	Maine	01	Manhattan	New York	13
Austin	Texas	74	Milwaukee	Wisconsin	39
Baltimore	Maryland	52	Nashville	Tennessee	62
Birmingham	Alabama	63	Newark	New Jersey	22
Boise	Idaho	82	New Orleans	Louisiana	72
Boston	Massachusetts	04	Oklahoma City	Oklahoma	73
Brooklyn	New York	11	Omaha	Nebraska	47
Buffalo	New York	16	Parkersburg	West Virginia	55
Burlington	Massachusetts	03	Philadelphia	Pennsylvania	23
Cheyenne	Wyoming	83	Phoenix	Arizona	86
Chicago	Illinois	36	Pittsburgh	Pennsylvania	25
Cincinnati	Ohio	31	Portsmouth	New Hampshire	02
Cleveland	Ohio	34	Portland	Oregon	93
Columbia	South Carolina	57	Providence	Rhode Island	05
Dallas	Texas	74	Richmond	Virginia	54
Denver	Colorado	84	Reno	Nevada	88
Des Moines	Iowa	42	Salt Lake City	Utah	87
Detroit	Michigan	38	San Francisco	California	94
Fargo	North Dakota	45	Seattle	Washington	91
Greensboro	North Carolina	56	Springfield	Illinois	37
Hartford	Connecticut	06	St. Louis	Missouri	43
Helena	Montana	81	St. Paul	Minnesota	41
Honolulu	Hawaii	99	Wichita	Kansas	48
Indianapolis	Indiana	35	Wilmington	Delaware	51

one giving the phone number; this indicates an answering service.

Finally, the loan officer should note certain types of information concerning financial data.

- Closed or canceled credit accounts could indicate a front for established credit, especially if the accounts were recent or short term.
- The applicant refers to a recent large deposit in a liquid account.
- An applicant with no credit history or new credit

should be asked to explain, especially if the person is not young and has had sufficient time to establish credit. In fact, a lender's written policy may require some minimum credit history to qualify for a loan.
- The credit report shows excessive recent inquires. This might indicate a changing life-style, or it may signal that the applicant is trying to accumulate as much credit as he or she can. In the latter instance, the applicant may be planning to file for bankruptcy soon.

When someone claims to have worked or lived in the same area for a number of years, the credit bureau report should also go back for that length of time.

Many lenders maintain a list of professional license agencies. Such agencies can verify whether or not the applicant is indeed a registered nurse, doctor, pharmacist or certified public accountant. Also, lenders may keep a fraud file that employees can cross-reference by the applicant's name, job and/or home address.

ANALYZING CREDIT INFORMATION

After the application is received and all the necessary information verified, the consumer loan officer or credit manager must analyze the information and decide whether or not to extend credit. When analyzing an applicant's information, the consumer loan officer reviews and analyzes several important factors such as the applicant's payment history, income, employment history and debt. After reviewing the information, the loan officer assesses the borrower's ability to repay. A competent review and analysis of the credit information is determined by the loan officer's experience and reliance on proven policies and procedures. Although it is impossible to screen out all potential bad debt, it is a good practice to follow established guidelines to identify the characteristics of credit worthy and noncredit worthy applicants.

One of the first things the loan officer checks is whether the applicant has had a satisfactory payment history. A satisfactory history tends to improve the likelihood that future payments also will be met. An unsatisfactory history, as evidenced by amounts reported past due, unfavorable ratings, judgment liens or bankruptcies, might indicate similar problems in the future. At this stage, the loan officer may ask the applicant for additional information to clarify the results of the credit investigation or refer to written explanations submitted by the applicant.

Throughout the evaluation process, the loan officer must abide by the Equal Credit Opportunity Act. The ECOA prohibits discrimination in credit decisions on the basis of:
- race;
- color;
- religion;
- national origin;
- sex;
- marital status;
- age;
- whether all or part of income comes from public assistance; or
- if the applicant has in good faith exercised any right under the Consumer Protection Act.

The Credit Report

The basic reason to examine the credit bureau report is to check on the applicant's honesty and credit history. From the application, the four Cs of credit (character, capacity, capital and collateral) that characterize the applicant are usually apparent. However, the loan officer needs to check that the information given is indeed accurate and complete. The credit report can be an important verification tool.

Credit bureau reports tell the loan officer a number of things. When analyzed, the report can show borrowing trends, whether or not the customer has been spending heavily or whether prior repayments were poor. The report can also signal a change in life-style. For example, if there are many recent inquiries, the customer may have just obtained several new credit cards. Sometimes, however, several inquiries shown in a credit bureau report may be unrelated to the applicant's credit use, such as those made without the applicant's knowledge. For example, car dealers commonly offer an application to several lenders at the same time. When in doubt, the loan officer should ask the borrower if he or she recently attempted to purchase something of this nature.

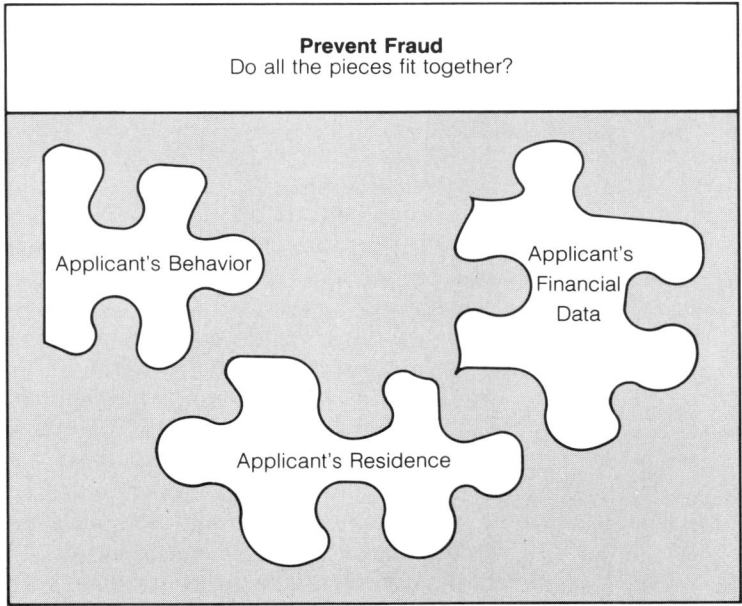

Additionally, credit reports should be analyzed differently for different types of applicants. The profiles of credit reports typically resemble the financial circumstances of applicants in similar life-cycle stages. For example, a credit report for a young married couple is likely to differ from that of a single person who has worked for a number of years. Profiles that do not match the applicant may indicate fraud. Finally, the report should be searched for negative factors, such as bankruptcies, judgments, collections and charge-offs. The report may indicate undisclosed debts. In addition, recent local and out-of-state inquiries by banks, savings institutions or finance companies may warrant further investigation.

Two items of importance that usually are not found in a credit bureau report are mortgage payment history and credit union loans. Mortgage payments are usually the last obligation a person will fall behind on; if all other credit has been good, chances are the mortgage history will be good, too. If the applicant has no credit history, but has a mortgage, a recent mortgage statement will show whether payments have been on time. A credit union loan can be spotted on a paycheck stub. If the applicant claims the credit union deduction is for savings, ask for proof of deposit.

Income Analysis

Income should be consistent and stable. Frequent changes in residence or employment without sound reasons are a cause for concern because they may result in fluctuating income. Changes in income (more importantly decreases in income) reflect unfavorably on the applicant because they indicate a reduced ability to repay debt.

The amount of verifiable income should be sufficient to cover all obligations and expenses, including the applied-for loan. When confirming that verifiable income is adequate, several precautions should be observed. Paycheck stubs can verify past income but do not necessarily indicate that commissions or overtime pay will continue. The top of the paycheck stub should be scrutinized also to check the name of the payor and verify that payments are for payroll and not for disability, which may stop soon.

The type of income is important as well. A retired applicant, for example, may have an income that is only marginally sufficient to qualify for a loan, but the majority of that income may be derived from interest and dividends received from a substantial capital base. Someone earning $12,000 in interest income is generally in better financial shape than someone earning $12,000 from wages. Therefore, the source of income could show that the applicant is strong in capital, which could also be used to make loan payments, if necessary.

Debt Analysis

The *debt-to-income ratio* relates the applicant's monthly credit obligations (including the applied-for loan) to monthly income. For example, if Jack Mitchell has $500 in monthly debts and $2,000 in monthly income, his debt-to-income ratio is 25%—$500/$2,000.

Sometimes debt-to-income ratios are computed using the applicant's net income which is the applicant's take-home pay after deductions for income tax and Social Security have been taken. This is called *debt-to-net income ratio*. If Jack's net income, or take-home pay, is $1,500, his debt-to-net income ratio is 33%—$500/$1,500.

Total debts include house or rental payments, real estate taxes, installment loans, bank and department store credit card charges and any other recurring obligations, such as child support, alimony, etc. When considering credit card charges in the debt ratio, the amount used for the calculation should be the largest payment that would be required if the full line of credit were to be used, and not simply the current balance at the time of the application. Short-term obligations may be exceptions; for instance, if there are six or fewer mortgage payments remaining, these would be not counted. Similarly, none of the above mentioned obligations would be considered if fewer than four payments remained.

Lenders have written policies regarding acceptable debt-to-income ratios that work well for the majority of applicants. However, for exceptional cases, such as applicants with very high or very low incomes, broad policies may not apply. In these cases, the loan officer may want to consider the applicant's absolute ability to make payments. For example, someone earning a high salary may have a debt-to-income ratio that exceeds the lender's guidelines, yet still be able to afford the loan payments quite easily. In another example, someone whose income falls within the lender's guidelines but has a large family to support may not be able to handle routine loan payments. In these cases, the loan officer can consider the family size and assign cost of living expenses per family member to determine if there is sufficient income left over to cover the loan payments. This is referred to as *margin* and is determined by subtracting all debt payments and living expenses per person (which can vary with regions and types of loans) from take home pay to arrive at spendable income.

Risk Analysis

Another ratio that lenders consider when evaluating a loan request is the loan-to-value ratio. The *loan-to-value ratio* is the relationship of the total amount of loans secured by the same collateral to the value of the collateral. This ratio is most often used on secured loans for real estate and automobiles.

Assume that an automobile valued at $10,000 is used to secure $5,000 in financing and has a loan-to-value ratio of 50%—$5,000/10,000. To determine if a loan-to-value ratio is acceptable, the lending institution refers to its own underwriting standards that give the range of acceptable ratio limits for evaluating applications. If the loan-to-value ratio for a requested loan is too high, the loan officer may suggest a higher downpayment from the applicant. To verify market values of collateral, lenders can check dealer invoices or price guidebooks.

Credit Scoring Systems

A *credit scoring system* is an objective method of evaluating applicant information or attributes to determine credit worthiness. Some attributes that might be used in an evaluation are martial status, number of years at the same address, whether a dwelling is owned or rented, years with an employer, deposit relationship and ownership of an automobile. On scoring systems, applicant attributes are assigned a number of points; the more points assigned, the more the attribute signifies a good credit risk. The credit manager rates an applicant on each attribute and then totals the points. Applicants are accepted if they achieve a point score at or above an established minimum. The minimum acceptable score is listed as part of the lender's underwriting standards.

Credit scoring systems must meet the nondiscriminatory standards of ECOA and other requirements set forth in Regulation B. Regulation B states that credit scoring systems must be empirically derived (that is, based on observation) and statistically sound. The data used to develop such systems must be obtained from actual applicant files. The data also may be derived from the lender's files. This includes charge-offs, delinquencies, denials, repossessions, etc. The attributes on which applicants are rated must separate credit worthy from noncredit worthy borrowers at a statistically significant rate. In addition, the first group of applicants rated according to a new credit scoring system should prove to validate the system; the new credit scoring system should have some impact on maintaining or, preferably, reducing the percentage of problem loans. In practice, because of the stringent requirements of ECOA and Regulation B, acceptable credit scoring systems are very difficult for a lender to develop. However, private companies have developed credit scoring systems with regulatory requirements in mind.

Another method of credit scoring can be designed from the lender's written policy guidelines. The guidelines can be given to a credit bureau to screen and obtain a list of potential applicants. Then the lender can market the loan product to preapproved, desirable applicants.

NOTIFYING THE APPLICANT OF THE CREDIT DECISION

After the information about an applicant is analyzed and a credit decision has been reached, the applicant should be notified as soon as possible. Institutions are required to notify all applicants of the approval or denial of credit within 30 days of the receipt of an application, although often today's turnaround time between application and approval or denial is much faster, perhaps a matter of a few hours within the same day. A desire for good customer service and the intense competition among lenders require an effort to respond quickly and efficiently.

Applicants approved for credit are notified either by telephone or in writing. Applicants for whom credit is denied must be notified in writing. In the interest of good customer service, applicants denied credit also may be called prior to written notification. This enables the loan officer to discuss alternative loan terms or types that may satisfy the customer's needs.

A denial of credit to an applicant is called an *adverse action*. If, after the initial application is taken, the lender decides to change the rate, amount, time or terms of the loan, such as requiring a co-borrower, the lender must give the applicant a notice of adverse action. If more than one applicant requested credit on a single application, the notice of adverse action need only be delivered to one of them.

In addition to written notification of an adverse action, Regulation B requires lenders to give applicants the following: an explanation as to why the adverse action was taken and a list of the outside credit sources that supplied informa-

FIGURE 5-6
Statement of Credit Denial, Termination on Charge

EQUAL OPPORTUNITY LENDER

Applicant's Name(s) _____

Mailing Address _____ Transaction _____

City, State, Zip _____ Reference _____

Indicated below are the reasons supporting our decision to deny credit per the application submitted in conjunction with the above referenced transaction.

PRINCIPAL REASON(S) FOR ADVERSE ACTION CONCERNING CREDIT

A. CREDIT
- ☐ Credit Application Incomplete (If you wish further consideration, please let us know when you can complete your application)
- ☐ No Credit File
- ☐ Insufficient Credit References
- ☐ Insufficient Credit File
- ☐ Unable to Verify Credit References
- ☐ Garnishment, Attachment, Foreclosure, Repossession or Suit
- ☐ Excessive Obligations
  - ☐ Insufficient Income for Total Obligations
  - ☐ Unacceptable Payment Record on Previous Mortgage
  - ☐ Lack of Cash Reserves
- ☐ Delinquent Credit Obligations
- ☐ Bankruptcy
- ☐ Information From a Consumer Reporting Agency

B. INCOME
- ☐ Insufficient Income for Mortgage Payments
- ☐ Unable to Verify Income

C. EMPLOYMENT STATUS
- ☐ Unable to Verify Employment
- ☐ Length of Employment
- ☐ Temporary or Irregular Employment
  - ☐ Insufficient Stability of Income

D. RESIDENCY
- ☐ Temporary Residence
- ☐ Too Short a Period of Residence
- ☐ Unable to Verify Residence

E. INSURANCE GUARANTY or PURCHASE DENIED BY:
- ☐ Department of Housing and Urban Development
- ☐ Veterans Administration
- ☐ Federal National Mortgage Association
- ☐ Federal Home Loan Mortgage Corporation
- ☐ _____
- ☐ _____

F. OTHER
- ☐ Insufficient Funds to Close the Loan
- ☐ Inadequate Collateral
  - ☐ Property doesn't meet minimum building code standards
  - ☐ Unsatisfactory condition of property
  - ☐ Cost to Appraisal Ratio too high
  - ☐ Unacceptable Leasehold Estate
- ☐ We do not grant credit to any applicant on the terms and conditions you have requested.
- ☐ Other, Specify _____

DISCLOSURE OF USE OF INFORMATION OBTAINED FROM AN OUTSIDE SOURCE

☐ Information furnished by the following consumer reporting agency:

_____
Name of Consumer Reporting Agency   Phone

_____
Address of Consumer Reporting Agency

☐ Information obtained from an outside source other than a consumer reporting agency.

NOTE: Under the Fair Credit Reporting Act, you have the right to make a written request within 60 days of receipt of this notice, for disclosure of the nature of the adverse information obtained from outside sources other than consumer reporting agencies.

You are hereby provided the following "Equal Credit Opportunity Act" notice as required under Section 202.9(a)(2) of Regulation B of the Consumer Credit Protection Act.

The Federal Equal Credit Opportunity Act prohibits creditors from discriminating against credit applicants on the basis of race, religion, national origin, sex, marital status, age (provided that the applicant has the capacity to enter into a binding contract); because all or part of the applicant's income derives from any public assistance program; or because the applicant has in good faith exercised any right under the Consumer Credit Protection Act. The Federal Agency that administers compliance with this law concerning this creditor is:

If there are any major factors which you feel could substantially affect this evaluation of your application, we would be pleased to discuss them with you.

_____   _____
Authorized Signature   Date

45023 (1/80)
Statement of Reasons for Denial of Credit and ECOA Notice   SAF Systems and Forms

FIGURE 5-7
Statement of Denial and Counteroffer

> FORM C-6—STATEMENT OF DENIAL AND COUNTEROFFER
>
> Date
>
> Dear Applicant:
>
> Thank you for your application for a home improvement loan in the amount of $45,000.
>
> I regret that we are unable to grant you the amount of credit you have requested. It is the policy of our firm to grant home improvement loans for a maximum term of 15 years and you have requested the loan for 20 years.
>
> We would be pleased to make you the loan in the amount you requested for a term of 15 years at a rate of _____% which would require monthly payments of $_____ for 180 months. If you would like to accept this offer please notify us no later than _____.
>
> You should know that the federal government prohibits creditors, such as ourselves, from discriminating against credit applicants on the basis of their race, color, religion, national origin, sex, marital status, age, or because they receive income from a public assistance program or because they may have exercised their rights under the Consumer Credit Protection Act. If you believe there has been discrimination in handling your application you should contact the [name of agency], XXX Street, Anytown, Anystate XXXXX, (XXX) XXX-XXXX.
>
> We look forward to hearing from you by _____.
>
> Sincerely,
>
> Credit Officer

tion used in making the credit decision. Samples of credit denial statements that comply with Regulation B are shown in Figures 5-6 through 5-9.

When preparing the adverse action notification, the loan officer should check off every reason that applies. This is to avoid unnecessary embarrassment. For example, if the applicant was denied credit for a number of reasons, but only one reason, such as insufficient income, for instance, was checked on the adverse action notification, that applicant might return with additional verifiable income and expect to receive a loan.

Sometimes credit denial decisions are made on the basis of incorrect or damaging information contained in a credit bureau report, such as a disputed bill that is being shown as past due. In these cases, the loan officer cannot let the customer see the report but is required to give the customer the name and telephone number of the credit bureau issuing

FIGURE 5-8
Statement of Reasons for Denial (Credit Scoring)

FORM C-7—STATEMENT OF REASONS FOR DENIAL (CREDIT SCORING)

Date

Dear Applicant:

Thank you for your recent application for _____.
We regret that we are unable to approve your request.

Your application was processed by a credit scoring system which assigns a numerical value to the various items of information we consider in evaluating an application. These numerical values are based upon the results of analyses of repayment histories of large numbers of customers.

The information you provided in your application did not score a sufficient number of points for approval of the application. The areas in which you did not score well compared to other applicants were:

*Bank references

*Occupation

*Credit rating

In evaluating your application we obtained information from a credit reporting agency that in whole or in part influenced our decision. The credit reporting agency played no part in our decision other than providing us with credit information about you. You have a right to know the information provided to us. It can be obtained by contacting:

Name: _____

Address: _____

_____

Telephone: _____

Sincerely,

NOTICE: The federal Equal Credit Opportunity Act prohibits creditors from discriminating against credit applicants on the basis of race, color, religion, national origin, sex, marital status, age (provided that the applicant has the capacity to enter into a binding contract), because all or part of the applicant's income derives from any public assistance program; or because the applicant has in good faith exercised any right under the Consumer Credit Protection Act. The federal agency that administers compliance with this law concerning this creditor is (name and address as specified by the appropriate agency listed in Appendix A).

the report. It then becomes the customer's responsibility to clear up any incorrect and/or damaging information that appears on his or her credit report.

UNDERWRITING INDIRECT LOANS

Some consumer loans are originated by dealers. These may be either on a direct loan referral or an indirect basis. A *direct referral* occurs when a dealer regularly sends purchasers to a particular institution for financing. With both direct referral and indirect loans, the Holder in Due Course Notice (presented in Chapter 3) must be a part of the retail installment contract or note.

This section discusses several aspects of indirect loans. First, the advantages and disadvantages of direct versus indirect loans are listed. Next, the importance of carefully selecting a dealer is explained. After selecting a dealer, the lender will have various indirect credit activities to perform.

FIGURE 5-9
Notice Regarding Incomplete Application and Request for Additional Information

---

FORM C-10—NOTICE REGARDING INCOMPLETE APPLICATION
AND REQUEST FOR ADDITIONAL INFORMATION

Date

Dear Applicant:

Thank you for your application for a loan in the amount of $8,500 to purchase a new car.

In order to make a decision on whether we can grant you the amount you have requested we need some additional information about your income. Since you are self-employed we would like to have copies of your tax returns for the past two years. As soon as we receive this information we will resume consideration of your request.

If we do not receive the information from you by _____, I regret we will be unable to grant you the loan on the basis of the current application.

Sincerely,

Credit Officer

The section ends with a description of how lenders purchase dealer paper, after a credit decision has been made.

Advantages and Disadvantages of Direct Versus Indirect Loans

Before becoming involved with indirect loans, lenders should consider the advantages and disadvantages of indirect lending by comparing it with direct loans. Lenders enjoy the following advantages with direct loans.
- The lender typically sees the applicant in a face-to-face interview.
- Direct lending provides a good way for lenders to begin offering a new loan product.
- The lender can closely monitor all steps in the process to make sure that credit policies and correct procedures are being followed.
- The loan volume can be controlled by adjusting terms or changing credit policies.
- The lender can cross-sell other services to the customer.

By contrast, with indirect loans involving a dealer, the lender will not be able to enjoy the above advantages to the same extent. Typically, interviews are conducted at the dealership, and such an off-site interview reduces the institution's control over procedures and eliminates the opportunity to cross-sell other institution products. Also, the dealer expects the lender to act in a consistent manner, making it more difficult for the lender to fine tune loan volume by altering loan terms.

Additional disadvantages of indirect lending include the following:
- dealer pressure to influence the lender's credit decisions;
- the need for more experienced staff to handle indirect lending than is required for direct lending; and
- loan volumes subject to a dealer's marketing efforts may be volatile.

The essential advantage of indirect loans over direct loans is volume. With indirect lending, a lender may purchase a large volume of profitable contracts efficiently and rapidly, thus building up a substantial loan portfolio in a short period of time. A productive dealer provides a second advantage—to widen the lender's market. A third advantage is that various dealer endorsements may protect the lender against some losses. Endorsements are explained later in this section.

Importance of Evaluating a Dealer

Before a lender buys dealer paper (loans originated indirectly) and accepts applications, the dealer should be approved by the lender's board of directors. In approving a new dealer, a lender investigates the dealer's financial stability and character and obtains the dealer's financial statements and a credit report. Other companies that do business with the dealer also may be contacted. After the dealer is approved, an agreement containing the terms of the arrangement is signed by both dealer and lender management.

A thorough investigation of a new dealer is important because some dealers can be unscrupulous. Among the various ploys of unscruplous dealers are drawing up fictitious contracts and trying to sell them to lenders; filing duplicate loan applications with more than one institution; deliberately stating inaccurate downpayment amounts; and delivering to a buyer merchandise other than that stated in a contract. A thorough credit investigation could reveal evidence of these acts and, thus, prevent loss to the institution.

The lender's management should make a thorough, personal examination of the dealer's ownership and management. The lender should require that the dealer be:
- available for the lender to call on;
- financially able to meet all obligations;
- staffed by friendly, amicable people;
- stable with a good local reputation;
- capable both in business and technical skills; and
- developed with a management depth that could prove able to continue the business in the owner's absence.

In addition, the dealer's products should be investigated for quality, service and value. Product quality should be high so that the collateral does not depreciate in market value faster than the loan balance is reduced. Service is very important as well. Warranties should be backed by manufacturers or a dependable third party. This is especially important because the lender is now subject to all claims and defenses that the borrower can assert against the dealer. For example, if the lender finances an extended warranty and the dealer goes out of business, the lender could find itself in the service business if no arrangements for service were otherwise made available to the borrower. It should also be remembered that the value of a product is affected by the market demand for it. The demand for some products (e.g., recreational vehicles) will change more drastically with changes in economic conditions than demand for other products.

Forming the Dealer Relationship

After selecting a dealer, the lender and dealer agree on how they will operate. A formal, written dealer agreement normally will spell out all of the business operating conditions. The dealer agreement will specify which party is responsible for compliance with regulations and bad credit losses. Before determining the particulars of the agreement, the lender must know what arrangements exist in the market. The worst place to find this out is from a dealer, who may mention only the points that are to the dealer's advantage.

The lender agrees to purchase dealer paper at a specific rate, called the *buy rate*. The dealer may charge the customer a higher rate, called the *customer rate*. The dealer agreement specifies to whom the difference between the buy rate and the customer rate will go, and how it will be paid. Frequently a portion of the difference is held in a reserve for losses. When the reserve exceeds some specified amount, the excess is paid to the appropriate party according to the specified frequency, such as monthly, quarterly, etc. The reserve also serves as a source of funds to return unearned interest when the customer is charged add-on interest and prepays the loan.

The dealer expects the lender to buy dealer paper in a consistent manner. Many times the lender and dealer begin their relationship with a trial period. During the trial period, the dealer submits to the lenders its typical deals, and the lender buys those that meet its standards. After the trial period, the dealer will have learned which deals a particular lender will buy. During this trial period, and even afterwards, the lender may randomly call the dealer's customers to check on their satisfaction.

In establishing a relationship with a dealer, another important fact to consider is that the lender who provides financing for the dealer's inventory (known as *floor planning*) will get the dealer's best consumer paper. Lenders who do not floor plan will get the second best. On the other hand, floor planning requires a great deal more planning and expertise in order to control risk than many lenders are willing or capable of providing.

Indirect Credit Activities
As noted earlier in dealer-originated loans, a financial institution's consumer loan officers do not have the opportunity to interview the applicants. Instead, the dealer asks consumers who request financing to complete an application form. Lenders may then handle the application in one of two ways.

One arrangement is for the completed application form to be sent directly to the institution. The institution's credit manager supervises the credit investigation and makes the credit decision. Under this arrangement, direct and indirect credit activities are performed in the same manner except for the interview.

Another arrangement is for the dealer to perform the credit investigation. The information collected is forwarded to the institution along with the application form. The institution's credit manager then makes the final credit decision. Under this arrangement, the institution relies on the dealer's ability to investigate credit as well as interview applicants. However, the credit manager still should obtain a credit report independently or verify the information on the report by phone. In other words, the lender should not put too much trust in the dealer and should do its own homework.

No matter what arrangement an institution uses, applications must be received quickly so that processing can be completed promptly. Application information may be sent from the dealer to the institution over a telecopier, by telephone or by messenger. A telecopier is a copying machine that sends and receives images on paper over telephone lines.

Buying Dealer Paper
When a consumer makes a purchase and finances it through a dealer, a *retail installment contract* is executed and signed by both parties. This contract is a legally binding agreement that

sets forth the terms of the sale and the terms of the purchaser's payment (see Figure 5-10). Dealers may not want to finance consumers' purchases with their own resources. In this case, they assign or sell their rights in these contracts to a third party, the lending institution. In effect, the institution buys a contract (called dealer paper) for a price negotiated with the dealer. The transfer of this contract from the dealer to the institution is evidenced by the execution of the assignment section of the contract (see Figure 5-10).

The assignment section identifies the institution and spells out dealer warranties and conditions. Conditions explain the rights of both parties to the contract in the event problems arise with the loan. Usually, the dealer agreement states how the contracts are to be assigned. It also states that the dealer is totally responsible for the identification of the applicant.

Conditions are of two major types: recourse and repurchase. *Recourse* is the institution's right to seek loan repayment from the dealer in the event of borrower default. *Repurchase* is the institution's right to seek loan repayment from the dealer if conditions set forth in the retail installment contract are not met. The amount of protection from recourse and repurchase agreements ranges from full protection to none at all.

Types of conditions include full recourse, full repayment, partial or limited recourse or repayment, and no recourse. Buying dealer paper *with full recourse* means that the dealer is obligated to buy back a contract for the loan payoff balance in the event the borrower defaults. With full recourse, the dealer is responsible for collecting from the delinquent borrower and incurs any repossession costs. If the signature on the application turns out to be a forgery, or if the dealer falsifies information about the size of the downpayment or other facts that would influence a positive decision, then the contract will become full recourse, regardless of the agreement. *With partial recourse* depends on what the dealer agreement specifies. There may be time or dollar limits on the dealer's obligations both with partial recourse and with repurchase agreements. Under a *partial repurchase* agreement, if the customer defaults, for example, on an automobile loan, the dealer repurchases the repossessed car. Buying dealer paper *without recourse* means that the dealer is not obligated to buy back the contract under any circumstances.

As noted earlier, lenders are reimbursed for loan losses from the dealer's holdback reserve. The reserve also holds part of the loans' interest for refunding prepayments. If the holdback reserve has an insufficient balance, the dealer is obligated to pay the lender according to the dealer agreement. Full recourse deals are usually made on loans that the lender would probably not have made if the customer had applied directly. They might, for instance, involve younger applicants who lack a sufficient credit history. If a dealer sells too many loans with full recourse and if a number of borrowers then default, the dealer may exhaust the reserve balance. If that happens, the lender's ability to collect from the dealer will only be as good as the dealer's financial condition, which is another reason why the lender must thoroughly know a dealer before doing business.

SUMMARY

The loan underwriting process includes taking a loan application, verifying credit information, analyzing credit risk, and approving or denying credit. These important activities attempt to determine the risks involved in making a specific consumer loan. They also establish suitable terms and conditions for the loan.

Loan policies provide guidelines as to the types of loans made, who may take applications, and the procedures for accepting and processing applications. Institutions use loan underwriting standards to evaluate applicants and determine their credit worthiness. FHLBB regulations impose no specific restrictions on consumer loans, except that they consistently must conform to the institution's written loan underwriting standards and that these standards be made available to the public upon request.

Loan applications may be accepted by mail, over the telephone or through an interview with a consumer loan officer. Regardless of the method of taking applications, interested consumers have the right to file applications. Institutions are specifically prohibited by FHLBB regulations and Regulation B from discouraging customer inquiries or loan applications.

FIGURE 5-10, Side 1
Retail Installment Contract

FIGURE 5-10, Side 2
Retail Installment Contract

ADDITIONAL PROVISIONS

Further Warranties and Covenants of The Buyer. The Buyer hereby warrants and covenants that:

1. The Buyer will not sell or offer to sell, assign, pledge, lease or otherwise transfer or encumber the Goods or any interest therein, or operate the Goods or any part thereof for hire without the prior written consent of the Seller.

2. The Buyer will immediately notify the Seller in writing of any change in address from that shown in this agreement and will also upon demand furnish to the Seller such further information and will execute and deliver to the Seller such financing statements and other documents and will do all such acts and things as the Seller may at any time or from time to time reasonably request or as may be necessary or appropriate to establish and maintain a perfected security interest in the Goods as security for the Obligations, subject to no adverse liens, or encumbrances. A carbon, photographic or other reproduction of this agreement is sufficient as a financing statement.

3. To the extent that full insurance coverage is not provided for in the schedule of charges comprising the Total of Payments as shown on the reverse hereof, Buyer will purchase and at all times maintain insurance on the Goods which, together with any insurance coverage provided for on the reverse hereof will insure against risks of loss or damage by collision, fire (including so-called extended coverage), theft and such other casualties as the Seller may reasonably require, all in such amounts, under such forms of policies, upon such terms, for such periods, and written by such companies or underwriters as the Seller may approve, losses in all cases to be payable to the Seller and the Buyer as their interests may appear. All policies of insurance shall provide for at least ten days' prior written notice of cancellation to the Seller, and the Buyer shall furnish the Seller with certificates of such insurance or other evidence satisfactory to the Seller as to compliance with the provisions of this paragraph. The Seller may act as attorney for the Buyer in making, adjusting and settling claims under and cancelling such insurance and endorsing the Buyer's name on any drafts drawn by insurers of the Goods.

4. The Buyer will keep the Goods free from any adverse lien, security interest or encumbrance and in good order and repair, will not waste or destroy the Goods or any part thereof and will not use the Goods in violation of any applicable statute, ordinance or policy of insurance thereon. The Seller may examine and inspect the Goods at any reasonable time or times wherever located. In no event, shall injury or destruction of the Goods release the Buyer from his obligations hereunder.

5. The Buyer will pay promptly when due all taxes and assessments upon the Goods or for its use or operation or upon this agreement.

Additional Rights of Parties. The Buyer authorizes the Seller, in its discretion, to discharge taxes, liens or security interests or other encumbrances at any time levied or placed on the Goods; to place and pay for insurance thereon upon failure by the Buyer, after having been requested so to do, to provide insurance satisfactory to the Seller; to order and pay for the repair, maintenance and preservation thereof; and to pay any necessary filing or recording fees. To the extent permitted by applicable law, the Buyer agrees to reimburse the Seller on demand for any payment made or any expenses incurred by the Seller pursuant to the foregoing authorization. Until default the Buyer may have possession of the Goods and use the same in any lawful manner not inconsistent with this agreement. If dual interest insurance on the Goods is provided for and a separate charge therefor is included in the Total of Payments as shown on the reverse hereof, Seller shall within 30 days after execution of this agreement send, or cause to be sent, to the Buyer the policy or certificate of insurance clearly setting forth the terms of such insurance.

Events of Default — Remedies. Upon the occurrence of any of the following events or conditions, namely: (i) default in the payment or performance of any of the Obligations or of any covenant or liability contained or referred to herein; (ii) any warranty, representation or statement made or furnished to the Seller by or on behalf of the Buyer in connection with this agreement proving to have been false in any material respect when made or furnished; (iii) loss, theft, substantial damage, destruction, sale or encumbrance to or of the Goods, or the making of any levy, seizure or attachment thereof or thereon; (iv) or death, insolvency, business failure, appointment of a receiver of any part of the property of, or assignment for the benefit of creditors by, the Buyer; — thereupon, or at any time thereafter (such default not having previously been cured), the Seller at its option may declare all of the Obligations to be immediately due and payable and shall then have the remedies of a secured party under the Uniform Commercial Code of Illinois (subject to the Retail Installment Sales Act of Illinois or Motor Vehicle Retail Installment Sales Act, or other applicable law), including, without limitation thereto, the right to take immediate and exclusive possession of the Goods and for that purpose the Seller may, so far as the Buyer can give authority therefor, enter upon any premises on which the Goods may be situated and remove the same therefrom if this can be done without breach of the peace (provided that if the Goods are affixed to real estate, such removal shall be subject to the conditions stated in the Uniform Commercial Code of Illinois); and the Seller shall be entitled to hold, maintain, preserve and prepare the Goods for sale, until disposed of, or may propose to retain the Goods subject to Buyer's right of redemption, in satisfaction of Buyer's Obligations, as provided in the Uniform Commercial Code of Illinois and the Retail Installment Sales Act of Illinois or Motor Vehicle Retail Installment Sales Act. Seller may require Buyer to assemble the Goods and make them available to Seller for its possession at a place to be designated by Seller which is reasonably convenient to both parties. Unless the Goods are perishable or threaten to decline speedily in value or are of a type customarily sold on a recognized market, Seller will give Buyer reasonable notice of the time and place of any public sale thereof or of the time after which any private sale or any other intended disposition thereof is to be made. The requirements of reasonable notice shall be met if such notice is mailed, postage prepaid, to the address of Buyer shown at the beginning of this agreement at least ten (10) days before the time of the sale or disposition. Seller may buy at any public sale and if the Goods are of a type customarily sold in a recognized market or are of a type which is the subject of widely distributed standard price quotations, he may buy at private sale. The net proceeds realized upon any such disposition, after deduction for the expenses of retaking, holding, preparing for sale or lease, selling, leasing and the like and the reasonable attorney's fees and legal expenses incurred by Seller and to which he shall be entitled, shall be applied in satisfaction of the Obligations secured hereby. The Seller will account to the Buyer for any surplus realized on such disposition and the Buyer shall remain liable for any deficiency. The remedies of the Seller hereunder are cumulative, and the exercise of any one or more of the remedies provided for herein or under the Uniform Commercial Code of Illinois shall not be construed as a waiver of any other remedies of Seller so long as any part of the Buyer's Obligations remains unsatisfied. All rights and remedies under this agreement are subject to applicable bankruptcy law.

General. This agreement and the security interest in the Goods and all additions and accessions thereto created hereby shall terminate and title therein shall vest in the Buyer only when all Obligations have been paid in full. No waiver by the Seller of any default shall be effective unless in writing nor operate as a waiver of any other default or of the same default on a future occasion. All rights of the Seller hereunder shall inure to the benefit of its successors and assigns; and all obligations of the Buyer shall bind the heirs, legal representatives, successors and assigns of the Buyer. If there be more than one Buyer, their obligations hereunder shall be joint and several. If Goods are not delivered to Buyer at time of execution of this contract, the identifying number of marks of the Goods or similar information and due date of first installment may be inserted in Seller's counterpart of this contract after it has been signed by Buyer.

If any provision of this agreement shall be prohibited by or invalid under applicable law, such provision shall be ineffective to the extent of such prohibition or invalidity, without invalidating the remainder of such provision or the remaining provisions of this agreement.

ASSIGNMENT

FOR VALUE RECEIVED, the Seller hereby sells, assigns and transfer to ______________________________

____

its successors and assigns, all right, title and interest in, to and under the foregoing agreement and in and to the Goods therein described, with authority to take either in its own name or in the name of the Seller, but for its own benefit, all such proceedings, legal, or equitable, as the Seller might have taken but for this assignment.

The Seller hereby warrants that the foregoing agreement represents a valid retail installment contract as provided under the laws of the State of Illinois and

that the Total of Payments shown due in the agreement is correct and remains unpaid ______________________________

____

and is the valid obligation of the Buyer; that the Buyer is the purchaser of the Goods in good faith, that his true name is signed to the foregoing agreement, and that all parties to this instrument have legal capacity to contract; that the agreement and all accompanying agreements and other documents submitted herewith are genuine in all respects and what they respectively purport to be; that to the best of Seller's knowledge all statements of fact contained in the agreement are true; that the description of the property is adequate to enforce the rights created therein; that the Goods were delivered and accepted by the Buyer in good faith and satisfactory condition, and that at the time of execution of the agreement Seller acquired good title to the Goods and the right to transfer such Goods free and clear of any adverse interest therein; that Seller's security interest is a perfected security interest; that Seller has no knowledge of any facts which would impair the validity of the agreement or other accompanying agreements and documents or render them less valuable or valueless; and that he knows of no defense to the payment of the Obligations of the Buyer thereunder, or counterclaims, or set-offs; that the down payment was made in full in cash or by trade-in as described and that no portion of the down payment is owing by separate note or open account.

The Seller hereby waives all demands and notices of default and consents that without notice to Seller, the assignee may extend time to or compound or release, by operation of law or otherwise, any rights against Buyer or any other obligor under said agreement.

The Seller hereby assumes to take any steps necessary to preserve any rights of the assignee or otherwise in the foregoing agreement or any accompanying agreements or documents against prior parties, and the assignee shall not be bound to take any steps to preserve such rights.

The Seller agrees that if any warranty or representation contained in this assignment should prove to be untrue or incorrect in any material respect when made, the Seller will upon demand of the assignee, at its election, accept a reassignment of the agreement or repurchase the property and in either event pay therefor the amount unpaid thereon, plus costs and expenses including reasonable attorney's fees incurred by the assignee in attempting to enforce the agreement.

______________________________, 19______ ______________________________
Seller

By ______________________________

The loan application interview should be conducted in a way that reduces any reluctance an applicant may have about providing information about personal finances and credit history. While completing the loan application, the applicant must be provided an ECOA Notice. The interview is also an excellent opportunity to cross-sell other services.

The application form provides important information about borrower characteristics. The application typically requests the purpose of the loan and personal information, as well as information about employment, assets, liabilities, credit references, real estate owned, insurance and collateral. It also provides space for the applicant's permission to investigate and verify the information provided.

In determining which parts of the application require verification, loan officers must consider the need for timely credit processing and decision making. Even so, speedy processing must not be substituted for a thorough investigation. Information about the applicant's character and capacity may be verified by institution files and records, other lenders, employers, financial statements and credit reporting agencies. Reporting agencies use three basic types of credit reports: in-file reports, trade reports and special reports. For secured loans, the ownership and value of the collateral is usually verified from title reports and certificates of title registration.

The credit approval decision is made only after credit risk has been analyzed. Risk analysis involves an evaluation of credit information, such as the applicant's payment history, income and employment. Three objective tools used to quantify the credit risk decision are the debt-to-income ratio, the loan-to-value ratio and credit scoring systems. A credit scoring system objectively evaluates applicant information to determine credit worthiness according to empirical evidence.

Lenders must notify an applicant of the credit decision within 30 days after the receipt of the application. An adverse action is a denial of credit. Lenders must notify an applicant as to the reasons for any adverse actions and provide a list of the credit sources used.

A consumer credit transaction financed through a dealer usually involves a retail installment contract. A dealer may then assign or sell the rights in these contracts to a third party, such as a lending institution. With indirect loans, consumer loan officers do not have the opportunity to interview applicants. However, credit investigation and loan approval may be performed in several ways. The best arrangement is the one that results in cost effective and timely credit processing for the institution.

CHAPTER QUESTIONS

1. Why is it important to match an applicant's loan needs to the most appropriate loan that falls within an institution's loan policies?

2. Define the six Cs of credit and relate the information requested on an application to four characteristics of the borrower.

3. How is a face-to-face interview beneficial for both the loan applicant and the loan officer?

4. Briefly explain how and why personal credit information should be verified.

5. List seven warning signals of possible fraud.

6. Compare and contrast three ways of analyzing debt.

7. Under what circumstances must an adverse action be given to an applicant?

8. What does a lender look for when evaluating a dealer's management?

9. For what should a dealer's products be investigated?

10. Under what conditions is full recourse dealer paper usually purchased? Describe a lender's considerations before doing so.

FOOTNOTE

[1] *Federal Guide*, Consumer Protection Unit, Regulations Section, Section 202.6.

6

Establishing and Perfecting Security Interest in Collateral

Objectives

After studying this chapter, you should be able to:
- ☐ Differentiate among consumer goods, motor vehicles and negotiable instruments used as collateral;
- ☐ Explain how an institution can establish a security interest in collateral;
- ☐ Describe and explain the importance of the procedures an institution must follow to perfect a security interest in collateral by filing a financing statement;
- ☐ Outline the conditions that must exist before attachment can occur;
- ☐ Differentiate perfection by filing from perfection by possession and automatic perfection;
- ☐ Give examples of problems that may arise when an institution takes a security interest in instruments or negotiable documents;
- ☐ Explain the difference between perfecting a security interest in a motor vehicle and perfecting a security interest in an appliance or television set; and
- ☐ Differentiate between the concepts of attachment and perfection as they relate to security interest in collateral.

INTRODUCTION

Savings institution employees involved in consumer lending activities should understand the principles and practices surrounding loans secured by collateral. A lender's right to seize collateral to satisfy a debt is defined by the laws of secured transactions. Although these laws can be extremely complex, the underlying principles and everyday practices required to protect a lender's rights in collateral are not difficult to understand.

This chapter focuses on how a lending institution can protect its right to obtain collateral if a borrower defaults. Before this happens, an institution must be certain that it has established an enforceable right against the borrower and that this right has attained priority over any rights to the same collateral by other creditors. Failure to properly establish and record such rights can either prevent the institution from taking possession of collateral or make another creditor's rights in the collateral superior to those of the institution.

LOANS SECURED BY COLLATERAL

Loans secured by collateral are loans in which the borrower has agreed to turn over a specific asset, such as an automobile, to the lender if the borrower fails to repay the loan as stipulated in the loan document. Collateral is something of value given or pledged as security for a debt or obligation. If the collateral is an automobile, boat or other item of tangible personal property, the lender generally does not take possession at the time the loan is made. In most cases, the asset that is pledged as security was purchased by the borrower with the loan proceeds. The borrower usually wants to use this asset and, therefore, retains possession. As long as the borrower continues to make timely loan payments, he or she will retain possession. However, if the borrower stops making payments and the lender has sufficient cause to believe that the loan will not or cannot be repaid, the lender may assert its claim against the asset by physically taking possession and selling the asset to satisfy the remaining debt.

Secured loans may represent less of a credit risk than unsecured loans, but this is not necessarily the case. Although secured loans give the lender an added measure of safety, any loan is only as good as the individual borrower's willingness and ability to pay. Some borrowers have excellent credit ratings and strong financial positions. Loans to borrowers with excellent credit ratings are generally very secure whether made on a secured or unsecured basis. Other borrowers may have only marginal qualifications or may be weak in one area of the important Cs of borrowers' characteristics (character, capacity and capital). Thus, to qualify for a loan, a borrower with marginal qualifications may be required to furnish collateral.

Sometimes secured loans are made to borrowers who would not qualify for an unsecured loan of the same amount. For instance, suppose that Christine Rose wants to borrow $10,000 to purchase a recreational vehicle. A lending institution might be willing to lend her the money to purchase a new RV if she agrees to offer the vehicle as collateral. However, the institution might not be willing to grant her a $10,000 unsecured loan. Therefore, in many cases the collateral is what qualifies the borrower for the loan.

If a secured loan goes into default (that is, the borrower either cannot or will not pay), the only remaining source of repayment is the collateral. This is collateral's major importance and the reason why an institution's right to the collateral must be clear. An institution that does not properly protect its right to seize and sell collateral in satisfaction of a debt may suffer material loan losses as a result. Therefore, a lending institution should properly establish and make public its claim to the collateral in which it has obtained rights as security for a consumer loan.

Limitations of Using Collateral for Repayment

Although having rights in collateral may lessen the risk of loss to a lender if default occurs, it does not completely eliminate this risk. When a borrower fails to repay a loan, an institution has the right to seize any collateral to which it has been granted a security interest and may then begin liquidation proceedings. To liquidate collateral means to sell it. The proceeds from the sale are then applied to the outstanding loan balance and related expenses; any remaining amounts must be returned to the borrower.

The process of seizing and liquidating collateral is expensive, however. Repossession agencies, companies that specialize in seizing collateral, are expensive to hire. Furthermore, once the collateral is seized, attempts must be made to find a buyer, and this, too, is expensive. As a result, in consumer lending, the proceeds generated by the liquidation of collateral are seldom large enough to fully satisfy both the remaining debt and the expenses incurred while disposing of the collateral. Thus, collateral cannot be viewed as a primary source of repayment; a lender typically will seize and liquidate collateral only as a last resort when all other options have been exhausted.

When a lender extends a loan on the strength of collateral, it neither expects nor wishes to take possession to liquidate it. Although the primary source of loan security is still the borrower's character, capacity and capital, collateral is taken to impress upon the borrower the necessity of repaying the loan, to give the borrower an added incentive (or added pressure) to repay and to minimize the loss to the institution upon default. Therefore, collateral is actually viewed as a secondary source of repayment that may reduce a loan loss but usually will not prevent one. Thus, an institution is wise to place high importance on determining whether the collateral is adequate security for the loan.

Determining Collateral Adequacy

Before concerning itself with protecting its rights in collateral, a lender must first decide whether to accept a given piece of collateral. In many instances, the collateral offered, or proposed, by a borrower may be insufficient for one or more reasons.

Before accepting any given asset as collateral, four major characteristics of the asset must be established:
- its condition and identification;
- its value;
- its ownership; and
- whether or not any prior liens are held against it.

First, the collateral should be properly identified, by serial or vehicle identification number if possible, and viewed to see that it is in good condition. Second, a lender should be certain that the collateral possesses sufficient value to secure the debt and to cover any collection costs that may be incurred if the borrower defaults on the loan. Ideally, the value should be high enough to cover debt, liquidation costs, legal fees, etc. and still provide a cushion for depreciation. The latter is especially important with consumer loans because personal property, the most common type of collateral for consumer loans, often is subject to rapid and steady depreciation. If the value of the collateral drops below the outstanding debt balance, the institution faces the possibility of a material loss, and the borrower may lose the incentive to continue making payments. Information on fair market values for a given collateral may be readily available, as in the case of automobiles, or it may be more difficult to obtain, (jewelry, for example), in which case the collateral will require appraisal by experts. Whatever method is used, obtaining an accurate valuation is necessary.

The third asset characteristic that must be determined is whether the borrower actually owns the collateral offered as security. A lender cannot obtain rights in collateral that is not legally owned by the borrower. Ownership is more difficult to determine for personal property than it is for real estate. In real estate lending, determining ownership poses no great problem because all states have statutes and regulations that govern the recording of deeds (representing ownership) that must be filed in the appropriate government offices for public inspection. Furthermore, mortgage lenders can purchase title insurance to protect themselves against the possibility of accepting collateral that is not actually owned by the borrower.

Unfortunately, determining ownership interest is not so simple when it comes to personal property. Although certain types of personal property, like motor vehicles and aircraft, require certificates of title to verify ownership, most types do not. Nor is title insurance generally available to lenders when they accept personal property as collateral.

A lending institution can use several methods to verify the borrower's ownership of collateral. For instance, if the asset being offered as collateral is already owned by the applicant and is not being purchased with the loan funds, certificates of title can be verified for items covered under such statutes. These statutes mainly apply to motor vehicles, aircraft, and, in some states, mobile homes and boats. For items not covered by these statutes, the lender often must rely on the applicant's honesty, integrity and moral character when attempting to ascertain ownership.

Finally, before a lending institution decides to accept collateral, the institution should determine that there are no prior liens or encumbrances existing against that collateral. A lien or *encumbrance* is a right given by law to retain the property of another for the purpose of securing a debt. A *lien holder*, then, holds the right to seize the property of a delinquent debtor, liquidate that property and use the proceeds to satisfy the unpaid debt. Since collateral sold in this manner rarely generates enough cash to completely erase the debt balance and associated collection costs, many lenders do not accept collateral that is already subject to another creditor's lien or encumbrance.

Therefore, a loan officer must know how to search for existing liens or encumbrances on proposed collateral. A good place to start is in the appropriate central filing office for a given state. Outstanding prior liens (liens that currently exist) are kept on file in this central office, along with applicable certificates of title.

Certain liens, however, may not show up in the public records. For example, a lien in which a retailer is automatically granted first rights in a consumer good that it has financed through an installment sales contract is commonly known as a *purchase money security interest*. This type of lien becomes effective immediately upon sale. A dealer is not required to file this claim in a public office.

Purchase money security interests are sometimes referred to as "secret liens," since there is no public record of their existence. In these cases, the retail dealer is automatically granted first rights in the collateral involved. For instance, assume a customer purchases a refrigerator worth $800 from a retail department store and agrees to pay for it according to the terms of an installment contract drawn up by the store. In this instance, according to provisions of the Uniform Commercial Code (UCC), the store will automatically be granted first rights in the refrigerator. This means that if the customer fails to make installment payments as stipulated in the agreement, the store will have the right to take physical possession of the refrigerator to satisfy the remaining debt.

First rights exist regardless of any other claims by subsequent lenders. For instance, assume that the customer has purchased the refrigerator and entered into an installment agreement with the store. A week later, the same customer obtains a consumer loan from a lending institution with that institution being granted a security interest in the refrigerator as collateral. If the borrower were to default on both of these debt obligations, the retail department store would be given the first opportunity to repossess the refrigerator. Since the store would almost certainly do so, the lending institution would be left with a loss.

Sometimes a search of public records will not turn up evidence of any "secret liens." Fortunately, an unfiled purchase money security interest is effective only for consumer goods with a value of $2,500 or less. All claims to collateral with a value of more than $2,500 must be filed in a central filing office in order to attain priority over the rights of subsequent creditors.

As a practical matter, institutions usually lend money to consumers to purchase large-ticket items such as automobiles, boats or recreational vehicles. There is little danger of any "secret liens" existing on these types of collateral both because of the price level and because the loan proceeds are usually used directly for the purchase of the specific piece of collateral involved.

A consumer lender should never assume that no prior liens exist on the collateral. Because of the complexity of the law surrounding secured transactions, even an honest borrower may not now that a lien exists on the proposed collateral. Consequently, an independent verification of prior liens is warranted. Creditors with existing claims to collateral may include other financial institutions; retail merchants; or governmental units. Also, the consumer lender should examine federal tax lien files, since federal tax liens can have priority over all claims to personal or real property.

Searching for prior liens and encumbrances can be difficult, but a thorough search of the public records by an experienced person will uncover most prior liens. Since many institutions will not accept collateral that is encumbered by a prior lien, these searches are usually indispensable. If a records search indicates that the proposed collateral is encumbered, the lender generally will ask for other collateral that is not subject to any prior liens or encumbrances.

To summarize, before deciding whether to accept a given piece of collateral, an institution should ascertain that:
- the borrower is credit worthy;
- the collateral has been properly identified and is in good condition;
- the collateral value is sufficient to secure the debt;
- the borrower's ownership interest in the collateral has been confirmed; and
- no prior liens have been placed against the collateral.

Once these factors have been substantiated, the institution can decide whether to accept or reject the proposed collateral. If the collateral is accepted, the lender must then properly establish its interest in the collateral and assure the enforceability of this interest against the borrower in a court of law.

ESTABLISHING A VALID SECURITY INTEREST

The process by which a lender makes its claim to collateral legally enforceable is referred to as establishing a valid security interest in collateral. A *security interest* is an interest in collateral that secures payment or performance of an obligation. This process is governed by the rules and regulations stipulated in Article 9 of the Uniform Commercial Code. Under Article 9, to create a valid security interest in collateral, the debtor and creditor must enter into a security agreement; they must reduce the agreement to writing; and the debtor must sign the agreement and, in some cases, give possession of the collateral to the creditor.

A *security agreement* is a document that represents a transfer of property from a borrower to a creditor given in fulfillment or satisfaction of a debt. The exact nature of the security agreement will vary, depending on the type of collateral being secured. However, a typical security agreement identifies the creditor and the borrower and contains a description of the collateral. Additionally, the terms and conditions of the agreement and any special provisions required by state or federal statutes are listed.

The security agreement will not create an enforceable right unless attachment occurs. An *attachment of security interest* is the obtainment of the secured party's rights in the collateral. In a secured transaction, attachment makes the security interest enforceable against the borrower. Generally, three conditions must be met to create attachment.

- The borrower must have signed a written security agreement describing the collateral. In the case of stocks, bonds, certificate accounts and other negotiable instruments, a "pledge arrangement" may be substituted for the security agreement. A *pledge arrangement* exists when the borrower has transferred actual possession of these instruments to the lender. However, even

when a pledge agreement is executed, a written security agreement setting forth the terms and conditions of the loan should also be executed.
- The institution—the secured lender—must give "value" to the borrower. Usually, this means that the lender has agreed to make a binding commitment to loan money or extend credit.
- The borrower must have "rights" in the collateral. Generally, this means that the borrower must own the collateral or have obtained some legal right to it.

When the above conditions are fully met, attachment occurs and the security interest becomes enforceable against the borrower.

However, attachment usually makes the security interest enforceable only against the borrower—not against claims of other lenders, creditors or trustees in bankruptcy. Attachment, then, is only half the battle. A lending institution, once it has established a valid, enforceable security interest in collateral against the borrower, must next seek to protect that interest from claims made against the same collateral by other competing lenders and creditors. This second protection is acquired through perfecting a security interest.

PERFECTING SECURITY INTEREST

Perfecting security interest helps a lender protect its rights in the collateral against the competing claims of third parties. An example of a time when this is very important to a lender is when a borrower files for bankruptcy. *Perfection of security interest* is the act of obtaining priority over claims of third parties. The secured interest is thus protected from court appointed trustees in bankruptcy. Perfection insures that the lender's rights in the collateral will have priority over the rights of subsequent creditors and third parties.

The following example explains why perfection is necessary.

Lee Michaels is a consumer debtor who has just filed for bankruptcy. Michaels owes creditors $75,000, and his only personal asset is an expensive sports car worth $30,000. The creditors include a savings institution that loaned Michaels $25,000 to purchase the vehicle and that has a perfected security interest in the vehicle as of April 15; a consumer finance company that loaned Michaels $25,000 for personal use and that has established a valid security interest in the vehicle by entering into a security agreement with Michaels on April 4; and various other creditors whom Michaels owes $25,000 collectively. Which party, if any, will receive any money?

Based on the information given in this example, only the savings institution will get anything. Since it has a properly perfected security interest in the sports car, a bankruptcy court will award it the vehicle. The institution will then be able to sell the vehicle for satisfaction of the remaining debt. Assuming the proceeds of the sale do not exceed the remaining debt, the institution will keep it all. Because the consumer finance company did not perfect its security interest, its rights in the collateral became secondary to those of the savings institution. If the finance company had perfected its security interest before the savings institution did, it would have been given first right to the sports car. The various other creditors, since they have no security interest in the vehicle, would only get money if the proceeds from the sale of the vehicle exceeded the remaining debt balances of both the savings institution and the consumer finance company.

This situation illustrates the importance of perfecting security interest in collateral. As shown, the date that a security agreement was entered into is irrelevant in determining priorities for rights in collateral. The determining factor is the date a security interest is perfected.

Occasionally, two lending institutions issue loans to a borrower and take as collateral the same specific item. As long as the borrower continues to repay the loan on a timely basis, no difficulties will develop. But if the borrower goes into default, only one institution will have the first right to seize the collateral. Since proceeds from the sale of collateral seldom cover the full cost associated with even one loan default, the question of who gets first chance to take possession becomes critical. Establishing a valid security interest, including attachment, only protects a lender against the borrower, not necessarily against the competing claims of other creditors.

Two, three or more valid security interests may be established in the same piece of collateral by several creditors. However, this situation rarely arises because lenders normally use collateral that is subject to certificate of title laws (automobiles, boats, recreational vehicles, aircraft) that require the lienholder to be noted on the title. If a search of the public records turns up a prior lienholder, a lender will usually not accept the collateral. Additionally, if stocks and bonds are accepted as collateral, the institution will usually take physical possession of these securities until the loan is paid.

Perfecting security interest in collateral insures that a lender's security interest, or lien, is protected against those of other creditors. The term "perfected" is taken from federal bankruptcy statutes and in effect means that a security interest is protected from a borrower's trustee in bankruptcy. Therefore, when an institution perfects security interest in collateral, it is protecting its claim against trustees in bankruptcy as well as establishing prior claim over subsequent creditors and third parties in the event a borrower defaults. Third parties can include purchasers who have knowledge of the unperfected security interest, as well as other lending institutions, creditors and a debtor's trustee in bankruptcy.

This action is important because a *trustee in bankruptcy* can be a formidable opponent to a secured creditor. When bankruptcy is declared, a court can appoint a trustee in bankruptcy who generally acts as a special representative of all creditors, but who also serves the interests of unsecured creditors. In fact, one of the trustee's most important functions is to maximize the recovery by unsecured creditors. To achieve this end, the trustee is given the status of a *perfected lien creditor* in all of the debtor's property as of the date the bankruptcy petition is filed. This means that the trustee can gain priority over all security interests and other liens that were not properly perfected as of the bankruptcy filing date. Therefore, a lender should be certain to perfect its security interest in collateral before a debtor has the opportunity to file a bankruptcy petition.

METHODS OF PERFECTING SECURITY INTEREST

The UCC allows three methods for perfecting security interest in collateral. Perfection may be achieved by filing a financing statement in the appropriate central filing office or by having the secured party take physical possession of the collateral. Or, perfection may occur "automatically" upon attachment.

The particular circumstances surrounding the transaction and the nature of the collateral involved will determine the method used.

Perfection by Filing a Financing Statement

The most important and commonly used method of perfection is the filing of a financing statement in the appropriate public office as designated by state law. A *financing statement* is a document filed at a designated public office that serves as a public notice to third parties that a creditor has established a security interest in some collateral. The financing statement, which provides the identities and mailing addresses of the borrower and creditor, also includes a description of the collateral. Most filings are done on the standard financing statement, called the UCC-1 (see Figure 6-1).

Once a lending institution files this statement, that institution attains priority over the rights of subsequent creditors in the same collateral. Claim priority is established at the date of filing—hence, if two or more institutions establish a valid security interest in the same collateral and a financing statement is required, the institution that files the financing statement first will usually achieve top priority in the collateral—regardless of which institution was first to establish the security interest.

A financing statement must not be confused with a security agreement. Generally, a financing statement may not be substituted for a proper security agreement, and both documents are normally required to properly establish and perfect an institution's rights in collateral.

Before filing a financing statement, an institution must become familiar with its own state's version of Article 9 of the UCC. By examining Article 9, an institution can find information on where to file, when to file and the consequences of erroneous filings.

Where to File

The state government normally designates the proper filing office. Some states prefer a centralized filing system, while others prefer a local filing system. Generally, central filing is with the secretary of state and local filing is with the county registrar of deeds, county clerk and/or recorder. If there is

FIGURE 6-1
Financing Statement—Form UCC-1

George E. Cole® Legal Forms, reprinted by permission of Boise Cascade Corporation.

uncertainty about the proper place to file, institutions should file more than one financing statement to insure that security interest is perfected.

When to File

A financing statement may be filed before, after or at the time the loan proceeds are disbursed. Because claim priority over subsequent creditors dates from the time of filing, however, an institution may wish to file before the loan proceeds are disbursed. But, a note of caution should be taken when filing before loan disbursement. The financing statement should accurately describe the nature of the transaction, but the amount of indebtedness should not be specified since it may change prior to loan disbursement. An incorrect amount could result in a portion of the loan remaining unsecured.

Normally, a time lag exists between the effective date of the financing statement search and the date upon which the new creditor's financing statement is filed. Hence, another creditor may file a financing statement during this lag period without the knowledge of the savings institution. For example, a savings institution conducts a search of the public records and finds no financing statement encumbering a piece of collateral. The search is effective through May 10. Accordingly, the institution agrees to accept the collateral and establishes a valid security interest in it. The loan proceeds are immediately disbursed and a financing statement is subsequently filed on May 15. Unknown to the institution, another creditor filed a financing statement against the same collateral on May 11. As a result, the savings institution does not have first priority in the collateral.

This risk can be eliminated by filing a financing statement before the loan proceeds are disbursed and by determining that no other financing statements were filed during the lag time. Filing after the loan proceeds have been disbursed is generally not advisable.

Erroneous Filings
Due to the complexities of many state rules and regulations that govern the filing of financing statements, sometimes an institution may unknowingly file a financing statement in the wrong place. For instance, an institution may file a financing statement in a central filing office, such as the office of the secretary of state, when it should have filed in a local or county office. If the secured lender files in the wrong place, however, its rights in the collateral still may be perfected as against the rights of other competing parties. The UCC provides that a filing made in good faith in an improper place "is still effective with regard to any collateral as to which the filing was correct, and with regard to collateral covered by the financing statement against any person who has knowledge of the contents of such financing statement."

The first part of the rule stated above is the easier one, legally. If a lender takes a security interest in construction equipment and farm equipment and properly files a financing statement with the secretary of state, the interest is perfected for the construction equipment even if a local filing is required for the farm equipment. In this case, the security interest in the construction equipment will achieve priority over claims of subsequent third parties. However, a subsequent creditor may achieve priority in the farm equipment by filing a financing statement in the local filing office if he or she filed in good faith and had no knowledge of the incorrect filing. Thus, the original filer has priority only in the collateral that was filed properly and has priority in the incorrectly filed collateral only if the subsequent creditor has knowledge of the existence of this improperly filed security interest.

The second part can be more complicated legally, depending on the circumstances. Generally, however, if a lender files centrally when the lender should have filed locally and if a competing creditor discovers the financing statement in a search of the central records, the improper local filing is clearly perfected as against this creditor. Additionally, if a competing creditor has received a copy of the improperly filed financing statement from the filing officer or someone else, the erroneous filing should probably also be effective.

Legal difficulties arise when the competing third party never sees the improperly filed financing statement but learns of the existence of the competing security interest. Which party has priority? The courts are split on this issue. Some cases hold that mere knowledge of the existing security interest makes the improper filing effective, even though the competing creditor never saw the actual financing statement. Other cases find the filing ineffective, citing that more specific knowledge is required.[1]

Perfecting Security Interest in Personal Property

Perfection of security interest in personal property, such as a motor vehicle, is generally accomplished by noting the lienholder on the certificate of title. All lienholders must be noted on the certificate of title to perfect a security interest in motor vehicles. Perfection by filing a financing statement alone is not sufficient.

The method of perfecting security interest in marine craft will vary depending on how this property is classified by state statutes. In many states, marine craft are classified as vehicles, and, as such, are subject to certificate of title laws.

Perfection is accomplished by noting the institution's lien on the certificate of title and filing it with the appropriate state or local government office, just as for other vehicles. However, in some states, marine craft are considered consumer goods. In that event, perfection can still be achieved easily. For instance, if the loan proceeds are to be used to buy marine craft, a purchase money security interest arises and perfection becomes automatic. As long as the value of the craft is under $2,500, a financing statement need not be filed. However, if the craft's value is over $2,500, or if the loan proceeds are not to be used to purchase the collateral, then a financing statement must be filed.

Security interest in aircraft is perfected by filing. The filing requirements for aircraft are subject to federal regulations, and filing occurs at the federal level at the Federal Aviation Administration (FAA) in Oklahoma City.

The methods for perfecting security interest in mobile homes vary depending on how the homes are classified by individual state statutes. Mobile homes may be classified as motor vehicles, consumer goods, fixtures, or, in some states, real estate if fixed to real property.

If a mobile home is classified as a motor vehicle, perfection is completed according to state certificate of title statutes. If a mobile home is considered a consumer good, perfection is accomplished either automatically or by filing a financing statement. If a mobile home is treated as a fixture, a financing statement must be filed. Finally, if a mobile home is classified as real estate, perfection is generally accomplished by recording a mortgage instrument with the appropriate county officer, usually the county clerk or recorder. A *mortgage instrument* is a document that represents a conveyance of real property offered as security for a debt. When recording, an institution should indicate whether the instrument is a first or second mortgage. In the case of a second, or junior, mortgage, the lender's rights in the property are subordinate to the claims of the first mortgage holder.

In many instances, a mortgage instrument will contain a future advances clause. This allows a lender to advance additional funds without executing a new mortgage instrument. In this case, perfection would be accomplished by noting the amount of the new debt on the original mortgage instrument.

Perfection is effective for a period of five years from the date of filing. It will automatically lapse at this time unless a continuation statement is properly filed. The continuation statement is a document that extends perfection for an additional five years from the last date on which the initial filing was effective. It lists the original file number and states that the original statement is still in effect.

Perfection by Possession

The oldest form of perfecting a security interest involves taking possession of the collateral. In fact, security interest in money or other negotiable financial instruments (stocks, securities, etc.) can only be perfected by the secured party taking possession.

Financial instruments held in this way generally include stocks, bonds, checks, drafts, notes, certificates of deposit and other items representing a right to monetary payment. As previously discussed, a pledge arrangement must exist to create an enforceable security interest against the borrower. This pledge arrangement may be evidenced by a written security agreement or by the mere physical transfer of the instruments to the secured party (or its agent).

In addition to a security agreement or pledge, an institu-

> Mr. Rogers, a consumer debtor, borrows $1,000 each from two friends, Bob and Jim, to be repaid in six weeks. Mr. Rogers agrees to give Bob $200 as collateral and does so. Jim does not ask for collateral. Six weeks later, Mr. Rogers notifies both creditors that he cannot and will not repay the debts. Bob, therefore, applies the $200 in his possession to the loan and realizes a loss of $800. Jim realizes a loss of $1,000 and has no claim to the $200 in Bob's possession.
>
> The same principle generally holds true when lending institutions are given possession of money or instruments as collateral for a loan. Here, too, perfection is accomplished by possession.

tion normally executes two other documents: a power to hypothecate and a collateral receipt. (see Figures 6-2 and 6-3). A *power to hypothecate* represents a pledge of stocks, bonds or other financial instruments to a lender without transfer of title. If an institution holds collateral in its possession, a *collateral receipt* also must be issued. This document serves as evidence to a borrower that the creditor has physical possession of the collateral. The Uniform Commercial Code does not define "possession." However, the length of time a security interest is perfected extends from the time of actual possession and continues as long as possession is retained.

A security interest in instruments generally may be perfected without filing and by taking possession within a certain number of days from the time security interest attaches. The number of days varies from state to state, but a common number of days is 21. In effect, if possession of instruments takes place within this 21-day period from the time the loan is made and the security agreement is signed, interest is perfected as of the date the loan is made. Thus, the institution is protected from other creditors and trustees in bankruptcy during this prescribed period. However, if during this 21-day grace period the borrower sells the instruments to a purchaser who is unaware of the pledge to the institution (bona fide purchaser), the purchaser has priority over the institution. In addition, if the borrower pledges the instruments to a competing creditor during this period, and the competing creditor takes possession and a security agreement is signed, the competing creditor will probably have priority over the institution. The competing creditor in this case is also considered a bona fide purchaser.

Automatic Perfection

In some instances, for certain kinds of collateral, perfection occurs automatically upon attachment. *Automatic perfection* happens when a creditor takes a purchase money security interest in collateral that is classified as a consumer good.

The UCC treats consumers and consumer goods differently from the way it treats businesses and assets used for business purposes. Difficulty distinguishing between a consumer good and a business asset often exists because these

FIGURE 6-2
Hypothecation Authorization

HYPOTHECATION AUTHORIZATION
(Securing All Present and Future Liabilities of Debtor)

To: _____   Date _____, 19___

    The undersigned hereby authorizes _____
(herein called "Debtor") to hypothecate, pledge and/or deliver the securities described below belonging to the undersigned, and the undersigned agrees that when so hypothecated, pledged and/or delivered said securities shall be collateral to secure any present or future indebtedness, obligation or liability howsoever evidenced, owing by Debtor to you, or any extension or renewal thereof, hereby consenting to the extension, or renewal from time to time of any such indebtedness, obligation or liability, and waiving any notice of any such indebtedness, obligation, liability, extension or renewal.

    The undersigned further agrees that said securities shall be subject to disposition in accordance with the terms and conditions of the instruments evidencing such indebtedness, obligation and liabilities, and/or the direction of Debtor and further authorizes you at any time and from time to time to transfer said securities, or any thereof, into your name or into the name of any nominee of yours, without disclosing, if you so desire, that the same are pledged or hypothecated, and without any indication, if you so desire, on any new certificate or other document issued to evidence such securities, or any thereof that such securities are pledged or hypothecated, and any corporation or association, or any of the managers or trustees of any trust, issuing any of said securities, or its or their transfer agent, shall not be bound to inquire, in the event that you or said nominee makes any further transfer of such securities, or any thereof, as to whether you or your nominee has the right to make such further transfers, and shall not be liable for transferring the same.

    This agreement shall be binding upon the undersigned and the heirs, personal representatives, successors and assigns of the undersigned, and shall inure to your benefit and the benefit of your successors and assigns.

In Presence of _____

                                              Signature

                                              Signature

42571-0 (1/82)
Hypothecation Agreement   SAF Systems and Forms

---

items may actually be the same. For instance, a television set in the hands of a consumer is considered to be a consumer good. However, that same television set in the hands of a retail dealer is considered inventory, a business asset. Often, the classification of a particular item will depend on the intent of the user. For instance, if a retail dealer in television sets purchases one on credit for his own personal use, then that

FIGURE 6-3
Collateral Receipt

particular set is considered to be a consumer good for that specific transaction. The automatic perfection provisions of the UCC apply only to consumer goods purchased by consumer borrowers.

A common example of automatic perfection occurs when a retail dealer sells a consumer an appliance on an installment contract. The dealer retains a security interest in the appliance and perfection is automatic upon attachment. This would also hold true if the consumer obtained a direct loan from an institution to purchase the appliance. The institution would retain a security interest in the appliance and perfection would be complete upon attachment.

The Uniform Commercial Code provides for automatic

> A customer executes a written security agreement in support of a $10,000 loan from a lending institution on May 1. The collateral consists of stocks and bonds that the customer promises to deliver to the institution within one week. Instead, the customer sells and delivers the stock certificates to a bona fide purchaser 10 days after the loan was issued, on May 11. In this case, the bona fide purchaser, who had no knowledge of the pledge, would retain possession. Similarly, if the customer instead of selling the stock certificates, had pledged and delivered them to another lender, that lender would retain possession. Hence, a lending institution should make certain it obtains possession of collateral within the prescribed grace period specified by state law before disbursing loan proceeds.

perfection of certain types of collateral for several reasons. Primarily, the automatic perfection provision reflects the opinion that consumers are usually aware that when they purchase consumer goods on an installment basis they are doing so on a secured basis. In addition, automatic perfection eliminates the cost and inconvenience of filing financing statements for a large number of small-ticket goods.

An automatic perfection carries risks to a lending institution. For instance, if a purchase money security interest is taken in consumer goods, and automatic perfection is relied upon, the consumer borrower could sell the collateral to another consumer. This buyer would retain possession and ownership if he or she bought without knowledge of the institution's "secret lien," paid the current market value, and used the item for personal, family or household purposes. This holds true only if the purchaser buys without knowledge of the security interest and before a financing statement is filed. This reiterates the necessity for a lender to file a financing statement.

Another problem may arise if the institution makes a mistake relating to the intended use of the collateral. For example, if automatic perfection is relied upon to perfect a security interest in a television set, the institution must be certain that the borrower intends to use that set for personal or household use. If the borrower uses the set in his or her business office, the collateral may be considered "equipment" rather than "consumer goods." In this case, the perfection would not be automatic and the institution would be left with an unperfected security interest in equipment.

Finally, if an institution makes a loan to a consumer to purchase furniture or appliances, but the loan proceeds are used for another unauthorized purpose (to purchase a used car, for example), the institution cannot rely on automatic perfection because it does not have a true purchase money security interest. By not filing a financing statement, the institution would be left with an unperfected security interest, and, should bankruptcy occur, priority would be given to the trustee in bankruptcy.

If the institution does not file a financing statement and wants to rely on automatic perfection, it must be certain that any check written for loan proceeds is made payable to the retail dealer as well as to the consumer. The institution might require that the loan proceeds be paid directly to the seller and that the seller sign a receipt. Or, the borrower might be required to produce a canceled check, paid invoice or bill of sale as evidence of purchase. Additionally, a signed, written statement by the seller indicating that title has passed to the buyer would be especially useful.

Occasionally, a borrower will offer a lender as collateral consumer goods that he or she already owns, such as appliances, furniture or television sets. In these cases, a direct inquiry to the debtor's seller is probably the only way to be certain that the collateral is not subject to any prior unfiled purchase money security interests.

Another problem may arise when a lender advances funds to the borrower to acquire proposed collateral, and the funds represent only a portion of the purchase price. In this instance, the lender should be certain that the balance of the purchase price comes directly from the borrower and that no other lender becomes involved. Otherwise, another lender may acquire a purchase money security interest in the same collateral.

Other surprises can also arise. For instance, a purchase money security interest in collateral is generally considered valid for 20 days after the borrower takes possession, and perfection relates back to the date of the security agreement if the financing statement is filed prior to the expiration of the 20-day period. Although a financing statement is not required for perfection, if one is filed during this 20-day period, then perfection becomes effective as of the date of the security agreement. Thus, if there is reason to believe that the proposed collateral has been acquired recently by the borrower, the lender would want to make sure that possession was obtained by the borrower more than 20 days prior to the issuance of any loan funds. Also, the filing of a financing statement should be effected prior to the loan disbursement.

ATTACHMENT VS. PERFECTION

The concepts of attachment and perfection are different. Attachment establishes a valid security interest in collateral that is enforceable against the borrower. Perfection, on the other hand, affects only an institution's rights in collateral against other competing creditors, good faith purchasers or trustees in bankruptcy.

For example, consider a situation in which a consumer lending institution issued a loan to a borrower to purchase a new motorcycle. A security agreement was properly executed and the conditions for attachment were met, but the institution failed to get its lien noted on the certificate of title. Subsequently, when the borrower skipped town with the new motorcycle, the loan officer recommended that the institution not seek him out because of the failure to note the lien. The loan officer thought that this omission left the institution without any enforceable security interest in or right to the motorcycle. However, since the security interest had already attached, the failure to perfect only affected the institution's rights against competing third parties. But in this situation, there were no other creditors, good faith purchasers or trustees in bankruptcy who had laid claim to the motorcycle. The failure to perfect had no bearing whatever against the borrower, and the institution had every legal right to seek out and take possession of the vehicle.

In a similar case, another lender forgot that it had rights to the collateral even in the absence of perfection. In this case, a savings institution made a direct purchase money loan to enable a borrower to buy a fancy sports car. The borrower executed a security agreement with the institution. The dealer to whom the loan proceeds check was payable expressly agreed to see that the institution had a "recorded first lien" on the certificate of title. However, the dealer failed to do this, and the dealer's name was mistakenly shown as the lienholder. When the borrower skipped town, the institution assumed it had no rights in the vehicle and sued the dealer for breach of contract in failing to get the proper lien noted on the title.

Since there was no indication of any competing third-party claims against the sports car, failure to perfect was not a problem; the institution's security interest would have been enforceable against the debtor irrespective of the certificate of title. The institution may not have had perfection, but it had enforceability under Article 9 of the UCC. Therefore, since the dealer's breach of contract did not cause the institution's injury, the lawsuit was dismissed. Knowing how to differentiate between attachment and perfection can mean the difference between loan recovery and loan loss.

PERFECTING SECURITY INTEREST WHEN MAKING INDIRECT LOANS

Generally, when an institution makes an indirect loan through a dealer, the dealer prepares all documents necessary to satisfy compliance with statutes and institution loan underwriting standards. In addition, the dealer is usually responsible for perfecting security interest in collateral. The method used by the dealer to perfect security interest is the same as if an institution were perfecting interest itself, that is, by filing a financing statement, certificate of title or taking possession of instruments.

If a dealer initially has no intention of selling a retail installment contract to a third party, perfection will occur in the dealer's name. However, should the dealer later decide to sell the contract to a third party, perfection of the security interest will transfer automatically to the third party. No additional filing is necessary on the part of the third party.

Regardless of whether an institution has an ongoing affiliation with a dealer or customarily buys retail installment contracts from dealers, the institution should carefully check all documents and dealer procedures to assure that perfection has taken place. An institution should never assume that the dealer has completed this important procedure.

TERMINATING THE FINANCING ARRANGEMENT

After a financing arrangement has been terminated and when a borrower has no further obligations to a secured creditor, the creditor, upon written request of the borrower, is obligated to send a termination statement to the borrower. A termination statement indicates that the creditor no longer has a security interest in the collateral. If the collateral is a consumer good, the secured party is obligated to file a termination statement with the filing officer within one month after the loan is repaid or within 10 days of the borrower's demand.

A secured lender may also file a statement of release of any collateral covered in the original filing. This usually involves only a partial release, and the statement must contain a description of the collateral being released, the names and addresses of the borrower and lender, and the file number of the financing statement. The statement need be signed only by the secured party.

SUMMARY

Typically, lenders accept collateral to reduce the risk of loss from loan default. Although collateralized loans represent a reduced risk, lenders must protect their interests in collateral to justify the lower interest rates they charge for secured loans. In addition, failure to protect one's rights in collateral can lead to a loss of rights or loss of priority in that collateral. This is important since collateral values are seldom sufficient to cover the costs of even one loan default.

For this reason, collateral should not be viewed as a primary source of repayment; instead, it should be considered as an extra measure of safety that will serve to reduce any loan loss resulting from default. Thus, collateral is more appropriately viewed as a secondary source of repayment.

Before accepting collateral, a lending institution should do four things to determine whether the collateral is adequate. First, the collateral should be properly identified and viewed, if necessary, to determine that it is in good condition. Identification should be specific, and each item should be described separately. Second, the collateral value should be determined. Ideally, this value should be high enough to cover the loan balance and any associated collection costs. Also, the projected depreciation in value should be considered. Third, it should be ascertained that the borrower actually owns the collateral, since a lender cannot establish a claim to collateral unless the borrower owns it. Fourth, a search of the appropriate central filing offices is required to determine if any prior liens or encumbrances have been placed against the proposed collateral. Many lenders will not accept collateral that is subject to prior liens.

Once collateral is accepted, the lender's next task is to create an enforceable right or claim to the collateral against the borrower. This is achieved by establishing a valid security interest in the collateral and is effected by entering into a security agreement with the borrower. Upon attachment, the security interest becomes enforceable. Attachment generally occurs when the borrower signs a written security agreement describing the collateral, the lender gives value to the borrower and the borrower has rights in the collateral.

An established security interest enforceable against the borrower (i.e., attachment) does not protect a lender's rights in collateral against the rights of other creditors in the same collateral. To assure top priority among creditors in the event of default or bankruptcy, the institution must perfect its security interest against certain purchasers, creditors and trustees in bankruptcy. A perfected security interest protects the lender against competing claims of third parties, most notably, the trustee in bankruptcy. A bankruptcy trustee immediately takes first priority in all assets not subject to a perfected security interest at the moment a bankruptcy petition is filed.

There are several methods of perfecting a security interest, depending on the nature and type of collateral involved. The most common form of perfection is to file a financing statement in the appropriate public filing office. Before filing a financing statement, an institution must become familiar with its state's version of Article 9 of the UCC, which governs these matters. By examining Article 9, an institution can determine where and when to file and the consequences of an erroneous filing. Generally, an institution should file prior to the disbursement of the loan proceeds.

Another method of perfection is achieved by possession. This is usually done for cash or monetary instruments and requires the creation of a pledge arrangement between the lender and borrower.

A third method of perfection, usually effected by a purchase money security interest in collateral, is referred to as automatic perfection. Automatic perfection becomes effective upon attachment, but an institution should still file a financing statement. If no financing statement is filed, a "good faith" purchaser who is not aware of the "secret lien" takes priority and retains possession in most cases.

In indirect loans, perfection is usually accomplished by the dealer. However, institutions should check to insure that perfection has taken place. When buying dealer paper in which a financing statement has been filed in the dealer's name, no further filing is necessary; the perfected security interest is automatically transferred at the time of purchase.

The concepts of attachment and perfection are different. Attachment creates an enforceable right against a borrower; perfection protects a lender's rights in collateral against competing claims of third parties.

When a financing arrangement is terminated, a termination statement should be sent to the borrower upon request. Such a statement is mandatory if the collateral is considered to be a consumer good. A lender may also file a statement of release of any collateral covered by the original filing.

CHAPTER QUESTIONS

1. Differentiate between a secured loan and an unsecured loan. Which type of loan represents a reduced credit risk and why?

2. Does collateral guarantee repayment of a loan? Why?

3. Why must an institution inspect the certificate of title before accepting a motor vehicle as collateral?

4. A borrower pledged personal property as collateral for a

consumer loan at a savings institution. It was later learned that the property belonged to an unrelated third party. What rights does the institution have in this collateral? Why?

5. After identifying the proposed collateral, what four things should be ascertained before it is accepted by a savings institution?

6. Differentiate between an established security interest and a perfected security interest. Which would give a higher level of comfort to a lending institution?

7. What is a financing statement? Detail the requirements needed to make a financing statement effective. For what types of collateral must a financing statement be utilized?

8. Compare and contrast the methods of filing, possession and automatic perfection as they relate to perfecting a security interest in collateral. Give examples of the types of collateral associated with each method.

9. A savings institution accepts common stock certificates as collateral for a consumer loan. What is necessary for attachment to occur? What documents, if any, should be executed by the institution?

10. A borrower pledges common stock certificates to a savings institution as collateral for a consumer loan. Before the institution takes possession, and during the 21-day grace period, the borrower pledges the same certificates to a commercial bank as collateral for another consumer loan. The bank, unaware of the previous pledge to the savings institution, takes physical possession of the certificates. Which lender has priority? Why?

11. What is meant by the term "bona fide purchaser"? Can a lending institution be considered one? What rights can a bona fide purchaser acquire in a savings institution's collateral and under what circumstances?

12. What is a security agreement? Detail the requirements to make it effective against a borrower.

FOOTNOTE

[1]The Law of Secured Transactions Under The Uniform Commercial Code by Barkley Clark; Warren, Gorham and Lamont, 1980.

7

Document Preparation and Loan Closing

Objectives

After studying this chapter, you should be able to:
- ☐ Outline the provisions of a promissory note, and explain the importance of the provisions;
- ☐ Describe the truth-in-lending disclosures commonly found on a promissory note;
- ☐ Identify and describe the forms for perfecting security interest;
- ☐ Differentiate between first and junior mortgage instruments;
- ☐ Name three internal consumer loan forms;
- ☐ State the purpose of loan closing activities; and
- ☐ Explain three ways in which loan proceeds can be disbursed.

INTRODUCTION

A major responsibility of a consumer lending operation is the accurate execution of all the documents required for an approved loan. Before loan proceeds can be disbursed, the proper documents must be completed, the borrower's authorization obtained and the lender's interest in any collateral secured. Many consumer credit department personnel are involved in these tasks.

All consumer credit department personnel, especially those who actually prepare loan documents, should be aware of the purpose and use of the basic documents needed to complete a loan file. Although the structure and wording of many documents will vary according to state law, the major documents contain similar provisions. The various documents also require similar information about the borrower, the loan amount, the loan terms and the collateral.

Chapter 7 presents a number of the more typical consumer loan documents that comprise a consumer loan file. The promissory note is a statement of a borrower's promise to repay a loan. Every loan has some form of promissory note. In addition, the security interest in the collateral securing a loan must be perfected by filing or recording documents with the appropriate agency to establish the lender as lienholder. When personal property such as motor vehicles, aircraft or household appliances are used as collateral, a lender completes the required forms or gathers the necessary information and forwards it to the appropriate government agency. When real property is used as collateral (for equity and home improvement loans), a mortgage instrument (or deed of trust) must be completed and recorded with the appropriate government office.

Each lender has its own set of internal forms that need to be completed to establish a new loan record. Forms for entering borrower information on a computer system (for both on-line and off-line systems) also need to be carefully completed. If a coupon payment system is used, the borrower must be issued a coupon book. In addition, institutions often send form letters to new borrowers to welcome them to the institution.

All documents and internal forms may be prepared in advance of a loan closing. Loan proceeds are disbursed when the borrower signs the documents and receives copies of them. Funds are disbursed in various ways depending upon whether the loan is direct or indirect. Internal forms are usually prepared before closing, but are not dispatched until after closing in order to avoid unnecessary work should the borrower happen to change his or her mind about the loan.

PROMISE TO REPAY

After analyzing a borrower's credit risk and approving an application, the lender requires the borrower or co-borrowers to sign a written promise to repay the loan. This written promise is a *promissory note*, also called a note or installment note. The note serves as evidence of the borrower's debt and renders the borrower and only the borrower personally liable for repayment.

The promissory note states the loan amount and describes the terms and any other conditions that may apply to repayment. Its exact wording may vary from lender to lender and from state to state and may depend upon the type of credit that is being granted. However, most notes will have only slight variations in their wording. The note includes an acknowledgement of indebtedness, a promise to repay, a description of the repayment method, an acceleration clause, a description of late charges, a prepayment clause, other general provisions, the purpose of the loan, and a section for the signature of the borrower or borrowers (see Figure 7-1). No note is needed with indirect loans, since retail installment contracts carry similar provisions and perform the same functions as a note.

The *acknowledgement of indebtedness* is a statement that identifies both the borrower and the lender and recognizes their debtor/creditor relationship. All co-borrowers are identified because they, too, are obligated to repay the debt both jointly and individually. Since a lender can collect payment from any co-borrower, all parties must be named in this section. The addresses of all borrowers along with the name and address of the lender and the date and place of the transaction also appear here.

The *promise to repay clause* is a statement in which the borrower agrees to repay and to be liable for the debt. For closed-end loans, this section lists the sum of money lent to the borrower and describes how the amount will be repaid.

FIGURE 7-1, Side 1
Promissory Note

NOTE

...., 19......... ....,................................
  [City]   [State]

....
[Property Address]

1. BORROWER'S PROMISE TO PAY
In return for a loan that I have received, I promise to pay U.S. $................................ (this amount is called "principal"), plus interest, to the order of the Lender. The Lender is .... I understand that the Lender may transfer this Note. The Lender or anyone who takes this Note by transfer and who is entitled to receive payments under this Note is called the "Note Holder."

2. INTEREST
Interest will be charged on unpaid principal until the full amount of principal has been paid. I will pay interest at a yearly rate of .... %.
The interest rate required by this Section 2 is the rate I will pay both before and after any default described in Section 6(B) of this Note.

3. PAYMENTS
(A) Time and Place of Payments
I will pay principal and interest by making payments every month.
I will make my monthly payments on the .... day of each month beginning on ...., 19......... I will make these payments every month until I have paid all of the principal and interest and any other charges described below that I may owe under this Note. My monthly payments will be applied to interest before principal. If, on ...., ..., I still owe amounts under this Note, I will pay those amounts in full on that date, which is called the "maturity date."
I will make my monthly payments at ....
.... or at a different place if required by the Note Holder.
(B) Amount of Monthly Payments
My monthly payment will be in the amount of U.S. $................................

4. BORROWER'S RIGHT TO PREPAY
I have the right to make payments of principal at any time before they are due. A payment of principal only is known as a "prepayment." When I make a prepayment, I will tell the Note Holder in writing that I am doing so.
I may make a full prepayment or partial prepayments without paying any prepayment charge. The Note Holder will use all of my prepayments to reduce the amount of principal that I owe under this Note. If I make a partial prepayment, there will be no changes in the due date or in the amount of my monthly payment unless the Note Holder agrees in writing to those changes.

5. LOAN CHARGES
If a law, which applies to this loan and which sets maximum loan charges, is finally interpreted so that the interest or other loan charges collected or to be collected in connection with this loan exceed the permitted limits, then: (i) any such loan charge shall be reduced by the amount necessary to reduce the charge to the permitted limit; and (ii) any sums already collected from me which exceeded permitted limits will be refunded to me. The Note Holder may choose to make this refund by reducing the principal I owe under this Note or by making a direct payment to me. If a refund reduces principal, the reduction will be treated as a partial prepayment.

6. BORROWER'S FAILURE TO PAY AS REQUIRED
(A) Late Charge for Overdue Payments
If the Note Holder has not received the full amount of any monthly payment by the end of .... calendar days after the date it is due, I will pay a late charge to the Note Holder. The amount of the charge will be .... % of my overdue payment of principal and interest. I will pay this late charge promptly but only once on each late payment.
(B) Default
If I do not pay the full amount of each monthly payment on the date it is due, I will be in default.
(C) Notice of Default
If I am in default, the Note Holder may send me a written notice telling me that if I do not pay the overdue amount by a certain date, the Note Holder may require me to pay immediately the full amount of principal which has not been paid and all the interest that I owe on that amount. That date must be at least 30 days after the date on which the notice is delivered or mailed to me.
(D) No Waiver By Note Holder
Even if, at a time when I am in default, the Note Holder does not require me to pay immediately in full as described above, the Note Holder will still have the right to do so if I am in default at a later time.
(E) Payment of Note Holder's Costs and Expenses
If the Note Holder has required me to pay immediately in full as described above, the Note Holder will have the right to be paid back by me for all of its costs and expenses in enforcing this Note to the extent not prohibited by applicable law. Those expenses include, for example, reasonable attorneys' fees.

7. GIVING OF NOTICES
Unless applicable law requires a different method, any notice that must be given to me under this Note will be given by delivering it or by mailing it by first class mail to me at the Property Address above or at a different address if I give the Note Holder a notice of my different address.
Any notice that must be given to the Note Holder under this Note will be given by mailing it by first class mail to the Note Holder at the address stated in Section 3(A) above or at a different address if I am given a notice of that different address.

MULTISTATE FIXED RATE NOTE—Single Family—**FNMA/FHLMC UNIFORM INSTRUMENT**   Form 3200 12/83
44601 SAF SYSTEMS AND FORMS
CHICAGO, IL

George E. Cole® Legal Forms reprinted by permission of Boise Cascade Corporation.

FIGURE 7-1, Side 2
Promissory Note

> **8. OBLIGATIONS OF PERSONS UNDER THIS NOTE**
> If more than one person signs this Note, each person is fully and personally obligated to keep all of the promises made in this Note, including the promise to pay the full amount owed. Any person who is a guarantor, surety or endorser of this Note is also obligated to do these things. Any person who takes over these obligations, including the obligations of a guarantor, surety or endorser of this Note, is also obligated to keep all of the promises made in this Note. The Note Holder may enforce its rights under this Note against each person individually or against all of us together. This means that any one of us may be required to pay all of the amounts owed under this Note.
>
> **9. WAIVERS**
> I and any other person who has obligations under this Note waive the rights of presentment and notice of dishonor. "Presentment" means the right to require the Note Holder to demand payment of amounts due. "Notice of dishonor" means the right to require the Note Holder to give notice to other persons that amounts due have not been paid.
>
> **10. UNIFORM SECURED NOTE**
> This Note is a uniform instrument with limited variations in some jurisdictions. In addition to the protections given to the Note Holder under this Note, a Mortgage, Deed of Trust or Security Deed (the "Security Instrument"), dated the same date as this Note, protects the Note Holder from possible losses which might result if I do not keep the promises which I make in this Note. That Security Instrument describes how and under what conditions I may be required to make immediate payment in full of all amounts I owe under this Note. Some of those conditions are described as follows:
>
> **Transfer of the Property or a Beneficial Interest in Borrower.** If all or any part of the Property or any interest in it is sold or transferred (or if a beneficial interest in Borrower is sold or transferred and Borrower is not a natural person) without Lender's prior written consent, Lender may, at its option, require immediate payment in full of all sums secured by this Security Instrument. However, this option shall not be exercised by Lender if exercise is prohibited by federal law as of the date of this Security Instrument.
> If Lender exercises this option, Lender shall give Borrower notice of acceleration. The notice shall provide a period of not less than 30 days from the date the notice is delivered or mailed within which Borrower must pay all sums secured by this Security Instrument. If Borrower fails to pay these sums prior to the expiration of this period, Lender may invoke any remedies permitted by this Security Instrument without further notice or demand on Borrower.
>
> WITNESS THE HAND(S) AND SEAL(S) OF THE UNDERSIGNED.
>
> ....(Seal)
> -Borrower
>
> ....(Seal)
> -Borrower
>
> ....(Seal)
> -Borrower
>
> *[Sign Original Only]*

The description includes the number of payments and the amount of each payment. Also included are the date of the first and subsequent payments and the number of days in the year used to calculate interest. Recall that lenders may choose to compute interest on the basis of a 360 or 365 day year; borrowers are entitled to know this when they accept the loan. If this basis for determining interest is not already preprinted, a blank is provided for the lender to fill in.

Since open-end loans do not involve specific sums, fixed loan amounts and repayment figures cannot be determined at the time credit is granted. The amount of each loan transaction varies according to the borrower's use of the loan account. Since the borrower is approved for a line of credit with a specified maximum, however, the borrower's original promise is to repay all amounts pertaining to this line of credit. The minimum monthly payment amount and the due date are included. Also, a description is given of how the amount of the monthly payment is determined. If a minimum transaction amount is established (generally for overdraft protection or check credit), this amount is also listed.

An *acceleration clause* states the lender's right to demand full payment of the debt in the event of default. To prevent problems later, default should be defined to the fullest extent. Events of default might include a missed due date, the death of the borrower, the borrower's written admission of inability to repay or bankruptcy. An acceleration clause is important when a borrower's behavior appears to reflect no intention of making further payments. Invoking this clause allows the lender to begin full collection procedures immediately.

Lenders may assess a late or default charge for payments that are made after the specified payment date (due date) stated in the promise to repay section. The late charge may be a percentage of the payment amount or a fixed fee. All of the conditions involving the assessment of late charges should be described in the note.

Sometimes lenders grant a grace period, a period of time (number of days) after the due date during which no late charge is assessed if the borrower makes a payment. For payments made after the grace period, the borrower must pay a late charge. If there is a grace period, its terms will be specified on the note. At times, a borrower may think that if there is a grace period, it is not necessary to pay on the due date and that merely paying within the grace period is acceptable. This is not true. Lending personnel should stress that payments are to be made on the due date and that after a certain date a late charge will be assessed.

A *prepayment clause* in the note lists any fees the lender may charge for full or partial prepayment. Full prepayment means the loan is paid off in advance of the maturity date; partial prepayment refers to one or several payments made before their due dates. With add-on loans, partial prepayment does not entitle the borrower to a rebate of interest, while full prepayment does. With simple interest loans, both full and partial prepayments reduce the total interest charged. Rebates of insurance premiums are generally only given with full prepayment.

In accepting prepayments, the lender incurs the additional operating costs of computing the reduced interest amount or rebate and recording the prepayment transaction, all of which are nonroutine procedures. Some states allow these costs to be passed along to the borrower through fees or penalties while other states do not permit prepayment fees or penalties.

In addition to covering additional operating costs, prepayment fees are meant to discourage borrowers from paying off a high interest rate loan to obtain a loan at a lower rate. For example, a borrower is granted an automobile loan for three years at 15% interest. In the second year, when the interest rates are lowered to 10%, the borrower prepays the 15% loan and applies for another loan at 10%. The process of approving and setting up new loan accounts is costly to the lender. Thus fees are established, where state laws and market conditions permit, to discourage loan turnover due to decreased interest rates.

Lenders set forth other terms and conditions pertaining to the debt in the general provisions section. This section will usually have a statement that insures the borrower's liability for the debt even if future changes are made to alter the original note. For variable rate loans, this section might include a statement of the lender's right to modify terms and conditions of the note in the future. All conditions or rights that a lender describes in the general provision section must be in accordance with applicable laws and regulations, of course.

The purpose of the loan section describes how the borrower intends to use the loan proceeds. Since regulations allow institutions to make consumer loans only for personal, family or household purposes, institutions may require the borrower to attest to the intended purpose of the loan. The purpose of the loan also indicates the type of loan granted to the borrower and dictates other regulations with which the lender must comply. Either the lender or the borrower completes this section of the application form. The borrower must sign it.

The final section of the note has a place for the signatures of all borrowers and the date the note is signed. If the loan is secured by collateral, the note may contain a brief description of the collateral and may mention the existence of a security agreement. (Security agreements are covered later in this chapter.) Borrowers should sign and date the note in the same manner that they sign the security agreement and other loan documents.

If the borrower's promise to pay is secured by a guarantor, the guarantor should sign the note and execute a guarantor's statement. (As you read in Chapter 3, whenever such a guarantor or cosigner is required by the lender, the lender must give the co-signer proper notice.) A guarantor's statement indicates that in exchange for a loan to the borrower from the lender, the guarantor promises full and prompt payment of the loan in the event the original borrower defaults. The guarantor also may be liable for legal fees resulting from the lender's attempt to collect payment. The statement outlines the conditions under which payment is expected from the guarantor. The guarantor is required to sign and date this completed agreement.

TRUTH-IN-LENDING DISCLOSURES

Under the Truth-in-Lending Act (see Chapter 3), lenders are required to disclose certain information to loan applicants. To save time in preparing documents, many lenders include the disclosures as part of the note. The Act requires that any disclosures that are included in the note be grouped together and be clearly separated from other material. This separation is achieved by putting these disclosures in boxes, sometimes referred to as "federal boxes." As of April 1, 1982, Regulation Z requires that the annual percentage rate (APR), finance charge, amount financed and total of payments be presented separately (see Figure 7-2).

Disclosures must be written in language that is easily understood by the borrower, that is, in "simple English." Simple English documents may describe the finance charge as "the dollar amount the credit will cost you" and the annual percentage rate as "the cost of your credit as a yearly rate." The total of payments is described as "the amount you will have paid after you have made all payments as scheduled."

Certain costs are specifically excluded from finance charges. For example, costs that are the same for a cash purchase and a credit purchase are not considered finance charges. Sales taxes and license or registration fees are specific instances. If the charge in a credit transaction exceeds the charge imposed in a comparable cash transaction, only the difference is a finance charge. Suppose, for example, that an escrow agent is used in both cash and credit sales of real estate, and that the agent's charge is $100 in a cash transac-

FIGURE 7-2
Federal Truth-in-Lending Disclosure Statement

FEDERAL TRUTH-IN-LENDING DISCLOSURE STATEMENT

ANNUAL PERCENTAGE RATE The cost of your credit as a yearly rate.	FINANCE CHARGE The dollar amount the credit will cost you.	Amount Financed The amount of credit provided to you or on your behalf.	Total of Payments The amount you will have paid after you have made all payments as scheduled.
_____ %	$ _____	$ _____	$ _____

You have the right to receive at this time an itemization of the Amount Financed.
☐ I want an itemization.   ☐ I do not want an itemization.

Your payment schedule will be:

Number of Payments	Amount of Payments	When Payments are Due
	$	
	$	
	$	

☐ This obligation has a demand Feature.   ☐ **Required Deposit:** The annual percentage rate does not take into account your required deposit.

Security: You are giving a security interest in:
☐ the goods or property being purchased   ☐ _____

Filing fees $ _____   Non-filing insurance $ _____

Late Charge: If payment is _____ late, you will be charged $ _____ / _____ % of the payment.

Prepayment: If you pay off early, you may be entitled to a refund of part of the finance charge.

See the Note and Security Agreement documents for any additional information about non-payment, default, any required repayment in full before the scheduled date, and prepayment refunds and penalties.

e means an estimate

---

tion and $150 in a credit transaction. Here, only $50 is a finance charge in the credit transaction.

Another possible exclusion is insurance. Premiums or other charges for insurance protecting the lender against the borrower's default or other credit loss are part of the finance charge only if the lender requires such insurance. The insurance section states whether or not the lender requires the borrower to obtain credit life or credit disability insurance. When lenders require insurance, they must comply with the following three conditions.

> A reminder: The finance charge is the cost of credit expressed as a dollar amount. It includes any charge that is payable directly or indirectly by the consumer and that is imposed directly or indirectly by the lender as an incident to or a condition of the extension of credit.

- The premium must be shown as a finance charge and be included in the APR.
- The insurance requirement must be unilateral, uniformly applied, very clear and nondiscriminatory.
- The lender cannot require the borrower to buy the insurance from the lender.

Premiums for credit life, accident and health or loss of income insurance may be excluded from the finance charge if the following three conditions are met.

- The lender does not require insurance coverage as a condition of the extension of credit and discloses this fact.
- The premium for the initial term of insurance is disclosed, and if the term of insurance is less than the length of the loan, the term of insurance is also disclosed.
- The borrower signs or initials and dates a written request for the insurance after receiving the required disclosures and being informed of the added cost.

Lenders are not required to itemize the amount financed unless the customer requests this breakdown. However, as a customer service, it is a good idea to do so.

Because the note is a legal contract, it is essential for it to be completed correctly and neatly. It need not be typed although many notes are. Whether it is handwritten or typed, any changes or corrections must be initialed by *both* the lender and the borrower.

DOCUMENTS FOR LOANS SECURED BY PERSONAL PROPERTY

In addition to the promissory note, all loans secured by personal property require documentation of the property and the lender's security interest in it. In this context, personal property includes stocks and bonds, motor vehicles, aircraft, or household furniture and appliances. For each type of personal property used as collateral, a different form is completed and a different set of procedures followed for perfecting security interest. This section explains the responsibilities of the filing officer and the necessary follow-up actions for documenting security interest in both direct and indirect loans.

Responsibilities of the Filing Officer

Filing is official at the time the financing statement and appropriate filing fee are presented to and accepted by the filing officer. Upon presentation of the financing statement, the filing officer assigns it a file number and marks the number, date and hour of filing on the statement. In addition, the filing officer examines the statement for errors. Common errors include the omission of signatures and/or addresses, collateral descriptions and fixture descriptions for real estate. If the filing officer finds errors, he or she will reject the financing statement. Rejections alert secured parties to correct any errors before their security interests can be perfected. As you read in the previous chapter, lenders who do not perfect their security interests may lose their collateral to other claiming creditors. Once approved, a copy of the statement with the date and time of filing is given to filers so they have a clear record of their priority claim to collateral.

As noted, filing fees are due when the financing statement is presented. Every state's version of Article 9 of the Uniform Commercial Code contains a list of the required filing fees. It is important that fee payments are for the appropriate amount because perfection is not realized without this consideration.

After the financing statements have been presented and the appropriate fees paid, the statements are filed alphabetically and stored for public inspection. A third-party searcher, for instance, might personally inspect the files and obtain

> In an actual case a bank tendered a check for $4.50 when the appropriate fee was $6.00. The filing officer returned the check two years after it was presented. In the meantime, the borrower filed for bankruptcy, and the bank lost the collateral to the trustee. The court's ruling was that, even though the filing officer improperly kept the check for two years, the bank erred more seriously in submitting an insufficient amount. If the tender had been proper and the only error had been on the part of the filing officer, then the filing would have been official and the bank's interests protected.

either a certificate showing other creditors who have filed against the borrower or copies of previously filed statements (a fee is generally charged for these copies). If searchers feel that they need more information than is found on a financing statement, they may contact the creditor whose name appears on the financing statement.

Security Agreement

As you read in Chapter 6, the security agreement establishes the lender's security interest in the personal property given as collateral for a secured loan. The Uniform Commercial Code specifies that the security agreement must contain the debtor's signature and a description of the collateral. Since some of the standard clauses on the security agreement are identical to the clauses on the promissory note, the two documents can be combined on a single form (see Figure 7-3).

The security agreement identifies the borrower and the lender and describes both the collateral and the debt secured by the collateral. The debt secured by the collateral is expressed by the loan amount and loan terms. If a separate security agreement is used, mention is made of the existence of the promissory note, which, in turn, mentions the security agreement.

The collateral description should be as complete and precise as possible. The ways of describing collateral vary with the type of collateral. A vehicle description generally includes the type of item (automobile, airplane or boat); year, make and model; mechanical features (number of cylinders, motor size); physical characteristics (color, body style); serial numbers; vehicle capacity; and a description of any options (power steering, power brakes). A description of household goods generally covers the type of item (refrigerator, dining room set), the manufacturer's name, the serial number, and other physical characteristics. A description of stocks or bonds refers to the type, the name of the issuing company or agency, the par value and the interest rate. A description of a deposit account or certificate of deposit includes the type and the number of the account and the name of the depository institution.

Along with a physical description of collateral, the note and security agreement also asks for the location of collateral.

FIGURE 7-3
Installment Note and Security Agreement

INSTALLMENT NOTE AND SECURITY AGREEMENT

Loan No. ____________
Date ____________, 19____

In this Note and Security Agreement the words, YOU, YOUR and YOURS mean anyone who signed it. WE, OUR and US mean

You promise to pay To repay our loan, you promise to pay us $____________(U.S.) plus interest at the rate of ________per cent per year. You will pay this amount in ________ consecutive ☐ **monthly** ☐ ____________ **(other mode of payment)** installment(s) of $____________each and a final installment of $____________. Your payment(s) will begin on ____________, 19____, and continue on the same day of each consecutive installment period until your loan is paid in full. Annual interest will be calculated on the basis of a ____________day year and charged for the actual number of days elapsed. The amount of the FINANCE CHARGE and the final installment shown below is based on all payments being made on the due date. Early payments will reduce your interest charge but late payments will increase it.

Collateral for Your loan ☐ Your loan is unsecured.

As collateral for your loan you grant us a security interest in the following goods or property: (Check all boxes that apply)

☐ Vehicle (against which we will place a lien)

☐ motor vehicle ☐ farm equipment ☐ boat ☐ airplane ☐ motorcycle ☐ recreational vehicle

New/Used	Year, Make and Model	No. Cyl.	Body Style	Manufacturers' Serial Number	Color	Ignition Number

☐ Auto Trans. ☐ Power Steering ☐ Power Locks ☐ Bucket Seats ☐ AM/FM Stereo ☐ Sun Roof
☐ 4-Speed ☐ Power Brakes ☐ Cruise Control ☐ Leather Seats ☐ Tape Deck ☐ T-Top
☐ Diesel Engine ☐ Power Seats ☐ Air Conditioning ☐ Vinyl Top ☐ Rear Defogger ☐ ________

☐ Your Household Goods (against which we will place a lien) listed below: ____________

☐ Other types of collateral such as savings or certificate accounts, stocks, and bonds (which we will take possession of) listed below: ____________

Collateral Address The collateral will be kept at the following address: ____________

Insurance Credit life insurance and credit disability insurance are not required to obtain credit, and will not be provided unless you sign below and agree to pay the additional cost.

Type	Premium	Term	Signature
Credit Life	$		I want to apply for credit life insurance. Signature ________
Credit Disability	$		I want to apply for credit disability insurance. Signature ________
Credit Life and Credit Disability	$		I want to apply for credit life and disability insurance. Signature ________

FEDERAL TRUTH-IN-LENDING DISCLOSURE STATEMENT

ANNUAL PERCENTAGE RATE The cost of your credit as a yearly rate.	**FINANCE CHARGE** The dollar amount the credit will cost you.	Amount Financed The amount of credit provided to you or on your behalf.	Total of Payments The amount you will have paid after you have made all payments as scheduled.
%	$	$	$

You have the right to receive at this time an itemization of the Amount Financed.

☐ I want an itemization. ☐ I do not want an itemization.

Your payment schedule will be:

Number of Payments	Amount of Payments	When Payments are Due
	$	
	$	
	$	

☐ This obligation has a demand Feature. ☐ **Required Deposit**: The annual percentage rate does not take into account your required deposit.

Security: You are giving a security interest in:
☐ the goods or property being purchased ☐ ____________
Filing fees $ ________ Non-filing insurance $ ________

Late Charge: If payment is ________late, you will be charged $ ________/ ________% of the payment.

Prepayment: If you pay off early, you may be entitled to a refund of part of the finance charge.

See the Note and Security Agreement documents for any additional information about non-payment, default, any required repayment in full before the scheduled date, and prepayment refunds and penalties.
e means an estimate

Repossession We will also have other legal rights such as the right to repossess collateral after giving you ________days' notice. We can use the proceeds of the sale toward what you owe us on this loan and any other debts you may then owe us.

Collection Costs We can add to what you owe us the costs of repossession, storage, sale, court costs and reasonable attorney's fees, if any. You agree to pay our attorney's fees equal to ________% of the total amount due plus court costs if we have to sue you. You also agree to pay any difference between the sales proceeds of the collateral and what you owe us. You are entitled to any excess if the sales proceeds are more than you owe us. If we owe you any money, we can use it to pay off this difference.

Late Charges If you don't pay any installment within ________days after the day it's due, you will have to pay a late charge of ________% of the unpaid installment, but not more than $____________, which you promise to pay promptly. The sum total of late charges on all installments cannot be more than________% of the total payments or $____________, whichever is less.

Right to Prepay Your Loan You can prepay your loan in part or in full at any time. We will apply all prepayments first to the finance charge and then to the principal balance If you make a partial payment we'll credit it to your principal balance but you'll have to make all your regular payments until your loan is paid in full

Law that Applies This note will be governed by____________law. If any part of this note is unenforceable, this will not make other parts unenforceable. Liens will be placed on all collateral according to the Uniform Commercial Code of this state and any other particular state laws.

Copy Received You acknowledge receipt of a completed copy of this note and security agreement. You promise to fulfill the terms of this note and give us the security interest in the collateral described above.

NOTICE: SEE OTHER SIDE FOR ADDITIONAL TERMS AND PROVISIONS

NOTICE: See Reverse Side Before Signing

Borrower	Address
Borrower	Address
Comaker	Address
Comaker	Address

45955-2 (1/83)
Installment Note and Security Agreement
Simple Interest

The location further helps to identify the collateral and provides the lender with information that would be helpful in the event of default. The location is stated as the address where the collateral is held (either the borrower's or the lender's address).

The security agreement also should contain a granting clause, an acceleration clause, a list of the events of default and other covenants of the borrower. The *granting clause* assigns a security interest in the collateral to the borrower. The acceleration clause, like the one in the note, makes the loan immediately due in full upon any one of the events of default. Other covenants of the borrower cover the borrower's agreement to purchase or own the collateral and to protect the lender's security interest. This section also contains the borrower's promise to keep the collateral insured and to pay taxes and authorized fees on it.

Consumer protection legislation may require some added provisions, such as statements indicating that borrowers should read the agreement before signing it, notification that borrowers are entitled to a copy, and an explanation of whether or not prepayment is allowed and if it is subject to penalties.

The final section of the agreement provides for the borrowers' signatures. All owners of the collateral should sign the agreement or the lender could be prevented from obtaining the collateral if the borrowers default. As with the note, any changes made to the signed agreement must be initialed by the borrowers or the signatures may be held to be invalid.

If securities such as stocks and bonds are used as collateral, the lender must complete additional forms besides the security or pledge agreement. Two of these forms are the power to hypothecate and the collateral receipt. The power to hypothecate is a contract that designates the pledged stocks or bonds as security for the borrower's repayment without a transfer of title or possession. It must be completed by the lender and signed by the borrower. This form includes the names of the borrower (owner) and the lender, a description of the stocks or bonds, the amount of the debt, and the date and amount of the note. The power to hypothecate form is shown in Chapter 6.

The collateral receipt is issued only when the lender holds the collateral in its possession. The receipt contains the name of the lender and the borrower, the date on which the collateral was received, a description of the collateral, the date of signing, and the signatures of the borrowers and the lender.

Lenders that make stock loans are required to state the purpose of a loan secured with stock on another form. This is to determine whether the stock pledged is also the stock being purchased. If it is, a proper margin must be maintained.

Forms for Perfecting Security Interest

As was described in the preceding chapter, depending on the type of collateral used to secure a loan and prevailing state laws, different types of forms are completed and different sets of procedures are followed for perfecting security interest. This section describes the certificate of title, aircraft registration and financing statement that are used to perfect lenders' security interests for both direct and indirect loans.

Certificate of Title Notation

Perfecting security interest for personal property that is subject to state certificate of title laws requires placing a lien against the title itself. State laws usually require that the identity of lienholders (lenders) be placed directly on the certificates of title. Liens on certificates of title often are filed with the secretary of state or department of motor vehicles.

Filing liens on motor vehicles for both direct and indirect loans may be done by either the lender or the dealer. If the dealer is responsible for completing the forms and submitting them, the lender may use a special endorsement stamp on the back of the disbursement check. By endorsing the check with a signature, the dealer then warrants that the lien has been recorded in the lender's name. A prompt follow-up should be performed if certificates of title for liens recorded by dealers are not received within a reasonable period of time.

To file a lien, the required information is submitted to either the secretary of state or the proper state agency along with the certificate of title. The required information about the lien may be submitted as a separate form or placed on the certificate of title itself. This varies from state to state. If a form is required, it may be used for other purposes besides filing liens, such as changing information about the owner (name or address). Most states charge a fee for filing liens, which must also be submitted.

In addition to state by state variations, the procedure for perfecting security interest in motor vehicles will vary depending upon whether the vehicle is new or used and whether the existing title was originated in the state or in another state.

Usually, certificates of title do not exist on new vehicles. New vehicles are purchased from dealers who generally are not required to obtain certificates of title on vehicles. Vehicles held by dealers for sale or resale are considered to be inventory, and certificate of title laws do not apply to collateral classified as inventory.

When a new vehicle is financed, an application for a certificate of title is submitted to the state. Often the application form contains a section that notes the lender as a lienholder. Along with the application form, the lender (or dealer) submits the *manufacturer's certificate of origination*. This form certifies that the vehicle is new and has never before been issued a certificate of title.

All used vehicles, therefore, already have a certificate of title. Lienholders are noted on the existing certificate. In some states, the secured party rather than the owner of the vehicle will retain possession of the certificate. In other states, for example Arizona, the lender receives a lien filing receipt and the borrower receives the title with the lien noted on it. Some states require that the creditor's name and address be entered on the front of the existing certificate and the certificate forwarded to the secretary of state's office or the department of motor vehicles. Subsequently, the state issues a new or first certificate of title, noting the existing lienholder and the new owner.

In some situations, a motor vehicle owner may possess a certificate of title that is registered in another state, either because it was purchased from an out-of-state dealer or because the owner moved from one state to another. In order to satisfy the laws of any given state, information that establishes ownership of the vehicle and identifies existing lienholders may be required. A lender securing interest in such a vehicle needs to complete and execute an application for a first certificate of title. This, along with the additional information noted above, is sent to the proper state department. The lender should also check with the state title agency to be sure that all of the proper documents and correct fees are submitted.

Filing for Aircraft
Perfecting a security interest in aircraft is outlined by the Federal Aviation Act of 1958. To perfect the lender's interest, the aircraft must be registered with the Federal Aviation Administration (FAA). (Aircraft owners may register by submitting an aircraft registration form together with the bill of sale.) The lender submits an aircraft security agreement to the FAA along with the proper filing fees. This agreement identifies the borrowers and the lender, describes the collateral and the conditions of the loan and requires the signatures of all parties. The FAA retains the security agreement in its files and returns to the lender a *conveyance recordation notice*, noting the lender's security interest in the aircraft.

Financing Statement
Perfecting a security interest in personal property that is not covered by state certificate of title laws or federal agencies is performed by filing a financing statement with a designated state office. The financing statement identifies the borrower and the lender and describes the collateral. The Uniform Commercial Code provides a standard financing statement that has been adopted by many states.

The financing statement is submitted to the secretary of state or other state agency. It requires the borrower's (debtor's) and the lender's (secured party's) name and address. The name of the borrower is listed and filed with the last name first. If the last name is not listed first, other parties searching for evidence of security interest may be unable to locate the statement because it has been misfiled. This can result in a legal suit against the lender, if the lender should be accused of misleading third parties. The lender's name as listed provides a source of additional information to researchers about the property's use as collateral. The lender's address listed on the statement should be the address where information about the security interest in collateral can be obtained. An improper borrower or lender address can cause a financing statement to be deemed invalid. This means that the security interest would not be perfected. Additionally, the financing statement should be signed by the borrower.

The financing statement must contain a collateral description that "reasonably identifies" the collateral. While there is no specific definition of reasonable identification, the use of broad descriptions such as "all personal property of the debtor" should be avoided. Personal property attached to real estate or recognized as a fixture (such as lighting fixtures or aluminum siding) should be described along with a brief legal description of the real property. The description on the financing statement should match that on the security agreement. Detailed requirements of collateral descriptions usually are given in state statutes.

Perfecting Security Interest when Making Indirect Loans

Generally, when a lender makes an indirect loan through a dealer, the dealer prepares all documents necessary to satisfy compliance with statutes and the lender's loan underwriting standards. In addition, the dealer usually is responsible for perfecting security interest in collateral. The method the dealer uses to perfect security interest is the same as if the lender were perfecting interest itself, that is, by filing a financing statement or certificate of title or by taking possession of negotiable instruments.

If a dealer initially has no intention of selling a retail negotiable installment contract to a third party, perfection will occur in the dealer's name. However, if the dealer should decide later to sell the contract to a third party, perfection of the security interest will automatically transfer to the third party. No additional filing is necessary by the third party.

Regardless of whether a lender has an ongoing affiliation with a dealer or customarily buys retail installment contracts from dealers, the lender should carefully check all documents and procedures of the dealer to assure that perfection has taken place. A lender should never assume that the dealer has completed this important procedure.

DOCUMENTS FOR LOANS SECURED BY REAL PROPERTY

Loans secured by real property also require special documentation of the property and the lender's security interest. Real estate is often used as collateral for home improvement loans and equity loans. If the borrower defaults on this type of loan, the lender must show evidence of its security interest in the property and have a recorded claim to it.

Mortgage Instruments

To secure interest on a junior mortgage, an institution completes a promissory note and a mortgage instrument, either a regular mortgage document or a deed of trust. A *regular mortgage document* is a deed or conveyance of real property that describes the debt and other conditions of repayment. A *deed of trust* conveys title of real estate to a third party or trustee. Whether an institution uses a regular mortgage document or a deed of trust depends on state laws. Both documents basically function in the same way.

A first mortgage instrument may contain a *future advances clause*. With this clause in the original instrument, additional funds may be loaned to the borrowers without executing a second mortgage instrument. If this clause does not appear, or if the borrower's first mortgage is held by another lender, however, the lender must execute another mortgage instrument.

Some institutions use the same documents for junior mortgages that they use for first mortgages. In this case, the note and mortgage instrument are stamped "second mortgage." Other institutions use separate forms for first and second mortgages. These forms may have some minor differences in the wording of the provisions. For example, the first mortgage instrument may contain a provision for establishing an escrow account for taxes and insurance. By contrast, the junior mortgage instrument may only include the borrower's promise to pay all taxes and insurance when due. Other forms, such as those for flood insurance, often are identical to those used for a first mortgage.

All mortgage instruments identify the borrower and the lender and contain a reference to the promissory note. They also include a statement of the borrower's pledge of the property securing the debt to the institution. The terms of repayment of the debt are given, along with a legal description of the property. The description can be obtained from a title report or deed.

The junior mortgage instrument often contains other conditions of the agreement between the borrower and the institution. One condition is that the borrower promises to pay the first mortgage as agreed and to comply with all the provisions of the first mortgage instrument. The borrower may also promise to forward all notices from the institution holding the first mortgage to the holder of the junior mortgage.

To secure the lender's junior lien position, two additional clauses are usually found in the mortgage: a prior mortgage default clause and a subordination clause. The *prior mortgage default clause* states that if the borrower defaults in payment of interest, principal or taxes on the first mortgage, the lender reserves the right to pay the amount in default to the first lienholder. This amount is then added to the amount of the second mortgage. By including this clause in the junior mortgage, a lender protects its security interest in the property and prevents losses due to foreclosure by prior lienholders.

A lender offering junior mortgages may want to have its lien position recorded directly on the original title. For example, the lender is granted a second lien position at the time of recording. To insure the second position, a subordination clause is inserted in the mortgage. A *subordination clause* states the preference of the lender in retaining a particular lien position. Thus the lender is establishing a lien position subordinate to another but potentially superior to other claims that might come later.

The last section of all mortgages usually provides a place for the borrowers' signatures and acknowledgements. Borrowers sign their full names (as shown on the note and title to the property). In states where witnesses are required, a notary public acknowledges the mortgage instrument.

Uniform mortgage documents for home improvement loans have been developed and approved by the Federal National Mortgage Association and the Federal Home Loan Mortgage Corporation. The use of uniform documents among lenders nationwide facilitates the sale of loans in the secondary mortgage market, not only to the two agencies that developed them but also to other institutions. The regular mortgage document is shown in Figure 7-4. It contains 16 standard provisions or covenants and any additional covenants required by state statutes. It may be used for either first or junior mortgages (see Covenant No. 4).

A sample deed of trust document is shown in Figure 7-5. Many institutions have begun adopting "simple English" mortgage documents. These documents avoid legal-sounding language in favor of a style that consumers generally find easier to read and understand.

Notice of Right to Rescission

Besides preparing notes and mortgage instruments for loans secured by real property, loan processors must prepare a document called the notice of *right of rescission* (see Chapter 3, Figure 3-1). This notice informs borrowers of their right to cancel the loan within three business days from whichever of the following events occurs last:
- the date of the transaction;
- the date that the truth-in-lending disclosures are received; or
- the date that the notice of their right to cancel is received.

The right of rescission must be disclosed to any borrower applying for a loan secured by property that is his or her primary residence.

The loan processor completes the form by filling in the last date on which the borrower may cancel the loan. The borrower signs and dates the form only if the loan is to be canceled. A space is provided on the form for the borrower's acknowledgement of receipt of the notice.

Insurance

If a borrower purchases credit life or any other type of insurance (such as property damage, homeowners or personal property insurance) for the loan, an application to draw up the insurance policy must be completed. Often an institution has an insurance expert or a separate department handle these details. Some institutions have service corporations that sell and process insurance. Even when these conditions exist, however, the consumer loan officer must be knowledgeable about the types of insurance the institution offers or requires and be able to explain them to applicants.

The application form for insurance varies with the type of insurance and the particular insuring company. Most require some standard information about a borrower, including basic identifying information such as name, address and age.

FIGURE 7-4, Side 1
Mortgage

MORTGAGE

THIS MORTGAGE is made this .... day of ....
19...., between the Mortgagor, ...
.... (herein "Borrower"), and the Mortgagee, ...
...., a corporation organized and existing under the laws of ....
whose address is ....
.... (herein "Lender").

WHEREAS, Borrower is indebted to Lender in the principal sum of U.S. $ ....
which indebtedness is evidenced by Borrower's note dated .... and extensions and renewals thereof (herein "Note"), providing for monthly installments of principal and interest, with the balance of the indebtedness, if not sooner paid, due and payable on .... ;

To SECURE to Lender the repayment of the indebtedness evidenced by the Note, with interest thereon; the payment of all other sums, with interest thereon, advanced in accordance herewith to protect the security of this Mortgage; and the performance of the covenants and agreements of Borrower herein contained, Borrower does hereby mortgage, grant and convey to Lender the following described property located in the County of ...., State of Indiana:

which has the address of ....
                              [Street]   [City]
Indiana .... (herein "Property Address");
    [Zip Code]

TOGETHER with all the improvements now or hereafter erected on the property, and all easements, rights, appurtenances and rents, all of which shall be deemed to be and remain a part of the property covered by this Mortgage; and all of the foregoing, together with said property (or the leasehold estate if this Mortgage is on a leasehold) are hereinafter referred to as the "Property."

Borrower covenants that Borrower is lawfully seised of the estate hereby conveyed and has the right to mortgage, grant and convey the Property, and that the Property is unencumbered, except for encumbrances of record. Borrower covenants that Borrower warrants and will defend generally the title to the Property against all claims and demands, subject to encumbrances of record.

INDIANA—SECOND MORTGAGE—1/80—FNMA/FHLMC UNIFORM INSTRUMENT   Form 3815

Source: FNMA/FHLMC

FIGURE 7-4, Continued
Mortgage

UNIFORM COVENANTS. Borrower and Lender covenant and agree as follows:

1. Payment of Principal and Interest. Borrower shall promptly pay when due the principal and interest indebtedness evidenced by the Note and late charges as provided in the Note.

2. Funds for Taxes and Insurance. Subject to applicable law or a written waiver by Lender, Borrower shall pay to Lender on the day monthly payments of principal and interest are payable under the Note, until the Note is paid in full, a sum (herein "Funds") equal to one-twelfth of the yearly taxes and assessments (including condominium and planned unit development assessments, if any) which may attain priority over this Mortgage and ground rents on the Property, if any, plus one-twelfth of yearly premium installments for hazard insurance, plus one-twelfth of yearly premium installments for mortgage insurance, if any, all as reasonably estimated initially and from time to time by Lender on the basis of assessments and bills and reasonable estimates thereof. Borrower shall not be obligated to make such payments of Funds to Lender to the extent that Borrower makes such payments to the holder of a prior mortgage or deed of trust if such holder is an institutional lender.

If Borrower pays Funds to Lender, the Funds shall be held in an institution the deposits or accounts of which are insured or guaranteed by a Federal or state agency (including Lender if Lender is such an institution). Lender shall apply the Funds to pay said taxes, assessments, insurance premiums and ground rents. Lender may not charge for so holding and applying the Funds, analyzing said account or verifying and compiling said assessments and bills, unless Lender pays Borrower interest on the Funds and applicable law permits Lender to make such a charge. Borrower and Lender may agree in writing at the time of execution of this Mortgage that interest on the Funds shall be paid to Borrower, and unless such agreement is made or applicable law requires such interest to be paid, Lender shall not be required to pay Borrower any interest or earnings on the Funds. Lender shall give to Borrower, without charge, an annual accounting of the Funds showing credits and debits to the Funds and the purpose for which each debit to the Funds was made. The Funds are pledged as additional security for the sums secured by this Mortgage.

If the amount of the Funds held by Lender, together with the future monthly installments of Funds payable prior to the due dates of taxes, assessments, insurance premiums and ground rents, shall exceed the amount required to pay said taxes, assessments, insurance premiums and ground rents as they fall due, such excess shall be, at Borrower's option, either promptly repaid to Borrower or credited to Borrower on monthly installments of Funds. If the amount of the Funds held by Lender shall not be sufficient to pay taxes, assessments, insurance premiums and ground rents as they fall due, Borrower shall pay to Lender any amount necessary to make up the deficiency in one or more payments as Lender may require.

Upon payment in full of all sums secured by this Mortgage, Lender shall promptly refund to Borrower any Funds held by Lender. If under paragraph 17 hereof the Property is sold or the Property is otherwise acquired by Lender, Lender shall apply, no later than immediately prior to the sale of the Property or its acquisition by Lender, any Funds held by Lender at the time of application as a credit against the sums secured by this Mortgage.

3. Application of Payments. Unless applicable law provides otherwise, all payments received by Lender under the Note and paragraphs 1 and 2 hereof shall be applied by Lender first in payment of amounts payable to Lender by Borrower under paragraph 2 hereof, then to interest payable on the Note, and then to the principal of the Note.

4. Prior Mortgages and Deeds of Trust; Charges; Liens. Borrower shall perform all of Borrower's obligations under any mortgage, deed of trust or other security agreement with a lien which has priority over this Mortgage, including Borrower's covenants to make payments when due. Borrower shall pay or cause to be paid all taxes, assessments and other charges, fines and impositions attributable to the Property which may attain a priority over this Mortgage, and leasehold payments or ground rents, if any.

5. Hazard Insurance. Borrower shall keep the improvements now existing or hereafter erected on the Property insured against loss by fire, hazards included within the term "extended coverage", and such other hazards as Lender may require and in such amounts and for such periods as Lender may require.

The insurance carrier providing the insurance shall be chosen by Borrower subject to approval by Lender; provided, that such approval shall not be unreasonably withheld. All insurance policies and renewals thereof shall be in a form acceptable to Lender and shall include a standard mortgage clause in favor of and in a form acceptable to Lender. Lender shall have the right to hold the policies and renewals thereof, subject to the terms of any mortgage, deed of trust or other security agreement with a lien which has priority over this Mortgage.

In the event of loss, Borrower shall give prompt notice to the insurance carrier and Lender. Lender may make proof of loss if not made promptly by Borrower.

If the Property is abandoned by Borrower, or if Borrower fails to respond to Lender within 30 days from the date notice is mailed by Lender to Borrower that the insurance carrier offers to settle a claim for insurance benefits, Lender is authorized to collect and apply the insurance proceeds at Lender's option either to restoration or repair of the Property or to the sums secured by this Mortgage.

Borrower shall give Notice to Lender, at Lender's address set forth on page one of this Mortgage, of any prior encumbrance and of any sale or other foreclosure action.

IN WITNESS WHEREOF, Borrower has executed this Mortgage.

.... (Seal)
—Borrower

.... (Seal)
—Borrower

STATE OF INDIANA, ... County ss:

On this .... day of ...., 19...., before me, the undersigned, a Notary Public in and for said County, personally appeared ....
...., and acknowledged the execution of the foregoing instrument.

WITNESS my hand and official seal.

My Commission expires:

....
....
Notary Public

Resident of .... County, Indiana.

This instrument was prepared by:..,
attorney at law.

FIGURE 7-5
Trust Deed

GEORGE E. COLE®
LEGAL FORMS

FORM NO. 206
April, 1980

TRUST DEED (ILLINOIS)
For Use With Note Form 1448
(Monthly Payments Including Interest)

CAUTION: Consult a lawyer before using or acting under this form.
All warranties, including merchantability and fitness, are excluded.

The Above Space For Recorder's Use Only

THIS INDENTURE, made ______________________ 19____,

between ______________________

____

____
(NO. AND STREET) (CITY) (STATE)

herein referred to as "Mortgagors," and ______________________

____

____
(NO. AND STREET) (CITY) (STATE)

herein referred to as "Trustee," witnesseth: That Whereas Mortgagors are justly indebted to the legal holder of a principal promissory note, termed "Installment Note," of even date herewith, executed by Mortgagors, made payable to Bearer and delivered, in and by which note Mortgagors promise to pay the principal sum of ______________________ Dollars, and interest from ______________ on the balance of principal remaining from time to time unpaid at the rate of ______ per cent per annum, such principal sum and interest to be payable in installments as follows: ______________________ Dollars on the ______ day of ______________, 19___, and ______________________ Dollars on the ______ day of each and every month thereafter until said note is fully paid, except that the final payment of principal and interest, if not sooner paid, shall be due on the ______ day of ______________, 19___; all such payments on account of the indebtedness evidenced by said note to be applied first to accrued and unpaid interest on the unpaid principal balance and the remainder to principal; the portion of each of said installments constituting principal, to the extent not paid when due, to bear interest after the date for payment thereof, at the rate of ______ per cent per annum, and all such payments being made payable at ______________________ or at such other place as the legal holder of the note may, from time to time, in writing appoint, which note further provides that at the election of the legal holder thereof and without notice, the principal sum remaining unpaid thereon, together with accrued interest thereon, shall become at once due and payable, at the place of payment aforesaid, in case default shall occur in the payment, when due, of any installment of principal or interest in accordance with the terms thereof or in case default shall occur and continue for three days in the performance of any other agreement contained in this Trust Deed (in which event election may be made at any time after the expiration of said three days, without notice), and that all parties thereto severally waive presentment for payment, notice of dishonor, protest and notice of protest.

NOW THEREFORE, to secure the payment of the said principal sum of money and interest in accordance with the terms, provisions and limitations of the above mentioned note and of this Trust Deed, and the performance of the covenants and agreements herein contained, by the Mortgagors to be performed, and also in consideration of the sum of One Dollar in hand paid, the receipt whereof is hereby acknowledged, Mortgagors by these presents CONVEY AND WARRANT unto the Trustee, its or his successors and assigns, the following described Real Estate and all of their estate, right, title and interest therein, situate, lying and being in the ______________________, COUNTY OF ______________ AND STATE OF ILLINOIS, to wit:

which, with the property hereinafter described, is referred to herein as the "premises,"

TOGETHER with all improvements, tenements, easements, and appurtenances thereto belonging, and all rents, issues and profits thereof for so long and during all such times as Mortgagors may be entitled thereto (which rents, issues and profits are pledged primarily and on a parity with said real estate and not secondarily), and all fixtures, apparatus, equipment or articles now or hereafter therein or thereon used to supply heat, gas, water, light, power, refrigeration and air conditioning (whether single units or centrally controlled), and ventilation, including (without restricting the foregoing), screens, window shades, awnings, storm doors and windows, floor coverings, inador beds, stoves and water heaters. All of the foregoing are declared and agreed to be a part of the mortgaged premises whether physically attached thereto or not, and it is agreed that all buildings and additions and all similar or other apparatus, equipment or articles hereafter placed in the premises by Mortgagors or their successors or assigns shall be part of the mortgaged premises.

TO HAVE AND TO HOLD the premises unto the said Trustee, its or his successors and assigns, forever, for the purposes, and upon the uses and trusts herein set forth, free from all rights and benefits under and by virtue of the Homestead Exemption Laws of the State of Illinois, which said rights and benefits Mortgagors do hereby expressly release and waive.

The name of a record owner is: ______________________

This Trust Deed consists of two pages. The covenants, conditions and provisions appearing on page 2 (the reverse side of this Trust Deed) are incorporated herein by reference and hereby are made a part hereof the same as though they were here set out in full and shall be binding on Mortgagors, their heirs, successors and assigns.

Witness the hands and seals of Mortgagors the day and year first above written.

PLEASE PRINT OR TYPE NAME(S) BELOW SIGNATURE(S)

______________________(Seal) ______________________(Seal)

______________________ ______________________

______________________(Seal) ______________________(Seal)

______________________ ______________________

State of Illinois, County of ______________________ ss., I, the undersigned, a Notary Public in and for said County in the State aforesaid, **DO HEREBY CERTIFY** that ______________________

____

IMPRESS SEAL HERE

personally known to me to be the same person ____ whose name ____________ subscribed to the foregoing instrument, appeared before me this day in person, and acknowledged that ___h___ signed, sealed and delivered the said instrument as ____________ free and voluntary act, for the uses and purposes therein set forth, including the release and waiver of the right of homestead.

Given under my hand and official seal, this ______________ day of ______________________ 19____.

Commission expires ______________ 19____. ______________________
Notary Public

This instrument was prepared by ______________________
(NAME AND ADDRESS)

Mail this instrument to ______________________

____
(CITY) (STATE) (ZIP CODE)

OR RECORDER'S OFFICE BOX NO. __________

George E. Cole® Legal Forms, reprinted by permission of Boise Cascade Corporation.

The institution may require that a borrower establish a new insurance policy for a new loan or simply maintain established coverage. In both cases the institution may request a copy of the policy for the loan file and a paid receipt representing coverage for a specified length of time. For life insurance of a fixed benefit amount, the institution also may require that the benefit amount equals or exceeds the loan amount. Property damage insurance generally replaces the collateral at its current value rather than a fixed benefit amount. Also, in order for the institution to have a claim to the insurance benefits, the institution must be named loss payee on the borrower's new or existing policy. The loss payee is the party to whom benefits are payable.

Internal Documentation

When a loan has been approved, information about the borrowers and the loan must be entered into the lender's records system. This often is a computer system. Computer loan records make it possible to quickly and accurately account for every loan payment received and to credit each payment to the proper loan account in a timely manner.

Loan processors are usually responsible for setting up new loan records in a computerized system. If the loan department has an on-line system and direct access to customers' loan records, a loan processor may enter the new loan information through a computer terminal. If the institution uses a data center to input information, the loan processor may complete an input form that arranges the information to the data center's specifications.

The amount of information that is recorded about each borrower depends upon the policies of each institution and its computer capabilities. Generally, the borrower's name and address are recorded along with other pertinent identifying features (such as social security number, birth date and telephone number). Information about the loan amount and terms is also essential. The date and amount of the first payment, the interest rate and the annual percentage rate may be recorded. The type of collateral securing the loan is always named, and, if the loan is indirect, the code number for the dealer is listed. Often a code number designating the officer who approved the loan is also recorded. The entire computer record will then provide a handy reference for future information about the borrower as well as the loan.

Entering a new loan account on an institution's records has an impact on daily loan reports. For instance, new loans appear on the daily trial balance (a list of all loan accounts and their outstanding balances). First repayments may be recorded on the transaction journal. Loan processors may examine these reports to verify that all new loan records have indeed been entered into the computer system.

A welcome letter (see Figure 7-6) may be mailed to new borrowers. This letter can create a favorable image of the lender. A good welcome letter is friendly but businesslike in tone. It thanks the new borrower for using an institution's service but still firmly stresses repayment amounts and due dates.

LOAN CLOSING AND DISBURSEMENT

Direct, closed-end loans (such as automobile and home improvement) are the only loans that may require the borrowers to visit the lender in order to sign the documents. Indirect loans (loans originated by a dealer) do require the borrower's signature on the retail installment contract, but a personal visit from the borrower to the lender usually is not necessary. The same is true for open-end loans (such as overdraft, check credit or revolving credit). Borrowers may submit an application form by mail and receive the note or credit agreement that they sign and return by mail. How funds are disbursed, whether by check, wire transfer, or credit to the borrower's account, depends upon whether the loan is indirect, direct closed-end or direct open-end.

Before funds are disbursed, accounting entries may be made to the lender's general ledger account called *loans in process*. A loan processor fills out journal tickets (or vouchers) to set aside funds for paying loan proceeds to the borrower from this account. The tickets are usually completed after the loan is approved by the lender and confirmed and signed by the borrower. Making entries to this account insures that the funds have been reserved and will be available when the loan is closed. The loans in process account serves as a control and record of the loan proceeds for all the lender's consumer loans. The loan processor may also make accounting entries

FIGURE 7-6
Welcome Letter

April 30, 19--

Mr. and Mrs. John Logan
1501 W. Northern
Any Town, Any State

RE: Loan No. 099 040 8503525

Dear Mr. and Mrs. Logan:

Welcome to the family of First Federal Savings customers! Enclosed are your copies of the Installment Note and Security Agreement.

Your first payment of $157.94 is due on June 5. You will be receiving coupons shortly for your convenience in making your payments. If you do not receive the coupons by the time the next payment is due, please mail your check or money order for the amount indicated in the enclosed envelope. Or, if you prefer, you may make your payments at any First Federal branch office.

Please write your account number on the face of your check or money order. That way, if it becomes separated from the payment coupon, we can be sure to apply it to the correct account.

Your payment is due on the fifth of each month. Your account is considered delinquent if your payment is not received by this due date. The late charge is 5% of your net monthly payment or a maximum of $5.00.

If you have any questions, please do not hesitate to contact us.

Sincerely,

Gilda Matthews
Consumer Loan Officer

Encl.

by completing journal tickets to requisition disbursement checks, or wire transfers, or to authorize internal transfers. Journal tickets may be prepared in advance of the loan closing and held without posting them to the accounting or computer system until the loan is closed.

The purpose of a consumer loan closing is to make certain that the loan is properly executed. The closing should insure that the loan is enforceable against a defaulting borrower and that the lender has a legal claim to the collateral. A consumer loan closing takes place after the loan has been approved and all necessary documents have been prepared. The loan officer inspects the group of prepared documents for accuracy, consistency and completeness. At this time, the results of public searches for prior claims to the collateral and the perfection of security interest are also verified. Once the institution is satisfied that all documents are in place and properly completed, the borrower signs the documents and receives the truth-in-lending disclosures and, finally, the loan proceeds. The loan file is then turned over to the operations department where it is inspected by the loan review officer. Failure to properly complete these activities and procedures could jeopardize a lender's claim to repayment of the loan or to the collateral.

Proceeds from direct, closed-end loans can be disbursed either to the borrowers or to third parties. A disbursement to the borrower may be made by check or by an internal credit to the borrower's existing checking or deposit account at the institution. Another payout method is to issue a check payable to the borrower and a third party or only to the third party. For consumer loans, the third party will often be an automobile dealer, a boat dealer or a home improvement contractor. This is a control measure for lenders. Checks made payable to an automobile dealer, for example, must be cashed by the dealer. This insures that the loan proceeds are used for the intended purpose.

With open-end loans, borrowers may ask their lenders to increase the dollar amount available to them in their credit lines. To increase a credit line, lenders may go through the same procedures that they do for granting a new loan. In either case, all of the regulations previously discussed still apply.

Indirect loans are generally disbursed to dealers. Since the interest in a retail installment contract is assigned to a lender, the lender is, in effect, financing the purchase. Funds are commonly disbursed to dealers by draft, check, credit to the dealer's account or wire transfer.

With indirect loans, after the dealer has released merchandise and/or provided services to the borrower, all documents (including the retail installment contract) are delivered to the lender who inspects them for completeness, compliance with Regulation Z disclosure requirements and other requirements set forth in the initial agreement between the dealer and the lender. Then the lender decides whether or not to purchase the retail installment contract. If a contract is incomplete or in error, the dealer may need to make corrections before the lender will purchase it.

When the lender agrees to purchase a retail installment contract, the dealer executes a written assignment (see Figure 5-10). An assignment states that, in exchange for a sum of money, the dealer transfers to the lender the rights set forth in the contract and the coexisting security agreement. As part of the assignment, dealers usually warrant in writing that the contract is genuine and in good standing, that the rescission period has expired, and that compliance with all state and federal laws governing the transaction has been verified. To avoid costly claims against dealers or lenders, the dealers also guarantee that they will perform all of their obligations under this contract, such as promptly repairing or replacing defective merchandise.

Dealers' warranties serve as assurance to the lender that the contract is valid, enforceable and not defective in any way that would inhibit debt repayment. Documents on most properly executed assignments include the date of the assignment, the identity of the dealership (company) and authorized signatures. Authorized signatures identify persons selected by the dealership and approved by lenders at the time the dealer agreement is executed. Authorized signatures are verified for authenticity against a signature card that contains all signatures of those authorized to execute documents on behalf of the dealership.

A single check may be issued for every retail installment contract accepted, or one check may cover disbursement amounts for a group of contracts. If indirect loan volume is low and if generally few contracts are accepted at any one time, issuing one check for every contract may be feasible and it does have the benefit of providing a clear record of the amounts disbursed. However, as loan volume grows, issuing individual checks may become too costly for the lender. The high costs of printed checks, check preparation, and postage or other delivery charges may make it preferable to issue one check to cover a group of contracts, usually those accepted in the same time period.

Another method of payment is for an institution to require the dealer to establish a deposit account and to credit the account for the amount of any contracts accepted. If the dealer has a deposit account with a commercial bank, the funds may be disbursed to this account by electronic or wire transfer.

SUMMARY

The promissory note is a written promise to repay a loan. The note lists the loan amount and describes the loan terms. Some of its major provisions are an acknowledgement of indebtedness, a promise to repay, an acceleration clause, a statement of late charges and a prepayment clause. The borrower may be asked to attest to the purpose for which the loan is required and to sign the note. The note may include truth-in-lending disclosures, such as the finance charge and whether or not credit life insurance is required.

For all loans secured by personal property, institutions usually require a security agreement. The Uniform Commercial Code specifies that the security agreement must contain the borrower's signature and a description of the collateral; it may also contain other provisions. Often, the note and security agreement are combined into a single document. To perfect security interest in personal property, additional steps must be taken to establish the lender as a lienholder of the property.

If insurance is required on the collateral, the loan processor requests a paid receipt and a statement from the insurance company indicating the lender as loss payee.

Internal institution documents must be completed to put a new loan on the books. An input form may be used to enter the new loan record onto a computer. The loan processor arranges for the borrower's loan statement or coupon payment book to be produced and mailed and sends a welcome letter to a new borrower.

Prior to loan closing, the necessary forms and documents must be completed to insure that the loan is enforceable against a defaulted borrower and that the lender has a legal claim to the collateral. The loan closing occurs when the borrower signs the documents and receives copies of them. At or shortly after the loan closing, funds are disbursed to the borrower (for direct loans) or to the dealer (for indirect loans). The loan file is then turned over to the operations area to await the borrower's first payment.

CHAPTER QUESTIONS

1. List and briefly describe five provisions of a promissory note. What truth-in-lending disclosures do many institutions commonly include in the promissory note?

2. What information must be contained in a security agreement?

3. Under what circumstances does an institution issue a power to hypothecate and/or a collateral receipt?

4. Outline the information normally contained in a financing statement.

5. What is the purpose of a manufacturer's certificate of origination?

6. Describe the differences between first and junior mortgage instruments.

7. What types of information does your institution's welcome letter contain?

8. Briefly state the purpose of a consumer loan closing.

9. Explain why loan proceeds from indirect loans are disbursed to the dealer rather than the borrower. How are loan proceeds normally disbursed for direct, closed-end loans and for direct, open-end loans?

8

Servicing Consumer Loans

Objectives

After studying this chapter, you should be able to:
- ☐ Explain why maintaining security interest is important, and describe how it is done;
- ☐ Identify and describe three common payment systems for consumer loans;
- ☐ Compare and contrast the features and uses of six optional consumer loan reports;
- ☐ Explain why dealer reserves are established and why periodic dealer visits are important;
- ☐ Identify the major credit card operation activities; and
- ☐ List reasons for the common inquiries received by the consumer credit department, and explain how to handle these inquiries.

INTRODUCTION

Servicing activities begin as soon as a consumer loan is closed. These activities include maintaining security interest on collateral; inspecting insurance policies and making sure premiums are paid; accepting and processing loan payments; monitoring and verifying loan reports; and answering customer inquiries. Lenders who originate indirect consumer loans may conduct the additional servicing activities of maintaining dealer reserves and preserving sound dealer relationships. Lenders who provide a credit card service must be ready to accept payments, post transactions, prepare monthly statements for the card-issuing institution and solicit merchants to accept credit card payments.

A number of institution employees, including some outside of the consumer credit department, perform consumer loan servicing activities. For example, loan processors or clerks may complete most of the paperwork and handle customer inquiries on a daily basis. Consumer loan officers or accounting officers monitor loan reports, interest income totals, dealer activity and levels of dealer reserves. Tellers accept and process payments from walk-in customers. Business development officers may make periodic visits not only to dealers to maintain indirect loan programs, but also to local merchants to establish new current credit card programs. This chapter describes these loan servicing activities and identifies how they are performed and by whom.

MAINTAINING SECURITY INTEREST AND INSURANCE ON COLLATERAL

Secured consumer loans require a number of specific servicing tasks. When a consumer loan is closed and the lender is legally established as a lienholder to the collateral, loan processors must obtain evidence of perfected security interest for the loan file. Then, certain tasks must be performed in order to maintain the perfected security interest. In addition, if a borrower has been required to insure collateral, the lender will need to verify that sufficient insurance is maintained throughout the life of the loan. Finally, when a consumer loan is paid off, lending personnel must release the security interest.

Obtaining Evidence of Perfected Security Interest

A lender should obtain evidence of a perfected security interest after a loan is closed. This procedure may take from several days to several weeks, depending on the type of collateral. The manner of obtaining evidence of perfected security interest will also vary according to the type of collateral. Depending on state law and the type of collateral, evidence may consist of a financing statement, a certificate of title, a lien on real property or a pledge of securities.

If a financing statement is filed, the loan processor retains one copy and forwards any other copies to the proper government filing office. Filing office personnel stamp the date and time of filing on the financing statements they receive. However, they generally are not required to notify the lender of receipt. To receive a dated copy of the financing statement, the lender often must submit an extra copy along with a written request to have the date and time of original filing noted on the copy and returned to the lender.

When a motor vehicle is used as collateral for a loan, the lender generally retains possession of the certificate of title as evidence of the lien. This action prevents the unauthorized sale of the vehicle to a purchaser who is not aware of the lien. Most of the time, state officials return certificates of title to the recording lienholders. If the certificate of title is not received within the usual length of time, however, the loan processor may need to contact the state office to insure that the certificate has not been forwarded to the borrower by mistake. When the certificate of title is received by the lender, the loan processor inspects it to see that the lender is properly noted as lienholder and that the collateral is described with a vehicle identification number that was affixed by the manufacturer.

A conveyance recordation notice serves as evidence of security interest in aircraft. This notice is sent to the lender by the Federal Aviation Administration (FAA) after the security agreement is filed. The FAA retains the security agreement and sends a registration certificate to the borrower.

When a consumer loan is secured by real property, the mortgage instrument or junior mortgage instrument is mailed to the appropriate local government agency, which records the lien. Agency personnel date and number the document and return it (or a copy of it) to the lender. As with other evidence of perfected security, the loan processor is responsible for prompt follow-up procedures if the document is not returned to the lender within a reasonable amount of time.

When stocks or bonds are pledged as collateral, there is no filing procedure; however, a security agreement is executed. The lender takes physical possession of the securities. Borrowers are then issued a collateral receipt. Lenders must exercise care in storing pledged securities as outlined by the Uniform Commercial Code.

Maintaining Security Interest

Once evidence is received, it must be protected and managed. To maintain perfected security interest in personal property and motor vehicles, the loan processor or other loan department personnel must perform some maintenance tasks. Continuation statements must be filed, the location of motor vehicles must be tracked, and stock and bond prices must be monitored, for example.

When security interest in personal property is perfected by filing a financing statement, maintenance responsibilities center around keeping the security interest effective. Here, under the 1972 Uniform Commercial Code, the original perfection lasts for a maximum of five years from the date of filing.[1] To extend this date for loans with a maturity of more than five years, lenders must file a statement of continuation or Form UCC-3 (see Figure 8-1). The form is completed, signed by a lending officer and forwarded to the office where the original financing statement was filed.

It is important that extensions not be filed too late nor too early. The statement of continuation must be filed during the six months prior to expiration of the original term. Statements filed before the six-month period may be deemed invalid. And, if the continuation is not filed at all, intervening creditors may obtain a superior lien position.

Changes other than time also may trigger a need for refiling. For instance, within four months after a borrower moves out of state, a statement must be refiled in the new state.

Liens on motor vehicle certificates of title usually are not

FIGURE 8-1
Form UCC-3

STATE OF ILLINOIS
UNIFORM COMMERCIAL CODE
STATEMENTS OF CONTINUATION, PARTIAL RELEASE, ASSIGNMENT, ETC.—FORM UCC-3

INSTRUCTIONS:

1. PLEASE TYPE this form. Fold only along perroration for mailing.
2. Remove Secured Party and Debtor copies and send other 3 copies with interleaved carbon paper to the filing officer.
3. Enclose filing fee.
4. If the space provided for any item(s) on the form is inadequate the item(s) should be continued on additional sheets, preferably 5" x 8" or 8" x 10". Only one copy of such additional sheets need be presented to the filing officer with a set of three copies of Form UCC-3. Long schedules of collateral, etc., may be on any size paper that is convenient for the secured party.
5. At the time of filing, filing officer will return third copy as an acknowledgment.

This STATEMENT is presented to THE FILING OFFICER for filing pursuant to the Uniform Commercial Code:

Debtor(s) (Last Name First) and address(es)	Secured Party(ies) and address(es)	For Filing Officer (Date, Time, Number, and Filing Office)

This Statement refers to original Financing Statement No. ________

Date filed: ________, 19____ Filed with ________

A. ☐ CONTINUATION .... The original financing statement between the foregoing Debtor and Secured Party, bearing the file number shown above, is still effective.

B. ☐ PARTIAL RELEASE.. From the collateral described in the financing statement bearing the file number shown above, the Secured Party releases the the property indicated below.

C. ☐ ASSIGNMENT......... The Secured Party certifies that the Secured Party has assigned to the Assignee whose name and address is shown below, Secured Party's rights under the financing statement bearing the file number shown above in the property indicated below.

D. ☐ TERMINATION........ The Secured Party certifies that the Secured Party no longer claims a security interest under the financing statement bearing the file number shown above.

E. ☐ AMENDMENT........... The financing statement bearing the above file number is amended.
☐ To show the Secured Party's new address as indicated below:
☐ Tc show the Debtor's new address as indicated below:
☐ As set forth below:

________ (Debtor) ________ (Secured Party)
(Signature of Debtor, if required)

Dated: ________, 19____ By: ________
(Signature of Secured Party)

(1) Filing Officer Copy—Alphabetical *This form of financing statement is approved by the Secretary of State.*

STANDARD FORM—UNIFORM COMMERCIAL CODE—FORM UCC-3—REV. 11-75

George E. Cole® Legal Forms, reprinted by permission of Boise Cascade Corporation.

subject to time limitations. However, to protect its security interest and prevent fraudulent schemes, the lender should keep track of the borrower's current address. A common fraudulent scheme is for the borrower to move the motor vehicle to another state and obtain a second certificate of title. With a new title (that is one free of a lien notation), the vehicle can be sold to a purchaser who is unaware of the lien status. The lender's security interest may be legally challenged by unknowing purchasers if the lien is not noted on the title. To help prevent this kind of fraud, most states do not issue new certificates of title for vehicles without first obtaining the original one.

Returned mail is often the first clue that a borrower has moved out of state. Consumer loan servicing personnel should watch for correspondence that is returned by the post office marked "addressee unknown" or with a similar notation. Delinquent borrowers are not likely to notify the lender of changes in residence, making it difficult or even impossible for loan personnel to locate them.

Lenders try to maintain their security interest in loans secured by stocks and bonds by monitoring the stock's value. A stock's value can change quickly. Two events that illustrate this are stock splits and a substantial drop in the market value. A stock split is an increase in the number of outstanding shares of a corporation's stock; new shares are granted to each stockholder in proportion to the original number of shares held. Because security interest in stocks and bonds is perfected by possession of the certificates, any additional shares issued to borrowers due to stock splits should be in the possession of the lender. Without physical possession, the lender may not have a perfected security interest.

The safest way to protect this collateral is with a written agreement between the borrower and lender covering any loss of value. This should be executed at the time the stock is given as collateral. The agreement should state that, if the stock's market value drops below some specified amount, the borrower will provide additional collateral. The agreement should also state that, if there is a stock split, the customer will surrender the additional shares.

Maintaining Insurance

To protect the value of secured loans, lenders may require that borrowers obtain insurance on the collateral. The type of insurance depends upon the collateral. Borrowers can, for example, obtain automobile insurance, homeowner's insurance, marine insurance and so on. Flood insurance is required by federally chartered institutions for loans secured by real property (including mobile homes) that is located in designated flood areas.

For all of these loans, lenders should inspect the insurance policies to make sure there is a payee clause. The *payee clause* lists the lender as a lienholder to the collateral. If collateral is damaged, the insurance check is made payable to the lender; however, the lender may choose to endorse the check over to the borrower to make repairs.

Insurance premiums must be paid promptly to insure that the collateral is properly insured. The premium amount may be added to the borrower's regular loan payment. In this case, the full premium amount is calculated for the life of the loan, added to the total loan amount, and divided by the total number of payments to determine the amount of each payment.

In other cases, a lender may allow borrowers to pay their own insurance premiums. Borrowers make the premium payments when due and send evidence of payment to the lender. If borrowers fail to make the premium payments, the insurance company may cancel the policy but often will notify the lender in advance of cancellation. This notification gives the lender a chance to try to contact borrowers before the policy is canceled.

Generally, when a borrower allows the insurance on collateral to lapse or expire, he or she is technically in default. However, this is a situation in which lenders usually react courteously. The lender first evaluates the customer's relationship, character and capacity, and then, in a tactful way, contacts good customers with a reminder that insurance is still necessary. In some cases, when the remaining loan balance or collateral value is not substantial, the security interest in the collateral may be released, and the remaining balance treated as an unsecured loan. In other cases, depending on the loan agreement, the lending institution may itself obtain the required insurance and charge the borrower for it.

Releasing Security Interest

When a consumer loan is paid off, lending personnel mark the note "paid" or "canceled" and return it to the borrower. The security agreement may be kept on file in case there are questions regarding title or release of the documents. Canceled documents indicate that borrowers are no longer financially obligated to the lender under the agreement. To release the lender's claim to the collateral, a release document is prepared and filed for the public records. The documentation

> Mr. Michaels has a boat loan with Seaview Savings that requires him to maintain insurance on the boat. Mr. Michaels has been a customer with Seaview for many years, has several large CDs and has made all loan payments on time. He has an outstanding loan balance of $1,000 to be paid in five monthly payments. In this situation, if Mr. Michaels did not renew his boat insurance policy, the lender might not press him. On the other hand, if Mr. Michaels were a new customer who had just recently bought the boat and still had a substantial loan balance outstanding, the lender probably would insist that proper insurance coverage be maintained.

used for releasing security interest depends on the type of collateral and where the lien was originally filed.

For loans secured by personal property, the Uniform Commercial Code requires lenders to prepare a release form called a statement of release (see Figure 8-1). The statement of release, which is a part of Form UCC-3, indicates that the secured party (the lender) no longer claims a security interest in the property under the financing statement. It contains a description of the collateral, the name and address of the borrower and the lender, and the financing statement file number, which can be obtained from the filing office or from the copy retained in the lender's file. An authorized loan officer or manager must sign the statement. Although not required, the lender may also ask the borrower to sign the release.

Both the 1962 and 1972 versions of the UCC require lenders to prepare release statements and send them to borrowers upon written request. In addition, the 1972 Code requires that the statement be filed at the same filing office where the original financing statement was submitted. A fee may be charged for releasing the lien. If a fee is charged, it may then be passed on to the customer. Failure to prepare termination statements upon request or submit them to the proper filing office renders the lender liable for any loss to the borrower. The lender also is fined an automatic civil penalty of $100.[2]

For loans secured by motor vehicles, lenders prepare a release of lien form, sometimes printed on the certificate of title itself. Lending personnel fill in the lender's name and the date of the release. The signature of an authorized lending officer or manager must also appear to authorize the release. Some state regulations require lenders to file the release and additional documentation with the proper state agency. Other states allow lenders to pass the filing responsibility along to the borrower.

For loans secured by aircraft, the lender completes the release section of the conveyance recordation notice and forwards it to the borrower who files it with the Federal Aviation Administration. The information needed to complete the release is the date of release and the signature and title of an authorized officer or manager at the lending institution.

For loans secured by real property, lenders file a release with the recorder's office. A form called a Full Satisfaction and Release of Mortgage is completed with the names of the lending institution and the borrower, a description of the mortgage instrument and a description of the property (see Figure 8-2). It is signed by two lending officers, notarized and filed with the same office that originally recorded the lien.

Some states list instructions for filing the release statement on the form itself. Depending on state regulations, a lender either files the release and forwards the recorded release statement to the borrower or sends the unrecorded release to the borrower. In both cases, the title is not cleared until the recorder's office receives the form.

Release statements are not needed for loans secured by stocks or bonds. The lender simply returns the stocks or bonds to the borrower along with the original power to hypothecate form stamped "canceled."

PROCESSING CONSUMER LOAN PAYMENTS

Maintaining security interest and monitoring insurance on loan collateral is the first major responsibility in consumer loan servicing. A second major servicing responsibility is processing loan payments.

Lenders establish with their customers the manner in which payments are to be made. As payments are received,

FIGURE 8-2
Full Satisfaction and Release of Mortgage

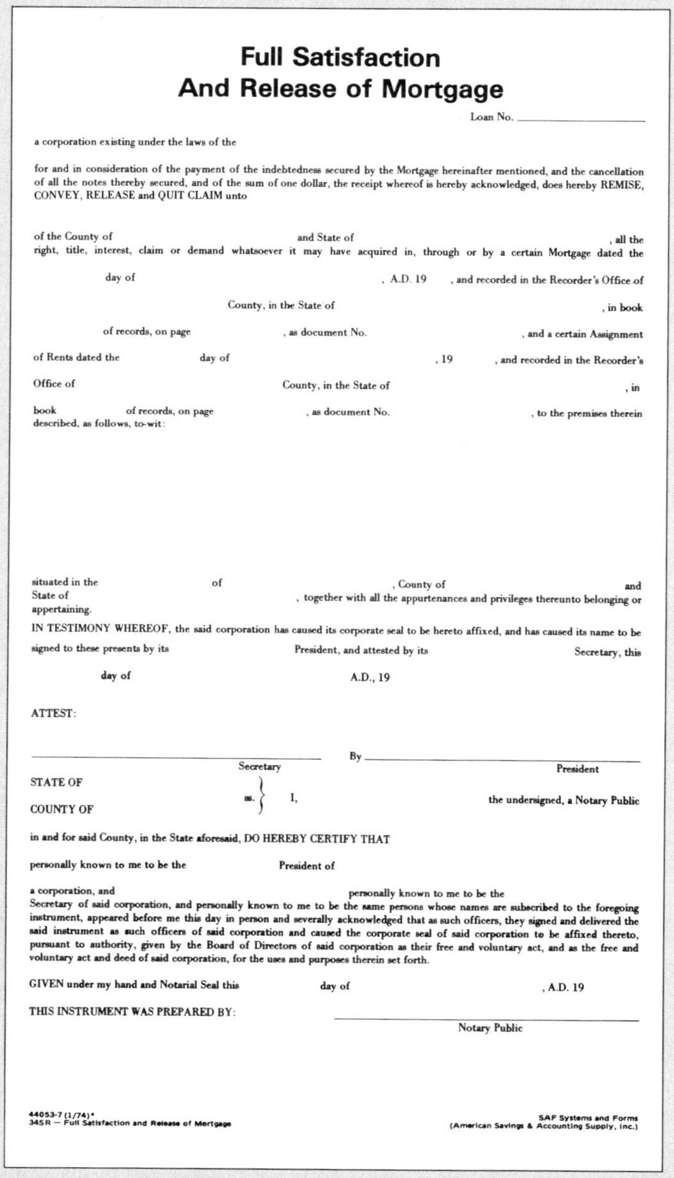

Full Satisfaction And Release of Mortgage

Loan No. ____________

a corporation existing under the laws of the

for and in consideration of the payment of the indebtedness secured by the Mortgage hereinafter mentioned, and the cancellation of all the notes thereby secured, and of the sum of one dollar, the receipt whereof is hereby acknowledged, does hereby REMISE, CONVEY, RELEASE and QUIT CLAIM unto

of the County of and State of , all the right, title, interest, claim or demand whatsoever it may have acquired in, through or by a certain Mortgage dated the

day of , A.D. 19 , and recorded in the Recorder's Office of

County, in the State of , in book

of records, on page , as document No. , and a certain Assignment

of Rents dated the day of , 19 , and recorded in the Recorder's

Office of County, in the State of , in

book of records, on page , as document No. , to the premises therein described, as follows, to-wit:

situated in the of , County of and State of , together with all the appurtenances and privileges thereunto belonging or appertaining.

IN TESTIMONY WHEREOF, the said corporation has caused its corporate seal to be hereto affixed, and has caused its name to be signed to these presents by its President, and attested by its Secretary, this

day of A.D., 19

ATTEST:

____________ Secretary

By ____________ President

STATE OF }
ss. } I, the undersigned, a Notary Public
COUNTY OF }

in and for said County, in the State aforesaid, DO HEREBY CERTIFY THAT

personally known to me to be the President of

a corporation, and personally known to me to be the Secretary of said corporation, and personally known to me to be the same persons whose names are subscribed to the foregoing instrument, appeared before me this day in person and severally acknowledged that as such officers, they signed and delivered the said instrument as such officers of said corporation and caused the corporate seal of said corporation to be affixed thereto, pursuant to authority, given by the Board of Directors of said corporation as their free and voluntary act, and as the free and voluntary act and deed of said corporation, for the uses and purposes therein set forth.

GIVEN under my hand and Notarial Seal this day of , A.D. 19

THIS INSTRUMENT WAS PREPARED BY:

____________ Notary Public

44053-7 (1/74)*
34SR — Full Satisfaction and Release of Mortgage

SAF Systems and Forms
(American Savings & Accounting Supply, Inc.)

lenders follow their own operational procedures that expedite payment processing most efficiently for their institutions. This section describes typical payment systems and processing procedures.

Payment Systems

Lenders use three common payment systems for consumer loans: coupons, statements and Transmatic® or other automatic transfer systems. With a coupon system, the borrower receives a book of coupons at closing or some time before the first payment is due. One coupon is submitted with each payment. Each coupon shows the payment amount (often broken down into principal, interest and possibly insurance); the date the payment is due; and the name and account number of the borrower. As part of the coupon system, the lender may send to the borrower a periodic statement that lists the dates prior payments were received, along with the amount applied to principal and interest. The outstanding loan balance after the last recorded payment may also be shown.

With a *statement system*, the lender sends to the borrower monthly statements that show the loan amount, the last payment made and how it was applied to principal and interest, the amount of the current payment and the date it is due. Statements also may explain when a payment is considered late and list any late charges. Often a detachable portion of the statement is returned to the lender with the borrower's check or cash payment. This "top" portion may also ask that any change in address be indicated.

With an automatic transfer or Transmatic® systems, loan payments can be deducted automatically from the borrower's checking or deposit accounts at that institution or at another financial institution. To have loan payments deducted from a deposit account, a borrower must sign a savings withdrawal authorization (see Figure 8-3). The institution automatically transfers the funds from the deposit account to cover the loan payment every month. To have loan payments deducted from a checking account, a borrower fills out a Transmatic® authorization form (see Figure 8-4) and submits a blank check from the account marked "void." Funds are transferred at a

FIGURE 8-3
Savings Withdrawal Application

specific time every month from the checking account to pay the loan.

Payment Processing

With coupon and statement systems, loan payments may be processed at a teller station, sent to a lock box for service or handled by an automatic transfer system. Each method has advantages and disadvantages.

On-site Payments

Tellers frequently handle loan payments from walk-in customers. With an on-line computer system, a teller can post the payment directly to a borrower's account by entering the loan account number and the payment amount on the computer terminal. The computer program then updates the borrower's account record and assigns the proper portions of the payment amount to interest, principal and insurance (if any).

If the amount remitted by a borrower is more or less than the regular monthly amount (advance or partial payments), tellers must follow a special procedure. This includes posting the payment to a general ledger account, rather than to the borrower's account, and notifying the collections department if some amount is past due. Many computer systems can handle advance and partial payments automatically. In this case, tellers may use the same posting procedure as for regular payments and enter transactions directly to the borrower's account record, but partial payments are automatically applied first to interest and then to principal. Advance payments are usually applied towards principal unless otherwise indicated.

For extra security, some lenders follow a policy that only collections personnel may handle advance or partial payments. One reason for this policy is that, if a loan account is in the process of foreclosure or repossession, acceptance of payment could delay legal proceedings. Thus, collection personnel have an opportunity to stop application of the funds. A second reason is that partial payments often signal the beginning of a delinquent loan, and collections department staff may want to flag the delinquent borrower's account for follow-up action. To alert tellers to this special status, a notation or code may appear on the computer terminal when the teller tries to post the payment, requesting referral of all attempted payments to a collector or the collections manager.

On-site payments have a number of advantages. They are convenient for customers and offer cross-selling opportunities. Situations that might cause problems are immediately noted and can be given special handling that matches the institution's policies. On-site payments also do not require special staff. On the other hand, they can be time-consuming.

Lock Box Payments

Under a *lock box* arrangement, borrowers send their loan payments to a post office box. The lender's depository bank has access to the box, and, acting according to prior agreement, picks up the payments and prepares a list of the

FIGURE 8-4
Transmatic® Authorization

```
                    AUTHORIZATION AND DIRECTIVE TO:
                                                    Date _____
A SAVINGS INSTITUTION TRANSMATIC® SYSTEMS LICENSEE AND BANKS IN WHICH UNDERSIGNED HAS ACCOUNTS
    Undersigned authorizes and directs said savings institution, as agent, to initiate TRANSMATIC checks or transfers payable
to savings institution for amounts, from time to time agreed upon between savings institution and Undersigned to be charged
against Undersigned's bank account. In the case of any TRANSMATIC check or other transfer initiated by the Savings
Institution in paper form, rights of Bank shall be the same as if these transfers were checks personally executed by the
Undersigned. On request of Undersigned, savings institution is authorized to transfer funds from savings institution to
Undersigned's bank account. (This agency authorization remains in effect until revoked in writing by Undersigned or savings
institution.) Savings Institution has sole responsibility that transfers payable to the savings institution are made pursuant
to proper authority.
    Responsibility for further transfer from Undersigned's bank account of funds originally transferred to it from Undersigned's
savings institution account shall not be that of the savings institution.
    By accepting this agency authorization, savings institution agrees that, as long as Undersigned's account shows a balance
sufficient to cover any payment authorized herein, Undersigned will not be deemed in default of any contractual payment
obligation to the savings institution.
    Undersigned's current bank account is identified by attached blank check marked "VOID."

_____
                    Print name(s) in which account is held

_____
        Authorized signature(s) exactly as it (they) appear(s) on Bank Account records
                            DO NOT WRITE BELOW
Bank Account Number: _____
Bank Name: _____
When the savings institution completes this section from the attached check marked "VOID", the check may be destroyed.

Using the TRANSMATIC System:
    ☐ I would like to save $_____ on _____ day(s) circled
                            beginning _____, 19_____.
    ☐ Savings Account Number _____. ☐ Please open a Savings Account.
    ☐ I would like to make the required payments on my loan number(s).
```

payment information (loan account number, date and amount of payment) for each one received. The bank totals the payment amounts, deposits the funds into the lender's account and forwards the list to the lender.

One advantage to a lock box arrangement is that funds from payments are made immediately available to the lender. Another is that the lender is relieved of the time-consuming operations involved in accepting and processing small individual payments. However, commercial banks that offer lock box processing often charge a fee for the service or require the lender to maintain a minimum or compensating balance in a noninterest bearing deposit account.

With automatic transfer or Transmatic® systems, the transfer of funds from the owner's checking or deposit account to make the loan payment can be initiated automatically each month by the computer system. In addition, the computer may generate a receipt to be mailed to the borrower. Under this system, the loan processor's only tasks for routine transactions may be to activate the program and to handle mailing the receipts. If there are insufficient funds in the designated account to make the loan payment, however, the loan processor may need to call the borrower and ask if there is another account from which the payment can be deducted.

Automatic transfer payments can be manually posted through on-line terminals or initiated by preparing debit and credit tickets in batch processing systems. In on-line posting, a teller or loan processor enters the transfer by computer terminal to records of both the borrower's deposit account and loan account. If source documents are used, the loan processor prepares a debit ticket for the borrower's deposit account and a credit ticket for the loan account.

Transmatic® payments may be initiated in a variety of ways, depending on the lender's internal data processing system. First, borrowers authorize the commercial bank (or other institution) to honor checks (sight drafts) drawn on their checking accounts written by the lender for the amount of the monthly payment. A borrower completes a directive to honor preauthorized payments and forwards it to the bank. Then each month when the payment is due, the lender prepares a check or preauthorized payment and credits the loan account. The check is processed for collection through the check-clearing system of the Federal Reserve Bank, where it is returned to the bank and debited from the borrower's checking account.

CONSUMER LOAN REPORTS

A number of reports are part of the consumer loan servicing function. Reports can be separated into two major types: required reports and optional reports.

Required Reports

In addition to the required disclosures described earlier, lenders are obligated to report regularly to borrowers and to the Internal Revenue Service on certain types of loans. These reporting requirements are based on the Tax Reform Act of

1984 and are covered in Section 6050H and 6050J of the Internal Revenue Code.[3]

Section 6050H: Forms 1098 and 1096
The underlying purpose of Section 6050H of the IRS Code is to insure that the IRS has the information it needs to match actual interest costs on loans against taxpayers' claims of deductions for loan interest. Section 6050H requires a lending institution to take two actions when it receives $600 or more of interest on one mortgage loan from a borrower within a calendar year. When this occurs, the lender must file an information return with the IRS. The lender also is required to send the borrower a statement showing that the report was filed and the amount of interest that was reported to the IRS on the loan for that calendar year.

The 1984 Tax Reform Act states that a mortgage is any obligation secured by real property. For reporting purposes, the law set up two categories of what is to be considered reportable interest: loans in existence on December 31, 1984 and loans made after December 31, 1984.

For loans in the first category interest reports are required if the loan is secured by real property and has been classified as a mortgage loan by the lender. For loans secured by real property that originated after December 31, 1984, the law requires reporting, regardless of the how the mortgage lender classifies the loans.

Lending institutions submit reports to the IRS for the interest received on IRS Form 1098 and an annual summary of all activity on IRS Form 1096. Lenders must file a separate report for each loan on which $600 or more of interest was received during a calendar year.

Form 1098 must include both the borrower's and lender's name, address and tax identification number, as well as the amount of interest received from the borrower during the calendar year. This report must be filed with the IRS by February 28 following the calendar year in which the mortgage interest was received. Lenders filing more than 50 forms do so on magnetic media.

A copy of Form 1098 that is sent to the IRS also must be sent to the borrower, or a notice containing the same information as Form 1098, along with statements declaring that: (a) the information shown on the form is being reported to the IRS; and (b) the amount reported on the statement is deductible by the interest payer for federal income tax purposes only to the extent the payer actually paid the amount and was not reimbursed by another person. Borrowers must receive this information by January 31 following the calendar year in which they paid the interest.

Section 6050J: Forms 1099 and 1096
Under the Tax Reform Act of 1984, the IRS is authorized to require reporting of abandonments and foreclosures of security property. An *abandonment* refers to those situations in which the borrower intends to and does permanently discard or give up the use of the security property. This law can be found in Section 6050J of the Internal Revenue Code. It applies to all acquisitions of property taken or received or abandonments occurring after December 31, 1984.

Section 6050J lists the specific circumstances that trigger the reporting requirements and how they are to be reported. Generally, the lender must report to the IRS on Forms 1099 and 1096 by February 28 following the calendar year that foreclosure or abandonment occurred.

The borrower must receive notification by January 31 following the calendar year that he or she gave up the property. The statement must include the name and address of the lender that is filing the informational return, the specific information the return contained and a statement that this information is being reported to the IRS.

Optional Reports

Lenders choose to prepare a number of reports on consumer loans to meet their own needs. These reports can verify the accuracy of data entered to borrowers' account records and can confirm that loan payments have been correctly recorded. They are often used to answer customer inquiries and to monitor the status of loans for other departments. Some examples of these reports are given below.

Trial Balance
The *trial balance* is a list of all loan accounts and their outstanding balances (see Figure 8-5). Usually accounts are listed in the order of their account numbers. Besides listing borrowers' names, addresses, account numbers and out-

standing balances, the trial balance may show the dates of the previous payment and next payments, late charges, late payments, late notices and unearned interest. Because the trial balance is usually a daily report, it often is used as a reference if on-line information is temporarily unavailable, if the computer is down or if the lender does not have on-line capabilities for consumer loans. Since it tells the consumer credit department manager the total dollar amount of outstanding loans on a given day, it also may be used to monitor loan activity.

Transaction Journal

The *transaction journal* or loan payment journal is usually generated by a computer and reports on all loan payments received the preceding business day (see Figure 8-6). Payments are usually listed in account number order. This journal identifies the borrowers, the number of the teller who accepted each payment, the office or branch where each payment was received and the payment amounts. A separate journal may be prepared for each branch office. The purpose

---

FIGURE 8-5
Consumer Loan Trial Balance

BRANCH CODE	ACCOUNT NUMBER	CUSTOMER'S NAME	PRINCIPAL BALANCE	LATE CHARGE	MONTHLY PAYMENT	INT. RATE
3			4,590.00		114.75	12.000
12			4,680.56		114.16	12.000
11			9,758.40		128.40	11.500
4			9,427.13		229.93	12.000
6			16,102.43		159.43	12.000
1			8,692.45		133.73	11.500
1			1,195.95		70.35	12.000
1			2,761.35		67.35	12.000
4			24,179.40		239.40	12.000
1			1,064.01		36.69	12.000
1			1,578.56	2.39	47.84	12.000
1			1,387.03		33.83	12.000
5			20,747.82		203.41	12.000
12			430.76		39.16	12.000
1			364.48		21.44	12.000

of this journal is to provide verification that a specific transaction has been made. It also is used to answer customer inquiries.

Loan processors or accounting personnel may be required to verify the amount of loan payments listed on this report. Errors made in entering the payment amount or in crediting the payment to the proper account can be detected and corrected. Any discrepancies discovered by comparing the journal to the coupons or statement stubs can be corrected by a manual transaction entered into the computer.

Loan History
A list of the transactions made to a particular borrower's loan account is called a *loan history*. A loan history may be taken from an on-line terminal, a copy of the borrower's statement or the loan ledger card, depending on the processing system the lender uses. Loan histories may take the form of computer-printed reports and may be available on a periodic basis (weekly or monthly) or by special request (printed immediately from a computer screen).

PAY CODE	PAID THROUGH	UNEARNED DISCOUNT	INSURANCE RESERVE		AHEAD OR BEHIND	DTE. LAST TRAN.
001	05/20/86	799.84			.00	04/20/86
001	05/15/86	823.17			.00	04/24/86
001	05/15/86	2,649.95			.00	04/30/86
001	05/15/86	1,637.76			.00	04/03/86
001	05/15/86	5,524.11			.00	04/08/86
001	05/05/86	2,110.46	.00	1	.00	03/31/86
001	05/05/86	99.28	.00	1	.00	04/03/86
001	05/20/86	485.55			.00	04/27/86
001	05/15/86	8,295.17	.00	1	.00	04/14/86
001	05/20/86	140.22	.00	1	.00	04/15/86
001	01/05/86	235.82	.00	1	.16	04/21/86
001	05/10/86	243.79			.00	04/06/86
001	04/20/86	7,187.28			.00	04/03/86
001	05/20/86	24.81			.00	04/16/86
001	05/10/86	30.24	.00	1	.00	04/10/86

FIGURE 8-6
Consumer Loan Transaction Journal

BRANCH CODE	ACCOUNT NUMBER	CUSTOMER'S NAME	TELLER CODE	OLD BALANCE
4			306	3,221.64
4			405	2,464.80
10			904	340.85
1			306	3,259.20
1			105	80.84
1			306	214.20
1			000	
1			000	4,347.60
1			000	
1			000	
1			000	
3			306	1,600.50
1			000	
1			107	7,827.52
1			000	

*Late charge

New Loans and Payoffs

Two other daily loan reports are common: the *new loan report* that lists information on new borrowers and the *payoff report* that identifies loan accounts on which the final payment has been made. Both reports list borrowers' names, loan account numbers and total loan amounts. In addition, the new loan report often gives borrowers' mailing addresses and the loan terms (interest rate, APR, loan amount, payment amount, and the dates that the first and last payments are due). A loan processor verifies that the information about new borrowers has been entered correctly on the computer by comparing this information with the loan application or other loan documents. Since the computer often prints mailing labels (or addresses envelopes) and figures interest and principal amounts from this stored information, the original entry must be accurate.

The payoff report shows the repayment history of a loan at the time the loan is paid in full. It lists the date the loan was approved (or the date of the first payment), the payoff date and the interest rate. To indicate whether payments have ever been late, the report may show the number of late payments

DEBITS WITHDRAWALS		CREDITS DEPOSITS	NEW BALANCE	TIME	DATE OF LST. TRAN.
		84.78	3,136.86	12-16	04-03-86
		63.20	2,401.60	17-50	04-03-86
		68.17	272.68	10-19	04-02-86
		67.90	3,191.30	12-16	03-18-86
		40.42	40.42	14-26	04-03-86
		71.40	142.80	12-16	03-26-86
L/C*	3.59			00-09	03-31-86
		84.74	4,262.86	00-11	04-01-86
L/C	8.50			00-09	03-18-86
L/C	2.38			00-09	03-31-86
L/C	5.74			00-09	03-31-86
		72.75	1,527.75	12-40	03-31-86
L/C	2.04			00-09	03-31-86
		128.32	7,699.20	16-02	04-15-86
L/C	5.97			00-09	04-08-86

made, the total amount of late charges, or a code number to identify repayment status (for example, 1 means no late payments; 2 means 1 to 3 late payments; 3, 4 to 9; 4, 10 or more).

Delinquencies

Delinquency reports are used by the collections department to identify delinquent borrowers and to provide a background for recommending the actions needed to collect back payments. Separate reports may be printed for loans at various stages of delinquency, for example, a 30-day report, a 60-day report or a 90-day report. The report lists borrower names and account numbers, outstanding balances and the number of notices sent in the collections process.

Other Report Data

If a lender has indirect loans, a code indicating the dealer may be part of each indirect borrower's account record. This code may appear on the trial balance. Separate reports, such as the transaction journal, new loans, closed loans and delinquencies may be printed out for the loans of each dealer. This helps consumer credit department managers monitor the activity on loans referred by a particular dealer. Dealers may receive copies of the trial balance for their loans and delinquency reports.

Lenders may use other reports to help managers assess loan profitability. One example is an *interest earned report*, which lists all loan accounts and the total interest charged on each or the interest charged for the past month. It also gives a total interest charged figure for all outstanding loans or each type of loan.

SERVICING INDIRECT LOANS

As explained in Chapter 5, indirect loans require that lenders take certain precautions. Since these precautions can be considered consumer loan servicing activities, they are reviewed in this section.

Maintaining Dealer Reserves

When a dealer executes an agreement with a lender for indirect loans, the dealer's rate of income is negotiated. The dealer's rate is usually expressed as the difference between the interest rate stated on the dealer's retail installment contract and the interest rate charged by the lender. For example, if the retail installment contract shows 15% and the lender charges 14% interest, the dealer's rate is 1%. This income compensates the dealer for the work involved in encouraging customers to finance and in preparing documents for the lender.

To protect lenders from dealers defaulting on their obligations as spelled out in the dealer's agreement, lenders hold a portion of each dealer's income in reserve. In this way, if a dealer fails to honor recourse or repurchase agreements, or fails to deliver collateral, the lender can use the reserves to repay the outstanding loan. Reserves also provide a convenient way for the lender to obtain the borrower's rebate of the dealer's unearned interest income when borrowers prepay their loans.

For dealers who just started selling dealer paper to a particular lender, reserve levels must be reached before income is remitted. A lender may begin to release a dealer's income only after the amount of reserves reaches an established percentage of the total amount of that dealer's outstanding loan balances.

Consumer loan or accounting employees monitor the reserve amounts for all dealers. Also monitored are the number of delinquencies and repossessions that the reserve amounts must adequately cover. When the reserve amounts are satisfied and all other agreements are satisfactorily met, interest income is disbursed to dealers.

A lender's exact procedures for monitoring reserves and disbursing income to dealers are dictated by department policy and the written dealer agreement. Among these duties are monitoring computer reports, reviewing the lender's general ledger account called "dealer reserves," making journal entries to add and subtract from reserves, and preparing checks to disburse income to dealers.

Maintaining Dealer Affiliations

A second major servicing responsibility for indirect loans is to maintain affiliations with dealers. Verifying that dealers are in sound financial condition and that the terms of the dealers' agreements are being met is the basis for a mutually beneficial relationship. By contrast, dealers in shaky financial condition may not be able to buy back dealer paper (under recourse or repurchase agreements) or might be tempted to commit fraudulent acts or declare bankruptcy to relieve themselves from liability to the lender.

To monitor the financial condition of a dealer, the lender should require that financial statements, such as balance sheets and income statements, be submitted frequently. These statements are examined for changes, such as decreases in income or increases in expenses or outstanding debt. Substantial changes of this kind may affect the ability of the dealer to accept liability.

Consumer loan or business development officers may visit dealers on a regular basis. These visits help maintain good working relationships by providing the opportunity to discuss possible problems such as consistent errors in dealer loan documentation or questionable items on financial statements. Personal visits also give dealers a chance to discuss problems they might have with the lender such as slow loan approval or tardy dealer income disbursement.

To verify the terms of retail installment contracts consumer loan officers and other employees often contact borrowers and inspect the collateral. A sample group of borrowers from a particular dealer is chosen at random, telephoned and questioned about contract terms. Loan officers may ask borrowers about the price of the merchandise, the amount of the downpayment and the total loan amount. They may ask for a description of the merchandise purchased (such as make, model, year, serial number). These questions verify that dealers are supplying accurate data. Any discrepancies may indicate fraudulent activity by the dealer and must be thoroughly investigated.

CREDIT CARDS

Savings institutions may offer established national bank credit cards in three ways: as card issuers, as agents or as participating agents. Generally, card issuers assume all responsibilities for servicing customer accounts. If the institution is a card agent, its primary activity is soliciting credit card applications and merchants. Institutions acting as participating agents may solicit applications and also evaluate applicants.

The activities involved in issuing a credit card include issuing new and renewed credit cards, processing payments, maintaining file information on customers, and responding to customer inquiries. Other activities are granting authorization requests, receiving and posting transactions from the card clearing system, and preparing and mailing statements.

Credit card operations are more expensive for small institutions that are unable to generate a volume large enough to be cost effective. Studies have shown that for small institutions, processing costs may amount to as much as 62% of credit card income, while costs amount to only 41% for large volume operations. To be more cost effective, some small institutions hire service companies to receive and process payments, rather than develop in-house operations. Generally, institutions need at least 350,000 to 500,000 cardholders to justify doing in-house processing.

Each major credit card company has its own authorization and interchange systems. *Authorization* is a procedure for notifying the card issuing institution when a cardholder makes a purchase over an established dollar amount called a *floor limit*. Different types of merchants that honor credit cards have different floor limits. Floor limits protect the merchant by guaranteeing that the cardholder's purchase does not exceed his or her personal credit limit. In addition, authorization provides a means of flagging lost or stolen credit cards to prevent their use by unauthorized persons.

When a credit card purchase is made, the merchant fills out a charge slip and deposits a copy with a financial institution. The charge slip information is routed electronically through a clearing system and is finally returned to the card-issuing institution. This clearing process, which operates in much the same way as check clearing through the Federal Reserve, is called *interchange*. Some companies have separate interchange systems to route transactions from the merchant back to the card issuer.

The card issuer accumulates transactions on individual cardholders' accounts and sends monthly statements. In recent years financial institutions have found that the cost of collecting, filing and returning charge slips with the statements are prohibitive; consequently descriptive statements are being used more often. A descriptive statement shows the previous (opening) balance; the descriptions, date and amount of each purchase; and merchants' names and addresses. In addition, it lists payments received during the period, finance charges, current amount due, required minimum payment and payment due date.

Institutions offering a credit card service often solicit and set up merchants for accepting credit card transactions. Merchants sign an agreement to accept payments by credit cards issued by the institution and affiliated members of the interchange system. Institutions arrange for the new merchant's supplies, such as charge slips, deposit slips and embossing plates (for imprinting the charge slips with the information embossed on the plastic credit card), and often train the merchant's employees to use them.

HANDLING INQUIRIES

Another important responsibility of a consumer credit servicing department is responding to inquiries from current borrowers and other lending institutions. Borrowers most often contact the lender by telephone to ask about the status of their loans or to request help in solving minor problems.

Lenders more often communicate in writing to inquire about a current borrower's loan status. To protect a customer's privacy, institutions often require that written requests from lenders carry the borrower's signature authorizing release of the information.

For lenders using coupon payment systems, new borrowers often telephone to say they have not received their coupon books. If the loan account number and amount are encoded in magnetic ink (called MICR encoding— *Magnetic Ink Character Recognition*) at the bottom of each coupon, coupon books for new borrowers must be ordered and may take several weeks to be printed. To avoid many unnecessary telephone calls, it is good practice to inform new borrowers of the date by which they should expect to receive their coupon books.

During the term of their loans, borrowers may call to report changes of name or address, lost disbursement checks or lost coupon books. Name and address changes must be recorded on the computer's files and, perhaps, on the loan documents in the loan files. For lost disbursement checks, lenders may issue stop payment orders (instructions to prohibit the commercial bank from honoring checks if they are presented for payment) as a matter of policy to prevent loss. Since lost coupon books do not generally represent a potential threat to either the lender or the borrower, the lender merely issues another coupon book.

Other less frequent inquiries are made to learn the total interest paid for the year and to question the information on audit notices. Because borrowers may use yearly interest figures to figure income tax returns these calls occur most frequently during the first three months of the year.[4] When a lender is audited, notices are sent to a sample group of borrowers to ask for confirmation of the outstanding loan amount and terms. Auditors ask borrowers to respond only if the information on the notice is incorrect.

Answering inquiries requires patient listening skills and efficient information retrieval on the part of consumer credit department personnel. In addition, employees must be able to carefully explain the lender's services and procedures. For example, if a borrower asks how the principal and interest amounts of a monthly payment change each month, the employee must be able to explain in a clear and concise manner how a loan amortizes.

Another inquiry concerns the possibility of a loan modification. A *loan modification* is any change in the loan term, interest rate or amortization schedule, made by agreement between both the borrower and the lender, to reduce the borrower's monthly payment amount. A lender can approve loan modifications to help borrowers in temporary financial difficulties. These borrowers have a history of submitting payments on time but suddenly find a smaller monthly payment more manageable. Some lenders offer a one month's extension at Christmas time to their preferred customers. Loan modifications may also be made for borrowers with a sudden increase in income who want to make an advance payment. The subsequent reduced principal balance can make later monthly payments fewer or smaller.

When a loan modification request is approved, loan processors prepare an agreement specifying the reason for modification and its effects on the terms of the original note. The agreement is signed by an authorized lending officer and all borrowers listed on the original note. The changes that are made are reflected on the note and on other documents in the borrower's loan file. Loan modifications are rare for consumer loans. They are more common for longer term loans such as real estate mortgages.

Another inquiry is for a borrower to ask if a substitution of collateral can be made. For example, suppose Ed has made 36 payments on his 48-month auto loan. Ed decides to sell the car and asks the lender if he can substitute another car as collateral for the remaining loan balance—in essence, swap titles. The lender may respond in several ways. The lender might look at Ed's account relationship with the institution, his payment history on this and other loans, and decide to return the car title to Ed, allowing an unsecured loan for the remaining balance. If the lender cannot justify an unsecured loan to Ed, a substitution of collateral might be feasible. Before switching titles, the lender checks the substitute car's value against car price guidebooks to make sure it is worth at least the remaining loan balance. Of course, the lien on the first car must be released and a new lien put on the second car.

In another example, suppose Sue, a novice water skier, borrowed funds to purchase a speed boat and boat motor. For a few years Sue paid her loan in a timely manner. Then, Sue, now an experienced water skier, wants to sell the boat motor so she can buy a faster one. She asks the lender to release the lien on the boat motor. The lender can do this with a partial release, using the UCC-3 form shown in Figure 8-1.

When borrowers want to pay off their loans, they may call the institution to obtain a payoff figure. In addition to providing the payoff figure, loan employees must be able to inform borrowers of the upcoming procedures for releasing the title to any collateral held by the institution. Callers might ask about the anticipated length of time before papers are released. For instance, a lender may wait for a time (anywhere from 3 to 15 days) to allow the borrower's final payment check to clear. This assures the lender that the funds will be collected before the title is released.

Commercial banks and finance companies, or credit reporting agencies might inquire about the current status of loans. This information may be helpful to them when they conduct credit evaluations or update credit agency files. When appropriate, lenders may inform inquirers in writing of the outstanding loan balance, the loan terms and the payoff date (see Figure 8-7).

Regulation B affects one aspect of responding to credit inquires; that of reporting credit information on spouses. Prior to 1976, lenders often reported credit only in the husband's name (even if the wife was also obligated to repay the debt). Because of this practice, in the past, a woman attempting to obtain credit in her own name often was hindered by the lack of her own credit history. Today, Section

FIGURE 8-7
Consumer Loan Status Report

```
BALANCE DUE   $4,956.97
DATE OPEN     December 12, 1984
TERMS         180 months                                    @ $    63.97
NEXT DUE      June 6, 1986
PAYOFF        2,987.88                          AS OF    May 29, 1986
DAILY FACTOR  + $2.98
LOAN TYPE:    [ ] ADD-ON    [X] SIMPLE INTEREST
CREDIT EXPERIENCE MAY BE OBTAINED FROM THE LOCAL CREDIT BUREAU.
QUOTED BY     S. Processor                      DATE     5/29/86
```

202.6 of Regulation B provides that if a loan account is one in which both an applicant and a spouse are contractually liable, the loan records must be designated to reflect the fact of participation by both spouses. When furnishing information to credit reporting agencies, then, lenders must provide information about the account in the name of both spouses.

SUMMARY

Consumer loan servicing duties involve a number of employees, including some who work outside of the consumer credit department. Loan processors are responsible for completing the loan file, a task that includes obtaining evidence that the security interest in collateral has been perfected, and verifying that collateral is properly insured and that the lender is named on the policy to receive the benefits.

Maintaining perfected security interest is especially important for collateral on which financing statements are filed because the financing statement will expire after five years. Lenders must periodically verify the location of motor vehicles to prevent the fraudulent practice of moving the vehicle to another state and obtaining a clear title. Lenders monitor stock dividends and splits to avoid a loss of collateral value. When a loan is paid off, the lender must execute a release to cancel its claim to the collateral.

Lenders use three common payment systems for consumer loans: coupons, statements and Transmatic® with a coupon system, borrowers receive a book of coupons and submit one with each payment. With a statement system, statements are mailed to borrowers every month indicating the payment amount and due date. Borrowers may submit payments to the lender through the mail, a teller window or a lock box arrangement. With an automatic transfer or Transmatic® service, borrowers execute an agreement that authorizes the lender to take loan payments from their checking or deposit accounts and credit their loan account. The lender initiates the payment every month.

For loans secured by mortgages, and for loans in which property has been foreclosed or abandoned, the lender may be required to submit informational reports to the IRS and the customer.

Consumer loan computer reports are common to lenders. The trial balance is a list of all loan accounts and their outstanding balances used to monitor loan activity. The transaction journal provides verification of posting by giving a report on all loan payments made the previous business day. The new loan report, loan history and payoff report are used to verify computer file information. Delinquency reports are used by collectors to identify delinquent borrowers as a basis for further action. The interest earned report aids in determining loan profitability and in completing required reports to the IRS and the customer.

Indirect loan servicing activities include monitoring and maintaining dealer reserves and disbursing dealer income. Periodic visits are made to dealers to check on operations and to monitor the dealer's financial condition.

Credit card operations involve many activities for the institution that issues its own credit card or cards from a national credit card service. Besides processing transactions and preparing monthly statements, institutions often solicit area merchants to accept payments by credit card.

Answering inquiries is a loan servicing activity that requires good listening skills and rapid information retrieval. Common borrower inquiries involve delays in receiving coupon books, reports of changes in name and address, and information such as the total interest paid for the year and the amount needed to pay off a loan.

CHAPTER QUESTIONS

1. Why is it important for a lender to carefully monitor and maintain security interest in a loan secured by an automobile, personal property, or stocks and bonds?

2. What steps must a lender take to release security interest in personal property, automobiles and real property?

3. Describe how payments are processed using a lock box service and the Transmatic® system.

4. List three common inquiries received by the consumer credit department.

5. Define dealer reserves and dealer rate.

6. Why is it important for a representative of the consumer credit department to make regular visits to affiliated dealers?

7. Outline the operations activities involved when an institution offers credit card services as an agent, participating agent or card issuer. List several items for which a card issuer should plan.

FOOTNOTES

[1] Under the 1962 version of the Uniform Commercial Code (§9-403(2)) "...a financing statement which states a maturity date of the obligation secured as five years or less is effective only until the stated maturity date and thereafter for sixty days; by comparison a financing statement containing no maturity date, or one exceeding five years or reflecting a demand obligation is always good for a full five years." Under the 1972 Code Rev (§9-403(2)), no exception is made for a stated maturity of less than five years.

[2] UCC §9-404(1); Rev. §9-404(1).

[3] Institutions should check with their legal counsel to find out which loans are covered. For greater detail see Title 26, Code of Federal Regulations, Parts 1 and 602 and the U.S. League's *Special Management Bulletin,* number S-241, dated 9-5-85.

[4] As of September 1986, proposed tax law changes would phase-out the deduction for consumer loan interest.

9

Collection Procedures and Remedies

Objectives

After studying this chapter, you should be able to:
- ☐ Name and explain factors that affect delinquency rates for consumer loans;
- ☐ Describe three methods of classifying delinquent borrowers;
- ☐ State the purpose of an established collections policy and give examples of characteristics of effective policies;
- ☐ Outline the prohibitions and effects on institution debt procedures of the Fair Debt Collection Practices Act;
- ☐ Name three general purposes of preliminary collection procedures;
- ☐ Describe the appropriate use of collection methods such as contacts by telephone, in writing and in person;
- ☐ Explain techniques to use in handling the special problems presented by "artful dodgers" and skips;
- ☐ Name and describe two remedial payment techniques and two methods of collateral acquisitions; and
- ☐ Explain when and why charge-offs of delinquent loans may be needed.

INTRODUCTION

All lenders expect a certain number of delinquent loans. Although most borrowers pay off their loans as agreed, a few make occasional late payments, while others are chronically late in making payments or stop making payments entirely. Therefore, all lenders must design collection policies and procedures to handle these recurring problems.

Collectors generally are responsible for contacting delinquent borrowers and working with them to collect payments. Although guided largely by institution policy, effective collectors also need interpersonal communication and customer relations skills to deal effectively with delinquent borrowers. If routine collection activities do not work, however, collectors or other institution personnel must then consider restructuring loan payment schedules; obtaining a portion of borrowers' wages from employers; or locating, acquiring and selling borrowers' collateral to satisfy the debt.

CONSUMER LOAN DELINQUENCY

A certain number of delinquent loans are inevitable in any consumer credit operation. Even institutions that employ experienced loan officers, follow sound underwriting procedures and require rigid adherence to their credit evaluation policies make some loans that become delinquent. An institution's *delinquency rate* is the percentage of delinquent loans to the total amount of loans outstanding. Certain factors that affect the rate and the seriousness of loan delinquencies are under the lender's control; other factors are external. Knowing these factors can help collectors make realistic plans.

Lender Controlled Factors

Two factors that the lending institution can control are its consumer loan marketing philosophy and the types of consumer loans it chooses to offer. Some lenders believe that a certain level of delinquencies is desirable, because this indicates that the institution is aggressively marketing its lending services. In this marketing approach, a delinquency level no lower than that of other institutions nationwide is viewed as appropriate. In contrast, an institution that is conservative in its lending policies may have a delinquency rate that is much lower than the national average. Although the second approach seems desirable, some view it as a sign that the institution turns away some marginal loans that might, on the whole, be profitable.

Since delinquency rates on different types of consumer loans vary, each institution's delinquency rates also depend in part on the types of consumer loans it offers. Historically, home appliance and mobile home loans rank among the higher risk consumer loans, revolving credit card and indirect automobile loans fall into the middle, and home improvement and direct automobile loans are among the lower risk types of consumer loans (see Figure 9-1).

As a general rule, unsecured credit products have a higher delinquency rate than secured credit products. Also a factor is the rate at which an asset purchased with loan funds depreciates. For example, home appliances depreciate more quickly and have shorter useful life spans than automobiles; this helps explain why the delinquency rate on appliances may be higher. The relative importance of the collateral to the borrower also contributes to the rate of delinquency: a home, for instance, represents a sizable and valued possession to the borrower, and so historically a home improvement loan is less often delinquent than an automobile loan.

External Factors

Certain events outside the control of the institution also affect loan delinquency rates. Over the years, rates have shown seasonal trends. For example, delinquency rates for most loans are highest either during the winter months because borrowers sometimes overextend themselves by spending excessively during the holiday season, or during late summer when borrowers must pay vacation expenses and bear the added expense of children returning to school.

More generally, economic and cyclical trends in business conditions also affect delinquency rates. For instance, unemployment rates, inflation levels, recession trends, and the level of interest rates or energy prices can cause delinquency rates to rise or fall for particular types of loans. Loans for recreational vehicles (RVs) will be negatively affected by

FIGURE 9-1
Percent of Loans Delinquent by Category

Type of Loan	Delinquency Rates*
Automobile	1.6%
Revolving Credit	1.6%
Home Improvement	1.9%
Recreational Vehicle	2.1%
Bank Cards	2.9%
Mobile Home	2.9%
Personal Loans	3.5%

*As of January 31, 1986

Source: *Consumer Credit Delinquency Bulletin*, American Bankers Association, First Quarter 1986.

rising energy prices, resulting in higher delinquency rates for the RV loans when the price of gasoline rises quickly. Similarly, rapidly rising interest rates may lead to an increase in defaults on revolving credit loans as people take on more debt than they can afford.

CLASSIFYING DELINQUENT BORROWERS

Collectors and institutions must keep delinquency rates in the proper perspective. Over 96% of the people who are granted consumer credit repay their loans as agreed; only the remaining fewer than 3% do not. Collectors must understand this small percentage of borrowers well, however, so they can handle repayment problems quickly and effectively.

Who are the delinquent borrowers and why do they become delinquent? Collectors may approach these questions by looking at borrowers from three perspectives: borrowers with different payment styles, borrowers experiencing financial distress and borrowers with differing attitudes toward their repayment responsibilities.

Payment Styles and Degree of Risk

Collectors often classify delinquent borrowers into three groups—good, fair or poor risks. Good risk borrowers are those who are willing and able to repay. They have established good credit ratings and are conscientious about maintaining them. Most often, if good risk borrowers have become delinquent, the reason is that they simply forgot to make a payment, the payment was lost in the mail, or it was received on time but was posted to the wrong loan account by mistake. These borrowers usually respond quickly when they learn of the real or perceived delinquency.

Fair risk borrowers are often able to pay but unwilling to repay as scheduled. People in this group respond to persistent collection attempts but too often seem to wait for a reminder from the collection department before remitting their payments.

Both good and fair risk borrowers may be unable to pay when unusual situations arise, such as temporary financial hardship. In this circumstance, good risk borrowers tend to seek financial counseling from collectors and to cooperate in setting up a reasonable repayment plan. Fair risk borrowers may not actively seek counseling services but will often respond to counseling if a collector or other responsible person suggests it.

In contrast to good risk and fair risk borrowers, poor risk borrowers often are unwilling and/or unable to pay. People in this group may have just narrowly met the institution's credit evaluation standards and may offer excuses rather than sound reasons for not repaying. Poor risk borrowers seldom respond to collection attempts, often express misdirected hostility or anger toward collectors. In addition, borrowers

\multicolumn{4}{c}{**Borrower Characteristics**}
Risk	Poor	Fair	Good
Payment Style	Unwilling and/or Unable	Able but Unwilling	Willing and Able
Reasons	Distressed • unemployed • illness • marital problems • excessive debts Chronic • cannot • will not	Distressed • unemployed • illness • marital problems • excessive debts	

may seem unconcerned with the effect of poor payments on their credit histories.

Often fair and poor risk borrowers become delinquent because of a lack of sound financial management. They have poor (or no) budgeting habits and demonstrate little knowledge of the amount of credit that they can safely assume. These inadequacies often lead to their contracting for larger monthly payments than they can afford which results in delinquencies.

The Distressed Delinquent

People who are normally good or fair risk borrowers sometimes get into situations in which they think they cannot repay the loan. Sudden unemployment or strikes are common examples. In these cases, a collector must determine if there are any other sources of funds available for repayment, such as deposit accounts or credit union accounts. Also, if the situation is temporary, the collector may suggest refinancing or recasting the loan.

Occasionally, illness may be a reason for delinquency. A collector must then determine if the borrower has adequate health and accident insurance and then approach the borrower to arrange repayment. Workers' compensation during unemployment is a source of funds for repayment in that situation.

Marital problems pose an especially difficult situation. A collector must be careful not to take sides. People who are divorced may sometimes claim that the divorce decree exempts them from repaying the debt, and that the spouse is responsible. A collector should know that a divorce decree is binding only between the two parties in a divorce and that it has no effect on the lending institution. Hence, a lender can legally seek repayment from either or both spouses if they signed for the credit jointly. This particular situation requires a firm yet diplomatic approach.

Excessive debts may also be a reason for delinquency. If a borrower claims to have excessive debts, a collector should verify this by calling a credit bureau. Sometimes a skillful collector may be able to show a borrower how the debts can be repaid from current income. The time expended in this effort may prove beneficial for both the lender and the borrower.

Attitudes of Repeat Delinquents

Chronically delinquent borrowers fall into two broad categories: those who cannot pay and those who will not pay. People suffering financial distress as just described often are among those who cannot pay as agreed. Their loan can usually be brought back to current status through counseling in financial management skills or by an arrangement with the lender for changes in the loan terms. For customers who have money but refuse to meet their debts responsibly, firmer measures are needed. These debtors must be convinced that the consequences of not paying are unacceptably high.

The typical collection process follows a sequence that helps the institution uncover creditor attitudes so that well-intentioned delinquent borrowers are given appropriate help while irresponsible delinquent borrowers are identified quickly to prevent significant loss to the institution.

THE COLLECTIONS POLICY

Every institution has its own *collections policy*. The purpose of a policy is to communicate to employees a systematic and legally correct method for identifying and contacting delinquent borrowers and for handling delinquent loans. With an established collections policy, the uniform treatment of borrowers is generally assured and the interests of the institution are protected.

Characteristics of Effective Practices

The overall goal of consumer loan collections is to protect the institution's financial investment in the loan. Ideally, the institution can collect all of the money still owed to it and also get loan payments back on schedule. If this is not possible, the next best alternative is to get as close to full repayment of the principal and interest due within a time frame as close to the original repayment schedule as possible.

The goal of collection efforts is to minimize the amount of loss. Certain polices and practices have proven most effective in meeting this goal. An effective collection system is prompt, fair, adaptable and results-oriented.

Prompt Response
Studies have shown that the longer a loan is delinquent the less chance a lender has of recovering payment. For this reason, prompt and consistent contact with delinquent borrowers must be established at the beginning of a delinquency to reduce the possibility of default. Early and regular contact indicates to the borrower that the institution is concerned about the cause of the delinquency and is serious about collecting payment.

Timing is especially crucial in attempting to recover delinquent payments on consumer loans. On mortgage loans, as time goes by, the value of the collateral tends to remain stable or even increase. By contrast, with a secured consumer loan, the collateral usually loses value quickly. Therefore, the collection process for consumer loans must be swift. Seriously delinquent consumer loans are unlikely to be repaid in full or to be recoverable in full by repossession of the collateral. A sample collection schedule is shown in Figure 9-2.

Fair Application
Since there can be many reasons for slow or missed payments, the institution's collection policy must be fair and not vindictive in its intent. Fair treatment of loan customers by collectors from the beginning to the end of the process is good customer relations, as well as legally required.

An example of fair treatment is to grant a grace period. Technically, borrowers are delinquent if a payment is not received by the due date, but institutions often allow a *grace period* of a number of days (10 is common) after the due date during which payments may be made without having to pay late charges. During this grace period, no collections procedures are begun, and payments submitted within this time generally do not reflect adversely on the borrower's permanent credit history.

A second example of fairness is to inform borrowers fully about late charges as specifically defined in the note. These *late charges* may be stated as a fixed fee or as a percentage of the loan payment due. The maximum permissible percentage generally is controlled by state law, with some states entirely prohibiting the use of late charges. Late charges are imposed to penalize borrowers for delinquent payments, thereby encouraging the habit of prompt payment. Income from late

FIGURE 9-2
Collection Schedules

	Institution A	Institution B
First Notice	5 days	10 days
Grace Period	10 days	15 days
Second Notice (Lists late charges)	10 days	20 days
Letters	Same as Second Notice	31 to 60 days— or telephone contact. (May contact employer at 31 days)
Telephone Contacts	15 days, and sends letter restating arrangements made	31 to 60 days
Personal Interviews	10 to 55 days a continuing option	15 to 120 (180) days Interviews whenever possible
Field Visits	25 days, and sends letter restating arrangements made	61 days Visits made by branch managers
Refer to Collections Manager	30 days, and sends letter threatening legal action at 35 and 45 days	61 to 120 (180) days Collections Manager reviews monthly
Legal Action	55 days	61 to 120 (180) days depending on situation
Recognized as a loss by FSLIC Regulations	Closed-end—120 days Open-end—180 days	Same

charges may help meet some of the administrative costs of nonstandard loan payments. However, late charges are effective only when regularly enforced. They should be waived only in appropriate situations.

Adaptable Procedures

While collectors follow standard rules for the collection process, they also need guidelines on how much they can tailor the standard process to a particular situation. Not all borrowers are alike, and collectors must work with each on an individual basis. This is especially true when establishing repayment plans, since collectors must consider a borrower's character, repayment history, current income and other debt, in order to set up a reasonable plan for ending the delinquency.

For first time delinquents, and particularly upon the first payment default, policy might suggest that the borrower be contacted first by telephone. During the conversation, the collector can obtain preliminary information about the borrower and check that the borrower understands the loan terms and the need for prompt payment.

Another instance of adapting policy to a particular situation is when a borrower has been granted an alternate (or remedial) repayment plan, but fails to submit payments as agreed. A collections policy might outline at what points the collector should continue to contact the borrower and when to refer the case to a superior for possible legal action.

Results-oriented
A well designed collections system will include a timely and accurate accounting of all results achieved by collection activities. The costs of using various collection devices and methods should be periodically compared to verifiable benefits obtained from them. Such comparisons may indicate a need to change collection policies and practices. Computer generated delinquency and scheduled items reports should be reviewed to identify trends or particular types of loans that may need further attention. Institution goals to maintain or lower delinquency rates need to be continually evaluated against the costs and benefits of attempting to achieve them. Policies should be in place to identify whether continued collection efforts or legal proceedings will be more cost effective for the lender. Generally, the sooner collection methods are begun on a delinquent loan, the better the chances are for collecting the debt.

Sequencing: Choosing the Right Device

A collections policy describes a sequence of events for collectors to follow. The policy names approved *collection devices* and outlines a schedule for the appropriate times to use each one. As the status of an overdue loan becomes more and more serious, increasingly severe devices are introduced.

For example, if a loan issued by First Federal to Frank

Meadows becomes 15 to 30 days past due, the institution's policy might be to use the devices of routine notices, telephone contacts and letters. During this time, collectors might counsel Frank or reinstate the loan without penalty once his payments are brought up-to-date. If Frank's delinquency continues and the loan becomes 91-120 days overdue, more severe devices might be approved. First Federal's policy might call for collectors to visit Frank's home personally and to consider appropriate legal action. With the more serious delinquency, collectors might present a new repayment plan to Frank or they might take steps to repossess the collateral.

A lender's collections policy also delineates the changing status of delinquent loans over time. An institution with a 30-day grace period might consider the loan in Frank's first situation (15 to 30 days overdue) as not delinquent, while its status at the second point in time (91-120 days overdue) might be that of a slow loan or a loan to be charged off as a loss.

Legal Constraints

If the institution has exhausted routine collection devices and has made numerous unsuccessful attempts to gain the borrower's cooperation, legal action may be needed. Here, the lenders' policy will insure that the action is legally correct in terms of the original contract and current laws and regulations.

Many state and federal laws and regulations influence collections policies. They place limits on actions the lenders can take to collect the debt and specify the steps that must be taken to enforce the contractual agreement between lender and borrower. One of the most important laws for collectors is the Fair Debt Collection Practices Act.

Fair Debt Collection Practices Act

The Fair Debt Collection Practices Act, a federal law, was adopted in 1977. Its major purposes are to protect borrowers from unfair, abusive or deceptive collection practices and to encourage states to pass similar laws to protect consumers.

FHLB regulations require member institutions to comply with the Act in those situations where an institution matches the Act's definition of collector. Specifically, savings institutions are debt collectors under the Act if:

- they are involved in a reciprocal service agreement whereby the institution acts as a third party to collect debts other than its own; or
- they use a name other than their own (in writing or orally) that might give the impression that a third party is collecting the debt.

Even though the Act's definition excludes collections practices of savings institutions, the FHLB encourages voluntary compliance with the Act for all of its member institutions. State laws may impose similar or even stricter requirements. Therefore, the Act's provisions are of concern for all collectors.

Contacting debtors. The Act requires that all contact with debtors should be at reasonable hours; generally, reasonable hours are said to be from 8:00 a.m. to 9:00 p.m. If collectors are aware that a debtor's employer does not allow collection efforts to be made at work, the efforts should not be made. Also, collectors should not contact the debtor at work if asked not to.

If the debtor disagrees with the amount of the debt or the statement that it is past due, collectors should refrain from further contact until they have again investigated the claim and reported back on the result. If the debtor continues to dispute the debt, contact may be resumed. Collectors must stop contacting the debtor if he or she writes and asks them to stop or refuses to pay. Collectors may, however, notify these resistant debtors that they plan to take legal action.

Contacting a third party to locate the debtor. When using a third party to locate the debtor, collectors should identify themselves and whom they are trying to contact. Collectors should not give the institution's name unless asked and should not tell the person that the borrower owes a debt.

A third person should not be contacted more than once unless the person allows it, or unless the collector has reason to believe that the information given originally was incorrect or incomplete and that the correct information is now available.

When contacting a third party by mail, the borrower's privacy must be protected. Nothing on the envelope should indicate that the communication relates to the collection of a debt, nor should postcards be used. All communication must be confidential.

Other practices. Collectors should not, while trying to collect the debt, use harassment. For example, the Act prohibits the use of abusive language, threats or physical force. The name of the debtor may not be publicly posted anywhere, and repeated telephone calls are prohibited.

False, deceptive or misleading representation in collecting the debt is not allowed. Collectors should not pretend to be attorneys, for example, nor should they threaten the seizure of property or garnishment of wages unless an action of this kind is lawful and is one they intend to take. Similarly, collectors cannot threaten to repossess collateral unless they have the right and intent to do so.

Federal and State Regulations
A number of additional laws and regulations affect the late stages of the collections process. Some areas of consequence are wage garnishment, repossession and foreclosure. State laws and regulations often are very relevant here. Therefore, institution policy might name relevant state statutes or agencies, or might direct collectors to managers or to the institution's legal counsel whenever a regulated point in the process is reached.

Preliminary Collections Procedures

In savings institutions, collectors take a number of steps before contacting borrowers. Preliminary procedures insure that collectors have full, correct information and they permit collectors to analyze the facts to decide on the most effective devices and actions to use.

Verification of Past-due Status

Before collectors contact a delinquent borrower, they must verify that the borrower has indeed failed to make a payment. Additionally, they should examine the borrower's past payment history on this and other loans, investigate additional information the institution has about the borrower and outline questions to ask during the contact.

Verifying that payments are past due avoids the problem of reporting borrowers as delinquent who are not, in fact, delinquent. If the institution has made an error in processing a payment, borrowers incorrectly reported as being delinquent may become angry when they receive a collector's call. This situation is embarrassing both for the collector and potentially harmful to the institution.

Review of Repayment History

Another important preliminary step is to review a borrower's repayment history. This can indicate to the collector whether the borrower is a good, fair or poor risk and thus help determine which collection device might be best. If the borrower is a long-term institution customer and has had no previous record of delinquency, the collector may suspect loan servicing problems or financial hardships rather than an unwillingness to repay. On the other hand, if the borrower has been delinquent from time to time throughout the life of the loan or frequently has broken promises to repay according to remedial plans, legal action may be the only answer. In the first case, the preferred device might be a friendly phone call to uncover the cause of this nontypical behavior. In the second case, the preferred device might be quick delivery of a letter signifying intent to begin legal proceedings unless full payment is received.

Review of Borrower's Situation

Other information gathered when the loan was approved may be studied before borrowers are contacted. Collectors might look for the basis of the borrower's income; whether income is derived from salary, hourly wages or commission, and whether or not income is likely to be temporarily reduced if work is not steady. The collector needs to know the dates on which the borrower receives paychecks and whether they coincide with the payment-due dates or whether other due dates would make on-time payments more manageable. If the loan has been delinquent before, the collector might see which collections devices were tried and proved effective.

Once collectors have gathered and analyzed the facts, they are ready to move to the collection process.

COLLECTIONS DEVICES AND TOOLS

Collections devices are arranged in a sequence from mild to severe. Some are more time-consuming than others and their costs also may differ by a considerable margin. These factors, plus institution policy and the specific delinquency situation, enter into the collector's plan of action.

Common devices and tools are telephone contacts, written notifications and personal interviews. When collectors face a particularly difficult delinquency, other strategies and tools may be needed. Whatever devices are used, prompt follow-up on any agreements is highly important. Collectors want borrowers to sense the urgency of keeping their promises. Throughout the process, collectors regularly monitor the status of the loan and continually respond to missed repayments or other unfulfilled agreements.

Telephone Contacts

Telephone contact with delinquent borrowers is an effective collections device because it commands the immediate attention of the borrower and permits two-way communication. The two purposes of the first telephone contact are to discover the reasons for delinquency and to persuade the borrower to make realistic arrangements to bring the loan back to current status.

The background information about the borrower that was gathered in the preliminary stage helps the collector determine the best time and place to call the borrower. In some institutions, collectors work during evening hours so that they can telephone delinquent borrowers at home. This often is helpful since many borrowers do not feel free to discuss personal financial matters at their place of business or have limited time for personal calls on the job.

Before telephoning a borrower, a collector may prepare a

brief outline of the intended conversation, including an opening statement and a list of important questions. Several possible remedial payment options may be designed if this seems necessary.

When using the telephone to contact delinquent borrowers, the collector should verify the identity of the borrower before stating the purpose of the call. This avoids giving an unknown person information about the delinquent borrower as prohibited under fair debt legislation.

A useful opening telephone technique is for collectors to simply identify themselves and then stop talking: "Is this Mrs. Helen Frederick? It is? Mrs. Frederick, this is Lee Williams from First Federal Savings." Then silence. The lack of small talk and explanation by the collector forces the borrower to respond without time to prepare an excuse. Often, feeling compelled to end the silence, the borrower quickly volunteers facts about the delinquency.

Once the borrower has responded, collectors may ask questions to fill in any gaps. While some questions might be

FIGURE 9-3
Collections Referral Card

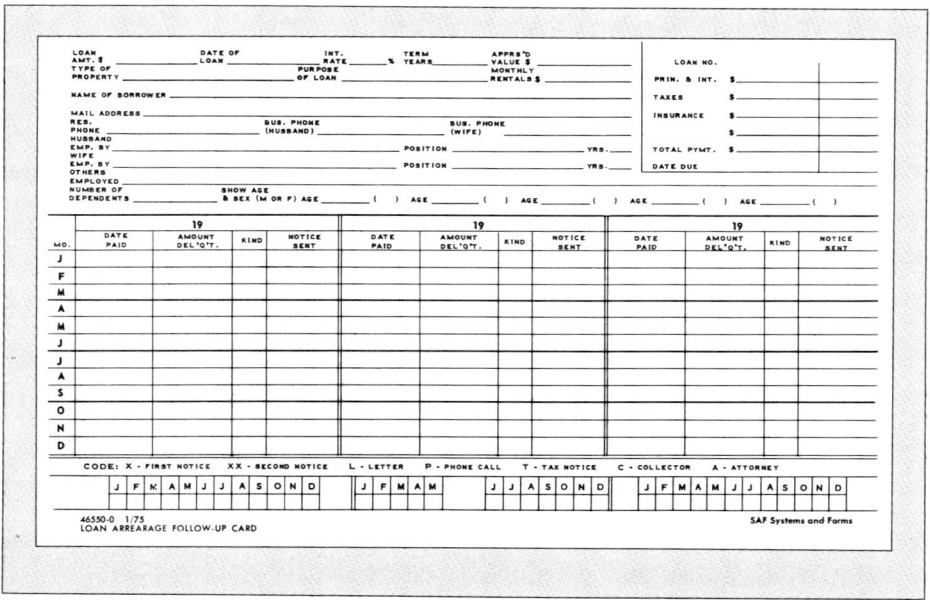

specific, collectors may find open-ended inquiries that cannot be answered by a single word or a *yes* or *no* more productive. Open-ended questions often begin with the words, *what, why, when, where* and *how*. Responses to a few good open-ended questions often contain more information than could be obtained from many yes/no questions.

By the end of the call, collectors should have received some commitment from the borrower for a payment. Here, collectors have two concerns: specific facts about when and how the payment will be made and information about the source of funds that will be used for repayment. When a borrower promises to make a payment, the collector should ask for a date, within the next few days, by which the payment can be expected. This adds to the borrower's sense of commitment and, if the payment is not made as agreed, gives the collector a justifiable reason for a prompt follow-up contact. Information concerning the source of the funds for repayment helps the collector estimate how realistic and serious the borrower's promise to pay is.

After the telephone call, the collector makes a permanent record of the conversation by entering the information into a computer file or by writing down the date of the contact and the agreed-upon repayment arrangements on a collections referral card (see Figure 9-3). This record is maintained throughout the collections process.

Written Notification

Written notifications are a convenient way to communicate with delinquent borrowers. Written notices do not take much staff time and demonstrate a good faith attempt by the lender to reach the borrower and solve the problem. In serious situations, they present a more formal appearance than a telephone call. They do not, however, permit two-way communication between delinquent borrowers and the institution, and borrowers might discard written notices without even opening or reading them.

Notices
The first contact with a delinquent borrower usually is a *late notice* that states that a payment has not been received (see

Figure 9-4). The notice is a brief preprinted form on which the past due amount and the due date are filled in. Its purpose is to bring the delinquent payment to the borrower's attention. Good risk borrowers often respond to the first late notice.

Some institutions use more than one late notice before trying another collection device. Second (or third) notices may notify the borrower of any late charges that have been assessed or mention that more serious action will follow unless payments are received.

Other institutions prefer not to send more than one late notice. Often, chronically slow-paying borrowers will learn to anticipate how many notices they will receive before more serious actions are taken and will deliberately wait before sending in a payment.

Letters
A collections letter is a serious, formal and personalized communication. Its purpose is to individualize the message in a way that preprinted forms do not do.

Institutions may send a series of collections letters to delinquent borrowers who do not remit payments. Early collections letters usually are brief, use simple but formal language, and specify the payment amount and the due date.

FIGURE 9-4
Late Notice

IMPORTANT

Your loan payment has not been received as yet. The account is now delinquent. We request that you remit by return mail.

PROTECT YOUR CREDIT RATING ... PAY PROMPTLY

DETACH HERE Enclose check or money order in envelope below—seal and mail.

46502-1 (9/83)
E 428-2R

SAF Systems and Forms

FIGURE 9-5
First Collections Letter

Mr. Henry A. Anderson
201 Greenleaf
Anytown, U.S.A. 12345

Dear Mr. Anderson:

Your loan payment of $240.00 due on September 1st has not been received. Late payments jeopardize your credit rating, and if this amount is not paid at once, other collection action may result.

Send $252.00 (which includes $12.00 in late charges) immediately or call our offices to make satisfactory arrangements for your payment.

Very truly yours,

Carl P. Corbett
Collections Manager
First Federal Savings

The first letter in the series might stress the importance of a good credit rating (see Figure 9-5). The second letter could emphasize the seriousness of the delinquency and the borrowers' responsibility for remitting payments on time (see Figure 9-6). The third letter might report that legal action will follow if the borrower does not respond (see Figure 9-7).

Other Written Messages

A variation on notices and letters are mailgrams and telegrams. A mailgram is a written message delivered by the U.S. Postal Service on the following business day. Its value as a collection device lies in its psychological impact and the impending sense of urgency it communicates. Mailgrams have some of the same psychological effects as telegrams but cost less to send. A disadvantage of both mailgrams and telegrams is that they release confidential information to a third party (e.g., postal worker) and, therefore, may be prohibited under the Fair Debt Collection Practices Act.

FIGURE 9-6
Second Collections Letter

> Mr. Henry A. Anderson
> 201 Greenleaf
> Anytown, U.S.A. 12345
>
> Dear Mr. Anderson:
>
> It is necessary for us to again remind you of the serious delinquent condition of your loan.
>
> You are to make payments every month on your due date, and it is your responsibility to make these payments on time.
>
> We cannot maintain your account on the basis upon which it has been carried. Please remit $252.00 by return mail and arrange your finances so that future payments are received on or before the monthly due date. Otherwise it will be necessary for us to take other steps to enforce the collection of the loan.
>
> Yours truly,
>
>
> Carl P. Corbett
> Collections Manager
> First Federal Savings

Personal Contacts

Two types of personal contacts may be used by collectors: field visits and office interviews. Because they are time-consuming for collectors, however, personal contacts typically are reserved for serious delinquencies.

Field Visits

Field visits are home visitations by collectors when borrowers do not respond to written notices or cannot be reached by telephone. A personal visit by a collector conveys the serious and concerned attitude of the institution. For secured consumer loans, these visits also allow for an examination of the

FIGURE 9-7
Third Collections Letter

Mr. Henry A. Anderson
201 Greenleaf
Anytown, U.S.A. 12345

Dear Mr. Anderson:

It appears that it may be necessary for us to refer your account to our attorneys for action. Whether or not that will happen depends on you.

Legal action means additional expenses and embarrassment for you. However, we feel that we have done everything possible to cooperate and are justified in bringing this matter to a conclusion.

Please contact me immediately to explain what arrangements you can make for payment.

Yours truly,

Carl P. Corbett
Collections Manager
First Federal Savings

---

real property, motor vehicle or other assets that were pledged as collateral.

Office Interviews

An *office interview* may be initiated at the suggestion of the collector or at the borrower's request. As with other contacts, the purpose of an office interview is to discover the reason for the delinquency and to establish a plan for bringing the loan current.

Office interviews often are more effective than telephone contacts, letters or field visits for two reasons. First, they take place in a formal setting. Institution offices convey a business-like atmosphere that encourages borrowers to respond in a responsible manner. Second, borrowers who agree to or initiate interviews are often those who will respond to the collector's counseling. In addition, an office interview incurs little or no added expense.

Legal Action

If the institution has exhausted all collection devices and has made numerous unsuccessful attempts to engage the borrower's cooperation, legal action may be required. Legal action is directed toward securing full satisfaction of the debt from the borrower and/or from the sale of collateral.

When collectors believe the time has come for legal action, the delinquent account and a full report of collections efforts to date are submitted to the collections manager, consumer loan manager or board of directors who then make the decision whether or not to begin legal proceedings. The institution's legal counsel is brought into the process and notification is sent to inform the borrower of the impending action.

SPECIAL PROBLEMS

At times, collectors face special problems that require persistent, intelligent application of nonroutine devices. Two examples are dealing with the "artful dodger" and locating missing borrowers through skiptracing.

The "Artful Dodger"

Collectors should distinguish between real, substantial problems that borrowers sometimes face and the minor excuses that typify the "artful dodger." The artful dodger usually intends to repay debts, but is generally slow or late with payments. Artful dodgers seldom offer any sound reason for being delinquent, although they always have an excuse, such as minor family illnesses, money tied up in long-term investments, "payment is in the mail," and so forth.

If the borrower says, "The payment is in the mail," a collector should challenge this statement by asking when the payment was mailed and by asking for the check number and amount. If the borrower wants to know why the collector needs this information, a good response is: "So that I can watch for it. Since it's a late payment, I don't want it to get lost. We want to make sure your account gets credited properly." By insisting on this information, a collector can determine how serious the borrower is. Additionally, if the payment was not actually sent but the borrower offers a date, check number and amount, most likely he or she will promptly write the check.

Some artful dodgers may excuse their delinquency by complaining about service from the dealer, especially on car loans. This is not a justification for failure to pay the debt. If a borrower was loaned money to purchase consumer goods (automobiles, appliances, etc.) and the institution has a purchase money security interest in those goods, the borrower is still legally obligated to repay the debt even if there is a dispute between the dealer and the borrower. A collector can explain that any problems with the dealer, although unfortunate, generally do not affect the borrower's obligation to repay the lender.

Owners of joint accounts sometimes respond to collectors' calls by reporting that the other joint account owner is the one who pays the bills and will ask the collector to contact that person. A collector should insist that the situation be resolved immediately. A good approach is to say, "Your name is listed on the account and you're just as liable for repayment as the co-owner. How do you plan to repay?" A good collector will then stop talking and let the borrower come up with a plan.

Sometimes borrowers claim to have misunderstood the terms and conditions of a loan. They may claim that they did not agree to the stated payment amounts and/or payment dates. In this case, a collector should determine whether this is an isolated incident or if there have been many similar claims. If the institution has experienced many of these incidents, then a problem exists with its loan closing process. If this is an isolated incident, chances are this is just another "artful dodge" that should be handled by firmly reminding the borrower of the legal obligation to abide by the loan agreement.

Sometimes the collector must contact third parties to obtain information to find the borrowers. However, bringing in a third party may bring the process under the Fair Debt Collection Practices Act, so collectors should first search the institution's own files for clues before moving to skiptracing.

Skiptracing

Delinquent borrowers who cannot be contacted by mail or telephone are called skips or skip debtors. *Skiptracing* is a process whereby collectors try to uncover information to help them locate missing debtors.

To protect borrowers' financial privacy, the Fair Debt Collection Practices Act limits skiptracing to "the acquisition of location information." Location information is defined as "the borrower's place of residence, the telephone number at the place of residence and the borrower's place of employment."

The Act requires certain activities directly related to skiptracing and prohibits others.

- Collectors must identify themselves, and they must identify their company if the party asks.
- Collectors cannot reveal to the third party that a borrower has an unpaid debt.
- A third party can be contacted only once unless the information obtained from that third party is incorrect or incomplete, whereupon, another contact may be made.
- Postcards cannot be used to communicate with the third party because they are considered to be an invasion of privacy.
- Envelopes and letterheads cannot display a logo or company name signifying that the collector is in the debt collection business or that there is a debt collection effort involved.

From the lender's viewpoint, the skiptracing techniques used and the intensity of the skip search depend on whether the skips are unintentional or intentional. Unintentional skips are usually borrowers who move and either simply forget to notify creditors or procrastinate in doing so. When unintentional skips are located promptly, debt repayments are usually recovered.

On the other hand, intentional skips purposely avoid repayment and literally attempt to hide from creditors. Two common types of intentional skips are people experiencing financial difficulties due to separation or divorce, and those with criminal intent. Skip debtors with marital problems usually have accumulated excessive amounts of debt or are experiencing a substantial reduction in income. This reduces the chance of prompt repayment. Skips with criminal intent never intended to repay the debt, and even if they are found, the likelihood of recovering payment is small.

Sources of Location Information
Collectors gathering location information must be persistent and ingenious, as well as conscious of the legal constraints of collection laws. The following items offer leads that collectors can pursue to locate a borrower. The list is not all inclusive but gives some sources of location information that illustrate the need for collectors to be persistent, creative and professional.

- Previous landlords: may provide names of friends or relatives used as referrals, or may have been contacted by new landlords checking up on references.
- Neighbors: may recall the moving company or, as friends, even know the current whereabouts of the skip.
- Neighboring businesses: mortgage companies and lending institutions may have forwarding addresses or phone numbers obtained when property was bought or sold; utility companies may have new addresses.
- Current or previous employers: management or co-workers may know of new job plans or have new addresses to which W-2 and other forms are to be sent.
- Past or current creditors: may be conducting skip-tracing activities, too, or may have additional names to add to the tracer's file.
- Government agencies: U.S. post offices may know a forwarding address, other agencies might provide motor vehicle registrations, real estate or personal property records, birth and death records, criminal and civil court records.
- Directories: telephone directories might show people with names similar to the skip or the skip's family; city directories serve as guides to addresses and business firms in unfamiliar cities.

Skiptracing by Telephone
Skiptracing can be done over the telephone or by mail. While the telephone is more expensive, it is also quick, direct and effective. Skiptracing by mail is less expensive, but it is slower and less direct than the telephone.

In a telephone conversation to third parties who might

have location information about the skip, collectors are most successful when they are friendly, considerate and persistent. A friendly approach puts third parties (known as informants) at ease and encourages them to respond favorably to questions. Collectors must be considerate of informants by calling at convenient times and keeping conversations short; but collectors must also be persistent and not easily discouraged. They must tactfully but firmly pursue their purpose: to get location information from third parties.

When making telephone calls, collectors first should identify third parties and themselves. They continue by stating the reason for the call. A good approach is: "I'm looking for John Jones. Can you help me? Nancy White, your neighbor, told me you have his telephone number and address." After this, one might pause and listen for information and possible leads.

All people, but particularly relatives or friends, may be hesitant to provide information if they think the person is in some kind of trouble. To place them more at ease, sometimes a member of the opposite sex is the best person to make the call. Suppose a collector is trying to find a man. If a male places the call to a possible informant, it may arouse suspicion and result in a defensive attitude. However, if a woman calls about a male skip, the informant may be more open.

When conducting skiptracing by telephone, a collector must listen carefully because information that seems unimportant at the time may in fact lead to the borrower. When all specific questions have been posed and enough information has been received, the collector should express appreciation and end the call promptly to avoid improperly giving information about the delinquency to a third party.

Skiptracing by Mail
Occasionally, a delinquent borrower cannot be reached by telephone. For these borrowers, skiptracing must be conducted by mail. The following facts and techniques may be helpful in this process.
- Add "Address Correction Requested" under the return address, a postal service that is available for a small fee.
- Use certified mail and ask for a receipt. If the skip signs the receipt, the institution has accurate location information. If someone else signs the receipt, that party might provide a lead.

- Know the limits of certified letters: someone must be home to accept them. If no one is home, the mail carrier leaves a notice of the letter in the recipient's mailbox. If it is not claimed within a specified time, the letter is returned to the sender.
- Inspect envelopes of returned letters. The postal stamp for undeliverable mail usually reads "Not There." Other messages, especially handwritten ("Not Here," "Doesn't Live Here"), might have been written by the skip to mislead the creditor. In such cases, or where the message reads, "Letter Refused," a visit to the address is indicated since the borrower may still reside there. Where the message reads, "Moved—Not Forwardable" or "Forwarding Order Expired," collectors can contact the post office to pay for obtaining the new address. The message, "Moved—Left No Address," tells the collector that other methods of skiptracing must be pursued.
- For borrowers in military service, contact the appropriate branch by mail and ask them to supply the current address. The Army, Navy, Marine Corps and Coast Guard will need the individual's name, rank and Social Security number. The Air Force requires name, date of birth, permanent home address and former organization.

REMEDIAL PAYMENT PLANS

If the collector believes the borrower cannot or will not pay under the existing loan terms, two remedial payment plans, forbearance or wage garnishment, may be considered. Obviously, these two approaches to problem solving are not rushed into as immediate solutions to a deliquent's problems.

Forbearance is appropriate for first time, seriously delinquent borrowers who are experiencing temporary financial hardships. Collectors generally use wage garnishment with delinquent borrowers who simply cannot manage their money. With forbearance, a collector relies on the borrower for repayment. With wage garnishment, the collector relies on both the borrower and the borrower's employer for repayment.

Forbearance

A *forbearance agreement* is a written or verbal statement whereby an institution grants a borrower additional time to make loan payments before pursuing a lawsuit, property repossession or garnishment of wages, as long as the borrower performs certain agreed-upon actions.

Forbearance agreements may vary as to the period of time or repayment methods. One method is for regular loan payments to be reduced or even suspended for a certain period of time (forbearance period), after which the borrower agrees to make higher than regular payments until the loan becomes current. To calculate the length of the forbearance period, the institution attempts to determine when the borrower will have recovered financial stability or when the borrower anticipates receiving additional income, such as a bonus or proceeds from the sale of property.

Another forbearance method is to restructure the loan. Here, the institution has two choices: adjust the monthly payments or alter the term. For instance, assume that Michael Monahan, a teacher, is delinquent on his home improvement loan. The problem started when the local school board cut back on the number of positions in the high school science department and Michael lost his job. Michael has some income from working part-time as a substitute teacher at the school and from taking on other part-time jobs while looking for another full-time teaching position.

During this time, Michael's loan payments of $100 a month (principal and interest) have stopped. The loan balance is now $3,000 including all late charges.

The institution might consider adjusting the monthly payments and agreeing to collect only the loan interest for a time. This would be the easiest option for the borrower and might be appropriate if Michael is a valued customer with a previously good repayment and employment record.

A second possible restructure is to capitalize the interest by adding it and the delinquent amount to the loan balance. Then the loan could be recast by dividing the new balance by the remaining term (it is better not to change the original term). The result is a higher new payment amount. This method is the preferred method of loan restructure when the borrower's financial situation is expected to improve and the higher payments will be affordable.

A third alternative is to increase the loan balance as just described but to lengthen the term of the loan. This is the least desirable method from the creditor's view, especially for consumer loans. The type of credit and the long-term value of any collateral securing the loan, as well as on the borrower's record, determine if this method should be used.

Recasting a loan may be worthwhile when dealing with a conscientious borrower undergoing a one-time, unusual circumstance, such as Michael Monahan, but it should not be done routinely. In effect, a recast loan "wipes the slate clean" and excuses any existing delinquency. Routine loan recasting is not sound business practice and could lead to problems with federal inspectors who might view it as deceptive financial reporting.

Wage Garnishment

Wage garnishment is a legal proceeding in which an institution seeks a court order to obtain funds for debt repayment from a third party (employer) who owes money (wages) to the borrower. There are several protections against abuse of this action. To protect borrowers, the Consumer Protection Act of 1968 states that "no employer may discharge any employee by reason of the fact that earnings have been subjected to garnishment for any one indebtedness." Also according to this Act, federally chartered institutions are limited in the amount of a borrower's weekly disposable income that can be subject to garnishment.

Under consumer protection regulations, a creditor must also determine a debtor's employment and income level before seeking a court judgment that will permit wages to be garnished. The extent to which wage garnishment can be used is also limited by state law. Some states prohibit the use of wage garnishment for state employees or establish monetary limits lower than those described in the Consumer Protection Act. Other states prohibit the use of wage garnishment entirely.

Even with potential restrictions, wage garnishment is a powerful collection tool in difficult cases. Where permitted by state law, collectors can inform stubborn debtors that the creditor has a legal right to seek this action. This comes as a surprise to some consumers who mistakenly believe their wages cannot be touched or their employers informed; news that these actions can be taken may prompt them to bring the loan back to current status.

This technique should be used with care, however. Once a creditor threatens that it will try to gain court approval for wage garnishment, the creditor must be prepared to take this action promptly if the borrower still resists repaying the loan.

COLLATERAL ACQUISITION

After all attempts to collect loan payments from the borrower of a secured loan fail, the lender must consider acquiring the collateral in order to repay the loan. Repossession and foreclosure are two methods used to acquire collateral. The method selected depends on whether the loan is secured by personal or by real property. If personal property is security for the loan, the lender repossesses the collateral; if real property is the security, the lender forecloses on the collateral or accepts a deed in lieu of foreclosure.

Repossession

Repossession is a remedy in which personal property used as security for a delinquent debt is acquired and disposed of for the purpose of repaying the loan in whole or in part. The point at which an institution actually repossesses collateral depends on its policy and the particular circumstances, although repossession may begin as early as 30 to 60 days after loan default.

The Process of Repossession
Prompt action is required when personal property is repossessed to avoid delinquent borrowers' moving, hiding or damaging collateral. Most personal property quickly loses value and usefulness over time, and so the borrower's incentive to repay a delinquent loan also diminishes over time. Therefore, the number of repossessions is higher with rapidly depreciating personal property than with property that retains value.

A court order may or may not be needed prior to repossession. If the borrower has signed a surrender of collateral statement, the institution has the right to acquire personal property without a court order (see Figure 9-8). Even when an executed surrender of collateral statement exists, however, the institution still should notify the borrower in writing of its intent to repossess.

State laws establish the method and procedure for repossession. These laws differ from state to state, but generally collectors conduct these activities prior to repossession.
- Inspect the documents to insure that the institution's rights to the property have been properly recorded. For example, the lien should be recorded and the title document properly filed.
- Notify all guarantors, co-signers and the dealer (if liable) of the intended action.
- Complete a report describing the condition of the collateral along with an estimate for repairs, when possible.
- Send the borrower advance notification. The notice should remind the borrower that the terms of the loan must be followed, that the institution has legitimate rights to the collateral and that the borrower is liable for any deficient amounts after the disposition of the collateral. (If any late payments are accepted after the original notice has been sent, a second notice must follow before the collateral is repossessed.)
- Anticipate and outline for management consideration any problems that might arise when trying to acquire the property and, where possible, propose ways to prevent or overcome the problems.
- Verify that physical damage insurance is in force.
- Determine how the collateral will be stored, repaired and sold.

Repossession Procedures for Auto Loans

Generally, about 2% of all car loans result in defaults. With automobile loans, repossession is a remedy that should be used only when there is no other viable alternative. Policy does not generally make repossession automatic when a car loan is delinquent for a given number of days, but rather only when no other method of repayment is forthcoming.

General guidelines. Policy guidelines from automobile repossession encompass the following parameters.

FIGURE 9-8
Collateral Pledge Agreement

FILE NO.

Collateral Pledge Agreement

NAME OF BORROWER ______________________

PROPERTY ADDRESS ______________________

DATE OF LOAN ______________ AMOUNT $ ______________ LOAN NO. ______________

DESCRIPTION OF COLLATERAL PLEDGED:

SAVINGS ACCOUNT NO. ______________ AMOUNT OF PLEDGE $ ______________

NAME ______________________

ADDRESS ______________________

WHEREAS:

is concurrently making a first mortgage loan on the property described above, identified as shown and evidenced by a note and mortgage which is hereby referred to as part of this Pledge Agreement, and requires additional security for said loan; therefore, In consideration of the making of said loan, the undersigned pledgor hereby pledges, assigns, transfers, and sets over to said Association his above described Savings Account in said Association to secure said indebtedness and the other obligations in said note and mortgage. It is hereby expressly agreed in consideration of the aforesaid matters that at anytime said indebtedness is in default or there is a default in any other obligation under said note and mortgage, before this pledge is used to remedy any such default said Association shall give the undersigned pledgor notice of such default at the address stated above or any other address supplied by the pledgor to the pledgee in writing by mail; and the depositing of such notice in the United States mail, postage prepaid, shall constitute service of such notice upon the undersigned pledgor. After such notice and within 30 days thereof, the undersigned pledgor shall have the privilege (1) of paying the amount of such default, or (2) of taking an assignment of said note and mortgage, without recourse, for the unpaid balance thereof, including such advances and costs, upon payment of such amount. If, within 30 days of such notice, such default is not remedied and such loan is not bought and transferred to the undersigned pledgor, then any officer of said Association is appointed attorney-in-fact for the undersigned pledgor and is expressly authorized to execute a withdrawal request against said Savings Account in the name of the undersigned pledgor and to withdraw any or all of the funds in said Savings Account and to apply the same to remedy such default by reducing the balance of the loan in such amount as it deems necessary and to repeat such process from time to time so long as funds remain in said account for such purpose. The pledge herein shall continue throughout the life of the mortgage herein and any extensions thereof or until all the pledged funds shall have been released by the Association, and shall in no way be affected by any transfer of the title to the premises covered by said mortgage, or by release of the mortgagors or change in their status; provided, that at any time said indebtedness, including any advances made under said note and mortgage, is not in default, that for each $______________ paid on the principal of such obligation by the mortgagors, the Association at the request of the pledgor will release the sum of $______________ from such Savings Account, or, if the principal balance of said indebtedness is at any time less than $______________, this pledge shall be released on demand. It is specifically agreed that at the option of the pledgee, it may exhaust the real estate security securing said indebtedness and retain this pledge to secure any deficiency and acting as above provided but without further notice, apply said Savings Account toward the liquidation of any deficiency, provided 30 days' notice is given of the foreclosure sale of the real estate security. Any dividends which may be declared on such Savings Account will be paid to the pledgor so long as the Association has not found it necessary to apply any portion of the principal amount evidenced thereby upon any loss suffered or incurred by the Association in connection with the said loan. In this instrument, the singular includes the plural and the masculine includes the feminine and neuter, and this pledge shall be binding on the undersigned, his heirs, assigns and personal representatives.

DATED: ______________________

______________________ BY ______________________

______________________ ATTEST: ______________________

Signature(s) of Pledgor(s)

—ALL PARTIES ON A JOINT ACCOUNT MUST SIGN—

PARTIAL RELEASE

DATE	BY	AMOUNT	LOAN BALANCE
		$	$
		$	$
		$	$
		$	$
		$	$
		$	$
		$	$

COMPLETE RELEASE AND RECEIPT

RELEASED BY ______________ DATE ______________

The undersigned hereby acknowledge(s) receipt of the above described collateral.

____
PLEDGOR(S)

____

____

42501-7 (2/71)
Collateral Pledge Agreement

SAF Systems and Forms
(American Savings & Accounting Supply, Inc.)

- Do not repossess this collateral unless it has value that exceeds repossession and other costs.
- Determine who in the institution will be authorized to order a repossession.

Collectors are not necessarily the best people for this. Someone in lending, who understands the value of automobiles, often is better able to determine if a repossession will be cost-effective. The person who is authorized to order repossession should be accessible to the staff and ready to make a quick decision.

Auto repossession agencies. Although occasionally a borrower will become convinced that he or she cannot afford an automobile and voluntarily turn over the keys (known as a voluntary repossession), this is rare. Often an institution needs an outside repossession agency for auto loans because some automobile repossessions are more difficult and require the services of seasoned professionals. For example, if the borrower refuses to cooperate, someone may need to be sent to the borrower's neighborhood, late at night, to locate and take the vehicle. Additionally, state laws may require bonding, insurance and licensing for people who carry out repossessions. These duties are beyond the scope of a lending institution's role and, therefore, require an outside repossession agency.

However, the services of a repossession agency may be expensive. A typical charge for an auto repossession can be $100 or more per vehicle. This price may be much higher if the vehicle is difficult to locate or if protective devices, such as new steering column locks, must be purchased.

In addition to basic physical repossession, some repossession agencies offer other services. They may make repairs, contact dealers for bids and see that personal property left in the automobile is returned to the borrower. Protecting the borrower's personal property is an important responsibility. Occasionally, a particularly difficult borrower will claim that jewelry, money, golf clubs or other expensive items were left in the car and were not returned after repossession. A reputable repossession agency can install systems to insure that personal property is located, protected and returned and that any unpleasant incidents are handled professionally.

Customers are entitled to a certain amount of time to reclaim repossessed property. To reduce any storage cost, some savings institutions keep repossessed vehicles in their own storage areas during the statutory redemption period. After this period, the institution must arrange for a protected storage area. For example, a vehicle should not be parked in an institution's regular parking lot where an angry delinquent owner might try to take it.

Selling repossessed automobiles. Another practical rule is to prohibit selling repossessed vehicles to institution employees. In many states an institution faces difficulty suing a borrower for a deficiency if the vehicle has been sold to an institution employee. The sale to an employee gives the appearance that the lender benefitted from the delinquency or that it took unfair advantage of the customer's payment problems. Therefore, it often is wisest to sell repossessed cars only through dealers.

Four follow-up activities are suggested for an institution that uses dealers to dispose of repossessed cars.

- The lender must insure that its repossessed collateral is properly displayed with other inventory for resale. A proper display means placing the collateral in a visible position, and displaying the collateral with items of similar value to help customers correctly perceive the collateral's value.
- Competitive pricing of repossessed collateral is essential. Overpricing the collateral may delay its sale, while underpricing collateral may result in a sales amount insufficient to cover the loan balance.
- The institution should submit all applicable insurance claims immediately. Payment from these claims often can pay for repairs that lead to a sale at the vehicle's highest value.
- The institution should periodically inspect the physical condition of the collateral. If damage occurs and is caused by dealer abuse or neglect, the institution may hold the dealer liable or may stop doing business with that dealer.

Out-of-state Repossessions
Dealers also are helpful partners in out-of-state repossessions. If a skip debtor is traced to an out-of-state location and if it becomes clear that the borrower has no intention of repaying, repossession of collateral must be considered. A

call to a repossession agency in the new location should be made promptly before the collateral can again be moved or hidden. The American Recovery Association publishes a useful resource book. It lists names and locations of members of this nationwide repossession agency trade group and state laws governing repossessions.

Out-of-state repossessions are not without dangers. Once an automobile is repossessed, the repossession agency customarily receives bids from area dealers and sells the car to the highest bidder. A portion of the sales proceeds are then kept by the agency, with the remainder sent to the savings institution. Since out-of-state institutions may have difficulty verifying actual bids, an unscrupulous agency might submit low bids and then sell the car for much more. If an institution has doubts about low bids, the only way to ascertain the true value of the vehicle is to send someone out to look at it or transport the vehicle back to the lending institution.

Foreclosure

Foreclosure is a legal procedure in which a lender extinguishes or cuts off any equitable rights (rights to the equity) of the borrower and legal rights of subsequent lienholders to the real property securing the loan. Foreclosure usually results in the secured property being sold at public auction. As with other collection procedures, once it has been decided on, foreclosure should be conducted quickly, because borrowers who know that an institution is contemplating foreclosure may neglect or damage the property.

In some states, strict foreclosure is permitted when the value of property involved is valued at no more than the unpaid loan balance. The lender asks a court to set a time by which a borrower must either pay the loan balance in full or lose the interest in the property. If that time period lapses without the borrower's action, the court can issue a decree giving title to the institution, subject to prior claims, without a public sale.

The basis for this kind of action is that, because the value of the property is equal to the loan amount due, borrowers have not acquired equity in the property. The equity value is realized through the sale of property. Consequently, if the court determines that equity value would not be realized through a public sale, the court may allow strict foreclosure.

If the foreclosed property is sold for more than the unpaid loan balance, the difference between the sale price and the unpaid loan balance (plus legal expenses) may go to the borrower or, in some cases, the institution. Again, this arrangement depends on state law. However, there are times when the proceeds of a property sale are not sufficient to cover an unpaid loan balance. The difference between the proceeds and the unpaid loan balance is called a *deficiency*.

In some states, if a deficiency occurs, the institution can file a *deficiency judgment* against the borrower for the amount of the deficiency and can seek satisfaction of the judgment by securing other assets belonging to the borrower. Other states have limited the amount of deficiency that lenders can seek, while still others prohibit deficiency judgments entirely.

All states grant borrowers a certain amount of time during which they can pay off their outstanding loan balances and recover their property before foreclosure sales occur. This privilege is known as the borrower's *equitable right of redemption*. Once the foreclosure sale is concluded, this right ceases.

In addition to the equitable right of redemption, which ends at the foreclosure sale, many states provide borrowers with a statutory right of redemption, which becomes effective after foreclosure. The *statutory right of redemption* refers to the period of time extended to borrowers to redeem property after the foreclosure sale and before the purchaser receives the title deed. If the borrower does not exercise his or her statutory right of redemption within the allowed period of time, the purchaser at the foreclosure sale will receive the deed that conveys title to the real property.

A *deed given in lieu of foreclosure* is generally the quickest and least expensive way of acquiring real property after borrowers default on loans. This deed is an instrument that voluntarily conveys ownership in the property to the institution in full satisfaction of the debt. It saves borrowers the embarrassment and pressures of public court proceedings.

CHARGE-OFF PROCEDURES

After a certain period of time elapses without the collection of payments, institutions charge off the delinquent loan balances. *Charge off* refers to the accounting procedure of reflecting losses from bad debts in institution records. By charging off the loan, the institution is removing the consumer loan from its assets. FSLIC regulations stipulate when this must be done in member institutions. Closed-end consumer credit loans that are delinquent for 120 days or more and open-end consumer credit accounts that are delinquent for 180 days or more (where no payments are expected) must be classified as losses and charged against the institution's current earnings. FSLIC regulations also require that "for the purposes of computing delinquencies, a payment of 90% or more of the contractual payment will be considered as a full payment."

SUMMARY

Some delinquency is inevitable in any consumer credit operation. Institutions use delinquency rates to assess the performance of their own operation. Delinquency rates are higher for some types of consumer credit depending on whether the credit is secured, how fast the collateral depreciates and the size of the downpayment. Economic conditions and cyclical business factors also affect delinquency rates.

Delinquent borrowers may be classified in three ways: as good, fair or poor risks. Good risk borrowers are usually conscientious about maintaining their credit ratings, while fair risk borrowers may be willing to repay but lack the ability to plan their finances. Poor risk borrowers are usually unwilling or unable to repay and are the least cooperative toward collection attempts.

An institution's collections policy prescribes a systematic method for contacting delinquent borrowers to assure uniform treatment of all delinquent loans. Policies establish the grace period, late charges and the collection devices appropriate at various stages of a delinquency. The provisions contained in the Fair Debt Collection Practices Act for contacting delinquent borrowers should be followed.

Collection devices include written notices, letters and mailgrams. More expensive tools include office and field visits and telephone contacts. Questions over the telephone should be phrased in such a manner as to elicit the maximum amount of information (i.e., "open-ended" questions).

Delinquent borrowers who cannot be located through routine mail or telephone contacts are called skips. Collectors use skiptracing techniques to locate skip debtors. Sources such as neighbors, friends, unions, directories, employers and others are consulted to accumulate location information.

For first-time, seriously delinquent borrowers, an institution may decide to establish a forbearance agreement. The institution grants additional time to make loan payments without exercising its right against the borrower as long as the borrower performs certain agreed upon actions.

Wage garnishment is another remedial payment plan by which an institution can acquire a part of the delinquent borrower's income. However, some states restrict or prohibit the use of this plan.

To acquire collateral on delinquent secured loans, institutions either repossess personal property or foreclose on real property. Institutions that make auto loans often have an outside repossession agency ready to help, if needed. Lines of authority should clearly spell out who can order repossessions, since speed is essential.

Institutions also can acquire real property through foreclosures. In some states strict foreclosure is permitted when the property involved is valued at no more than the unpaid loan balance. If foreclosed property is sold for more than the unpaid loan balance, the excess usually goes to the borrower. If there is a deficiency, the institution can file a judgment against the borrower for that amount.

For FSLIC member institutions, after a specified period of time elapses, uncollected loan balances must be charged off as losses.

CHAPTER QUESTIONS

1. What factors affect consumer loan delinquency? Why are certain types of consumer loans subject to greater delinquency rates than others?

2. List several legitimate reasons why a good risk borrower might become delinquent. Compare these reasons to the reasons offered by an "artful dodger."

3. How should a collector respond to a delinquent borrower's statement that "the payment is in the mail"? What specific collections actions would you consider appropriate for delinquent joint account loans?

4. Janice Morris, a good customer, has fallen behind in her loan payments. She is given several options by the collector, including the opportunity to either stretch out the payments or make slightly higher payments to get the loan current. Discuss the available options and the conditions under which you would consider each appropriate. Which option is ideal from the viewpoint of the lending institution?

5. Briefly explain provisions of the Fair Debt Collection Practices Act. Cite examples of prohibited actions according to the law.

6. Describe the advantages and disadvantages of telephone calls, written communication and interviews as collection devices. When might each be used?

7. How can a collector use silence to his or her benefit?

8. What is skiptracing? When is it used? What sources may be useful in helping a collector track down a skip?

9. Differentiate between a forbearance agreement and a wage garnishment. When might each be used?

10. What actions should a savings institution take before repossessing collateral?

11. At what point should an institution consider repossessing an automobile? Explain the role of repossession agencies in delinquent automobile loans.

12. Define foreclosure. What happens if foreclosed property is sold at a gain? A loss?

13. At what point must an FSLIC-member savings institution charge off uncollected delinquent loan balances as losses? Why do you think this rule was made?

10

Consumer Lending and Bankruptcy

Objectives

After studying this chapter, you should be able to:
- ☐ Explain the historical basis for consumer bankruptcy in the United States;
- ☐ Give examples of bankruptcy protections for debtors and creditors;
- ☐ Define basic terms in the consumer bankruptcy process;
- ☐ Describe the sequence of legal events in bankruptcy proceedings under Chapters 7 and 13 of the Bankruptcy Code;
- ☐ Give examples of creditor concerns in response to legal events during consumer bankruptcies; and
- ☐ Explain actions that consumer lenders can take to protect their interests during Chapter 7 and Chapter 13 bankruptcies.

INTRODUCTION

Consumer bankruptcy has risen dramatically in recent years; a fact that has serious consequences for all lenders. A major factor may have been a 1978 federal law that critics claim made bankruptcy an attractive alternative for individuals seeking to avoid repaying their debts. In the first 12 months after the 1978 law went into effect, bankruptcy filings rose nearly 60% and the increases continued into the early 1980s. Pressure from creditor groups during those years led Congress to enact amendments in 1984 designed to eliminate those provisions in the 1978 law that appeared to lead to abuse. Nevertheless, consumer bankruptcy filings in the 1980s remain substantially higher than their pre-1978 levels, and financial institutions continue to suffer significant losses as a result of consumer bankruptcy filings. Therefore, it is important that savings institution personnel have a basic understanding of the bankruptcy process and its ramifications for consumer lending institutions.

This chapter discusses elements of the federal bankruptcy laws and focuses on legal events in personal bankruptcy filings under Chapters 7 and 13 of the Bankruptcy Code. Bankruptcy law is a very complex subject and cannot be completely covered in a short chapter. The objective of this chapter is to give readers a basic understanding of the processes, terminology and issues of consumer bankruptcy. Also presented are some of the concerns and activities that an affected institution's consumer loan staff might become involved in when a loan customer files for personal bankruptcy.

HISTORICAL VIEW OF BANKRUPTCY LAWS

Today, *bankruptcy* can be defined as a legal process in which a person or business declares the inability to repay debts. When an individual files for bankruptcy, his or her assets may be liquidated or the person may follow a court-approved plan to repay debts. In either event, U.S. bankruptcy laws attempt to strike a balance between the rights of creditors to be paid and the rights of debtors to settle their debts and make a fresh start. In the 17th century, however, bankruptcy was viewed as a crime, and debtors were summarily tossed into debtor prisons. Georgia, one of the 13 original colonies, was founded as a refuge for English debtors who were sent to the new world to work off their debts. The criminal debtor of that time had few rights, whereas today overburdened debtors may try through the court system to make a "fresh start."

The Constitution of the United States grants Congress the power to make uniform laws regarding bankruptcy. Federal bankruptcy laws in the 1800s often followed periods of economic difficulty and were short in duration. In 1898, Congress passed the National Bankruptcy Act, which was the first piece of legislation that was not repealed when the immediate crisis was over. This act mainly used liquidation of assets rather than reorganization of debts as a remedy for bankruptcy. The debtor, therefore, had the right to a fresh start but only with limited means. If bankruptcy is viewed as an attempt to balance the rights of creditors and the rights of debtors, the balance leaned toward the rights of the creditors at the turn of the century.

The National Bankruptcy Act remained relatively unchanged until the Chandler Act amended it in 1938. This act tilted the balance on the scale toward the debtor by allowing for reorganization and other methods of relief besides liquidation. The Chandler Act remained relatively unchanged for 40 years.

By 1978, significant economic changes created pressure for further change. Consumer and commercial credit had expanded greatly since the Chandler Act of 1938, and bankruptcies had also increased in numbers. Both lenders and borrowers claimed the law was biased against them and was not uniformly enforced. The Bankruptcy Reform Act of 1978 instituted major changes that added to the rights of debtors. Following those changes came the dramatic increase in bank-

---

"Currently, one-fourth of all consumers who declare bankruptcy do so without needing financial relief, according to the National Coalition for Bankrupty Reform."

Comment prior to passage of 1984 legislation. Robert B. Lieberman, "Bankruptcy Bill Gives Protections to Creditors," *American Banker*, July 6, 1984, p. 1.

ruptcy cases mentioned earlier and another cry for reform, this time largely from creditors. Other issues, such as whether a bankrupt company had to negotiate with labor unions and in which court bankruptcy cases could be tried, also rose.

The result was the Bankruptcy Amendments and Federal Judgeship Act of 1984. Among the changes introduced in the 1984 law are the following:
- authorizing bankruptcy judges to take into account not only a debtor's assets and liabilities but also current income and expenses when approving a filing;
- permitting married couples to choose to take exemptions either under federal or state rules but not under both; and
- shortening the time allowed for debtors with secured loans to state what they proposed to do with collateral.

Figure 10-1 shows the number of filings for personal bankruptcy from the first year that the 1978 law went into effect through the early years under the 1984 law. A dip in numbers after 1984 was reversed with a new high by 1986. Factors blamed for continuing high totals include easy credit, economic events (recession; unemployment) and changes in social values that may attach less disgrace to bankruptcy filings than once was the case. Today's consumer bankruptcy laws aim to provide a fresh start to an overburdened debtor and yet to achieve the maximum possible reimbursement to the undercompensated creditor.

OVERVIEW OF CONSUMER BANKRUPTCY

Consumer bankruptcy is governed by the federal Bankruptcy Code. The Code, based on current law, now consists of eight sections or chapters. They are numbered consecutively, with odd numbers only, so that the final section is Chapter 15.

When filing for bankruptcy, an individual consumer debtor usually has two choices: a petition initiated under Chapter 7 or one initiated under Chapter 13 of the Code. (Although consumer debtors can file under Chapter 11, this usually is not done since the provisions of this bankruptcy chapter are primarily designed for businesses.)

In *Chapter 7* bankruptcies, the debtor's assets are liquidated and distributed among the creditors. Chapter 7 is also called straight bankruptcy. A *Chapter 13* bankruptcy is based

FIGURE 10-1
Personal Bankruptcy Filings (in thousands/year)

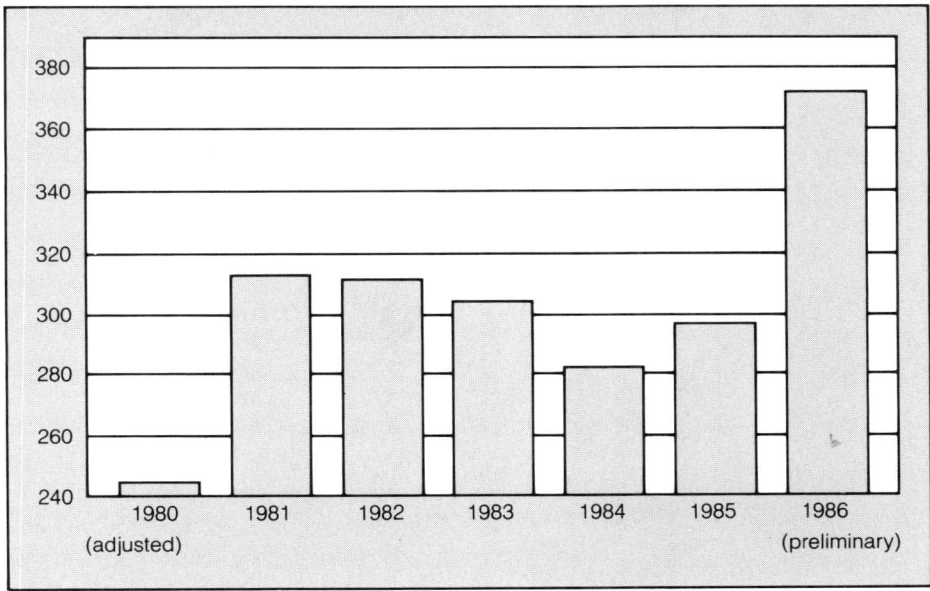

Source: Administrative Office of U.S. Courts.

on a plan in which the debtor proposes a way to repay debts (partially or fully) in order to keep his or her assets.

Although different in many ways, both Chapter 7 and Chapter 13 bankruptcies have much in common because of their similar goals. When filing a Chapter 7 or a Chapter 13 petition, a debtor seeks relief from debts that existed before the debtor filed for bankruptcy. If the debtor's petition is granted, creditors are repaid on less favorable terms than those of the original loan agreement. Therefore, the creditor's goal is to be reimbursed as fully as possible for the amount of debt still due. The duty of the bankruptcy court system, then, is to resolve these conflicting goals of debtors and creditors.

One way in which the bankruptcy system protects the rights of debtors is by assuring a full release from debts by the end of the bankruptcy process. At the end, the debtor is held responsible only for prebankruptcy debts that are assessed as payable during the bankruptcy proceedings even when creditors are not paid in full.

For example, in a particular case, assets available for

unsecured debts may be so limited that unsecured creditors are granted repayment of only 10¢ on the dollar. The obligation to repay the other 90¢ is discharged by the court. In many bankruptcy proceedings, unsecured creditors receive substantially less than "10¢ on the dollar," but it makes no difference as to discharge: the debtor is still legally released from any unpaid debt balances.

At the same time, many procedures followed by the bankruptcy court system assist creditors. Trustees appointed by the court or elected by creditors are chiefly responsible for obtaining maximum value for the debtor's estate and for orderly distribution among creditors' claims. In distribution, certain types of debts usually are given priority and, under specified conditions, some cannot be discharged through bankruptcy. These debts are called *nondischargeable*; they remain due according to the original agreement.

An example of a nondischargeable debt is one resulting from intentional consumer fraud. Assume that Adam Phillips has filed for Chapter 7 bankruptcy, with one of his prebankruptcy debts an automobile loan from Home Savings. On reviewing all the facts of the case, Home Savings discovers that in his loan application, Phillips listed income from both himself and his wife, even though only he was employed at the time. Phillips also falsely gave the name and business address of a friend as his wife's "employer" for the institution to contact to verify her employment and income. When Home Savings discovers these facts, it might challenge the discharge of this debt on the grounds that the debtor knowingly supplied false information on the application and that these false statements resulted in loan approval. The court then might rule that this particular debt is nondischargeable.

CHAPTER 7 BANKRUPTCIES: LIQUIDATION

Chapter 7 bankruptcies are of two general types: voluntary or involuntary liquidation of a debtor's assets. Voluntary bankruptcies, are, by far, more common.

In a *voluntary bankruptcy* preceeding, debtors who file are, in effect, voluntarily turning over their assets to the court for liquidation. In contrast to voluntarily choosing to petition for Chapter 7, an *involuntary bankruptcy* is initiated by a creditor or a group of creditors in an attempt to make the debtor liquidate assets to pay off debts. Involuntary bankruptcies are comparatively rare because creditors must persuade the court that bankruptcy is not only in their best interests, but also is in the interests of the debtor. Moreover, creditors may incur substantial legal costs during involuntary bankruptcy proceedings, which offset the amount of income from debt repayments awarded through the courts.

In all Chapter 7 bankruptcies, both voluntary and involuntary, liquidation is handled by a trustee. Trustees may be elected by creditors at the first creditors' meeting, but frequently the trustee initially appointed by the court is retained throughout the case. Trustees act as administrators of the estate and as unbiased representatives of all creditors. The trustee's role, powers and duties are described more fully later in the chapter.

In this text, the events that take place in voluntary Chapter 7 bankruptcies have been divided into four phases:
- initiation of the bankruptcy proceedings;
- meetings of creditors;
- administration of the estate; and
- closing of the estate.

For each of these phases, special emphasis is placed on the role and concerns of the lender.

Each of the principals in a voluntary bankruptcy —trustee, debtor and creditor—has certain options that may be exercised to meet the individual needs of the case. Additionally, the court is granted considerable latitude so that court representatives can respond to the particular circumstances of each case. Similarly, savings institutions may respond in different ways according to their lending policies and organization. As a result, not all bankruptcies proceed in

---

"The consumer bankruptcy provisions will allow bankruptcy judges for the first time ever to rule on whether a person filing for Chapter 7 bankruptcy relief represents substantial abuse of the bankruptcy system."

Comment in support of 1984 legislation by Robert B. Evans, president, American Financial Services Association, quoted by Robert B. Lieberman, "Bankruptcy Bill Gives Protections to Creditors," *American Banker*, July 6, 1984, p. 1.

exactly the same manner. The four phases described in this chapter represent typical events in a bankruptcy.

Initiation: Phase One

Debtors who voluntarily file a petition for Chapter 7 bankruptcy have reached a point at which their debts exceed their assets. By filing, the debtor acknowledges an inability to repay debts and seeks, through the courts, a new arrangement to handle contractual obligations. Because creditors are one party to the contract, the early events alert them to the changed status of the loan. Creditors must be prepared to give early notices prompt attention and to respond actively and defensively.

Phase One Legal Events

Many important events occur during the first stage of Chapter 7 bankruptcies. Early events include the petition, the automatic stay, the statement of intent and the court's authority to dismiss a case.

Petition. A Chapter 7 bankruptcy is initiated when a debtor files a petition for bankruptcy (see Figure 10-2). At the time of the filing, the debtor provides the court with information about his or her financial condition, including a list of assets, debts and creditors. The date on which the debtor petitions for bankruptcy, known as the filing date, is important for two reasons.
- The date establishes the time at which a debtor's bankruptcy *estate* is created. The initial estate usually includes all property held by the debtor at the time of filing.
- The filing date also establishes which debts qualify to a share in the distribution of funds at the conclusion of the case. In general, only those debts incurred before the filing date qualify for discharge by the court.

Automatic stay. It is the responsibility of the bankruptcy court to provide for the orderly and equitable distribution of a debtor's assets. To insure that no creditor has an unfair advantage in collecting on a debt, a stay order "freezing" the debtor's assets takes effect immediately and automatically when a debtor files for bankruptcy. Once the *automatic stay* order is in effect, all creditors must go through the bankruptcy court to make claims on a debtor's prebankruptcy dischargeable debts.

Statement of intent. Soon after petitioning for bankruptcy, a debtor must file a statement of intent. This statement is significant to creditors because it specifies how a debtor proposes to treat his or her property. The debtor's intent may be to return certain property to a creditor, to turn over some property to the trustee as part of the estate and/or to retain some property. Retained assets, called *available exemptions*, often are household items needed for day-to-day living.

A debtor also may propose to redeem certain assets. In bankruptcy, *redemption* means that a debtor has paid a creditor the cash value of the collateral in order to take possession of the property free of liens. As an alternate proposal, a debtor who wants to retain possession of a particular asset that is not exempt from collection may propose to reaffirm, or reinstate, that portion of the debt.

Dismissals. Both creditors and court officials review the information supplied by the debtor. Bankruptcy judges are authorized to dismiss a case if this appears warranted. A case might be dismissed, for instance, if in the court's judgement, the petitioner's financial condition was not serious enough to warrant Chapter 7 bankruptcy relief.

Another reason for possible dismissal is ***repetitive filing***. The general rule is that petitioners should not have filed earlier under Chapter 7 within 180 days of the latest petition. This rule would apply in a situation where the debtor filed but voluntarily withdrew within that time period. It also would cover a situation where the debtor acted in a way that caused the court to dismiss the case (such as the debtor failing to appear at the creditors' meeting). Cases like these would qualify as repetitive filing, symptoms of abuse of bankruptcy protection.

Phase One Creditor Concerns
Soon after a debtor files for Chapter 7 bankruptcy, a savings institution receives notice that the debtor has filed, that an automatic stay is in effect, and that a creditors' meeting will be held. To protect its rights as a creditor, a savings institution may take certain actions upon receiving notice of a bankruptcy filing.

FIGURE 10-2
Voluntary Petition for Personal Bankruptcy

Form 1
Voluntary Petition

UNITED STATES BANKRUPTCY COURT
For the .... District of ....

In re

Debtor*
Social Security No.
and Debtor's Employer's Tax
Identification No.

Case No. ....

VOLUNTARY PETITION

1. Petitioner's mailing address, including county, is ....
....

2. Petitioner has: **
    ( ) resided within this district for the preceding 180 days.
    ( ) had his domicile within this district for the preceding 180 days.
    ( ) had his principal place of business within this district for the preceding 180 days.
    ( ) had his principal assets within this district for the preceding 180 days.
    ( ) ☐ resided ☐ had his domicile ☐ had his principal place of business ☐ had his principal assets within this district for a longer portion of the preceding 180 days than in any other district.

3. Petitioner is qualified to file this petition and is entitled to the benefits of title 11, United States Code as a voluntary debtor.

4. *[If appropriate]* A copy of petitioner's proposed plan, dated ...., is attached *[or* Petitioner intends to file a plan pursuant to chapter 11 *or* chapter 13*]* of title 11, United States Code.

5. *[If petitioner is a corporation]* Exhibit "A" is attached to and made part of this petition.

6. *[If petitioner is an individual whose debts are primarily consumer debts]* Petitioner is aware that [he *or* she] may proceed under chapter 7 or 13 of title 11, United States Code, understands the relief available under each such chapter, and chooses to proceed under chapter 7 of such title.

7. *[If petitioner is an individual whose debts are primarily consumer debts and such petitioner is represented by an attorney]* A declaration or an affidavit in the form of Exhibit "B" is attached to and made a part of this petition.

WHEREFORE, petitioner prays for relief in accordance with chapter ....of title 11, United States Code.

Signed: ....,
                            Attorney for Petitioner.
Address: ....,
....
[Petitioner signs if not represented by attorney.]

....
                                                Petitioner.

I, ..., the petitioner named in the foregoing petition, declare under penalty of perjury that the foregoing is true and correct.

Executed on .... Signature: ....,
                                                                                               Petitioner.

*Include all names including trade names used by debtor within last 6 years.
**Indicate with an "x" the appropriate clause.

George E. Cole® Legal Forms, reprinted by permission of Boise Cascade Corporation.

Consumer lending personnel and other staff involved in the loan process may be notified, along with the institution's legal counsel and any insurance companies protecting the debtor's collateral. The institution also may contact the bankruptcy court to obtain a list of the debtor's bankruptcy files, including information on assets, debts, income and expenses (see Figure 10-3). Information supplied in this file may be compared to the institution's records. Sometimes, a comparison of the debtor's original loan application to the bankruptcy files uncovers discrepancies that are grounds for dismissal of the debtor's bankruptcy petition.

In the case of secured loans, the statement of intent may need to be examined to see how the debtor proposes to handle property, especially that serving as collateral for debts that are due to the institution. The institution can challenge the debtor's proposal and also should verify that the security property is awarded a fair value when the estate's assets are listed for eventual distribution. Any other data about the petitioner's financial situation (such as funds in deposit or checking accounts as of the date of filing) also can be gathered.

Institutions that offer such consumer loans as credit cards, checking accounts with an open line of credit, automobile loans or other loans for discretionary purposes, might review evidence of when funds were spent prior to the bankruptcy petition. Debts arising from purchases of luxury items *immediately prior to* the filing date (called "loading up") may be disallowed by the court.

First Meeting of Creditors: Phase Two

A savings institution receives information about the date and location of the first creditors' meeting in the original notification of Chapter 7 bankruptcy. For their own protection, it is essential that all creditors attend this meeting to obtain up-to-date information about the debtor's financial condition and to learn of other creditors' claims on the debtor's estate.

Before sending representatives to the first creditors' meeting, a savings institution should assemble loan data from its own records and determine if there are any questions to pose at the meeting to help prepare its claims or to justify its challenges.

FIGURE 10-3
Summary Statement of Debtor's Debts and Property

Form 6
Summary of Debts and Property

GEORGE E. COLE®
LEGAL FORMS

SUMMARY OF DEBTS AND PROPERTY

(From the statements of the debtor in Schedules A and B)

Schedule		Total
	DEBTS	
A-1/a,b	Wages, etc. having priority	
A-1(c)	Deposits of money	
A-1/d(1)	Taxes owing United States	
A-1/d(2)	Taxes owing states	
A-1/d(3)	Taxes owing other taxing authorities	
A-2	Secured claims	
A-3	Unsecured claims without priority	
	Schedule A total	
	PROPERTY	
B-1	Real property (total value)	
B-2/a	Cash on hand	
B-2/b	Deposits	
B-2/c	Household goods	
B-2/d	Books, pictures, and collections	
B-2/e	Wearing apparel and personal possessions	
B-2/f	Automobiles and other vehicles	
B-2/g	Boats, motors, and accessories	
B-2/h	Livestock and other animals	
B-2/i	Farming supplies and implements	
B-2/j	Office equipment and supplies	
B-2/k	Machinery, equipment, and supplies used in business	
B-2/l	Inventory	
B-2/m	Other tangible personal property	
B-2/n	Patents and other general intangibles	
B-2/o	Bonds and other instruments	
B-2/p	Other liquidated debts	
B-2/q	Contingent and unliquidated claims	
B-2/r	Interests in insurance policies	
B-2/s	Annuities	
B-2/t	Interests in corporations and unincorporated companies	
B-2/u	Interests in partnerships	
B-2/v	Equitable and future interests, rights, and powers in personalty	
B-3/a	Property assigned for benefit of creditors	
B-3/b	Property not otherwise scheduled	
	Schedule B total	

George E. Cole® Legal Forms, reprinted by permission of Boise Cascade Corporation.

Phase Two Legal Events
During the first creditors' meeting, two important activities take place. First, the permanent trustee, subject to the approval of creditors, is elected. (The role of the trustee is covered in the next section.) Second, the debtor, who is under oath, may be called on to answer creditors' questions about his or her debts, assets and financial condition.

Soon after the first creditors' meeting, creditors file a proof of claim. Filing establishes legal evidence concerning the size and validity of the claim. Information in the claim may help determine where each creditor's claim fits into the legal process of asset distribution. For example, a creditor who can present proof of a valid and properly perfected security interest might be permitted to reclaim the collateral immediately if it is established that the amount still due is more than the market value of the property. Since, in this case, the debtor does not have equity in the collateral, courts often release the collateral to the creditor during phase one rather than waiting until the estate is closed. If no interested party objects to the claim, it is considered to be allowed, and the creditor will be granted funds proportionate to the size and validity of the allowed claim.

Phase Two Creditor Concerns
The interests of a savings institution at the first creditors' meeting may be represented by consumer lending personnel and/or legal counsel. As noted earlier, representation at the meeting is important because the savings institution can gather important information about other creditors' claims on a debtor's assets as well as get answers to questions about the debtor's financial situation. Further, if a debtor fails to attend a meeting at which creditors are present, the court may dismiss the bankruptcy petition. Creditors may, therefore, win a reaffirmation of their debt simply because a debtor failed to attend the creditors' meeting.

Claims should be carefully prepared and submitted in the prescribed time period. Challenges about the accuracy of credit data, objections and requests for special handling also need to be submitted.

Unsecured creditors also should file a proof of claim (see Figure 10-4). While this is not required by law, priority is given to the creditors who file over those who do not. When the proceeds of the liquidated estate are distributed, unsecured creditors who have not filed a proof of claim are among the last to be paid, resulting in their receipt of few or no funds from the estate.

Administration of the Estate: Phase Three

Administration of the Chapter 7 debtor's bankruptcy estate is handled by the trustee, who is responsible for collecting assets, converting them into cash, distributing proceeds to creditors and fulfilling other administrative duties. The trustee, therefore, plays an especially important role during the administration of the estate, the third phase of the Chapter 7 bankruptcy process.

Phase Three Legal Events

A Chapter 7 bankruptcy trustee has two principal responsibilities: to act as a neutral representative of all creditors and to administer the estate for the bankruptcy court.

In assembling the estate, the trustee initially tries to gather all of the debtor's assets. However, as the administra-

---

FIGURE 10-4
Comparison of Claims of Creditors with Secured and Unsecured Claims

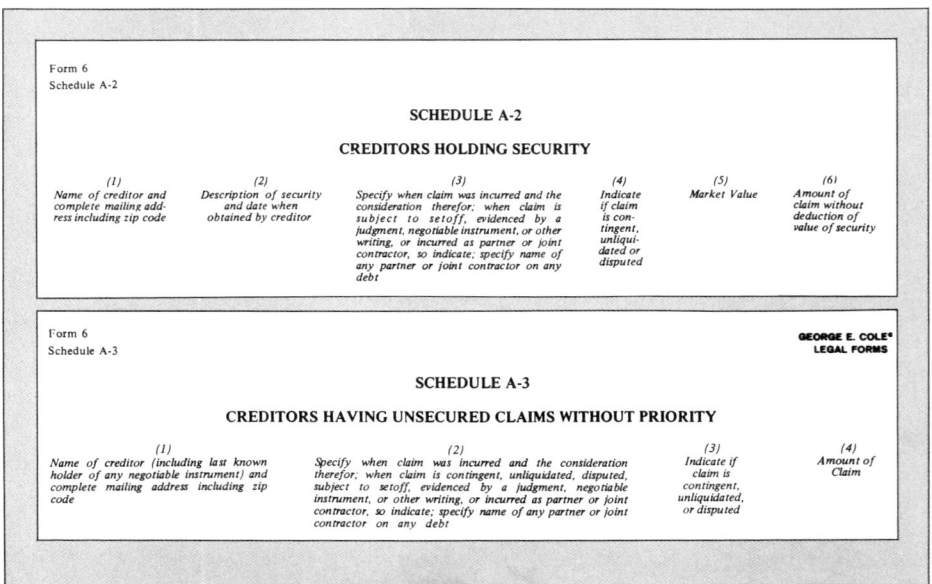

George E. Cole® Legal Forms, reprinted by permission of Boise Cascade Corporation.

tive process continues, certain assets may be removed from the estate. One method of removal is the use of available exemptions, such as the debtor's right to keep basic household possessions. Another method of removing assets from the estate is by *reaffirmation*, the debtor's agreement to repay the debt in full.

At the same time that certain assets are being removed, trustees may be locating other assets to add to the estate. As administrator of the estate, the trustee is empowered to require that debtors and creditors turn over to the estate any assets not exempt from collection. Trustees have considerable power to require others to deliver assets that the debtor partially owns or to obtain funds for the estate that others owed to the debtor at the time bankruptcy was initiated.

Once all nonexempt assets of the bankruptcy estate have been collected, the trustee may continue to meet with creditors to negotiate the liquidation of assets. For example, the trustee may decide to sell or lease property to raise cash for distribution to creditors. Depending upon the individual circumstances of the case, creditors may or may not have a voice in the manner in which assets are liquidated.

All of these responsibilities are handled by the trustee acting in the place of the debtor. In the role of neutral representative of creditors, the trustee has several other duties. The trustee verifies that a debtor qualifies for dischargement of pre-bankruptcy debts and has not illegally assigned assets to the benefit of any one creditor or group of creditors, since this would improperly place one creditor in a better position than the others (see Figure 10-5). To protect the rights of creditors, the trustee verifies the accuracy and completeness of each creditor's claims and objects to those claims deemed invalid. The trustee may also hire attorneys or other professional assistants to help during the process of collection, liquidation and distribution of proceeds from the estate.

Phase Three Creditor Concerns
The administration phase in Chapter 7 bankruptcies can be a busy time for creditors, particularly if there are questions about the priority of their claims relative to those of other creditors; about the facts provided by the debtor; or about the trustee's plan for accumulating assets.

Two-way communication between the institution's representative and the trustee helps during this process. Perhaps

FIGURE 10-5
Examples of Verification of Debtor's Assignments

> 11. (a) Payment of loans, installment purchases and other debts.
>
> What payments in whole or in part have you made during the year immediately preceding the filing of the original petition herein on any of the following: (1) loans; (2) installment purchases of goods and services; and (3) other debts? (Give the names and addresses of the persons receiving payment, the amounts of the loans or other debts and the purchase price of the goods and services, the dates of the original transactions, the amounts and dates of payments and, if any of the payees are your relatives or insiders, the relationship; if the debtor is a partnership and any of the payees is or was a partner or a relative of a partner, state the relationship; if the debtor is a corporation and any of the payees is or was an officer, director, or stockholder, or a relative of an officer, director, or stockholder, state the relationship.)
>
> (b) Setoffs.
>
> What debts have you owed to any creditor, including any bank, which were setoff by that creditor against a debt or deposit owing by the creditor to you during the year immediately preceding the filing of the original petition herein? (Give the names and addresses of the persons setting off such debts, the dates of the setoffs, the amounts of the debts owing by you and to you and, if any of the creditors are your relatives or insiders, the relationship.)
>
> 12. Transfers of property.
>
> a. Have you made any gifts, other than ordinary and usual presents to family members and charitable donations, during the year immediately preceding the filing of the original petition herein? (If so, give names and addresses of donees and dates, description, and value of gifts.)
>
> b. Have you made any other transfer, absolute or for the purpose of security, or any other disposition, of real or personal property during the year immediately preceding the filing of the original petition herein? (Give a description of the property, the date of the transfer or disposition, to whom transferred or how disposed of, and, if the transferee is a relative or insider, the relationship, the consideration, if any, received therefor, and the disposition of such consideration.)
>
> 13. Repossessions and returns.
>
> Has any property been returned to, or repossessed by, the seller or by a secured party during the year immediately preceding the filing of the original petition herein? (If so, give particulars, including the name and address of the party getting the property and its description and value.)

George E. Cole® Legal Forms, reprinted by permission of Boise Cascade Corporation.

through negotiation, the trustee's original plan to sell pledged collateral could be modified to a decision to rent, with income from the rental going to the lender. Negotiated agreements on a debtor's requests for exemptions and reaffirmations may also reduce the extent of a lender's loss. During this time, too, objections can be raised. Because of the complexity of rulings and the sometimes differing federal and state requirements, this process may call for the involvement of legal counsel (at least in an advisory capacity) or of another individual with considerable experience in bankruptcy law.

Distribution and Discharge: Phase Four

The final phase in Chapter 7 bankruptcies is the distribution of assets and discharge of debts. With a full discharge, the debtor is released from any remaining prebankruptcy debts, whether or not the distribution confers the full amounts that were due. This is the "fresh start" that is the debtor's goal in petitioning for a Chapter 7 bankruptcy.

Phase Four Legal Events
Decisions made earlier already have established certain priorities for the distribution of assets. The benefits of correct handling of liens and the perfection of security interest when the loan was made are very much apparent during distribution since these debts are placed higher in the order. Generally, too, creditors who have filed claims have priority over those who have not.

After all early considerations have been resolved, remaining claims against the estate are considered. Typically, certain types of debts are awarded higher priority than others. Administrative and court expenses rank high, followed by income taxes and pre-bankruptcy property taxes. Claims from unsecured creditors rank further down with those filed on time typically placed higher than those filed late. However, the bankruptcy court at all times has considerable power to subordinate claims if it judges this action to be appropriate.

Dissatisfied parties may challenge the full discharge of the debts. If there are no objections, the bankruptcy case is closed, and the debtor is fully released from dischargable pre-bankruptcy debts.

CHAPTER 13 BANKRUPTCIES: REPAYMENT

As explained above, Chapter 7 bankruptcies result in liquidation of debtor assets. By contrast, Chapter 13 bankruptcies offer a way for debtors to retain and continue to use their assets. To accomplish this, debtors propose a method by which they will repay debts. The plan may be to pay all debts in full but over a longer period of time than originally scheduled, or it may be for a partial repayment with no extension of the term.

Creditors may find Chapter 13 bankruptcies somewhat more acceptable than Chapter 7 because they tend to receive a greater proportion of the amount due them. Repayment, however, is very dependent on an accurate and realistic view of the debtor's present and future resources, and it succeeds only with debtors who are responsible about following through with their plans. Clearly, creditors lose whether they agree either to accept partial repayment or to grant an extended repayment term, since both actions have adverse effects on profits.

Not all debtors qualify for Chapter 13 bankruptcy. First, this option is available only to individuals. Second, to qualify, individuals must have a regular source of income. Third, a ceiling is placed on the amount of debt that Chapter 13 petitioners currently owe ($100,000 for unsecured debts and $350,000 for secured debts). Finally, Chapter 13 petitioners must not be guilty of repetitive filing for bankruptcy.

•The following sections provide an overview of a typical Chapter 13 sequence: initiation, plan proposal, plan fulfillment and the final discharge. Examples of legal events and lender concerns during each phase are given.

Initiation: Phase One

The initiation of a bankruptcy suit is a significant event to each of the people or companies who have extended credit to the petitioner. This early phase immediately changes the status of a loan and limits the legally correct actions that creditors may take to collect on their loans.

Phase One Legal Events

As with Chapter 7, the first action in a Chapter 13 bankruptcy is for the debtor to file a petition (see Figure 10-2). For Chapter 13 bankruptcies, filings are always voluntary. As with Chapter 7 bankruptcies, the filing triggers an automatic stay on the debtors' pre-bankruptcy debts. Chapter 13 debtors provide information about their current financial situation (see Figure 10-6) and, either at this time or soon thereafter, file their repayment plan.

Phase One Creditor Concerns

On learning that a borrower has filed a Chapter 13 petition, the savings institution stops its standard collections process (because of the automatic stay) and alerts all internal departments that could be involved. The institution's legal counsel and the insurance companies protecting this debtor's collateral also may be notified immediately.

Servicing and collections staff must gather data regarding

> "Having lectured on bankruptcy in 50 states, I can say with some authority that Chapter 13 programs are a crazy patchwork quilt across the nation."
>
> William R. Mapother, "Prepare to Defend Yourself in Chapter 13s," *Credit Union Magazine*, March 1986, p. 78.

the amount of money currently owed, the type of loan (secured, unsecured), the debtor's record of payments to date, and the age and value of collateral securing the loan, if any. Depending on circumstances, the institution may file its claim now or later but in either event must be prepared before the first creditors' meeting is held.

Plan Proposal: Phase Two

The second phase of Chapter 13 bankruptcies is the most demanding for creditors. At this time the debtor presents a repayment proposal for review by court officials and creditors. Many steps that creditors take (or ignore) at this time have long-term consequences regarding how well the lender's interests are protected.

Phase Two Legal Events

Shortly after a petition is filed, the court appoints a trustee. The trustee represents the interests of all parties, initiates and follows through on all legally required steps, and receives and distributes funds that the debtor sends to fulfill the repayment plan.

The repayment plan itself is a key element in Chapter 13 bankruptcies. Once confirmed, the plan functions as a new contract between debtors and creditors and substitutes a new arrangement for the original obligations. The repayment plan includes the proposed repayment amounts, debtor resources and budgets, and the proposed schedule for repayment.

In the plan, the debtor may propose to repay debts in full or in part. If the plan calls for only partial repayment, however, the debtor must commit all disposable income to

FIGURE 10-6
Statement of Financial Affairs for Personal Bankruptcy

Form 7
Statement of Financial Affairs
for Debtor Not Engaged in Business

GEORGE E. COLE*
LEGAL FORMS

UNITED STATES BANKRUPTCY COURT
For the................ District of ....

In re

Debtor*
Social Security No.
and Debtor's Employer's Tax
Identification No.

Case No. ....

STATEMENT OF FINANCIAL AFFAIRS FOR DEBTOR NOT ENGAGED IN BUSINESS

(Each question shall be answered or the failure to answer explained. If the answer is "none" or "not applicable" so state. If additional space is needed for the answer to any question, a separate sheet, properly identified and made a part hereof, should be used and attached.

The term, "original petition," used in the following questions, shall mean the petition filed under Rule 1002, 1003, or 1004.)

1. Name and residence.

a. What is your full name?

b. Have you used, or been known by, any other names within the 6 years immediately preceding the filing of the original petition herein? (If so, give particulars.)

c. Where do you now reside?

d. Where else have you resided during the 6 years immediately preceding the filing of the original petition herein?

2. Occupation and income.

a. What is your occupation?

b. Where are you now employed? (Give the name and address of your employer, or the address at which you carry on your trade or profession, and the length of time you have been so employed or engaged.)

c. Have you been in a partnership with anyone, or engaged in any business during the six years immediately preceding the filing of the original petition herein? (If so, give particulars, including names, dates, and places.)

d. What amount of income have you received from your trade or profession during each of the two calendar years immediately preceding the filing of the original petition herein?

e. What amount of income have you received from other sources during each of these two years? (Give particulars, including each source, and the amount received therefrom.)

*Include all names including trade names used by debtor within last 6 years.

Form 7 Statement of Financial Affairs (for debtor not engaged in business) Page No. 2

3. Tax returns and refunds.

a. Where did you file your federal, state and municipal income tax returns for the two years immediately preceding the filing of the original petition herein?

b. What tax refunds (income and other) have you received during the year immediately preceding the filing of the original petition herein?

c. To what tax refunds (income and other), if any, are you, or may you be, entitled? (Give particulars, including information as to any refund payable jointly to you and your spouse or any other person.)

George E. Cole® Legal Forms, reprinted by permission of Boise Cascade Corporation.

FIGURE 10-6, Continued
Statement of Financial Affairs for Personal Bankruptcy

4. *Financial accounts, certificates of deposit and safe deposit boxes.*

    a. What accounts or certificates of deposit or shares in banks, savings and loan, thrift, building and loan and homestead associations, credit unions, brokerage houses, pension funds and the like have you maintained, alone or together with any other person, and in your own or any other name within the two years immediately preceding the filing of the original petition herein? (Give the name and address of each institution, the name and number under which the account or certificate is maintained, and the name and address of every other person authorized to make withdrawals from such account.)

    b. What safe deposit box or boxes or other depository or depositories have you kept or used for your securities, cash, or other valuables within the two years immediately preceding the filing of the original petition herein? (Give the name and address of the bank or other depository, the name in which each box or other depository was kept, the name and address of every other person who had the right of access thereto, a brief description of the contents thereof, and, if the box has been surrendered, state when surrendered, or, if transferred, when transferred, and the name and address of the transferee.)

5. *Books and records.*

    a. Have you kept books of account or records relating to your affairs within the two years immediately preceding the filing of the original petition herein?

    b. In whose possession are these books or records? (Give names and addresses.)

    c. If any of these books or records are not available, explain.

    d. Have any books of account or records relating to your affairs been destroyed, lost, or otherwise disposed of within the two years immediately preceding the filing of the original petition herein? (If so, give particulars, including date of destruction, loss, or disposition, and reason therefor.)

6. *Property held for another person.*

    What property do you hold for any other person? (Give name and address of each person, and describe the property, or value thereof, and all writings relating thereto.)

7. *Property held by another.*

    Is any other person holding anything of value in which you have an interest? (Give name and address, location and description of the property, and circumstances of the holding.)

8. *Prior bankruptcy.*

    What cases under the Bankruptcy Act or title 11, United States Code have previously been brought by or against you? (State the location of the bankruptcy court, the nature and number of each case, the date when it was filed, and whether a discharge was granted or denied, the case was dismissed, or a composition, arrangement, or plan was confirmed.)

9. *Receiverships, general assignments, and other modes of liquidation.*

    a. Was any of your property, at the time of the filing of the original petition herein, in the hands of a receiver, trustee, or other liquidating agent? (If so, give a brief description of the property, the name and address of the receiver, trustee, or other agent, and, if the agent was appointed in a court proceeding, the name and location of the court, the title and number of the case, and the nature thereof.)

    b. Have you made any assignment of your property for the benefit of your creditors, or any general settlement with your creditors, within one year immediately preceding the filing of the original petition herein? (If so, give dates, the name and address of the assignee, and a brief statement of the terms of assignment or settlement.)

10. *Suits, executions, and attachments.*

    a. Were you a party to any suit pending at the time of the filing of the original petition herein? (If so, give the name and location of the court and the title and nature of the proceeding.)

    b. Were you a party to any suit terminated within the year immediately preceding the filing of the original petition herein? (If so, give the name and location of the court, the title and nature of the proceeding, and the result.)

    c. Has any of your property been attached, garnished, or seized under any legal or equitable process within the year immediately preceding the filing of the original petition herein? (If so, describe the property seized or person garnished, and at whose suit.)

George E. Cole® Legal Forms, reprinted by permission of Boise Cascade Corporation.

repayment for at least three years. For individuals, *disposable income* is defined as income that is not needed to support the debtor or his or her dependents. When the debtors own a business from which income is derived, the definition of disposable income also may include income beyond that needed to keep the business operational, since creditors would gain nothing if this source of debtor income disappears.

To document the source of funds pledged for repayment, the plan includes information on current income and expenses and lists the debtor's current assets. The plan also describes the proposed repayment process and terms. The repayment terms for Chapter 13 bankruptcies are somewhat flexible but cannot exceed three years without court approval.

If they were not due earlier, creditors prepare and file their claims during this time. The specific time allowed for claims after the petition has been filed may vary somewhat, but the maximum time period for this action is never extensive. A creditor should file claims on time since this may affect where its claims are placed in the order in which debtor funds are allotted (see Figure 10-7).

Also at this time, one or more creditors' meetings are held. The initial meeting often is conducted by the trustee who presents the debtor's repayment plan. Creditors may seek clarification of facts at the first meeting. Objections in written form will need to be submitted within a specified time.

The final action during this stage is a confirmation hearing and court approval of the plan. If no objections have been filed, the bankruptcy court probably will approve the trustee's recommendation to accept the plan. If objections are filed, the court considers these at the confirmation hearing. The debtor and other informed parties may be called on to give evidence to confirm or refute an objection. If a plan is confirmed over the continued objections of one or more creditors, the decision can be appealed to a higher court.

Phase Two Creditor Concerns
The fact that the repayment plan constitutes a new loan agreement is of primary importance to creditors at this time as they review the debtor's proposed plan, view his or her financial situation, and learn of other creditors' claims on

FIGURE 10-7
Creditor's Proof of Claim Form

No. 750
March, 1984

Form 19
Proof of Claim

CAUTION: Consult a lawyer before using or acting under this form. All warranties, including merchantability and fitness, are excluded.

UNITED STATES BANKRUPTCY COURT

For the _____ District of _____

In re

Case No. _____

Debtor*

PROOF OF CLAIM

1. [*If claimant is an individual claiming for himself*] The undersigned, who is the claimant herein, resides at**

[*If claimant is a partnership claiming through a member*] The undersigned, who resides at**
_____ , a partnership,
is a member of
composed of the undersigned and
of** _____ , and
doing business at**
and is authorized to make this proof of claim on behalf of the partnership.
   [*If claimant is a corporation claiming through an authorized officer*] The undersigned, who resides at**

is the _____ of
a corporation organized under the laws of
and doing business at**
and is authorized to make this proof of claim on behalf of the corporation.
   [*If claim is made by agent*] The undersigned, who resides at**
_____ , is the agent of
of** _____ , and is
authorized to make this proof of claim on behalf of the claimant.
2. The debtor was, at the time of the filing of the petition initiating this case, and still is indebted [*or* liable] to this claimant, in the sum of
$
3. The consideration for this debt [*or* ground of liability] is as follows:

   [*If filed in a chapter 7 or 13 case*] This claim consists of $_____ in principal amount and $_____ in additional charges [*or* no additional charges.] [Itemize all charges in addition to principal amount of debt, state basis for inclusion and computation, and set forth any other consideration relevant to the legality of the charge.]

4. [*If the claim is founded on a writing*] The writing on which this claim is founded (or a duplicate thereof) is attached hereto [*or* cannot be attached for the reason set forth in the statement attached hereto.]
5. [*If appropriate*] This claim is founded on an open account, which became [*or* will become] due on
_____ , as shown by the itemized statement attached hereto.
Unless it is attached hereto or its absence is explained in an attached statement, no note or other negotiable instrument has been received for the account or any part of it.
6. No judgment has been rendered on the claim except

7. The amount of all payments on this claim has been credited and deducted for the purpose of making this proof of claim.
8. This claim is not subject to any setoff or counter-claim except

9. No security interest is held for this claim except

[*If security interest in the property of the debtor is claimed*] The undersigned claims the security interest under the writing referred to in paragraph 4 hereof [*or* under a separate writing (or a duplicate of which) is attached hereto, *or* under a separate writing which cannot be attached for the reason set forth in the statement attached]. Evidence of perfection of such security interest is also attached.
10. This claim is a general unsecured claim, except to the extent that the security interest, if any, described in paragraph 9 is sufficient to satisfy the claim. [*If priority is claimed, state the amount and basis thereof.*]
                                      (Unsecured)
11. This claim is filed as a(n) (Secured)   claim.
                                      (Priority)
                                                                                                 $ _____
Claim Number   Total Amount Claimed
(For Office Use Only)

Name of Creditor: _____
(Print or Type Full Name of Creditor)

Dated: _____   Signed: _____

Penalty for Presenting Fraudulent Claim. Fine of not more than $5,000 or imprisonment for not more than 5 years or both—Title 18, U.S.C., ¶152.

*Include all names used by debtor within last 6 years.   **State mailing address.

debtor assets and income. Creditors can seek further information or raise objections at various times during this phase of the Chapter 13 bankruptcy process.

The debtor's repayment plan is critically important to lenders. The plan deserves careful review and analysis by each creditor because it details the debtor's resources and explains how the debtor proposes to repay the monies owed via the new debtor/creditor relationship.

Lenders must also carefully examine the financial data on which the debtor's budget is based to see if the budget is logical and workable. If not, creditors may wish to file an objection. For example, if a debtor reports take-home pay of $500 a month and living expenses of $400, but the plan calls for $200 in monthly repayments, the plan is not reasonable and workable. The likelihood is that the plan soon would fail and creditors would not receive the full amount of repayment. This type of weakness could be the basis for an objection. Considerable time may be needed to analyze the plan's financial data since it often is not easy to evaluate a debtor's financial situation and budget accurately.

Creditors also may object to the proposed repayment amounts and/or the percentage of debt coverage of a plan if they believe that the debtor is not making a serious commitment to repayment. Unfortunately, the law is not clear on exactly what proportion of income is appropriate for debtors to keep for their living expenses. Since debtor's living expenses are set aside before disposable income amounts are determined, however, the matter of debtors reserving a fair share of their income to contribute toward repayment is important to creditors and the court. The proposed length of the repayment term also may be challenged.

Plan Fulfillment: Phase Three

The fulfillment phase of a Chapter 13 repayment plan does not require as much attention from creditors as the first two phases. In one way, it is similar to the loan servicing process at savings institutions during which no special response is needed as long as payments arrive on time and in the right amount. A difference between routine loan servicing and Chapter 13 bankruptcy repayments is that action might be needed if the debtor's financial situation changes or if the debtor asks for a change.

Phase Three Legal Events

Chapter 13 debtors must begin to make payments toward their debts very soon after their petition is filed. Payments are sent to the trustee who holds early payments until the plan is confirmed. After confirmation, the trustee distributes the accumulated funds. The trustee continues to be responsible for accepting and distributing payments throughout the term.

From these payments, the trustee first pays out administrative and court expenses and then distributes the remainder of each payment to creditors according to the plan as confirmed by the court. An important responsibility for trustees during this time is to make sure that payments are made in full and on time. Nonpayment or late payments are grounds for dismissal in Chapter 13 bankruptcies.

Either the debtor or the creditor may petition the court to modify the original plan at any time. Reasons for considering modification might be a sudden increase or decrease in the debtor's income or expenses.

Phase Three Creditor Concerns

During repayment, lenders monitor the satisfactory repayments as channeled through the trustee. Special financial reports or accounting records may need to be used for this nonroutine income. Lenders continue to be concerned during this phase that any collateral securing their loans is properly protected.

"In terms of prevention, the best solution [to Chapter 13 problems] is a crystal ball to determine which applicants are Chapter 13 candidates. Short of that, your best hope is establishment of loan policies encouraging use of co-makers and collateral."

William R. Mapother, "Set Your Strategies for Chapter 13," *Credit Union Magazine*, April 1986, p. 86.

As noted, creditors may seek to modify the terms of the original plan if this seems appropriate. While trustees usually fulfill their function responsibly, a lender who observes that payments are not timely and who notes that the trustee has failed to act to dismiss the bankruptcy, might seek dismissal.

Discharge: Phase Four

A debtor's goal in bankruptcy is to be released from obligations for all dischargeable prepetition debts. Thus the final phase in Chapter 13, as in other bankruptcies, is for the debts to be discharged.

Phase Four Legal Events
The standard method of discharge for Chapter 13 bankruptcies is for the debtor to satisfactorily complete the repayment plan within the time approved by the court. A second possible method is for a debtor to ask for a hardship discharge sometime during the repayment term. The bankruptcy court determines whether or not to grant a hardship discharge, basing its decision chiefly on exceptions noted in the law. Certain debts remain dischargeable even in the case of a hardship discharge; the Bankruptcy Code specifies these exceptions.

Phase Four Creditor Concerns
Creditors will have few concerns for discharges that result from completion of the plan, since this is usually the repayment plan they agreed to originally. If the court permits a hardship discharge, creditors may file a complaint if they think the ruling is not appropriate or is contrary to the Code. Aside from any final accounting procedures, the creditors concern with a Chapter 13 bankruptcy ends with the discharge.

At best, a bankruptcy proceeding for a formerly approved consumer loan costs the lender a great deal of time and effort. While personal situations sometimes seem to make bankruptcy the only alternative to individual borrowers, the lending institution receives only a portion of the income and profit it had expected when the loan was made. The unhappy events surrounding bankruptcy, therefore, reinforce how valuable it is to savings institutions and their good customers when institutions follow sound underwriting, servicing and collection procedures for all of their consumer loans.

SUMMARY

The historical background of bankruptcy in the United States reveals a series of laws aimed at striking a balance between the rights of a hard-pressed debtor and the rights of creditors. Major laws and regulations today are the Bankruptcy Reform Act of 1978, the Bankruptcy Amendments and Federal Judgeship Act of 1984 and the Bankruptcy Code based on current federal law.

Consumer debtors normally file petitions in bankruptcy under Chapter 7 or Chapter 13 of the Code. Debtors can be held responsible for pre-bankruptcy debts as determined by the courts. A discharge is granted for amounts that remain unpaid.

A Chapter 7 bankruptcy involves the total liquidation of the debtor's estate whereas a Chapter 13 proceeding allows the debtor to keep assets while agreeing to a repayment plan.

Once a bankruptcy petition is filed, an automatic stay is put into effect that bars creditors from any further contact with the debtor except in conjunction with the bankruptcy proceeding. Soon after, a bankruptcy trustee is appointed by the court. This trustee is expected to serve as a neutral representative of all parties and to achieve a legally correct and equitable distribution of debtor assets. The trustee can achieve a superior position in collateral if a creditor's security interest was not properly perfected. Trustees have considerable authority to obtain estate assets from the debtor, the debtor's friends or preferred creditors for proper distribution to creditors; to liquidate the estate (in Chapter 7); and to discharge remaining debts.

In a Chapter 13 bankruptcy a compromise agreement is worked out in which the debtor and creditors agree to a plan of repayment. The plan may give creditors less than full repayment or may provide for full payment but over a longer period of time than under the original agreement. The debtor provides information about income and expenses to demonstrate that future payments can be made as proposed.

Repayment plans must provide either that all unsecured debts will be paid in full or that all of the debtor's disposable income over at least three years will be devoted to the loan's repayment.

For both types of bankruptcy, creditors must take certain actions at prescribed times for their claims to be recognized. They also have opportunities to file objections to rulings or proposals at various times during the process.

CHAPTER QUESTIONS

1. Trace the history of bankruptcy law in America from colonial times to the 1980s. How do the legal changes demonstrate the continuing conflict between the rights of debtors and creditors?

2. Compare voluntary and involuntary Chapter 7 bankruptcies. When might creditors initiate a suit for involuntary bankruptcy? What are its drawbacks?

3. Explain the following early events in a Chapter 7 bankruptcy: petition, automatic stay, statement of intent, court dismissal. In what ways do these events concern the lending institution?

4. In May, Alan Everett purchased a luxury car and charged expenses for a seven-day trip on a top-of-the-line cruise ship. A few weeks after returning from the cruise, he filed for Chapter 7 bankruptcy. Could the lending institution that held Everett's credit card and auto loan protect its interests in this case? Explain.

5. What legal events take place at a Chapter 7 creditors' meeting? What part should a lending institution play before, during and after the meeting?

6. Compare and contrast the role and duties of trustees in Chapter 7 and Chapter 13 bankruptcies.

7. How does a Chapter 7 bankruptcy case end? Which lenders probably receive a larger portion of their funds when the case is closed?

8. What is the benefit to debtors of Chapter 13 over Chapter 7 bankruptcy? What are its benefits and drawbacks to creditors?

9. How do early actions in Chapter 13 bankruptcies resemble those in Chapter 7? How are they different?

10. What is the significance of a Chapter 13 debtor's repayment plan? What elements might be of interest to the lending institution? Give examples of items that might be the basis for objection.

11. Describe the trustee's role during the plan fulfillment phase of Chapter 13 bankruptcies. What circumstances might be of concern to the lender during this time?

12. Name two ways in which a Chapter 13 bankruptcy case might be concluded.

Glossary

abandonment The situations, according to the Internal Revenue Code, in which the borrower intends to and does permanently discard or give up the use of the security property.

acceleration clause The clause of a legal contract that states the institution's right to demand full payment of the debt in the event of a default. It may appear on a promissory note, mortgage instrument or security agreement.

accident and health insurance The type of insurance that provides monthly loan payments to the lender on behalf of the borrower (the insured). The benefits are paid for a prescribed period of time if the borrower loses income as a result of an accident or illness.

acknowledgement of indebtedness A statement contained in the promissory note that identifies the borrower (or co-borrowers) and the lender and recognizes their debtor-creditor relationship.

actuarial method A method of recognizing simple interest income based on the outstanding principal balance for the unit of time between payment due dates.

add-on interest The interest on a loan that is computed by determining the interest charge for the term of the loan and adding that charge to the principal of the loan. The borrower agrees to repay the principal plus interest, although only principal is disbursed to the borrower. Also called precomputed interest.

adjusted balance method A creditor method of assessing finance charges after subtracting payments made during the billing period.

adverse action The denial of credit to an applicant.

aircraft insurance The type of insurance that covers physical damage on aircraft. The deductible feature on aircraft policies usually varies, depending on whether or not the aircraft is in use.

amortization The process of reducing principal and interest in equal installment payments at specific intervals over a set period.

amortization table A table that shows the monthly payment amount needed to amortize, or pay off, a borrowed sum at a given percent of interest over a period of time.

annual percentage rate (APR) A measure of the cost of credit, expressed as a yearly rate, that relates the amount and timing of payments made. The APR takes into account the amount of interest and all other types of finance charges. The APR is the percentage cost of credit on a yearly basis.

assets The tangible and/or intangible items of value that help determine a borrower's capital.

attachment of security interest The obtainment of the secured party's rights in the collateral. In a secured transaction, attachment makes the security interest enforceable against the borrower. *See also* security interest.

authorization A procedure for notifying the card-issuing institution when a cardholder makes a purchase over an established dollar amount called a floor limit. *See also* floor limit.

automatic perfection A purchase money security interest in collateral that is classified as a consumer good by the Uniform Commercial Code. The automatic perfection provision reflects the opinion that consumers are usually aware that when they purchase consumer goods on an installment basis they are doing so on a secured basis. *See also* perfection of security interest and purchase money security interest.

automatic stay A freeze on a debtor's assets after the filing of a bankruptcy petition; after this court action, creditors must go through the court to make claims on a debtor's assets.

available exemptions The retained assets, such as household items needed for daily living, that are not subject to liquidation in bankruptcy.

average daily balance method A creditor method of assessing finance charges in which creditors add borrowers' balances for each day in the billing period and then divide by the number of days in the billing period.

bankruptcy A legal process in which a person or business declares the inability to repay debts; any available assets are liquidated and the proceeds distributed among creditors; or the person or business may follow a court-approved plan to repay debts.

buy rate The interest rate at which a lender agrees to purchase indirect loans from a dealer (dealer paper).

capacity An applicant's "financial ability" to repay a loan according to scheduled payments. Capacity is determined by verifying the applicant's total income and total expenses and subtracting the latter from the former.

capital The assets or items of value owned by an applicant that could be a possible source of debt repayment.

capitalization The addition of accrued unpaid interest to the outstanding principal balance. Also called compounding of interest and negative amortization.

certificate of registration An evidence of ownership for aircraft. It gives a description of the property and lists any liens against it.

certificate of title An evidence of ownership for automobiles, recreational vehicles and, in some states, boats. It gives a description of the property and lists any liens against it.

Chapter 7 bankruptcy A form of bankruptcy in which the debtor's assets are liquidated and distributed among the creditors; also called straight bankruptcy.

Chapter 13 bankruptcy A form of bankruptcy in which a debtor proposes a method for partially or wholly repaying debts while retaining use of the assets.

character A borrower's reputation for repaying debt; it is determined from the borrower's credit history. It refers to the borrower's apparent or historically demonstrated "willingness," determination and commitment to pay. It reflects the applicant's integrity and honesty.

charge off An accounting procedure that reflects losses from bad debts in institution records. By charging off the loan, the institution is removing the consumer loan from its assets. FSLIC regulations stipulate when this must be done in member institutions.

closed-end credit A fixed-term credit whereby the amount of credit to be extended, the length of time for repayment, and the payment amounts are determined before purchase.

co-applicant A person who requests credit along with an applicant. Both applicant and co-applicant are contractually liable for repayment of the debt. Also called co-borrower.

cognovit or confession of judgment A clause prohibited by the FHLBB in consumer loans and certain equity loans made by Federal Home Loan Bank System members. A cognovit or confession of judgment declares the borrower's consent to future judgments against the borrower for the amount owed in case the borrower defaults on a loan. It waives both the borrower's right to prior notice and the right to be heard in a formal legal proceeding. In other words, a contract cannot require a borrower to waive these rights.

collateral An item of tangible or intangible value that is owned or being purchased by the individual, such as an automobile, real estate, deposit account or negotiable instrument, used to secure promise of future payments. A lender can repossess collateral if the loan is not repaid.

collateral receipt A document that serves as evidence to a borrower that the creditor has physical possession of the collateral.

collection device The means of contacting delinquent borrowers such as late notices, collections letters, telephone calls, field visits and office interviews.

collections letter A letter sent to delinquent borrowers to establish the lender's firm position in dealing with delinquency and to relay a sense of urgency to the borrower about submitting the past due amount.

collections policy A lender policy that communicates to employees a systematic and legally correct method for identifying and contacting delinquent borrowers and for handling delinquent loans.

commercial bank A privately owned and operated financial intermediary chartered by a state or federal agency for the purposes of facilitating commerce (buying and selling) and promoting industry, providing a safe place for deposited funds, and aiding in the transfer of those funds by check and credit extension.

commitments for title insurance The title reports from title insurance companies.

competition The rivalry between two or more businesses striving for the same customers or market.

conditions The economic climate affecting both the borrower and the lender. Conditions include inflation; interest rates; seasonal demand for an item; availability and price; and prospects for continued employment.

consumer credit classified as a loss According to FSLIC

regulations, closed-end consumer credit delinquent 120 days or more and open-end consumer credit delinquent 180 days or more.

consumer finance company A state-regulated company whose main purpose is to make installment credit available to consumers.

conveyance recordation notice The document that serves as evidence of the lender's security interest in aircraft. It is issued by the Federal Aviation Administration to the lender.

cosigner An individual who signs a legal document on an equal basis with the signer. On a promissory note, all cosigners are individually and jointly liable for repayment of the full debt.

credit life insurance The insurance that insures a borrower in the event of death. If death occurs, the insurance benefits will pay the lender the loan balance due. Credit life usually takes one of three forms: decreasing, level or joint.

credit scoring system An objective method of evaluating applicant information or attributes to determine credit worthiness. Applicant attributes are assigned a number of points; the more points assigned, the more the attribute signifies a good credit risk. The minimum acceptable score is listed as part of the lender's underwriting standards. Credit scoring systems must meet the nondiscriminatory standards of ECOA and other requirements set forth in Regulation B.

credit union A cooperative financial organization chartered by the state or federal government for the purpose of collecting savings from members and making loans to other members. Members of credit unions have a common bond, such as place of employment; membership in the same labor union, religious congregation or club; or place of residence.

customer rate The interest rate charged to a borrower. The customer rate may be higher than the buy rate for loans originated indirectly.

debt-to-income ratio The ratio that expresses the relationship of the sum of the applicant's monthly credit obligations to the applicant's monthly income.

debt-to-net income ratio The ratio that expresses the relationship of the sum of the applicant's monthly credit obligations to the applicant's take-home pay after deductions for income tax and Social Security have been taken.

decreasing credit life insurance A form of credit life insurance that begins on the first day of the loan term and ends when the loan is repaid fully. Throughout the life of the policy, the amount of coverage equals the outstanding loan balance.

deed given in lieu of foreclosure An instrument that voluntarily transfers ownership in real property, which is securing a debt, from a delinquent borrower to a lender in exchange for a canceled note and mortgage.

deed of trust A mortgage instrument that conveys title of real estate to a third party or trustee. Whether an institution uses a regular mortgage document or a deed of trust depends on state laws. Both documents basically function in the same way. *See also* mortgage instrument.

deficiency The difference between the proceeds from a public sale of foreclosed property and the unpaid loan balance. *See also* deficiency judgment.

deficiency judgment A court order that renders the defaulted borrower liable to the lender for the amount of deficiency. It is outlawed or restricted in some states. *See also* deficiency.

delinquency rate The percentage of the total amount of loans outstanding that are delinquent.

delinquency report A report used by the collections department to identify delinquent borrowers and to provide a background for recommending the actions needed to collect back payments.

deposit account loan A loan granted to a consumer who pledges a portion of his or her funds deposited with the institution as security for the loan.

direct loan A loan negotiated between a consumer and a lender.

direct referral A loan originated by the dealer in cooperation with a lender in which the dealer sends the purchaser to the lender for financing.

discount interest The type of interest that is determined by calculating the total amount of interest for the loan and subtracting it from the principal loan amount.

disposable income The income that is not needed to support the debtor or dependents involved in bankruptcy; when a business is owned, it includes income beyond that needed to keep the business operational.

dual interest coverage A type of physical damage insurance that offers protection for up to 100% of the value of the collateral. Both the lender and the borrower, who is presumed to have some equity in the item, are covered.

electronic funds transfer (EFT) Any transfer of funds, other than transactions originated by paper instruments, that is triggered through the use of an electronic terminal, telephone equipment, computer, or magnetic tape and orders or authorizes an institution to debit or credit an account.

encumbrance A claim or liability attached to real property, such as a mortgage or unpaid taxes. *See also* lien.

equitable right of redemption The privilege granted by states to borrowers allowing a certain amount of time before the foreclosure sale when borrowers can pay the outstanding loan balance and recover the property. *See also* statutory right of redemption.

equity The portion of real property owned by an individual.

equity loan A loan that uses the borrower's equity in real property as security. It may be made for a variety of purposes. Also known as a second or junior mortgage loan.

estate The property held by the debtor at the time of filing for bankruptcy.

exact interest-exact time The method of calculating interest that is based on a 365-day year and the exact number of days interest is earned or owed. In leap years this method uses 366 days. Also called the 365/365 method.

field visits The home visitations by collectors when borrowers do not respond to written notices or cannot be reached by telephone.

finance charges The sum of all charges payable directly or indirectly by the borrower and imposed directly or indirectly by the creditor as an incident to or as condition of the extension of credit.

financial intermediary A financial institution that accepts money from savers and investors and uses these funds to make loans and other investments in its own name. Financial intermediaries include savings and loan institutions, mutual savings banks, life insurance companies, credit unions and investment companies.

financing statement A document filed at a designated public office that serves as a public notice to third parties that a creditor has established a security interest in some collateral. It provides the identities and mailing addresses of the borrower and creditor, including a description of the collateral.

flood insurance The type of insurance that protects both the borrower and the lender from loss of property due to flood damage.

floor limit The established dollar amount of available credit over which a cardholder cannot make a purchase without the card-issuing institution being notified. *See also* **authorization**.

floor planning   The loans made to finance dealer's inventory purchases.

forbearance agreement   A written or verbal statement whereby an institution grants a borrower additional time to make loan payments before pursuing a lawsuit, property repossession or garnishment of wages, as long as the borrower performs certain agreed-upon actions.

foreclosure   A legal procedure in which a lender extinguishes or cuts off equitable rights (rights to equity) of the borrower and legal rights of subsequent lienholders to the real property securing the loan. Foreclosure usually results in the secured property being sold at public auction.

full-payout lease   A type of lease in which the total payment stream of the lease rental payments alone should cover the cost of the leased asset, the cost of financing, the lessor's overhead and a rate of return acceptable to the lessor.

future advances clause   A clause on a mortgage instrument that allows a lender to advance additional funds without executing a new mortgage instrument.

grace period   A specified number of days after the due date during which no late charge or other penalty is assessed if the borrower makes a payment. During this grace period, no collections procedures are begun, and payments submitted within this time generally do not reflect adversely on the borrower's permanent credit history.

granting clause   A clause contained in the security agreement that assigns a security interest in the collateral to the borrower.

guarantor   An individual, or entity, who promises to make payments to the lender in the event the borrower defaults on the loan.

hedge A counter-balancing transaction made to protect oneself against a possible investment loss.

home improvement loan A loan that provides funds for repairing, altering or restoring residential structures.

implied warranty An unwritten assurance that a product is fit for consumption.

inbound telemarketing A method of marketing by advertising a telephone number (for example, a toll-free number) and handling incoming customer calls.

indirect loan Any loan originated by a dealer, retailer, or seller of goods and services to finance the purchase of those goods and services. Also called third-party loans or dealer paper because the loans are assigned or sold to a lender by a third party.

in-file credit report A report from a credit reporting agency used to evaluate a loan applicant; it lists all information that the agency has on the applicant in question.

installment credit A repayment plan that involves two or more future payments. Payments are scheduled at periodic intervals (for example, monthly, quarterly or semi-annually) and must be continued until the full amount of the loan is satisfied. It allows consumers to obtain or enjoy the benefits of goods or services while paying for them in small amounts over a specified period of time.

interchange A clearing process for charges made by credit cards; it operates in much the same way as check clearing through the Federal Reserve.

interest The fee paid for the use of money.

interest earned report A report that lists all loan accounts and the total interest charged on each or the interest charged for the past month. It also gives a total interest charged figure for all outstanding loans or each type of loan.

involuntary bankruptcy A fairly rare legal proceeding in which a creditor or group of creditors attempt to make a debtor liquidate assets to pay off debts.

joint credit life insurance A form of credit life insurance that covers both husband and wife during the period of the loan.

judgment lien A charge against the real or personal property of a debtor as a result of a final ruling by a judicial court. Judgment liens give creditors a security interest in a debtor's property and can include the right to acquire and retain possession of the property until the debt is satisfied.

late charge A penalty imposed by the lender for delinquent repayments, as specified in the debt instrument. Late charges are usually stated as a fixed fee or as a percentage of the loan payment due.

late notice A notice sent to delinquent borrowers stating that the loan payment has not been received.

lease A contract that specifies the conditions by which an owner conveys the possession and use of an asset to another. The lease is a financing contract between a *lessee* (user of the asset) and a *lessor* (owner of the asset).

lessee A person or business that is granted use and possession of property in return for rent.

lessor An owner of property who allows another to use it in return for rent.

level credit life insurance A form of credit life insurance in which the amount of coverage stays the same over the life of the loan.

lien A claim that a lender has upon the property of another as security for the payment of a debt or charge. *See also* encumbrance.

lien holder A lender who holds the right to seize the property of a delinquent debtor, liquidate that property and use the proceeds to satisfy the unpaid debt.

loan application An oral or written request for an extension of credit that is made in accordance with procedures established by a creditor for the type of credit requested.

loan history A list of the transactions made to a borrower's loan account.

loan modification Any change in the loan term, interest rate or amortization schedule, made by agreement between both the borrower and the lender to reduce the borrower's monthly payment amount.

loan payment journal *See* transaction journal.

loan term The total length of time allowed for repayment of debt. Also called loan maturity.

loan-to-value ratio The relationship of the total amount of loans secured by the same collateral to the value of the collateral. This ratio is most often used on secured loans for real estate and automobiles.

loans in process A general ledger account from which loan funds are usually disbursed.

lock box A post office box to which customers mail payments to an institution. Payments are picked up for processing by either the institution itself or an institution that has contracted to provide these processing services.

magnetic ink character recognition (MICR) The electronic reading of machine-readable characters printed in magnetic ink, such as those appearing on checks.

manufacturer's certificate of origination The form used to obtain a certificate of title for a newly purchased motor vehicle that certifies that the vehicle is new and has never before been issued a certificate of title.

margin The method used to evaluate whether an applicant can handle proposed loan payments by considering the applicant's family size, living expenses per person and monthly credit obligations and subtracting debts from expenses.

marine loan The type of loan used to finance the purchase of boats.

marine insurance The type of insurance that covers boats.

marketing A management function whose purpose is to identify and provide products and services that customers want and need. A broad range of activities included in this function are: researching of needs, selecting from alternative ideas, planning, implementing, distributing, servicing, evaluating and revising of products and services.

mean An arithmetic average of all reported amounts.

median The middle value, above and below which lie an equal number of reported amounts.

mobile home loan A nonmortgage loan made to an individual for the purchase of a mobile home. It is secured by the lender's lien on the mobile home.

mortgage instrument The document that represents a conveyance of real property offered as security for a debt. *See also* deed of trust and regular mortgage instrument.

mutual savings bank A state-chartered or federally chartered financial intermediary incorporated to provide a secure place for individuals to save. It invests deposits primarily in mortgage loans, stocks, bonds and other securities.

net lease A lease in which the lessee assumes responsibility for the payment of all charges and expenses such as taxes, insurance and maintenance.

new loan report The report that lists new borrower information such as name, loan account number, loan amount, loan terms and mailing address.

nondischargeable debts The debts for which a person who has filed bankruptcy remains responsible even after the bankruptcy action; they remain due.

nonfiling insurance A type of insurance that protects the lender against a loss that results from unintentional errors or omissions in the filing or recording of a security interest.

nonpayout lease A type of lease in which the lessor's profits are in part dependent on the lease being renewed or on finding a second lessee to take over payment of the remaining expenses.

office interview A personal meeting at a lender's office between a delinquent borrower and collector. The purpose of an office interview is to discover the reason for the delinquency and to establish a plan for bringing the loan current.

open-end credit A type of credit whereby consumers request and receive an open line of credit up to a predetermined amount (dollar credit limit). Consumers can draw against their line of credit without having to make specific arrangements for each purchase. Consumers can make payments that most closely reflect their financial capabilities at a particular point in time. As the loan balance is reduced, the available credit increases back to the predetermined limit. The line of credit remains available (open) indefinitely until either the borrower or lender cancels it. *See also* retail open charge credit.

operating lease A lease in which the lessor or manufacturer is responsible for maintenance and services.

ordinary interest-exact time The method of calculating interest that is based on a 360-day year while considering the exact number of days interest is earned or owed. Also called the 365/360 method.

ordinary interest-ordinary time The method of calculating interest that is based on a 360-day year and considers each month to have exactly 30 days. Also called the 360/360 method.

outbound telemarketing A method of marketing whereby potential or existing customers are called to stimulate business.

overdraft revolving credit The protection against overdrawn checking accounts.

partial repurchase A term in a written agreement, used in lending, that gives the buyer in the event the borrower defaults, the right to reimbursement for an agreed-upon amount (usually market value).

payee clause An insurance policy clause that lists the lender as a lienholder to the collateral.

payoff report A report that lists loan accounts on which the final payment has been made (usually on the previous business day). It includes such information as name, loan account number, date loan was approved, payoff date, interest rate and whether payments were ever late.

perfected lien creditor A lien holder who has obtained priority over claims of third parties. *See also* lien, lien holder and perfection of security interest.

perfection of security interest The act to obtain priority over claims of third parties. The secured interest is thus protected from a court appointed trustee in bankruptcy. *See also* automatic perfection and security interst.

personal property The objects that are not permanently affixed to land. Personal property can be either tangible or intangible. Examples of tangible personal property include appliances, cars, boats and television sets. Examples of intangible personal property include stocks and bonds.

physical damage insurance A type of insurance that covers physical damage on automobiles, boats, recreational vehicles and aircraft used as collateral for the loan.

pledge arrangement The arrangement that exists when the borrower transfers possession of collateral to the lender.

power to hypothecate A document that represents a pledge of stocks, bonds or other financial instruments to a lender without transfer of title.

preauthorized EFTs The activities authorized by consumers in advance, such as when a transfer of funds occurs and recurs at regular periodic intervals. For example, preauthorized loan payments made through the automatic transfer of funds from a customer's savings or checking account.

prepayment clause A clause contained in a promissory note that lists any fees the lender may charge for prepayments (payments made in advance of the due date).

previous balance method A creditor method of assessing finance charges that gives no credit for payments made during the billing period.

principal An amount of money borrowed.

prior mortgage default clause A clause contained on a mortgage instrument that states that if the borrower defaults in payment of interest, principal or taxes on the first mortgage, the lender reserves the right to pay the amount in default to the first lienholder. This amount is then added to the amount of the second mortgage.

private mortgage insurance (PMI) A type of insurance on real property that protects the lender from a loss on a specified percentage of the unpaid loan balance. Regulations state that loans over 90% of the property value must be insured down to 80%. The actual percentage covered by private mortgage insurance is the difference between the loan-to-value ratio and 80%.

promise to repay clause A statement contained in the

promissory note that says the borrower agrees to repay and to be liable for the debt.

promissory note A written promise to pay a stipulated sum of money to a specified party under conditions mutually agreed upon. Also called a note or installment note.

purchase money security interest A lien in which a retailer is automatically granted first rights in a consumer good that it has been financed through an installment sales contract. *See also* automatic perfection.

pyramiding late charges The act of charging multiple late charges for one late payment. The FHLBB prohibits this type of clause in consumer loans and certain equity loans made by Federal Home Loan Bank System members.

reaffirmation An act by which the debtor who has filed for bankruptcy may retain a particular asset by promising to repay the debt in full as originally agreed.

real property The land along with any buildings or other objects permanently affixed to it.

recourse The right of a lending institution to seek loan repayment from the dealer in the event of borrower default.

recreational vehicles (RVs) Those units built or mounted on a chassis and intended for travel, vacationing, camping and other temporary living.

recognition of income A process by which lenders receive and account for interest payments as they are earned.

redemption An act in bankruptcy in which the debtor pays a creditor the cash value of collateral in order to take possession of the property free of liens.

regular mortgage document A mortgage instrument that conveys title of real property and describes the debt and other conditions of repayment. Whether an institution uses a regular mortgage document or a deed of trust depends on state laws. Both documents basically function in the same way. *See also* mortgage instrument.

repayment schedule   A list of the due dates and amounts of all loan payments needed to satisfy the debt.

repossession   A remedy available to lenders whereby personal property used as security for a delinquent debt is acquired and disposed of for the purpose of repaying the loan in whole or in part.

repurchase   The right of a lending institution to seek loan repayment from the dealer if conditions set forth in the retail installment contract are not met.

residual value   The estimated value of the asset at the end of the lease.

retail credit   A type of consumer credit extended a borrower to purchase goods or services. *See also* retail revolving credit and retail open charge credit.

retail firm   A business that facilitates the transfer of consumer goods from the manufacturer to the ultimate consumer. Also called retailer.

retail installment contract   Legally binding agreement that sets forth the terms of the sale and the terms of the purchaser's payment.

retail installment credit   A credit purchase in which a buyer and seller may reach an agreement in which payment for the goods can be extended over a longer period of time than for retail revolving credit. For the privilege of delayed payment, a carrying charge is generally levied on the customer. One or many items may be involved, and the installment account may be secured by an additional agreement on the merchandise purchased.

retail open charge credit   The credit extended to borrowers to acquire goods with the promise to pay in one lump sum, usually within a 30- to 60-day period. The consumer usually pays no additional fees for the privilege of the delayed payment. *See also* open-end credit and retail credit.

retail revolving credit A credit purchase in which a customer is permitted to purchase goods or services by agreeing to make full payment for them within 25 to 30 days or a monthly payment in which an interest charge for the privilege of using this type of credit is added. *See also* retail credit.

right of rescission The right of consumers to cancel any credit transaction where the collateral used to secure the transaction is their principal residence within three business days from whichever of the following events occurs last: the date of the transaction; the date that the truth-in-lending disclosures are received; or the date that the notice of their right to cancel is received.

Rule of 78s A method of recognizing add-on interest by using predetermined factors to the portion of total interest earned for the period. A declining ratio is applied to a fixed-loan amount to determine interest earned for the period. Also called the sum-of-the-digits method.

savings and loan institution The state-chartered or federally chartered financial intermediary that accepts savings from the public and invests those savings primarily in residential mortgage loans. Also known as co-operative banks, homestead societies, or building and loan associations.

scheduled items An FLSIC regulatory category in which every insured institution is required to include the total amount of its slow loans (including slow consumer credit loans), real estate owned in foreclosure, and real estate sold on contract or financed at a high loan-to-value ratio.

secured credit The credit granted when a consumer pledges collateral guaranteeing loan repayment.

security agreement A document that represents a transfer of property from a borrower to a creditor given in fulfillment or satisfaction of a debt. A typical security agreement identifies the creditor and the borrower and contains a description of the collateral. Additionally, the terms and conditions of the agreement and any special provisions required by state or federal statutes are listed.

security interest An interest in collateral that secures payment or performance of an obligation. *See also* attachment of security interest and perfection of security interest.

service credit The consumer credit used to acquire the benefits derived from nontangible items or services. Legal advice and medical or dental care are examples of services that can be obtained with this type of credit transaction.

simple interest A method of calculating interest in which the amount of interest is computed on the outstanding principal balance of a loan for each given period.

single payment credit A repayment plan in which full payment for a good or service is made in one lump sum. This sum is paid at a future date agreed upon by both consumer and creditor.

skip insurance A type of insurance that protects the lender from losses caused by the borrower changing the property securing the loan, embezzlement or someone hiding the collateral. Also called venders single interest (VSI) insurance.

skiptracing A process whereby collectors try to uncover information to help them locate missing debtors and collect repayment.

slow consumer credit According to FSLIC regulations closed-end consumer credit delinquent 90 to 119 days and open-end consumer credit delinquent 90 to 179 days.

special credit report A report from a credit reporting agency used to evaluate a loan applicant that gives only specific information on an applicant as requested by a lender.

statement system A system of reporting on the status of an account. This statement is mailed to the customer at specified periods and contains a record of any account action—deposits, withdrawals, interest and principal payments, etc.—that has taken place during that period.

statutory right of redemption The period of time extended to borrowers to redeem property after the foreclosure sale and before the purchaser receives the title deed. *See also* equitable right of redemption.

subordination clause A mortgage clause that states the preference of the lender in retaining a particular lien position. Thus a lender establishing a lien position subordinate to another but potentially superior to other claims that might come later.

sum-of-the-digits method See Rule of 78s.

telemarketing The act of marketing by telephone.

title report A report from a title search company that gives a description of real property and indicates if there are any liens against the title. It is used by the lender to investigate the ownership and value of the collateral. Also called commitment for title insurance.

tolerance range An accurate calculation of the APR to within ranges prescribed by federal regulations. Depending on the transaction type, the APR must be within either ⅛ or ¼ of 1% of the figures computed by the federal examiner.

trade report A report from a credit reporting agency used to evaluate a loan applicant that provides a record of the applicant's past and current credit accounts.

transaction journal A report that lists all loan payments received the preceding business day. Also called the loan payment journal.

Transmatic® The trade name of a franchised, preauthorized payment system for savings institutions that was developed and is offered by SAF Systems and Forms.

trial balance A list of all loan accounts and their outstanding balances.

trustee in bankruptcy A court appointed trustee who generally acts as a special representative of all creditors, but who also serves the interests of unsecured creditors. One of the trustee's most important functions is to maximize the recovery by unsecured creditors.

United States Rule A method of recognizing simple interest income based on the daily outstanding principal balance between the time payments are received.

unsecured credit The credit extended on the borrower's promise to repay and for which collateral is not required. It is usually extended to consumers possessing a good credit reputation.

voluntary bankruptcy A legal proceeding in which a debtor personally files for bankruptcy as a means of securing relief from debts; assets are turned over to the court for liquidation.

wage assignment A contract clause between a borrower and a lender stating that, upon default, the lender has the right to obtain a specific portion of the borrower's wages from a specific employer without notice or hearing. Wage assignments differ from wage garnishments in that garnishments require a court judgment while an assignment does not. The FHLBB prohibits this type of clause in consumer loans and certain equity loans made by Federal Home Loan Bank System members.

wage garnishment A legal proceeding in which an institution seeks a court order to obtain funds for debt repayment from a third party (employer) who owes money (wages) to the borrower.

waiver of exemption The FHLBB prohibits this type of clause in consumer loans and certain equity loans made by Federal Home Loan Bank System members. A waiver of exemption is a contract clause allowing a lender to waive a borrower's protection under state law from the attachment of real or personal property. The provision that prohibits lenders from disregarding exemptions does not apply to real or personal property that secures the loan.

warranty insurance A type of insurance that protects the lender and the borrower from losses sustained from the misrepresentation of goods by the seller. Misrepresentation is generally a violation of two implied warranties, merchantability and fitness for a particular purpose.

with full recourse A term in a written agreement, used in lending, that gives the buyer in a sale or other transaction the right to full reimbursement from the seller for any losses resulting from the loans or other items purchased.

with partial recourse A term in a written agreement, used in lending, that gives the buyer in a sale or other transaction the right to reimbursement for an agreed-upon portion of any losses resulting from the loans or other items purchased.

without recourse A term in a written agreement, used in lending, that abrogates the right of the buyer, in a sale or other transaction, to reimbursement from the seller for any subsequent losses resulting from the loans or other items purchased.

Index

Acceleration clause, 222
Accident and health insurance, 63–64
   elimination policy, 63
   retroactive policy, 63
Acknowledgment of indebtedness, 219
Actuarial method
   for calculating monthly payments, 118, 120–21
   comparison of, with United States Rule, 120
   and early repayment, 129
Add-on-interest, 109, 131–32
Adjusted balance method
   for calculating monthly payments, 117
   disclosure of, 119
Adverse action, notifying applicant of, 171–75
Age, correlation of, with credit use, 14
Aircraft
   obtaining evidence of perfected security interest in, 251
   perfecting security interest in, 202, 233
Aircraft insurance, 66
Aircraft loans, 54–55
American Express, 11, 23
Amortization, 107
Amortization table, use of, to calculate monthly payments, 113, 114–15
Annual percentage rate (APR), 121–22
   and early repayment, 129
   on open-end loans, 126–29
   for simple interest loans, 122–26
   tolerance range for closed-end loans, 122
Appliance loans, 55
Application form, 150–57
Application interview, 146–50
"Artful dodger," dealing with, 302–3
Assets, tangibility of, 154
ATM network, use of, to deliver consumer loan services, 28
Attachment of security interest, 194
   versus perfection, 209–10
Authorization, 272–73
Automatic perfection, 204–9
Automatic transfer loan payment system, 262–63

Automobiles
   financing of, through consumer credit, 23, 49–50
   repossession procedures for, 311, 313–15
Average daily balance method
   for calculating monthly payments, 117
   disclosure of, 119

Bankruptcy, 154. *See also* Chapter 7 bankruptcy; Chapter 13 bankruptcy
   laws regarding, 84–85, 322–24
   overview of, 324–25
Bankruptcy Amendments and Federal Judgeship Act (1984), 84, 324
Bankruptcy Reform Act (1978), 84, 97, 323–24
Billing errors, disclosure statement regarding, 90, 91

Capacity, evaluation of, in loan evaluation process, 143, 152
Capital, evaluation of, in loan evaluation process, 143–44, 152
Capitalization, 120
Carte Blanche, 23
Certificate of title notation, in perfecting security interest in loan secured by personal property, 231–33
Certificates of registration, 161
Certificates of title, 161
Chandler Act (1938), 323
Chapter 7 bankruptcy, 84, 322, 324, 326–28
   administration of the estate, 334–36
      creditor concerns, 335–36
      legal events, 334–35
   distribution and discharge, 336–37
      legal events, 337
   first meeting of creditors, 331, 333–34
      creditor concerns, 333–34
      legal events, 333
   initiation, 328
      automatic stay, 328–29
      creditor concerns, 329, 331
      dismissals, 329
      legal events, 328–29
      petition, 328, 330

statement of intent, 329
Chapter 13 bankruptcy, 84, 322, 324–25, 337–38
  discharge, 346–47
    creditor concerns, 346–47
    legal events, 346
  fulfillment, 344–45
    creditor concerns, 345–46
    legal events, 345
  initiation, 338–39
    creditor concerns, 338–39
    legal events, 338
  plan proposal, 339
    creditor concerns, 342, 344
    legal events, 339–42, 343
Character, evaluation of, in loan evaluation process, 142, 152
Charge-off procedures, 316–17
Check credit, 56
Closed-end loans, 8–9
  calculating monthly payments for, 113–16
  closing for, 242
  disbursements for, 244
  tolerance range for APR, 122
Co-applicant, 154
Cognovit or Confession of Judgment, 92
Collateral, 9–10
  acquisition, 310
    foreclosure, 315–16
    out-of-state repossessions, 315
    repossession, 310–11
      procedures for auto loans, 311, 313–15
  attachment versus perfection, 209–10
  determining adequacy of, 199–94
  evaluation of, in loan evaluation process, 144–45, 152
  handling inquiries on substitution of, 275–76
  institution policy regarding, 35–37
  investigating ownership and value of, 160–61
  limitations of using, for repayment, 189–99
  loans secured by, 188–94
  receipt, 204
  value of, and physical damage insurance, 64
Collections devices and tools, 295
  legal action, 302
  personal contacts, 300–2
  telephone contacts, 295–97
  written notification, 297–300
Collections policy, 287
  adaptable procedures, 289–90
  characteristics of effective practices, 287
  collateral acquisition, 310–15
  fair application, 288–89
  legal constraints, 291–93
  preliminary procedures, 293
    review of borrower's situation, 294–95

review of repayment history, 294
verification of past-due status, 293–94
prompt response, 288
remedial payment plans, 307–10
results orientation of, 290
sequencing, 290–91
skiptracing, 304–7
Commercial banks
  and credit card operations, 57–58
  as provider of consumer credit, 17–18
Commitments for title insurance, 161
Community Reinvestment Act (1977), 87–88, 96
Competition, evaluation of, in loan evaluation process, 145–46
Conditions, evaluation of, in loan evaluation process, 145
Constant ratio formula, for annual percentage rate, 123
Consumer credit. *See also* Consumer loans
  categories of, 6
    closed-end, 8–9
    installment, 6–8
    open-end, 8–9
    secured, 9–10
    single payment, 6–8
    unsecured, 9–10
  characteristics of users, 13–17
  classification of, as loss, 76–77
  history of, 4–5
  marketing of products, 4–5
  providers of, 17
    commercial banks, 17–19
    consumer finance companies, 19–20
    credit unions, 20
    retail firms, 22–24
    savings institutions, 21–22
  types of, 10
    direct loan, 12
    retail credit, 11–12
    service credit, 12
Consumer finance companies, as provider of consumer credit, 19–21
Consumer installment credit
  history of, 5–6
  outstanding amount of, 7
Consumer leasing, 56–57
  federal regulations regarding, 77–79
Consumer loan history report, 267
Consumer loan register, 157
Consumer loan reports, 263
  delinquency reports, 269
  loan history, 267
  new loan report, 268
  payoff report, 268–69
  required reports, 263–65
  transaction journal, 266–67
  trial balance, 265–66
Consumer loans
  classification of, 32

376 Consumer Lending

closing and disbursement, 242, 244–46
collateral, 35–37
delinquency, 282
 external factors, 283–84
 lender controlled factors, 282–83
documentation, 241–42
evaluation of, 140–81
modification of, 275
origination, 33–34
payments, 257–63
policies, 32–33
profitability, 37–38
regulations protecting consumers, 85
 Bankruptcy Reform Act (1978), 97
 Community Reinvestment Act (1977), 87–88, 99
 Consumer Protections rule (1985), 92–93, 97
 Electronic Funds Transfer Act (1978), 94–95, 97
 Equal Credit Opportunity Act (as amended 1976), 86–87, 96
 Fair Credit Billing Act (1974), 96, 98
 Fair Credit Reporting Act (1971), 95, 96, 98
 Fair Debt Collection Practices Act (1978), 99
 Fair Housing Act (1968), 86, 96
 Magnuson-Moss Warranty Act (1976), 96
 Right to Financial Privacy Act (1979), 97, 99–100
 Truth-in-Lending Act (1968), 88–91, 96
 Truth-in-Lending Simplification and Reform Act (1980), 91–94, 97
 Uniform Commercial Code—Holder-in-Due-Course Rule (1976), 96
regulations protecting lenders, 73
 Depository Institutions Deregulation and Monetary Control Act (1980), 73, 97
 federal bankruptcy laws, 84–85
 Garn-St Germain Depository Institutions Act (1982), 73–79, 97
 Magnuson-Moss Warranty Act (1976), 83–84
 state consumer warranties and contractual capacity 80–81
 state usury laws, 79–80
 Uniform Consumer Credit Code, 81–83
servicing, 250–63
term
 definition of, 107
 institution policy regarding, 34–35
 types of
 aircraft loans, 54–55
 automobile loans, 49–50
 check credit, 56
 consumer leasing, 56–57
 credit cards, 57–60

 deposit account loans, 41–42
 education loans, 45, 48–49
 equity loans, 50–52
 furniture and appliance loans, 55
 home improvement loans, 39–41
 marine loans, 53–54
 mobile home loans, 42–45, 46–47
 overdraft protection, 60–62
 personal loans, 55–56
 recreational vehicle loans, 52–53
Consumer Protections Rule; Unfair or Deceptive Credit Practices (1985), 92–94, 97
Consumers
 correlation of characteristics of, and credit use, 13
 age, 14
 education level, 15
 family income, 14
 family life cycle stage, 14
 reasons of, for using credit, 16–17
Consumer warranties and contractual capacity,
 state regulations on, 80–81
Cosigner, definition of, 93
Credit analysis, 165–66
 credit report, 166–68
 debt analysis, 168–69
 income analysis, 168
 risk analysis, 169–70
Credit cards, 57–60
 for consumer credit, 28
 federal regulations regarding, 77
 servicing of, 272–73
 use of, for consumer credit, 23
Credit decision, notifying applicant of, 171–75
Credit information, sources of, 158–60
Credit insurance, 62
 accident and health insurance, 63–64
 aircraft insurance, 66–67
 credit life insurance, 62–63
 decreasing life, 62–63
 joint life coverage, 63
 level life, 63
 flood insurance, 66
 marine insurance, 67
 nonfiling insurance, 65
 physical damage insurance, 64
 dual interest coverage, 64
 skip insurance, 65
 warranty insurance, 65–66
Credit investigation, role of dealer in performing, 179
Credit life insurance, 62–63
 decreasing life, 62–63
 joint life coverage, 63
 level life, 63
Credit line, versus installment loan, 141
Credit report, use of, in credit analysis, 166–68

Credit reporting agencies, as source of credit information, 159–60
Credit screening, 27
Credit unions, as provider of consumer credit, 20
Cross-selling, 141, 150, 261

Dealer
 evaluation of, in indirect loans, 177–78
 forming relationship with, 178–79
 maintaining affiliations with, 271–72
Dealer paper, 33
 buying, 180–81
Dealer reserves, maintaining, 270–71
Debt analysis, 168–69
Debtors, contacting, 292
Debt-to-income ratio, 168–69
Debt-to-net income ratio, 169
Deed given in lieu of foreclosure, 316
Deed of trust, 235
Deficiency, 316
Deficiency judgment, 316
Delinquency rate, 282
Delinquency reports, 269
Delinquent borrowers
 classifying, 284
  attitudes of repeat delinquents, 287
  distressed delinquent, 286
  payment style and degree of risk, 284–86
Deposit account loans, 41–42
 federal regulations regarding, 77
Depository Institutions Deregulation and Monetary Control Act of 1980 (DIDMCA), 4, 22, 38, 49, 57, 73, 97
 effect of, on usury regulations, 79–80
Diners Club, 23
Direct loans, 10, 12
 comparison of, with indirect loans, 176–77
 loan evaluation process, 140–75
 origination, 33, 34
Direct referral, 175
Discount interest, 109–10, 132–33
Documentation
 insurance, 241
 internal documentation, 241–42
Document preparation, 218–19
 for loans secured by personal property, 226–34
 for loans secured by real property, 234–42
 promissory note, 219–24
 truth-in-lending disclosures, 224–26
Dual interest insurance coverage, 64

Education level, correlation of, with credit use, 15–16
Education loans, 45, 48–49
 federal regulations regarding, 77
Electronic Funds Transfer Act (1978), 94–95, 97

Electronic funds transfer (EFT), 94
Encumbrance, 192
Equal Credit Opportunity Act (as amended 1976), 86–87, 96
 effect of, on loan application process, 155–56, 166
Equitable right of redemption, 316
Equity, definition of, 50
Equity loans, 50–52
 documents for, 235–36
 obtaining evidence of perfected security interest in, 251–52
Evaluation of credit request
 analysis of credit information, 165–66
  credit report, 166–68
  credit scoring systems, 170–71
  debt analysis, 168–69
  income analysis, 168
  risk analysis, 169–70
 credit decision notification, 171–75
 purpose and policy, 140–41
 six Cs of credit, 141–42
  capacity, 143
  capital, 143–44
  character, 142
  collateral, 144–445
  competition, 145–46
  conditions, 145
 taking application, 146
  consumer loan register, 157
  form, 150–51, 154–57
  interview, 146–50
 underwriting of indirect loans, 175–81
 verifying personal credit information, 157–58
  detection of fraud, 161–65
  investigating ownership and value of collateral, 160–61
  sources of credit information, 158–60
Exact interest-exact time method of calculating interest, 112

Fair Credit Billing Act (1974), 96, 98
Fair Credit Reporting Act (1971), 95, 96, 98
Fair Debt Collection Practices Act (1978), 99, 291–93, 299, 303, 304
Fair Housing Act (1968), 86, 96
Family life cycle, correlation of, with credit use, 14–15
Farmers Home Administration (FmHA), insurance of mobile home loans by, 43
Federal Aviation Administration (FAA), inspection requirements, 54
Federal boxes, 224
Federal Home Loan Bank Board (FHLBB)
 on deposit account loans, 41
 on home improvement loans, 40–41
 on mobile home loans, 44–45
Federal Housing Administration Title I program, 39

success of, as program, 17
Federally Insured Student Loan Program, 48
Field visits, use of, for collections, 300–1
Filing officer, responsibilities of, in filing of financing statement, 227–28
Finance arrangement, terminating, 211
Finance charges, 121, 225
Financial intermediaries, 17
   total assets of, 19
Financial services delivery, 27
Financial services marketing
   of consumer lending products, 4–5
   determining customer needs, 24
      by mail, 26
      by personal contact, 24–25
      by telemarketing, 25–26
      using statistics, 26–27
   importance of, 24
Financial statements
   definition of, 198
   erroneous filings, 200–1
   perfection by filing, 198–200
   and perfection of security interest in personal property, 233–34
   as source of credit information, 160
Flood Disaster Protection Act (1973), 66
Flood insurance, 66
Floor limit, 272–73
Floor planning, 75, 179
Forebearance, 308–9
Foreclosure, 315–16
Fraud detection, 161
   characteristics of fraudulent applicant, 163–65
   inconsistent identification, 162–63
Full-payout lease, 78
Full Satisfaction and Release of Mortgage, 257, 258
Furniture loans, 55
Future advances clause, 202, 235

Garn-St Germain Depository Institutions Act (1982), 4, 22, 73, 97
   consumer leasing, 77–79
   credit cards, 77
   deposit account loans, 77
   education loans, 77
   percentage-of-assets, 73–76
   scheduled items, 76–77
Gasoline companies, provision of consumer credit by, 23
Grace period, 288
Guaranteed Student Loan Program, 48
Guarantor, use of, to secure loan, 36–37
Guarantor's statement, 223–24

Health insurance. See Accident and health insurance

Hedge, 74
Higher Education Act (1965), 45, 48

Home improvement loans, 39–41
   conventional, 40–41
   government insured, 39–40
   secured versus unsecured, 40–41
   uniform mortgage documents for, 236–37
Home Owner's Loan Act (1933), 39, 41
Housing Act (1964), 45
Housing and Development Act (1968), 43
Hull insurance, 66

Implied warranty, 80–81
Inbound telemarketing, 25–26
Income analysis, 168
Income level, correlation of, with credit use, 14
Indirect loans
   comparison of, with direct loans, 176–77
   disbursements for, 244–45
   origination, 33–34
   perfecting security interest, 210–12, 234
   servicing, 270
      maintaining dealer affiliations, 271–72
      maintaining dealer reserves, 270–71
   underwriting, 175–85
In-file report, 160
Inquiries, handling, 273–77
Installment credit plans, 6–8
Insurance. See also Credit insurance
   documentation for, 237, 241
   role of loan servicing department in maintaining, 254–55
Interchange, 273
Interchange fee, 58
Interest
   definition of, 106
   determination of, 34–35
   factors affecting totals
      add-on interest, 109
      discount interest, 109–10
      loan term, 107–8
   nature of, 106–10
   simple
      calculating monthly payments, 113–21
      exact interest-exact time, 112
      ordinary interest-exact time, 112
      ordinary interest-ordinary time, 112–13

Judgment lien, 154
Junior mortgage. See Equity loans

Late charges, 288
Legal action, use of, for collections, 302
Lender liability, regulations regarding, 81–85
Lessee, 56
Lessor, 56
Letters. See Mail
Lien, 42–43
Lien holder, 192
Loans in process, 243
Loan-to-value ratio, 169
Lock box loan payments, 261–62

Index 379

Magnuson-Moss Warranty Act (1976), 83–84, 96
Mail
  marketing of financial services through, 26
  skiptracing by, 306–7
  use of, for collections, 298–99
Mailgrams, use of, for collections, 299
Manufacturer's certificate of origination, 232
Margin, 169
Margin requirements, 36
Marine insurance, 67
Marine loans, 53–54
Marketing. *See* Financial services marketing
MasterCard, 11, 62
Merchandise credit, 11. *See also* Retail credit
Mobile homes
  loans for purchase of, 42–45, 46–47
  perfecting security interest in, 202
Mortgage instrument, 202
Mutual savings banks, as providers of consumer credit, 21–22

National Automobile Dealers Association Used Car Guide, 34, 49
National Bankruptcy Act (1898), 323
National Conference of Commissioners on Uniform State Laws, 81
National Direct Student Loan Program, 48
National Flood Insurance Program, 66
National Housing Act (1934), 39
Negative amortization, 120
Net lease, 78
New Boat Price Guide, 54
New loan report, 268
Nonfiling insurance, 65
Nonpayout lease, 78
Notice of right to rescission, 88, 89, 237
Notices, use of, for collections, 297–98

NOW account services, and overdraft protection, 60

Office interviews, use of, for collections, 301–2
On-site loan payments, 260–61
Open-end loans, 8–9
  annual percentage rate on, 126–29
  calculating monthly payments for, 117–21
  closing for, 242, 244
Operating lease, 78
Ordinary interest-exact time method of calculating interest, 112
Ordinary interest-ordinary time method of calculating interest, 112–13
Origination of loan
  direct, 33, 34
  indirect, 33–34
Outbound telemarketing, 25–26
Out-of-state repossessions, 315
Overdraft protection, 60–62

  single-account approach, 60–61
  two-account approach, 61–62
Partial repurchase agreement, 180–81
Payee clause, in insurance policy, 254–55
Payment plans, 257, 259
  handling inquiries on, 274
  payment processing, 260
    automatic transfer or Transmatic® systems, 262–63
    lock box payments, 261–62
    on-site payments, 260–61
  payment systems, 259–60
Payoff figure, 129
Payoff report, 268–69
Perfected lien creditor, 197
Perfection of security interest, 195
  versus attachment, 209–10
Personal contact
  and loan collections, 300–1
  marketing of financial services through, 24–25
Personal credit information, verification of, 157–65
Personal loans, 55–56
Personal property, 35–36
  documents for loans secured by, 226–34
  maintaining security interest in, 252–54
  perfecting security interest in, 201–3
Physical damage insurance, 64
Pledge arrangement, 194–95
Policy of Insured Real Title (PIRT), 161
Possession, perfection by, 203–4
Power to hypothecate, 204
Precomputed interest, 109
Prepayment clause, 222–23
Previous balance method of calculating monthly payments, 117
Principal, 106
Private mortgage insurance (PMI), 51
Profitability analysis
  acquisition cost, 37
  cost of funds, 37
  liquidation costs, 37
  servicing costs, 37
Promise to repay clause, 219, 221–22
Promissory note
  acceleration clause, 222
  acknowledgment of indebtedness, 219
  prepayment clause, 222–24
  promise to repay clause, 219, 221–22
  sample, 220–21
Purchase money security interest, 192
Pyramiding late charges, 93

Real property, 35
  documents for loans secured by, 234–42
Recognition of income process, 109
Recourse, 180
Recreational vehicle loans, 52–53
  delinquency of, 283–84

Regular mortgage document, 235
Regulation B, 146, 147, 151, 170, 276–77
Regulation E, 94–95
Regulation Z, 88, 90, 224. *See also*
   Truth-in-Lending Act
Remedial payment plans, 307
   forebearance, 308–9
   wage garnishment, 309–10
Repayment schedule, 106
Repurchase, 180
Residual value, 56
Retail credit, 10, 11–12
   installment credit, 12
   open charge credit, 12
   revolving credit, 11–12
Retail firms, as provider of consumer credit, 22–23
Retail installment contract, 180, 182–83
   purchase of, 245–46
Right to Financial Privacy Act (1979), 97, 99–100
Risk analysis, 169–70
Rule of 78s, 129, 133–37

Savings institutions
   effects of legislation on powers of, 22
   as provider of consumer credit, 21–22
Scheduled items, FSLIC regulations regarding, 76–77
Second mortgages. *See* Equity loans
Secret liens, 192–93
   and automatic perfection, 207
Secured credit, 9–10
Security agreement, 194
   in loan secured by personal property, 228–31
Security interest
   attachment versus perfection, 209–10
   definition of, 194
   establishing valid, 194–95
   forms for perfecting in loan secured by personal property, 231–35
   methods of perfecting, 197–98
      automatic perfection, 204–9
      filing a financing statement, 198–201
      in personal property, 201–3
      by possession, 203–4
   obtaining evidence of perfected, 251–52
   perfecting, 195–97
   perfecting, when making indirect loans, 210–11
   release of, 255–57
   role of loan servicing department in maintaining, 250–54
Security interest in household goods, 93
Service credit, 10, 12Servicing, 250
   consumer loans reports, 263
      delinquency reports, 269
      interest earned report, 270
      loan history, 267

new loan report, 268
optional reports, 265–70
payoff report, 268–69
required reports, 263–65
transaction journal, 266–67
trial balance, 265–66
   maintaining security interest and insurance on collateral, 250–57, 258
   processing consumer loan payments, 257, 259–63
Simple English documents, 224, 236–37
Simple interest loans, annual percentage rate for, 122–26
Singer Sewing Machine Company, offering of retail credit by, 23
Single-payment credit, 6–8
Skip insurance, 65
Skiptracing, 302, 304–5
   by mail, 306–7
   sources of location information, 305
   by telephone, 305–6
Slow consumer credit, 76
Special report, 160
Statistics, use of, to target market for consumer credit, 26–27
Statutory right of redemption, 316
Stocks and bonds, use of, in securing loans, 254
Straight bankruptcy, 324
Student Loan Marketing Association (Sallie Mae), 45
Sum-of-the-digits method, 133–37
Surrender value, 36

Tax Reform Act (1984), 263–64, 265
Telecopier, use of, to transmit credit information, 179
Telegrams, use of, for collections, 299
Telemarketing, 25–26
Telephone
   skiptracing by, 305–6
   use of, for collections, 295–97
Third party, contacting, to locate debtors, 292–93, 303
Third party disbursement, 244–45
Third-party loans, 33
Title reports, 161
Trade report, 160
Transaction journal, 266–67, 268
Transmatic® loan payment system, 262–63
Trial balance report, 265–66
Trustee in bankruptcy, 197
Truth-in-Lending Act (1968), 88–91, 96
   on annual percentage rate (APR), 121–22, 126
   and calculation of monthly payments, 117
   disclosures, 224–26
Truth-in-Lending Simplification and Reform Act (1980), 91–92, 97

Uniform Commercial Code (UCC), 66
    on automatic perfection, 204–7
    on perfecting security interest, 197–98
    Holder-in-Due-Course Rule, 82–83, 96
    and purchase money security interest, 192
Uniform Consumer Credit Code (UCCC), 81, 93
United States Rule
    and calculation of monthly payments, 118
    comparison of, with actuarial method, 120
    and early repayment, 129
Unsecured credit, 9–10
Used Boat Price Guide, 54
Usury, state regulations on, 79–80

Vendors Single Interest (VSI) insurance, 65
Veterans Administration, guaranteeing of mobile home loans by, 43
VISA, 11, 62
Voluntary repossession, 313

Wage assignment, 92–93
Wage garnishment, 309–10
Waiver or exemption, 93
Warranty insurance, 65–66
Welcome letter, 242, 243